WEST G
GL

MW01194248

The antiauthoritarian revolt of the 1960s and 1970s was a watershed in the history of the Federal Republic of Germany. The rebellion of the so-called "68ers" – against cultural conformity and the ideological imperatives of the Cold War; against the American war in Vietnam; in favor of a more open accounting for the crimes of the Nazi era – helped to inspire a dialogue on democratization with profound effects on German society. Timothy Scott Brown examines the unique synthesis of globalizing influences on West Germany to reveal how the presence of Third World students, imported pop culture from America and England, and the influence of new political doctrines worldwide all helped to precipitate the revolt. The book explains how the events in West Germany grew out of a new interplay of radical politics and popular culture, even as they drew on principles of direct democracy, self-organization, and self-determination, all still highly relevant in the present day.

TIMOTHY SCOTT BROWN is Associate Professor of History at Northeastern University. He is the author of *Weimar Radicals: Nazis and Communists between Authenticity and Performance* (2009) and co-editor of *Between the Avant-garde and the Everyday: Subversive Politics in Europe, 1957 to the Present* (with Lorena Anton, 2011).

WEST GERMANY AND THE GLOBAL SIXTIES

The Antiauthoritarian Revolt, 1962–1978

TIMOTHY SCOTT BROWN

CAMBRIDGE
UNIVERSITY PRESS

CAMBRIDGE
UNIVERSITY PRESS

University Printing House, Cambridge CB2 8BS, United Kingdom

Cambridge University Press is part of the University of Cambridge.

It furthers the University's mission by disseminating knowledge in the pursuit of education, learning and research at the highest international levels of excellence.

www.cambridge.org
Information on this title: www.cambridge.org/9781107519251

© Timothy Scott Brown 2013

First published 2013
First paperback edition 2015

A catalogue record for this publication is available from the British Library

Library of Congress Cataloguing in Publication data
Brown, Timothy Scott.
West Germany and the global sixties : the antiauthoritarian revolt, 1962–1978 / Timothy Scott Brown.
pages   cm. – (New studies in European history)
Includes bibliographical references and index.
ISBN 978-1-107-02255-3 (hardback)
1. Germany (West)–Politics and government.   2. Protest movements–Germany (West)   3. Opposition (Political science)–Germany (West)   4. Authoritarianism–Germany (West)–History.   5. Counterculture–Germany (West)–History.   6. Popular culture–Germany (West)–History.   7. Student movements–Germany (West)–History.   8. New Left–Germany (West)–History.   9. Nineteen sixties.   10. Nineteen seventies.   I. Title.   II. Title: Antiauthoritarian revolt, 1962–1978.
DD260.4.B78   2013
943.087′6–dc23   2013020829

ISBN 978-1-107-02255-3 Hardback
ISBN 978-1-107-51925-1 Paperback

Contents

Illustrations

Acknowledgments

I wish to express my gratitude to the Fulbright Foundation, the American Council on Germany, Pomona College, and Northeastern University for their generous support for this project. I also wish to offer heartfelt thanks to my friend, colleague, and research assistant extraordinaire Alexander Holmig. Thanks are also due to a number of scholars for their help and/ or inspiration: Martin Klimke, Joachim Scharloth, Kathrin Fahlenbrach, Detlef Siegfried, Uta Poiger, Robert Moeller, Geoff Eley, Jeremy Prestholdt, Mark Overmyer-Velazquez Diethelm Prowe, Jonathan Petropoulos, John Connelly, Ingo Cornils, Margaret Anderson, Gerald Feldman, Martin Jay, Jonathan Zatlin, Devin Pendas, Julian Bourg, James Cronin, Laura Frader, Tom Havens, Wilfried Mausbach, Philipp Gassert, Peter Fritzsche, Andrew Lison, Carla MacDougall, Mia Lee, and Nick Wolfinger. My sincere gratitude goes out to a group of very kind German archivists and interlocutors: Reinhart Schwarz of the Hamburger Institut für Sozialforschung; Siegward Lönnendonker of the Archiv "APO und soziale Bewegungen" at the Freie Universität Berlin; Peter Hein of the Archiv Peter Hein in Berlin; Heinz Korderer of the APO-Archiv München; Uwe Husslein of the Poparchiv Uwe Husslein in Cologne; Gert Möbius of the Rio-Reiser-Archiv in Berlin; Rainer Langhans and Christa Ritter, Michael Baumann, Florian Havemann, K. D. Wolff, and Antje Krüger. I am also grateful to the staff of the Papiertiger Archiv in Berlin, the Kreuzberg Museum in Berlin, the Landesarchiv Berlin, the Bundesarchiv in Berlin and Koblenz, and the Staatsarchiv München, as well as that of the International Institute for Social History in Amsterdam, the Hoover Institution, and the Green and Widener Libraries. I further wish to thank my students Samantha Christiansen, Zachary Scarlett, Burleigh Hendrickson, Andrew Jarboe, Sana Tannoury-Karam, Akin Sefer, Mikhail Rekun, Daniel Quaresma, Samuel Severson, and Christopher Hils. Thanks, finally, are due to my wife Donna McKean, who now knows far more about the 1960s in West Germany than she ever meant to.

Abbreviations

AAO	Action-Analytical Organization
AFN	Armed Forces Network
AGSS	Action Association of Spandau School Pupils
AHA	General Homosexual Working Group
APO	Extraparliamentary Opposition
ASH	Action School Pupil Self Help
AUSS	Action Center for Independent and Socialist School Pupils
BFBS	British Forces Broadcasting Service
BRD	Federal Republic of Germany
CDU	Christian Democratic Union
CSU	Christian Social Union
DAAD	German Academic Exchange Service
DDR	German Democratic Republic
DFFB	German Film and Television Academy Berlin
DGB	Confederation of German Trade Unions
DKP	German Communist Party
FDJ	Free German Youth
FDP	Free Democratic Party
HAW	Homosexual Action West Berlin
HIB	Homosexual Initiative Berlin
IEST	International Essen Song Days
InfoBUG	Info Berlin Undogmatic Groups
KBW	Communist League West Germany
KfA	Campaign for Disarmament
KPD	Communist Party of Germany
LSD	Liberal German Student League
MSB	Marxist Student League Spartakus
NATO	North Atlantic Treaty Organization
NPD	National Democratic Party of Germany
NSDAP	National Socialist German Workers Party

OAS	Secret Armed Organization
RAF	Red Army Faction
SDAJ	Socialist German Worker Youth
SDS	Socialist German Student League
SED	Socialist Unity Party of Germany
SEW	Socialist Unity Party West Berlin
SFB	Socialist Women's League West Berlin
SPD	Social Democratic Party of Germany
SRP	Socialist Reich Party
SSK	Socialist Self-Help Cologne
USG	Independent School Pupils' Association

Introduction: West Germany in the world

In early 2009, researchers digging through the files of the former East German state security ministry (the Stasi) unearthed a political bombshell: The police officer whose fatal shooting of a West German student on June 2, 1967, helped launch the West German student movement on a fatal collision course with the authorities was not simply a West German police officer – he was also an East German spy.[1] Commentators were quick to declare that the revelation of the shooter's real identity discredited, once and for all, left-wing claims about the repressive nature of West German society; the "fascist cop" had been a Communist all along! This response, notable for its attempt to reimpose the very Cold War boundaries that the "68ers" sought to challenge, suggests the extent to which the 1960s are still a sore spot in Germany; far from being a dead letter, they remain central to the politics of memory. For the historian, the events of June 2, once again in the news, are of critical importance; Karl-Heinz Kurras's shooting of the unarmed Benno Ohnesorg during the protest against the state visit of Shah Mohammed Reza Pahlavi of Iran helped spread the radicalism of the West Berlin student movement to the rest of the country and played a major role in the radicalization of the left, leading to the formation of terrorist groups such as the Rote Armee Fraktion (RAF; Red Army Faction). That Ohnesorg's killer was working for East Germany reinforces the extent to which the West German "1968" must be considered in the broader context of German–German relations, not just at the level of state policy but also, as we will see, in the minds of both the 68ers and the establishment.[2]

---

[1] Helmut Müller-Enbergs and Cornelia Jabs, "Der 2 Juni 1967 und die Staatssicherheit," *Deutschland-archiv: Zeitschrift für das vereinigte Deutschland*, March 2009.

[2] On the killing of Ohnesorg, see Uwe Soukup, *Wie starb Benno Ohnesorg? Der 2 Juni 1967* (Berlin: Verlag 1900, 2007). See also the interview with Soukup about the Kurras revelation, available online at www.dradio.de/dlf/sendungen/interview_dlf/969932 (accessed June 1, 2009).

Yet in the media storm over the revelation of the identity of Ohnesorg's killer, the events of June 2 – and the ideological either/or position with which they are so easily connected – are made to bear too much heuristic weight. The reduction of the West German "1968" to this single frozen tableau – a decontextualized confrontation between university students and police – precludes any meaningful attempt to assess its nature and legacy. Not only does it erase the motivations and goals of the events' myriad actors – not just students, after all, but bohemians and artists, apprentices and young workers, established intellectuals and average citizens – but it ignores the multilayered causes and consequences of their actions. This reductionist tendency has been exaggerated by the overrepresentation, among historians of the events, of veterans of the student movement, whose lack of critical distance from events readily results in a mixing up of historical events and personal biographies. In the most egregious cases (one thinks here of the attempt by a certain ex-Maoist to cast his entire generation as latter-day Nazis), this process results in a kind of historiographical psychotherapy in which personal crimes of conscience are projected onto others and used as the basis of historical interpretation.[3] Stilted and fruitless debates about whether "1968" was good or bad (Was the French Revolution good or bad?) hinder, rather than facilitate, genuine historical inquiry. A new perspective requires a new approach, one that captures more fully the breadth of "1968" (rendered hereafter without quotation marks) as an event driven by participants of widely different backgrounds, orientations, and experiences.

The very complexity and richness of 1968 has contributed to making it a major area of scholarly activity in disciplines ranging from history to art history, from media and cultural studies to literature, from film studies to linguistics, sociology, and musicology.[4] The forty-year anniversary of 1968 brought with it a major surge in scholarly activity, producing a veritable explosion of scholarly conferences and publications. Equally important has been a growing sense that the time has come to historicize the 1960s, freeing them from the grip of partisan polemicists and opening up perspectives missing in the work of the participant-historians who have largely dominated the historiography. The West German 1968, for obvious

---

[3] Götz Aly, *Unser Kampf: 1968* (Frankfurt: Fischer-Verlag, 2008).

[4] See, for example, the essays in Timothy Brown and Lorena Anton, eds., *Between the Avant-garde and the Everyday: Subversive Politics in Europe, 1957 to the Present* (New York: Berghahn Books, 2011).

reasons a much-treated topic in the German literature, has only recently begun to figure in the anglophone literature.[5] The faint outlines of a future consensus interpretation, around the key importance of the global and transnational, the interpenetration of the cultural and the political, and so on, is only now beginning to emerge on the horizon.[6]

The designation 1968 is, of course, a terminological convention, one that enfolds certain analytic assumptions. It is aimed at suggesting a world-historic conjuncture, centered roughly around the year 1968, which took place over a sufficiently large expanse of the globe – from Paris to Mexico City, from Berkeley to Dhaka, from Prague to Tokyo – so as to figure as a "global" event. The actual content of this globality – inscribed as much by its participants as by historians – is a point to which we shall return momentarily. Important here is that 1968 operates not merely as a temporal designation but as a spatial one; through the combined weight of similar events taking place across the world around the same time, the date 1968, or the decade of the 1960s, are transformed into the world-historical event "1968." Increasingly, scholars have adopted the term "global sixties" (or "global 1960s") to capture the breadth of this conjuncture. In this work, the terms "global sixties" and "1968" will be used interchangeably, with the understanding that "1968" in West Germany refers to the German case in a larger event understood as "1968" or the "global sixties."

It should go without saying that the term "global" in these formulations is not be taken literally to suggest that student or countercultural uprisings took place in every quarter of the globe in the 1960s. Nevertheless, scholarship is demonstrating, the uprisings of the decade, if not literally global, did in fact encompass much of the globe, certainly much more than has previously been thought.[7] Moreover, radicals in West Germany and elsewhere believed themselves, with some justification, to be actors in a global uprising that shaped both their self-conception and their activism.

---

[5] To date, the only dedicated English-language monographs are those by Nick Thomas and Martin Klimke, the latter a comparative-transnational treatment of West Germany and the USA; see Nick Thomas, *Protest Movements in 1960s West Germany: A Social History of Dissent and Democracy* (New York: Berg, 2003); Martin Klimke, *The "Other Alliance": Global Protest and Student Unrest in West Germany and the US, 1962–72* (Princeton University Press, 2010).

[6] See, for example, the essays in the two-part forum on 1968 in the *American Historical Review*; AHR Forum, *The International 1968*, Parts I and II, vol. 114, no. 1 (February 2009) and vol. 114, no. 2 (April 2011).

[7] Samantha Christiansen and Zachary Scarlett, *The Third World in the Global 1960s* (New York and Oxford: Berghahn Books, 2011).

"Global" here thus refers to both literal (i.e. geographic) space and to conceptual space. "Global" is also occasionally used in a third way, as one half of the global/local antinomy common to cultural-and-media-studies approaches to cultural globalization. "Global/local intersections," in this sense, refer to moments in which transnational exchanges result in actors in one local terrain (e.g. West Germany, West Berlin, etc.) coming into contact with, adopting, rejecting, or otherwise responding to, exogenous influences. In these instances, "global" refers not to a literal condition but to a theoretical model useful in conceptualizing the transnational.

In terms of historical periodization, it is obvious that terms such as "1968" or "the global sixties" can only be imprecise; not only did main events often take place before or after the year 1968 – in West Germany, for example, the first ten-year anniversary commemorated not the protests of the year 1968 but the killing of Benno Ohnesorg in 1967 – but they often unfolded over a period of a decade or more, a fact that accounts for the widespread adoption of the "long sixties" periodization proposed by the British historian Arthur Marwick.[8] Marwick's model is not unproblematic, for reasons that will become clear in due time; here it is sufficient to call attention to an unresolved tension encoded in the choice of nomenclature. Whereas the term "1968" suggests the importance of big events, the notion of the (long) 1960s connotes process; and, indeed, there has developed in the historiography something of a split between scholars emphasizing the importance of longer-term social and cultural developments and those insisting on the importance of ideology, volition, and the power of the revolutionary moment. Obviously, these positions hardly need be mutually exclusive, and one goal of this study is to reconcile two sides of what has perhaps become an unnecessarily schematic distinction.

In the historiography on West Germany, 1968 is clearly established as a watershed event. Rebelling against a stifling atmosphere of cultural conformity, challenging anti-Communist Cold War hysteria, and demanding an accounting with the crimes of the Nazi era, young West Germans demanded nothing less than a democratic renewal of society from the ground up. Such demands, explosive wherever they were made, acquired a special potency in a West Germany poised precipitously on the front line of the Cold War and struggling with the legacy of a recent past marked by fascism, war, and genocide. In challenging the older generation about its complicity in the crimes of the Nazi era, the 68ers helped

---

[8] Arthur Marwick, *The Sixties: Cultural Revolution in Britain, France, Italy, and the United States, c. 1958–c. 1974* (Oxford University Press, 1998).

spur a dialogue on democratization that profoundly affects German society to the present day.[9]

Yet, if the importance of 1968 as a national event/process is firmly established (even if commentators and scholars differ on both its content and legacy), the relationship between the West German 1968 and the global 1968 of which it is understood to be a part – that is, of the content of its globality – remains unsatisfactorily resolved. Our very use of the term "1968" is, after all, bound up with the idea that something of worldwide scope occurred in the late 1960s; it is the status of 1968 as a *global* event that organizes and confers meaning on the individual *national* events. The concept of a global sixties has informed a number of works written from either a European/transatlantic or a worldwide perspective.[10] All of these works pay greater or lesser attention to transnational factors, as indeed they must, given the nature of the topic; but each nevertheless approaches the global primarily through the multiplication of individual national cases, whether these are inserted into some sort of meta-framework (e.g. the Cold War) or treated in broadly comparative terms (normally in terms of connections between Europe and North America).

This book takes a different approach. It seeks to capture the globality of 1968 not in the multiplication of individual national scenarios but in the intersection of global vectors across one local terrain.[11] One advantage of this approach is that it enables us to write the history of an individual national 1968 (with all the detail and historiographic specificity this implies) without falling victim to the limitations of purely national history. In the West German case, the latter approach would leave critically important factors – the presence of the Third World student diaspora in the Federal Republic, for example, or the importation of American protest

---

[9] See Ingo Cornils, "Successful Failure? The Impact of the German Student Movement on the Federal Republic of Germany," in Stuart Taberner and Frank Finlay, eds., *Recasting German Identity: Culture, Politics and Literature in the Berlin Republic* (Rochester: Camden House, 2002), pp. 107–126.

[10] See Gerd-Rainer Horn, *The Spirit of '68: Rebellion in Western Europe and North America, 1956–1976* (Oxford University Press, 2006); Michael Schmidtke, *Der Aufbruch der jungen Intelligenz: Die 68er Jahre in der Bundesrepublik und den USA* (Frankfurt: Campus Verlag, 2003); Jeremy Varon, *Bringing the War Home: The Weather Underground, the Red Army Faction, and Revolutionary Violence in the Sixties and Seventies* (Berkeley, Calif.: University of California Press, 2004); Klimke, *The "Other Alliance"*; Jeremy Suri, *Power and Protest: Global Revolution and the Rise of Détente* (Cambridge, Mass.: Harvard University Press, 2003); George Katsiaficas, *The Imagination of the New Left: A Global Analysis of 1968* (Boston, Mass.: South End Press, 1987).

[11] See Timothy S. Brown, "1968 East and West: Divided Germany as a Case Study in Transnational History," *American Historical Review*, 114 (1) (2009); AHR Forum on the "International 1968."

repertoires – out of the picture. A second advantage is that it allows us to add historical specificity and concreteness to theoretical talk about transnational flows and cultural globalization. Critical raw material of the 1960s cultural revolution – the writings of the Beat poets, for example, or the music of Bob Dylan – did not appear in West Germany or anywhere else by magic, nor because the agentless mechanisms of transnational consumer capitalism increasingly made everything available everywhere; they appeared in many cases for highly contingent reasons, often through the actions of key individuals who made choices about what was important (to import, to translate, to recreate) and thus played a crucial role in mediating transnational interactions.

This study pays careful attention to the role of these individuals, and not only for reasons of narrative interest. In recent years, scholars working in cultural and media studies, history and other disciplines, have emphasized the importance of an "active" model of cultural reception in which local actors employ globalized culture in ways that empower them.[12] This is a part of the story in the West German 1968, to be sure; but even more telling and characteristic is the way that (sub)cultural activists reached out to embrace – and literally bring into West Germany – the cultural components necessary for the integration of the Federal Republic into the global youth revolution. In seizing agency in this way, they took part in a new democratic politics of self-invention from below, a process marked by an explosion of creativity across a range of artistic and political media. This explosion, stretching from the underground press, film, and music to the creation of alternative educational, political, and cultural institutions, is a central focus of this book. The important point here is that transnational connections and cultural transfer did not just *contribute* to the activism of the 1960s and 1970s or determine the conditions in which it took place – they were a *part* of it.

From this perspective, the study of global – local intersections in 1968 becomes intimately bound up with the study of 1968 itself, and not only because of the salience of the (sub)cultural connection-forging just described. First of all, the political *charge* of globalized culture was determined less by its meaning at the point of origin than by how it resonated

---

[12] See the discussion in Timothy S. Brown, "'Keeping It Real' in a Different 'Hood: (African)-Americanization and Hip Hop in Germany," in Dipannita Basu and Sidney Lemelle, eds., *The Vinyl Ain't Final: Hip Hop and the Globalization of Black Culture* (London: Pluto, 2006), pp. 137–150; see also Timothy S. Brown, "Subcultures, Pop Music and Politics: Skinheads and Nazi Rock in England and Germany," *Journal of Social History*, 38 (1) (2004): 157–178.

with the needs of those on the receiving end. Yet the local appropriation of global cultural products was only one side of the coin, for the function of popular culture in the local setting involved a process of imagination through which young people became connected to a global youth culture. This global imagined community of youth, organized around music, fashion, and lifestyle, represents the complementary aspect of the local appropriation of globalized culture, for through it young people imagined themselves across and outside the boundaries of the nation-state. This is one sense in which this book seeks to place West Germany into the world, even as, in tracing the local appropriation of global culture, it seeks to locate the world in West Germany.

But there were other equally important ways in which young West Germans imagined themselves into the world, as well as ways in which the world came to them. If transnational connections pulled West Germany into the world at the level of popular culture and daily life, global structures and processes (e.g. the Cold War) and transnational vectors (military presences, student exchange networks, state visits), created many-sided connections and produced profound local effects. Operating in a situation in which distinctions between the foreign and the domestic, between the internal and the external, seemed to fade away, young West Germans undertook a principled engagement with the problems of Germany's position in the world. Here the aims of the counterculture and the student movement dovetailed, for if one goal of the former was the search for an *authentic* existence, this was also the aim of 68er politics more broadly; their roots lay in the perceived gap between the democratic and humanitarian claims of the parent generation and the reality of Cold War politics. Key events in the development and radicalization of the West German 1968 – the visit of the African strongman Moïse Tshombe in December 1964, for example, or that of the Iranian Shah Mohammad Reza Pahlavi in June 1967 – were important precisely because they called attention to the gap between official rhetoric of democracy and human rights, on the one hand, and the reality of state oppression on the other.

Here again the transnational became important, in two ways. First, in broad terms, the integration of the Federal Republic into the Cold War alliance system meant that issues of democratic legitimacy abroad became intertwined with issues of democratic legitimacy at home. The West German state's relationship with its American benefactors, and with Third World dictators, meant that young West Germans were part of the world whether they wanted to be or not. At the same time, the substantial presence of Third World students in the Federal Republic helped synergize protest around Third World issues.[13] Attention to their presence both underlines the new importance in the 1960s of increased human mobility and gives the links between the Third World and the First a concrete importance that is often overlooked. These linkages, combined with the growing propensity of young radicals to look to the Third World for the solutions to revolutionary problems at home, meant that a hallmark of the West German 1968 became a multifaceted global engagement.

If the 68er movement was global in its orientation, it was, simultaneously, intensely local, not only in the spaces in which it was played out (the school, the neighborhood, the street, the home, the body) but in the concerns with which it engaged. Nowhere does this come out more clearly than in the new focus, in the 1960s, on the personal sphere. This reorientation, which represented a shift away from the iron laws and dour demeanor of twentieth-century Marxist collectivism, was linked with a new emphasis on feelings and emotions, especially those feelings and emotions subversive of the time-honored emotional tropes of male warriordom. It was linked, in turn, both with a rediscovery of the early Marx and his focus on alienation and with a growing interest in psychoanalytic theory, especially the work of the renegade Marxist Wilhelm Reich. The shift in focus toward personal subjectivity provided the basis for an opening up of the definition of politics to encompass new fields of inquiry and action: interpersonal relationships and group dynamics; sex and relations between the sexes; child-rearing and education; and the whole range of personal subjectivity encoded in style.

The window of possibility in which these concerns were able to find expression was part of an unprecedented upsurge of prosperity in Western societies – a "golden age" in the words of the great British historian Eric Hobsbawm – that created the preconditions for a postmaterialist turn. The force of the rejection of life organized around the profit motive, careerism, and consumerism (even as its young adherents used consumption for their own ends) was reflected in the widespread popularity of the writings of Herbert Marcuse, the German-American philosopher of the Frankfurt School, who argued that a society organized around the striving after false needs masked a deep and profound spiritual oppression.[14]

---

[13] For the most comprehensive study of this phenomenon to date, see Quinn Slobodian, *Foreign Front: Third World Politics in Sixties West Germany* (Durham, NC: Duke University Press, 2012).

[14] For a cogent discussion of Marcuse's relationship to the West German student movement, see John Abromeit, "The Limits of Praxis: The Social-Psychological Foundations of Theodor Adorno and Herbert Marcuse's Interpretation of the 1960s Protest Movements," in Belinda

A not dissimilar point was made by the Situationists, a Paris-centered group of avant-garde intellectuals who, already at the end of the 1950s, sought to blur the boundaries between art, politics, and daily life. They assumed (prematurely, as it turned out) the victory of a technocratic post-work society as a jumping-off point for a comprehensive critique of the ways in which the "spectacle" of consumer capitalist society prevented authentic existence. Both Marcuse and the Situationists provided theoretical voices for a widespread feeling of skepticism about the primacy of work–family–duty–sobriety; about prescribed social roles; and – going deeper – about the authoritarian face of daily life. Much of the characteristic activity of the 1960s represented an attempt to escape from precisely these social roles and cultural strictures, through explorations inner (drugs, group therapy, Eastern mysticism) and outer (communal living, hitchhiking, travel abroad).

A key element in the breakout from prescribed social roles and thought patterns was the attempt to create an alternative sphere of knowledge in which the claims of authority could be put to rigorous test even as new values and ideas were put forward. This attempt involved a struggle over representation in which the left challenged the interpretations of events and ideas presented by the mainstream media. This critique of the means by which information was presented in society found its strongest expression, in West Germany, in the campaign against the Springer Press monopoly which, alongside the Vietnam War, formed the centerpiece of student engagement during the crisis year of 1968; but this was only the most visible element in a wider emphasis on the expansion of consciousness and the development of a critical intelligence. This emphasis, which expressed itself in attempts at developing antiauthoritarian educational practice and new possibilities of self-representation, came to particularly pronounced expression in the underground press, which expressed the new intellectual combativeness in a precocious cut-and-paste style.

The underground press was a key site in the development of a more general phenomenon central to 1968: the interpenetration of radical politics and popular culture. A crucial development in the transformation of politics in the 1960s was, of course, the incorporation of the myriad concerns of daily life into the analytic repertoire of the left. One of the things that was *new* about the New Left, beyond its attempt to overcome

Davis, Martin Klimke, Carla MacDougall, and Wilfried Mausbach, eds., *Changing the World, Changing Oneself: Political Protest and Collective Identities in West Germany and the U.S. in the 1960s and 1970s* (New York and Oxford: Berghahn Books, 2010).

the authoritarianism, compromises, and analytical poverty of the older Communist and Social Democratic parties, was a focus on personal subjectivity linked to the erasure of the distinctions between public and private. Expressed through lifestyle generally, and as several scholars have recently pointed out, through consumer choices in particular, this subjectivity transformed the broad palette of daily life into a field of political identity.[15] It was against this background that popular culture, in the form, especially, of popular music, developed into a crucial factor in the elaboration of a distinctive "youth culture," which, in the course of the unparalleled politicization of the 1960s, came to be seen (and experienced) as inseparable from the political agenda(s) of the New Left.[16] At the same time, the multisided link between youth culture, politics, and consumption became – partly as a result of consumer capitalism's ability to recuperate and commodify symbolic challenges to its hegemony, partly as a result of the willingness of authorities to tolerate (and of cultural elites to embrace) aspects of youth rebellion – the basis of a broader "cultural revolution."[17] In simultaneously pushing back the boundaries of the permissible and expanding the cultural palette of lifestyle and artistic possibility, this broad cultural revolution had a decisive impact on Western societies.[18]

Yet it would be a mistake to reduce 1968 to the level of its accommodation by mainstream society, ignoring in the process the principled engagement of its young protagonists with problems that, in many cases, remain urgently unsolved some four decades later. The very process of capitalist appropriation that helped drive the broader evolutionary moment was itself the object of fierce resistance, as anyone with even a passing familiarity with the West German scene is aware. Such resistance is significant not only in marking out popular culture as a field of conflict as well as consensus but also in hinting at the function of popular culture as an active category of political engagement. Popular culture supplied the raw material for the creation of youth identities that, over the course of the 1960s, increasingly became *political* identities. This was especially true, for example, of popular music. Functioning not as the harbinger of

---

[15] See, for example, the essays in Axel Schildt and Detlef Siegfried, eds., *Between Marx and Coca-Cola: Youth Cultures in Changing European Societies, 1960–1980*, Oxford University Press, 2005.
[16] Detlef Siegfried, *Time Is on My Side: Konsum und Politik in der westdeutschen Jugendkultur der 6oer Jahre* (Göttingen: Wallstein, 2006).
[17] A concept associated with Arthur Marwick; see Marwick, *The Sixties.*
[18] Axel Schildt, Detlef Siegfried, and Karl Christian Lammers, eds., *Dynamische Zeiten: Die 6oer Jahre in den beiden deutschen Gesellschaften* (Hamburg: Christians, 2000).

depoliticized mass taste predicted by the theorists of the Frankfurt School but as the vehicle of life feelings and expressive codes with strong emancipatory potential, popular music articulated with the radicalism of the student left in an increasingly thoroughgoing way from the mid 1960s.[19] This mutual interpenetration created a field of political-cultural experimentation, which, by the end of the decade, helped fuel the revolutionary fantasies of self-styled urban guerrillas combining notions of Third World revolution with cultural identities drawn from the comic books and the movies.[20]

A second key feature of the interpenetration of culture and politics in the West German 1968 was the intrusion of artists or people motivated by theories of action drawn from the artistic avant-garde into politics. Artists across a variety of media – painting, film, photography, music, dance, and theater – elaborated a new "revolutionary" art, which attempted to free itself from the constraints of the old, to make itself available as part of a broader project of democratic renewal, and in some cases to spur or to serve as activism in its own right. Even more telling, however, was the blending of artistic theory and praxis with political theory and praxis. The characteristic actor of 1968 was the bohemian nonconformist, typically but not exclusively male, armed with theories drawn from the artistic avant-garde, attempting (like the Situationists, and often in direct imitation of or cooperation with them) to erase the distinctions between art, politics, and everyday life. This tendency was central to one of the most important initiatives undertaken in the West German 1968, the founding of a revolutionary "commune" in West Berlin. The activists of the so-called Kommune I attempted to *live* theory, incorporating Situationism's concern with daily life with its emphasis on shattering the complacent assumptions of capitalist normality. In doing so, they upset the apple cart of sober theoretical student politics, dragging the chief West German student movement kicking and screaming into a new realm of play, pranks, and provocations.[21]

---

[19] See Detlef Siegfried, "Music and Protest in 1960s Europe," in Martin Klimke and Joachim Scharloth, eds., *1968 in Europe: A History of Protest and Activism* (New York: Palgrave Macmillan, 2008), pp. 57–70; Detlef Siegfried, *Sound der Revolte: Studien zur Kulturrevolution um 1968* (Weinheim: Juventa, 2008); Timothy S. Brown and Beate Kutschke, "Politisierung, Pop und postmoderne E-Musik," in Tobias Schaffrik and Sebastian Wienges, eds., *68er-Spätlese: Was bleibt von 1968?* (Münster: LIT-Verlag, 2008), pp. 83–101.

[20] See Brown, "1968 East and West."

[21] See the section on West Berlin's Kommune I in Timothy S. Brown, "A Tale of Two Communes: The Private and the Political in Divided Berlin, 1967–1973," in Martin Klimke, Jacco Pekelder, and Joachim Scharloth, eds., *Between Prague Spring and French May*, pp. 132–140.

The Kommune I became a clearing house for the elaboration of new concerns (most famously the politics of sexuality and the body) and for the breaking down of boundaries between formerly separate areas of engagement (not least between the "underground" and the "mainstream"). It also helped pioneer a third key feature of the fusion of culture and politics in the West German 1968: a democratization of expressive action in which popular culture, more than simply providing raw material for the creation of oppositional identities, became itself a field for political action. From the printing presses of underground publishers to the electric guitars of politicized rock groups, the possession of the cultural means of production helped fuel an unprecedented outburst of creativity from below that was instrumental in the creation of identities both personal and political.

In contrast to studies focusing more or less narrowly on the politics of the student movement, this study expands the ambit of "politics" to encompass this wider range of activities, activities that neither conformed to the boundaries (or the politics!) of organizations such as the Sozialistischer Deutscher Studentenbund (SDS; Socialist German Student League) nor fit easily within the overused category of "protest." Protest – against university administrations, against governments – represents only the barest fraction of what 1968 was about; not only does an exclusive focus on protest reduce the focus to an area so narrow that it excludes important parts of the picture – until, indeed, all that is left is a binary of opposition between "protest" and "power" – but it also robs the agency of the protagonists, reducing them to a defensive posture in the face of the state's initiatives.[22] This study expands the picture to include new actors (not only the students of the SDS but also artists, freaks, hippies, intellectual fellow travelers, and subcultural entrepreneurs); and new activities (not just marches, street battles, congresses, and proclamations but also radical democratic self-invention from below using the raw material of globalized popular culture). Most important of all, it focuses attention on the critical importance of a diverse set of (often overlooked) transnational influences and global–local intersections that gave the West German 1968 its distinctive shape.

The complex interplay of global and local factors is teased out through a narrative stretching across eight thematic chapters. Each chapter opens with a key event, either political, cultural, or, in many cases, both. Chapters 1 (Space) and 2 (Time) plot the spatial and temporal vectors

---

[22] Suri, *Power and Protest.*

against which the West German 1968 unfolded. Chapter 1 situates the Federal Republic in the context of a bipolar, Cold War world, paying special attention to the consequences of division and occupation for political action. Using the December 1964 visit of Moïse Tshombe as a centerpiece, the chapter introduces two sets of actors: on the one hand, the Third World students who helped synergize the protest against Tshombe; on the other, the West German students they influenced. Among the latter, the circles around the Marxist student radical Rudi Dutschke and the bohemian Situationist Dieter Kunzelmann are introduced as archetypical examples of, respectively, the political and the cultural elements in the distinctive activism of the 1960s. The chapter also explores the relationship between urban space, youth activism, and habitus, examining those actors (e.g. *Gammler*, or hippies) who, in contrast to the main thrust of the student movement, enacted their rebellion at the level of daily life.

Chapter 2 opens with the famous trial of the defendants in the Frankfurt department-store arsons of April 1968, using it as a lens through which to view the relationship of the antiauthoritarian revolt to history and historical consciousness. The influence of the past is examined on two levels: (1) the attempt to respond to the ever-present Nazi past; (2) the attempt to mine the left-wing German past – erased by National Socialism – by rediscovering lost radical traditions and histories. This impulse to recover a lost past functioned especially strongly in West Germany, in two ways. First, the looming history of war and fascism – and the "silence of the fathers" about that history – made the attempt to come to grips with the Nazi past a central component of the 1960s rebellion in West Germany. The National Socialist past functioned in the present in a number of ways, not least as a tool of juxtaposition and analysis in the political struggle with the West German establishment. If the history of National Socialism had been, as it were, "erased" (although the extent of this erasure is disputed) so had that of the German revolutionary tradition. The German left had been forced into exile or exterminated, its works and the works of its illustrious forebears burned, banned, and largely erased from public memory. The desire to recover this lost revolutionary past – to recover usable traditions, bodies of theory, and radical practices – became a central component of the West German 1968.

Tellingly, the German past became fused, in the cultural productions of the West German student movement, with the global present, the history of National Socialism in particular serving as a ready template for assessments of the contemporary political situation. Indeed, the recovery of the past became bound up with the attempt to elaborate an antiauthoritarian politics in the present. The question of organizing a new politics outside of established models – in direct opposition to the parliamentary politics of compromise – provided no clear paths toward the future. For this reason, the mining of the past for revolutionary traditions (Marxism, Leninism, anarchism, psychoanalysis) produced contradictory results that mirrored contradictory lines of practice. This study examines how the project of recovering a usable past dovetailed with the active reception of transnational influences in the present.

Chapters 3, 4, and 5 deal with the local appropriation of globalized culture. Chapter 3 (Word) focuses primarily on print media. Analyzing 1968 in Germany as part of a movement for media democracy (a main continuity between the 68er movement and the anti-globalization movement of today), the chapter examines the creation of alternative media, especially the underground press, which played a critical role in the fusion of culture and politics characteristic of 1968. The underground press became the site at which the artistic and political avant-garde of the early 1960s, the student movement of the late 1960s, and the left-wing terrorism of the 1970s came together and overlapped. The chapter pays special attention to the way in which the underground press served as a clearing house for transnational connections, through its appropriation of ideas and imagery drawn from the globally available. At the same time, the study examines the phenomenon of left-wing publishing, in particular the career of Rolf Dieter Brinkmann, an activist who played a major role in first importing literature such as the work of the Beats into West Germany. The chapter also explores the creation of left-wing printing houses, one of the most salient phenomena of the West German 1968, and one that has received comparatively little attention given its importance.

Chapter 4 (Sound) extends the analysis of Chapter 3 to include popular music, which, it will be argued, was a key nexus for the intersection of the cultural and the political, the global and the local. The chapter will explore in particular the rise of politicized rock groups from the end of the 1960s, especially the West Berlin rock group Ton Steine Scherben, which held a salient position in the West Berlin anarchist scene at the moment (1969–1973) that marked the transition from the student movement to the later Sponti and terrorist scenes. Simultaneously, the chapter will explore the role of countercultural entrepreneurs such as Rolf Ulrich Kaiser, who both promoted the importation of foreign musical acts into the Federal Republic and helped foster a homegrown German music scene with its own events, record labels, and bands.

Chapter 5 (Vision) examines the role of visuality in the counterculture and in the antiauthoritarian revolt more generally. Opening with the showing of film student Holger Meins' infamous *The Making of a Molotov Cocktail* short at the February 1968 Springer Tribunal in Berlin, the chapter emphasizes not only the power of images but also their ambiguity. Owing to advances in technological reproduction and a democratization of access to media, the visual represented a field of action that the New Left was able to exploit in a way never seen before. Film and the visual arts became heavily politicized, meanwhile, while icons drawn from the increasingly rich global image sphere became central elements of the construction of radical identity. Yet the prominence of images in the antiauthoritarian revolt, particularly in the cultural productions of the underground press, helped to blur rather than to sharpen the ideological outlines of the antiauthoritarian revolt. Visual codes central to countercultural or left-wing identity were, moreover, easily and quickly coopted by consumer capitalism so that the visual became a site of recuperation as well as rebellion.

Chapter 6 (Power) takes as its starting point the International Vietnam Congress of 1968, an event followed closely by a massive anti-student citizens' demonstration in West Berlin and the attempted assassination of student leader Rudi Dutschke. Exploring the impasse the student movement and extraparliamentary opposition found themselves facing during the second half of 1968, the chapter examines attempts to find a way forward via new venues of struggle and new revolutionary subjects. Ranging from the politicization of ever-younger sections of the population (school pupils and children in group homes) and non-students (young workers and apprentices) to the creation of a host of independent projects from self-organized drug-treatment programs to rural communes, the chapter explores the different ways in which activists tried to enact the "revolution." Paying special attention to the splintering of the movement into dogmatic and "undogmatic" groups from 1968 on, the chapter teases out the different strands of a movement grasping toward elements of the past even as it strove toward the future.

Chapter 7 (Sex) deals with the gender and sexuality aspects of the 68er movement, from the so-called "sexual revolution" to the birth of autonomous women's- and gay-rights movements. Led respectively by female activists dissatisfied with their subordinate position in the male-dominated 68er movement and gays and lesbians seeking to come out of the closet while negotiating the line between Marxist politics and personal liberation, these movements characteristically drew on key imperatives of the antiauthoritarian revolt, even as they strove to broaden the ambit of its politics. Highlighting the ambiguous relationship of these groups to a sexual revolution that existed both in a mainstream, commodified form and in a radical form in which sex and sexual theory became weapons of antiauthoritarian renewal, the chapter also demonstrates that these movements were heavily transnational in both makeup and orientation, highlighting, again, the extent to which the West German 1968 must be placed in a broader, world perspective.

Chapter 8 (Death) deals with the issue of political violence, examining the development of left-wing terrorism out of the conflict between the antiauthoritarian revolt and the state's response to it. Opening with the 1977 "Buback Obituary," an anonymous student's ambiguous rejection of terrorist methods that was nevertheless used by the state as the basis of a witch hunt against terrorist "sympathizers," the chapter places the development of left-wing violence in discursive context, showing how terrorism was used to justify the state's attempt to shut down the alternative public sphere that had accompanied the antiauthoritarian revolt. Concluding with the TUNIX Congress of February 1978, an event that marked the end of the revolt, the chapter shows how the principles of direct-democratic self-management that had underpinned the revolt gained a new lease of life in the transition to the "alternative movement" of the 1970s and 1980s.

The reader will notice a degree of overlap in the chapters; there will be some "word" in "sound," some "sex" in "vision," and some "space" in "death." This is on one level merely an inevitable consequence of the organization of the book; the attempt to trace parallel narrative threads across a range of thematic areas must necessarily see the themes reemerge and flow into each other. But on a deeper level this overlap is exactly the point, for the dynamism of 1968 derived precisely from the way in which a host of radical impulses converged with and synergized each other. Debates about what 1968 *was* frequently operate as if there is but one event or process in need of definition. Is 1968 a generation upheaval? A product of student movements based in universities? A cultural revolution driven by a counterculture, subcultures, or broad social changes rooted in the growth of consumer societies? Recent scholarship has made attempts to move past unnecessary antinomies – e.g. the distinction between politics and culture, between students and hippies – through imperfect formulae such as "the intersection of culture and politics"; but it is perhaps more helpful to think about the revolution of 1968 as a collection of revolutions, cutting across each other, influencing each other, synergizing each other. In its thematic and empirical concerns, its theoretical approach, and its organizational structure, this book is an attempt to trace the revolutions within the revolution.[23]

Two key terms used in this book merit attention at the outset. The first, "extraparliamentary opposition" (*Ausserparlamentarische Opposition*; APO), is used to suggest the (self-described) alliance of the student movement with other forces in society (e.g. the remnants of the 1950s peace and antiauthoritarian nuclear movements, trade unions, and journalists). The second – "the antiauthoritarian revolt" of the book's subtitle – best captures the essence of the 68er project and of the book's; for it will be argued here that 1968 was nothing less than a wide-ranging attempt to dismantle the usually taken-for-granted authority relations in society. The antiauthoritarian impulse was operative not just at the level of politics (with respect, for example, to state policy) but across the whole range of cultural production in the arts and media. It also unfolded at the level of "daily life," a term that will be used here to capture those aspects of human existence (from the possibility of moving and being in the city to the whole vista of gender relations, child-rearing, and sexuality) that, before the 1960s, were typically considered to fall outside the ambit of politics.

The preeminence of the antiauthoritarian dynamic so heavily on display in the West German 1968 represents, moreover, one of the key factors linking the West German revolt to the rest of the global sixties. To be sure, national conditions differed greatly, as, for example, on the two sides of the Iron Curtain. But whether directed against ossified Communist parties in the East, capitalist establishments in the West, or the myriad (Cold War) political arrangements of the Third World, the antiauthoritarian impulse typically challenged both local orthodoxies and the larger strictures of the Cold War simultaneously.

In West Germany, antiauthoritarianism represented one of five imperatives governing the revolt: (1) the antiauthoritarian; (2) the self-organizational; (3) the communicative; (4) the scholarly-scientific; and (5) the transnational. The *antiauthoritarian imperative*, as mentioned above, dictated the questioning of all authority relations in society. As the revolt in West Germany progressed, this imperative opened up more and more of

---

[23] A similar point has been made by Uta Poiger in Uta Poiger, "Generations: The 'Revolutions' of the 1960s," in Helmut Walser Smith, ed., *The Oxford Handbook of Modern German History* (Oxford University Press, 2011), pp. 640–662.

the social landscape to the antiauthoritarian gaze, so that, by 1969 at the latest, there was hardly an institution or area of human activity in the Federal Republic in which authority relations were not being challenged and upset. This antiauthoritarian imperative embodied a key contradiction, however: one that cut through the entire antiauthoritarian revolt, for the revolutionary traditions and sources that activists inherited or sought to draw on, whether from the Old Left legacy or from contemporary postcolonial struggles, were ambiguous at precisely this point – even as they challenged power relations at every level, activists worked with source materials (e.g. Marxism-Leninism, Maoism) in which authoritarian and antiauthoritarianism were heavily intertwined. To be sure, the working through of the basic contradiction at the heart of the antiauthoritarian movement represented one of the main discursive features of 1968. A reinvented anarchist tradition, moreover, represented an important counterweight to the authoritarian tendencies present in aspects of the Marxist tradition. Still, the failure, or perhaps inability, to come to terms with the dichotomy at the heart of this mixed legacy may be seen to represent the blind spot in the antiauthoritarian gaze.

An additional blind spot existed alongside the first, one having to do with gender. For all that activists attempted to upset authority relationships in society, one such relationship – the one between men and women – proved remarkably resistant to such interventions. Initially, the so-called "sexual revolution" seemed to offer, certainly for many male activists, the field for a sustained and potent attack on traditional mores and authority relationships. This was not the same thing, however, as an analysis of the subordinate status of women, not just within society as a whole but within the antiauthoritarian movement itself. It was not until the end of the 1960s, and not really until the 1970s, that a movement – pioneered by women – emerged to extend the revolt's antiauthoritarian analysis to the realm of gender. During the entire period of the revolt, this gender critique existed uneasily with other critiques with which it was connected (e.g. class). These tensions give evidence of the fundamental strength of the antiauthoritarian imperative, even where it challenged unwritten orthodoxies – the preeminence of the male theoretician, or the assumption that women play their part in the sexual revolution by always being sexually available to male comrades – that unsettled the antiauthoritarian revolt itself.

The second key imperative, one that accompanied the gender critique prominent from the end of the 1960s, was the *self-organizational*. A practical analog to the antiauthoritarian imperative with which it was closely linked, it corresponded to the impetus toward participatory democracy and autonomous social organization in the antiauthoritarian revolt, driving the search for radical-democratic alternatives to top-down models of social organization. This attempt came to expression in the school, the workplace, and in all the autonomous initiatives – underground publishers and bookstores; independent youth centers and child-care collectives; film, music, and theatrical collectives – where radical politics met independent cultural production. It also dovetailed, crucially, with the search for the revolutionary subject that drove the mobilization of an ever-wider segment of the young population, from school pupils to young workers and apprentices. Self-organization was the organizational trope and mobilizing method par excellence, one that could help paper over, at least temporarily, political contradictions at the heart of the antiauthoritarian project.

The third imperative, the *communicative*, refers to the privileging of communication as political action, not just in verbal terms but in visual and performative acts as well. The communicative possibilities of any action – a political demonstration, the publication of a tract, smoking pot, or making love – was one of the primary litmus tests by which activists judged its relative worth. In this sense, "communication" served as a trope for justifying the merit of particular actions, but it also signifies the actual content of the antiauthoritarian revolt, for 1968 was above all an act of speech: an assertion of the right to break silence, to challenge authority's monopoly on truth, to dispute the legitimacy of official lines of communication and to forge alternatives.

A fourth imperative, the *scholarly scientific* (*wissenschaftliche*), governed the relationship of activists to their activism as well as to the society in which it took place.[24] The antiauthoritarian revolt took place during the social-scientific moment of the 1960s, in which fields such as sociology and psychology were coming into their own as means of explaining rapid social change, and in which sociologically minded thinkers such as C. Wright Mills and Herbert Marcuse enjoyed unprecedented status among the student left intelligentsia. The leading role played by students in the movements of 1968 ensured that political action would be grounded in theory; and the primacy of theory meant that all acts of rebellion, even those rooted in primal drives, would be justified in accordance with key texts and intellectual traditions. The fashionability of theory allowed it

---

[24] The adjective *wissenschaftlich* (knowledge-creating) is used in German to refer to both scientific and scholarly enterprises. I have thus chosen to use the term "scholarly-scientific" to suggest this twofold meaning.

to spread beyond student circles, supplying a ready-made justification for whatever acts of revolt young people envisioned. At the same time, the primacy of fields of knowledge and practice such as psychology and social pedagogy supplied a common language in which activists could communicate the needs of activism to the liberalizing intelligentsia in government agencies. It thus provided one of the key linkages between revolt and reform, the former, as we will see, often unfolding in the context of the latter. Indeed, a notable feature of the antiauthoritarian revolt, the willingness of authorities to go along with and support all sorts of independent initiatives at the local level, is a prime example of what Arthur Marwick has called "measured judgment," the tendency of authorities in the 1960s to negotiate conflict by avoiding overt repression, responding in a nuanced way to challenges from below.[25] In many cases, measured judgment bled over into a sort of "cooperative radicalism," in which sympathetic authorities made possible the establishment and maintenance of radical initiatives.

The fifth imperative, the *transnational*, was an inevitable response to the reality of the moment in which border-crossing ideas, goods, and activists were the order of the day. More fundamentally, however, it was a response to the perceived deficits, political and cultural, of the Federal Republic itself. Where necessary, activists looked abroad for inspiration, in both the political and the cultural realms; that it was so frequently necessary was a product of the extent to which fascism had succeeded in destroying left-wing traditions in Germany, but it was also a product of the richness of the offerings elsewhere. Whether drawing on radical ideas and practices from the Continent, popular and underground culture from England and America, or theories of guerrilla warfare from the Third World, activists sought out the locally needed from the globally available. Although the transnational was operative everywhere in 1968, the special requirements of the West German situation made it simultaneously emblematic of key trends and a special case.

[25] Marwick, *The Sixties*.

CHAPTER I

Space

On December 18, 1964, authorities in West Berlin played host to a would-be ally in the global Cold War against Communism. Their guest was Moïse Tshombe, ruler of the copper-rich Katanga province in the newly decolonized Congo. Friend to Belgian mining interests, recipient of aid from the Belgian military as well as from assorted European mercenaries (among them former members of Nazi Germany's wartime armed forces), Tshombe helped to sabotage the creation of a unified, decolonized Congo by announcing the secession of Katanga province in July 1960. Precipitating a civil war that ultimately killed tens of thousands, the secession contributed to an internationalization of the crisis in the Congo that saw the involvement of both superpowers (one of the first extensions of the Cold War into the African continent) and the intervention of the United Nations, called in at the request of Prime Minister Patrice Lumumba. Deposed by a Central Intelligence Agency coup, Lumumba was delivered to Katanga, where he was tortured and killed, possibly – as rumor has long held – by Tshombe personally.[1] Appearing in West Germany uninvited in hopes of gaining additional Western aid, Tshombe was received with state honors. His visit on December 18 to the Berlin Wall, where he was photographed looking solemnly outward over the death strip separating the capitalist and Communist worlds, was meant to symbolize his commitment – and that of his hosts – to defend against Communist aggression wherever it might occur. The symbolic essence of the relationship was expressed succinctly by the editorial in a West German daily that described Tshombe as a friend who was "preventing the building of another Berlin Wall across the Congo."[2]

---

[1] The grounds for the coup were both political and commercial; Lumumba had appealed to the Soviet Union for aid and was seen as a threat by both Belgian and American mining interests. On the US decision to depose Lumumba, see David N. Gibbs, *The Political Economy of Third World Intervention: Mines, Money and US Policy in the Congo Crisis* (Chicago University Press, 1991).
[2] *Welt am Sonntag.*

Figure 1.1 Moïse Tshombe at the Berlin Wall, December 18, 1964. Landesarchiv Berlin.

The projection of West Germany onto the map of Africa was hardly unusual; on the contrary, it was typical of the cognitive cartography of the Cold War. What was unusual was that Tshombe's visit provided the occasion for the presentation of an alternative scheme in which the dictator appeared not as a friend but as an enemy. This alternative was posed by student protesters who openly challenged the status quo in the streets. Taking to the streets, as such, was nothing new; the movement against West German rearmament in the 1950s had involved massive protests, and, indeed, the death of Lumumba the year before had seen demonstrations throughout the Federal Republic.[3] What was new in the Tshombe protest was the appearance of a self-consciously radical avant-garde that sought to use the protest as a means to larger, more thoroughgoing ends. Among the organizers, in addition to the SDS and other student groups, including the African Student League, was a small radical group calling itself Subversive Aktion. Formed the previous fall, Subversive Aktion brought together two future key figures of the West German 1968: the *Münchener* Dieter Kunzelmann, who would go on to found the notorious

[3] Nikolaus Jungwirth, *DEMO: Eine Bildgeschichte des Protests in der Bundesrepublik* (Weinheim and Basel: Beltz Verlag, 1986), p. 49.

Kommune I in West Berlin, and the *Berliner* Rudi Dutschke, who, along with his colleague Bernd Rabehl, would become a leading force in the "antiauthoritarian" faction of the SDS and eventually *the* face of the student revolt in West Germany.[4]

Subversive Aktion helped stage protests against Tshombe's visits to Munich on December 14 and to West Berlin on December 18. In a leaflet printed for the occasions, the group called attention to Tshombe's use of American and Belgian military equipment, his reliance on mercenaries – not only from Germany's Hitler-era Waffen SS but also from the French Organisation de l'Armée Secrète (OAS; Secret Armed Organization, the proto-fascist French paramilitary terror group), which had so bloodily prolonged the colonial conflict in Algeria. Drawing a connection between Germany's Nazi past and recent and current anticolonial struggles, the flyer concluded by articulating an alternative to the anti-Communist coalition linking cold warriors in the First and Third Worlds: "The oppressors of the Congolese people are also our oppressors."[5]

The inverse of the Cold War principle by which brutal Third World dictators became valuable friends in the struggle to defend democracy, this formulation sought to establish a new moral geography linking opponents of imperial domination across the hard boundaries of the bloc system. More than simply a protest against Tshombe's dismal human-rights record, it was a protest against the persistence of colonial domination in the Third World symbolized by Western elites' support of Tshombe. Situating Tshombe with respect to global structures of oppression, a persistent colonial domination that encompassed the First as well as the Third World, the action was a protest against colonialism, against the Cold War, and against anti-Communism as an organizing principle. This fusion of the global and the local was strikingly captured in the blunt rhetorical question posed in the flyer created for the protest: "What business does the murderer Tshombe have here?"[6]

In asking this question, Subversive Aktion did more than challenge the West German establishment in a new register of moral outrage and truculent self-confidence; it acknowledged the arrival of a new globalized

---

[4] On Kunzelmann, see Aribert Reimann, *Dieter Kunzelmann: Avantgardist, Protestler, Radikaler* (Göttingen: Vandenhoeck & Ruprecht, 2009); on Dutschke, see Ulrich Chaussy, *Die drei Leben des Rudi Dutschke* (Berlin: Fischer, 1993).

[5] "Was hat der Mörder Tshombe bei uns zu suchen?" in Frank Böckelmann and Herbert Nagel, eds., *Subversive Aktion: Der Sinn der Organisation ist ihr Scheitern* (Frankfurt: Verlag Neue Kritik, 1976), p. 281.

[6] *Ibid*. On the situation in the Congo, see Gibbs, *Political Economy*.

politics, one which its activists embraced for reasons of temperament and ideology, but one to which they were also forced by the nature of the situation; for, as Tshombe's visit to the Federal Republic illustrated, the line between West Germany's domestic politics, the politics of the Cold War bloc system, and the politics of anticolonial liberation were thin indeed.

The anti-Tshombe protest demands the attention of the historian for several reasons. To begin with, it established a model that would recur repeatedly in 1960s West Germany: the protest against a foreign dignitary invited to (or in Tshombe's case, merely received in) West Germany for Cold War *raisons d'état*. This occurred most famously in the visit of the Shah Mohammad Reza Pahlavi of Iran to West Berlin in June 1967, an event that launched the antiauthoritarian revolt to a more intense level of conflict. At the same time, for the Subversive Aktion members who took part in it, the Tshombe protest represented a watershed moment when new actors, new tactics, and a new consciousness came to the fore. This view was expressed most clearly by Rudi Dutschke, who wrote, "With the anti-Tshombe demonstration, we have for the first time seized the political initiative in this city. We can see it as the beginning of our cultural revolution, in which ... all prior values and norms are called into question."[7]

In a broader sense, however, the response to Tshombe's visit underlines the differing conceptions of democratic legitimacy motivating protesters and members of the establishment in 1960s West Germany. The protest against Tshombe took place in what, in a meaningful sense, was an era of liberalization. From its founding in 1949, the Federal Republic of Germany had been governed under the liberal-conservative chancellorship of Konrad Adenauer. Adenauer's Christian Democratic Union (CDU), in alliance with the Christian Social Union (CSU) and sometimes also with the liberal Free Democratic Party (FDP), oversaw a period of relative stability, one marked, however, by a fierce anti-Communism and a conservative cultural atmosphere. The administration of Adenauer's successor, the CDU politician Ludwig Ehrhard (1963–1966), gave way in 1966 to the so-called "Grand Coalition" of the CDU with the Sozialdemokratische Partei Deutschlands (SPD; Social Democratic Party). This coalition, representing the first entry of the SPD into government in the postwar

---

[7] Uwe Bergmann, Rudi Dutschke, Wolfgang Lefèvre, and Bernd Rabehl, *Rebellion der Studenten oder die neue Opposition* (Hamburg: Rororo Aktuell, 1968), p. 63. This notion of "cultural revolution," as Richard Hinton Thomas and Keith Bullivant point out, was "not a substitute for revolution but a preparation for it, aiming to liberate the masses from the 'false consciousness' generated by the 'consciousness industry'." Richard Hinton Thomas and Keith Bullivant, *Literature in Upheaval: West German Writers and the Challenge of the 1960s* (Manchester University Press, 1974), p. 57.

period, was only possible because of the party's gradual eradication of its Marxist roots, a fact that caused many former supporters to reject it and helped fuel the development of the extraparliamentary opposition.

The SPD's support for the so-called Emergency Laws (*Notstandgesetze*) was a particular cause of left-liberal outrage. Proposed in October 1958 as a "safeguard" against future civil unrest, the Emergency Laws were seen by the government as a step in the direction of German sovereignty since they would gather into German hands powers heretofore held by the Allied occupation authority. Nonetheless, the laws provoked widespread opposition, not only among youth but also among a spectrum of intellectual opinion. The laws figured prominently in the famous polemic of the philosopher Karl Jaspers published in 1966, *What Is Becoming of the Federal Republic?*, and were criticized by a wide range of other intellectuals as a dangerous return to authoritarian type.[8]

Yet the SPD's passage into government nevertheless set the stage for an era of liberalization, both nationally and in regions and locales where left SPD politicians held office. The Social Democratic mayor of West Berlin at the time of the Tshombe protest was Willy Brandt, a politician who would go on to build the foundations of rapprochement with Communist East Germany as Foreign Minister in the Grand Coalition. Sympathetic to the argument of the African Student League that Tshombe's visit reflected poorly on West Germany, Brandt gave him a relatively curt reception, prompting him to end his visit early.[9] Five years later, in 1969, in no small part on the strength of the votes of portions of the 68er generation, Brandt assumed the chancellorship of West Germany under the slogan "Dare More Democracy." That the antiauthoritarian revolt was assuming evermore radical forms at the time of Brandt's accession to the chancellorship suggests not only the extent to which the "authoritarianism" targeted by the antiauthoritarian revolt was always a relative matter but also the extent to which terms such as "democracy" and "liberation" were susceptible to more than one meaning.[10] More importantly, it illustrates the fact that, for activists, the goal was never to achieve top-down reforms enacted by liberal politicians but to realize new forms of collective action and social life.

Because it marked the moment at which a host of previously separate forces and influences began to coalesce into the form that they would

---

[8] Karl Jaspers, *Wohin treibt die Bundesrepublik? Tatsachen, Gefahren, Chancen* (Munich: Piper, 1966).

[9] Slobodian, *Foreign Front*, p. 70.

[10] The latter is a point made by Thomas, *Protest Movements*.

assume for the better part of the next decade, providing the motor force for the rise of the extraparliamentary opposition in West Germany and all that followed from it, the anti-Tshombe protest marks a natural starting point for the narrative account that will unfold over the course of this study. But the protest is also important as a moment in which we may trace the outlines of 1968 in its *spatial* aspect; for, in the events of December 18, 1964, we can detect the imprint of the cartographical conceptions and communities of the imagination in which 1968 was situated, trace out transnational lines of influence to their convergence (exposing the new formations created out of the intersection of global and local), and uncover the outlines of a new relationship to authority in which the disposition of space – both discursive and physical – conditioned the possibilities of radical action.

MAPPING 1968 IN WEST GERMANY

What might a map of 1968 in West Germany look like? What sort of places and spaces, streets and alleys would it depict? What terrain, cognitive or concrete? Where would the Tshombe protest fit upon it? We might begin to think about these questions by considering an actual sort of map created by student activists at the Free University in Berlin a few short years after the Tshombe protest. Adorning the cover of the May 1968 issue of the *FU Spiegel*, published at the height of the student riots in Paris, the map depicts students dressed in jeans and parkas sprawling out in silhouette over a Europe in revolt. Berlin is merely one in a number of revolutionary capitals, designated by stars, stretching from Oslo in the north to Rome in the south, from London in the west to Warsaw in the east. Erasing distinctions between the southern dictatorships and the northwestern democracies, between the "free" West and the Communist East, the map depicts the revolt of a new historical agent – the revolutionary student – across the borders of the nation-state and the boundaries of the Cold War bloc system.

This depiction of youth in revolt corresponded to an easily identifiable reality in the spring of 1968; youth was indeed on the move, unsettling university and government administrations on both sides of the Iron Curtain. Yet the map is also important for illustrating a way of thinking about the world; in depicting the erasure of boundaries – an erasure of boundaries linked to an erasure of distinctions between one place (or thing) and another – it reproduces what may rightly be identified as *the* fundamental spatial-conceptual maneuver of 1968. The erasure of

Figure 1.2 International Student Revolt. *FU Spiegel*, no. 64, May 1968. APO-Archiv.

distinctions between *places* is simultaneously the erasure of distinctions between *concerns*; and encoded in the map's depiction of "international student revolt" is the (revolutionary) notion that what matters to students in London also matters to students in Prague, that the problems (and solutions) of one place are those of the other. The concern with the Third

World exhibited in the Tshombe protest – as a place where questions of democracy and human rights ought to have the same valence as in the Western metropoles (and later as a place that seemed to offer theoretical solutions to the revolutionary impasse in those metropoles) – represents merely an extension of this fundamental conceit.

The upsurge of global engagement on the part of the young intelligentsia was organized around notions of political authenticity: activists took at face value the claims of Western governments regarding democracy and human rights and probed at the gaps between official pronouncements and factual realities when the two did not meet up. In this connection, it is possible to interpret 1968 as an attempt to overcome the divergence between words and deeds, both in the public sphere (with respect to power's claims to legitimacy) and later, as we will see, in the private sphere as well. The critique of power and its claims was linked to a new vitality of the social imagination, characterized by an ability to envision the consequences of state policy across the borders of the nation-state. This act of the imagination was not created entirely from the side of student activists, however, but was made possible for them (sometimes imposed on them) by the cartographical structures in which West Germany was imbedded and by the avenues of communication and mobility that cut across these structures.

The spatial situation of Germany in the 1960s can be imagined in terms of a series of concentric circles: the middle circle, corresponding roughly to the defeated nation partitioned by the victorious Allies in 1949, represents divided Germany, its western half made up of the Bundesrepublik Deutschland (BRD; Federal Republic of Germany), its eastern half by the Deutsche Demokratische Republik (DDR; German Democratic Republic). Like an island in the middle of the latter lies a smaller circle corresponding to the divided city of Berlin, physically partitioned since late 1961 by a mined and barbwired concrete wall, its non-Communist half connected to the West by a thin umbilical highway stretching some 177 kilometers to its entry point in the Federal Republic at Helmstedt. Reproduced in microcosm in divided Berlin is not only the partitioned state of which it was formerly the capital but a still larger circle formed by the Cold War bloc system dividing Europe and much of the rest of the world into Soviet and American spheres of influence. A fundamental feature of this arrangement is that an action in one of the circles must necessarily resonate in the others, so that physical locations do not function independently of each other but rather mirror each other.

This phenomenon especially stands out in the case of US–West German relations. The role of the USA in founding the Federal Republic is difficult to overstate; in a divided Germany with a discredited past, the American attempt to stamp its influence on West Germany was constitutive in its profundity.[11] The official German–American alliance, rooted in the American military occupation at the end of World War II, was sealed by American backing for the formation of the Bundesrepublik in 1949 and the integration of West Germany into the NATO (North Atlantic Treaty Organization) alliance in 1955. This relationship was concretized in a hundred ways big and small, not least by continued American military governance in West Berlin and the presence of American military bases elsewhere throughout West Germany. For the West German establishment, the relationship with America was seen as a bulwark against the past and a guarantee for the future; yet the American presence in the Federal Republic had a dual effect, for while the American guarantee against Communist aggression made the USA the object of heartfelt gratitude (nowhere more than in West Berlin), it also meant that American actions anywhere in the world automatically resonated, for good or ill, in West Germany.

The effect of the US war in Vietnam offers the example par excellence of this phenomenon. The war was one of the most important globalizing factors of 1968. Killing over 2 million civilians and wounding another 5 million, in no small part through air sorties that unleashed the equivalent of 640 Hiroshima bombs, the war was widely seen as a crime against humanity of vast scale.[12] Opposition to the war helped create networks of affinity and notions of common struggle that focused on the global issue of the war even as they articulated with local concerns. Nowhere in Europe was the war of such immediate local concern as in West Germany. The prominence of opposition to the American war in Vietnam to the West German student movement makes it easy to forget how much young West Germans in the 1960s looked up to the USA. The USA was regarded as a beacon of democracy and a guarantor of Germany's turn away from its authoritarian past. The election of John F. Kennedy as President of the USA in 1960 reinforced notions of America as a source of modernizing liberalism whose democratic claims (problems of racism and structural inequality aside) could be regarded seriously.

[11] See Konrad H. Jarausch and Hannes Siegrist, eds., *Amerikanisierung und Sowjetisierung in Deutschland, 1945–1970* (Frankfurt: Campus, 1997).
[12] Nick Turse, *Kill Anything That Moves: The Real American War in Vietnam* (New York: Metropolitan Books, 2013).

The American playwright and journalist Alex Gross, a Berlin correspondent for the British underground newspaper *International Times*,
friend to many German artists, intellectuals, and student activists, recalls
the "worship" that his German friends lavished on America and its institutions. "I have sat through innumerable German student meetings," he
writes, "in which the words 'democracy' or 'freedom of expression' were
used almost ritualistically, not as the difficult realities we know them
to be ... but almost as magical open-sesame phrases, which if repeated
often and earnestly enough will come to fruition."[13] Gross recalls with
bemusement how his friend, the German-American writer Reinhard
Lettau, "waxed into absolute ecstasy about how pure and just and true the
American people were, unlike Germans, and how Americans always dealt
democratically and fairly with one another and were not subject to all
the petty prejudices Germans suffered from."[14] Lettau went on at length,
praising, among other things, the democratic qualities of "the great
American game of baseball," to the extent that, Gross wryly observes, "he
really began to sound like a Hearst editorial of ten years earlier."[15]

Such projections clearly said more about Germans' attitude toward
Germany than about their knowledge of America, but they also reflected
a democratic striving that, if constructed in terms of an overidealized
vision of America, was no less authentic for that. The key effect of this
regard for America, however, was to transform its descent into the violent
and morally compromised chaos of the Vietnam War into a major source
of cognitive dissonance. Disappointment over the Vietnam War was by
no means confined to the student movement, indeed, but was widely
shared. To be sure, many supported the war, either because they accepted
the argument that it was a necessary defense against Communist aggression or simply because the West German government supported it; but
wide strata of society, including Christian groups and trade unions, journalists and intellectuals, and many average citizens, opposed it. In every
case, the special relationship between West Germany and the USA gave a
diamond edge to the outrage. In this way, the concrete connections of the
Cold War alliance system, and the conceptual categories with which they
were connected, caused space both to expand (to encompass global concerns) and to collapse, reproducing global relationships at the local level.

[13] Alex Gross, *The Untold Sixties: When Hope Was Born – An Insider's Sixties on an International
Scale* (New York: Cross-Cultural Research Projects, 2009), p. 214.
[14] *Ibid.*
[15] Gross, *The Untold Sixties*, pp. 214–216. Lettau moved to California to take up a post in German
literature at the University of California, San Diego, in 1967.

Figure 1.3 "Americans in Vietnam make us guilty too." Anti-Vietnam War demonstration, Tauentzienstraße, Berlin-Schöneberg, October 21, 1967. The protest was part of a transatlantic event, timed to coincide with the march on the Pentagon in Washington, D.C. Landesarchiv Berlin.

This sort of spatial conflation reached its ultimate expression in the division of Berlin, a city that came to reproduce, in its very top-ography, the conceptual categories of the Cold War.[16] Prior to August 1961, Berlin provided the only significant space of exchange between the two Germanys; the inter-German border had been sealed, electrical grids severed, and telephone lines cut, nearly a decade before. Before the construction of the Wall (and to an extent afterwards as well), Berlin acted as a sort of permeable membrane between East and West.[17] Sixty thousand East Berliners worked in West Berlin in 1961, and roughly a million tickets to West Berlin theaters and cinemas were purchased by East Germans that year. Fifteen thousand East Germans decided to flee

[16] Wilfried Mausbach has used the term "relocation" to capture a similar idea; see Wilfried Mausbach, "America's Vietnam in Germany: On the Relocation of Spaces and the Appropriation of History," in Davis et al., *Changing the World*, pp. 41–64.
[17] Brian Ladd, *Ghosts of Berlin: Confronting German History in the Urban Landscape* (University of Chicago Press, 1997), p. 179.

to West Berlin permanently in January 1961, with numbers increasing month by month.[18]

The building of the wall transformed the situation in Berlin (literally) overnight. The Berlin population awoke on the morning of August 13, 1961, to find East German forces erecting crude wire barriers across a 43-kilometer stretch of the city from top to bottom. In response to threatening crowds of excited and angry West Berliners, members of the Volkspolizei (VoPos) deployed tear gas and water cannons along the Bethaniendamm in Kreuzberg and at the Brandenburger Tor. The first warning shots were fired the next day at the Brandenburger Tor and on the Wildenbruchstraße in Neukölln. In Treptow (and subsequently in other districts), buildings along the intercity border were walled in or nailed up.[19] By the end of August, some 25,000 people somehow managed to make it to West Berlin before the wall was hardened into the imposing concrete structure that it would remain for almost three decades.[20] Many more, unable or unwilling to escape, were doomed to be cut off from friends and family for the rest of the Cold War.[21]

Rudi Dutschke was already in West Berlin when the wall went up, one of many East Germans attending the Free University there. When the Wall was erected at the end of November 1961, Dutschke faced a difficult choice: separation from friends and family versus the opportunity to continue his education and live free of the strictures of an increasingly repressive East German regime. Dutschke opted to stay in the West, but his outlook and his politics were decisively shaped by his experiences in the DDR. "It's crazy," he wrote in April 1965 on the way to Moscow as part of an SDS delegation,

---

[18] Chaussy, *Die drei Leben des Rudi Dutschke*, p. 26. In June, the figure was 20,000; in July, 30,314; in August, 17,528; the last left the DDR on the night of August 12; *Ibid*. Some 2,691,270 persons were registered with the government of the Federal Republic as having fled from the DDR since September 1949; Bundesministerium für Gesamtdeutsche Fragen, "Die Flucht aus der Sowjetzone und die Sperrmassnahmen des Kommunistischen Regimes vom 13, August 1961 in Berlin, September 7, 1961," Bundesarchiv (hereafter BArch) Koblenz, B106, 36768.

[19] "Bericht über Ereignisse und Einsatz der Schutz- und Bereitschaaftspolizei vom. 13.8–13.11.1961," BArch Koblenz, B106, 36768, p. 3.

[20] The number reached over 51,000 by the end of the year; Alexandra Hildebrandt, *The Wall: Figures, Facts* (Berlin: Verlag Haus am Checkpoint Charlie, 2005), p. 55.

[21] "Even then the two Berlins were not entirely isolated from one another," points out Ladd, "but the extent of the remaining contacts was very limited: postal service, a teletype connection between the police forces, telephone connections between the transit systems and the fire departments, Western subway lines that travelled under Eastern territory without stopping, a train system in the West operated by the East, Eastern water serving a few corners of West Berlin, and sewage flowing freely under the wall wherever gravity dictated." Ladd, *Ghosts of Berlin*, p. 179.

I come from East Germany, from the DDR, and had to get out. Now I'm traveling through, can't get off the train anywhere. The comrades who are traveling with me probably can't comprehend this funny feeling ... Certainly I can't forget another experience: my youthful attempt to take in June 17, 1953, my prayers for the Hungarian uprising of 1956.[22]

Dutschke's mother, still living in the East German town of Luckenwalde, advised him to forget about politics and to concentrate on his studies. "I can't even go to Luckenwalde to visit," he lamented in his diary.[23] The trauma of separation was complicated by Dutschke's intellectual relationship to the East as both a birthplace and a burial place of revolution. "As an SDS member they can't simply arrest me," he wrote during the same trip; "they're not in the 1930s any more. Anyway, the era of *barbaric* Stalinism is over(?)."[24]

For the average citizen of West Berlin, especially anyone old enough to have had direct experience of the tactics employed by Soviet security forces in Berlin in the early postwar period (dragging hapless victims into waiting sedans never to be seen again), the situation was much less complicated. Outrage over the murders at the Wall of fellow Germans trying to escape from East Berlin was only the barest part of the picture. "They had lived through the time of rubble, blockade, airlift, revolts, waves of refugees, the building of the wall, fears of war, nightly gunshots, screams, searchlights, barking of dogs, dramatic scenes of every variety," writes Gerd Koenen, "and along with that the bullying of the VoPos whenever they wanted to leave the city ... That ... students could get more worked up about the [visit of] a Moïse Tshombe ... than about the situation of the city [was something they] could not grasp."[25]

An attitude of determined resistance to Soviet domination was personified in popular figures such as West Berlin's first mayor, Ernst Reuter, a former Communist with impeccable anti-Nazi credentials who helped build up the self-image of West Berlin as an isolated outpost of freedom.[26] Popular anti-Communism was amplified in the daily newspapers of the Springer Press, which reproduced, in sensationalist form, the Manichean worldview of the Cold War. The consensus view toward the "socialist"

[22] Rudi Dutschke, *Jeder hat sein Leben ganz zu leben: Diaries of Rudi Dutschke 1963–1979*, ed. Gretchen Dutschke (Cologne: Kiepenheuer & Witsch, 2003), undated entry, p. 26.

[23] Dutschke, *Diaries*, entry for April 19, 1965, pp. 26–27.

[24] Dutschke, *Diaries*, undated entry, p. 26.

[25] Gerd Koenen, *Das rote Jahrzehnt: Unsere kleine deutsche Kulturrevolution, 1967–1977* (Cologne, Kiepenheuer & Witsch, 2001), pp. 38–39.

[26] On Ernst Reuter, see David E. Barclay, *Schaut auf diese Stadt: Der unbekannte Ernst Reuter*, trans. Ilse Utz (Berlin: Siedler Verlag, 2000).

experiment taking place in the East was reflected in the practice, uniform in official publications, of referring to East Germany as the "so-called DDR," or more simply, as the *Sowjetische Besatzungszone* (SBZ; Soviet Occupation Zone).

For the West German student generation coming of age in the 1960s, anti-Communism of the sort that had characterized the Adenauer years, and that continued, in West Berlin, to operate as an organizing principle, was no longer tenable. The notion of West Berlin as a *Frontstadt* (front city) was symbolic of the sclerotic Cold War relations the student movement sought to challenge. Whatever the crimes of Eastern Bloc Communism – crimes that SDS members were typically ready to acknowledge, even if, for understandable reasons, they preferred not to be seen to stand ideologically shoulder to shoulder with the surviving representatives of a Nazi regime known for its anti-Marxist brutality – anti-Communism could too easily be instrumentalized to cancel out discussion of political alternatives. As a flyer produced by the group around Kunzelmann in December 1966 put it:

The free citizen, fed on *Bild* newspapers, recites his well-learned newspaper slogans at the Wall and swears to the eternal front-line atmosphere necessary for West Berlin's political preservation. A "democracy" conceived as an opposition to the East is not able to see its own contradictions. It becomes a dictatorship where everyone is his own cop.[27]

The policing of Cold War boundaries was expressed in fundamentally spatial terms. Constructing a West German identity oriented toward the *West* placed dissent automatically in the *East*. "From the beginning of the student movement," complained an activist in 1970, "protesters – no matter whether they were young Christians, trade unionists or Social Democrats – were painted as 'Mao Youth,' 'Red Guards,' 'FU-Chinese.'"[28] A primary culprit in this regard was the Springer Press, which routinely conflated West German students, East German agents, and Chinese Red Guards. This maneuver was notable for the way it tried to import conceptual categories for understanding the actions of West German youth from abroad (e.g. China), even as it simultaneously tried to force student dissidents across the wall into the ideological camp of West Germany's enemies.

[27] Reprinted in Peter Stansill and David Zane Mairowitz, eds., *BAMN (By Any Means Necessary): Outlaw Manifestos and Ephemera, 1965–1970* (New York: Autonomedia, 1999), pp. 116–117.
[28] Hannes Schwenger, "Literaturproduzenten: eine deutsche Kulturrevolution?" in Frank Benseler, Hannelore May, and Hannes Schwenger, eds., *Literaturproduzenten!* (Berlin: Edition Voltaire, 1970), p. 5.

Such attempts at virtual deportation, predicated on a heavily policed two-dimensional spatial scheme, were not infrequently accompanied by threats of the real thing. Protesters were advised by passersby to go to the DDR if they didn't like it in West Berlin. "A dog like you who can only murder, beat, and steal," wrote an anonymous correspondent to Rudi Dutschke, "belongs in the East, from whence you get your money. There's no place here for parasites. So piss off over there."[29] Comments like this were only an extreme and *ad hominem* variant of a more general response, which, although by no means uniform or monolithic, found expression from the highest government officials down to the man or woman in the streets of West Berlin. Elsewhere in the Federal Republic, naturally, the situation was less tense than in the divided former capital, but the conceptual boundary-policing that reached a white-hot intensity in the vicinity of the Wall exemplified a key aspect of the spatial politics of 1968; for, if one of the main thrusts of the 68er movement was the attempt to break out of the Cold War bloc system and its stifling anti-Communism, the hallmark of the establishment response was, for a variety of reasons, the attempt to reassert those boundaries.

Cold War boundaries were, in reality, far from being as solid as the conceptual categories of the Cold War would have had them. To begin with, they were constantly being challenged by new possibilities of mobility and communication. Many West German students had first-hand knowledge of the DDR and other Eastern Bloc countries. SDS delegates traveled to the World Youth Festival in Sofia, Bulgaria, in July 1968 (and were promptly disinvited when they clashed with their hosts over a protest at the US Embassy), and members of the Kommune I, including Dieter Kunzelmann, Fritz Teufel, and Rainer Langhans, traveled to East Berlin on a number of occasions, either to acquire copies of Mao Zedong's Red Book at the Chinese Embassy or to visit their opposite numbers in East German student circles, who were trying to enact their own rebellion against the strictures of Cold War politics.[30]

The exploits of the Kommune I had an impact far beyond the boundaries of West Berlin, and, like other aspects of the Western counterculture

---

[29] Anonymous letter in Stefan Reisner, ed., *Briefe an Rudi Dutschke* (Frankfurt: Edition Voltaire, 1968), p. 9.

[30] See the interview with Dieter Kunzelmann in Wolfgang Dreßen, Dieter Kunzelmann, and Eckhard Siepmann, eds., *Nilpferd des höllischen Urwalds: Situationisten, Gruppe Spur, Kommune I* (Giessen: Anabas), p. 197. Such visits took place under the nervous but watchful eye of the Stasi; see Tobias Wunschik, "Die Bewegung 2 Juni und ihre Protektion durch den Staatssicherheitsdienst der DDR," *Deutschland Archiv*, 6 (2007): 1014–1025, at p. 1017.

and student movement, its influence was strongly felt in the East.[31] Indeed, the visits of the Western communards to the Communist half of the city helped inspire the founding of a commune in East Berlin.[32] This so-called "K1-Ost," as it was dubbed by its founders, was the work of a small and relatively privileged group of children of leading cultural and political luminaries, prominent among them two sons and one daughter of the dissident scientist Robert Havemann. Members of this group were heavily influenced both by the ideas of the Western student movement and counterculture, of which they were well informed through Western media and personal contacts, and of contemporaneous attempts to develop a "Socialism with a Human Face" in neighboring Czechoslovakia.[33]

Members of this circle took part in the spontaneous wave of protests that greeted the Soviet invasion of Czechoslovakia in August 1968 and suffered jail terms and loss of educational privileges as a result. Shocked and disillusioned by the outcome of this all-too-brief foray into the public sphere, some of these would-be 68ers regrouped around the idea of a commune.[34] Founded in June 1969, the K1-Ost existed in different apartments in East Berlin until 1973.[35] It had a particularly important practical function, for, unlike West Berlin, with its left-wing bars and hangouts, East Berlin lacked semiprivate venues for oppositional sociability. Yet, as in the West, the goal of breaking through old strictures on personal behavior was at the forefront. In the face of a regime whose repressive moralizing and self-assured belief in its own rectitude was even more stifling than the "repressive tolerance" lamented by radicals in the West, the task

[31] Lutz Kirchenwitz, "1968 im Osten: was ging uns die Bundesrepublik an?" *UTOPIE kreativ*, 164 (June 2004).

[32] See Florian Havemann "68er Ost," *UTOPIE kreativ*, 164 (June 2004): 544–556, at p. 546; Frank Havemann, in Rainer Land and Ralf Possekel, *Fremde Welten: Die gegensätzliche Deutung der DDR durch SED-Reformer und Bürgerbewegung in den 80er Jahren* (Berlin: Kiepenheuer & Witsch, 1998), p. 220; Paul Kaiser, "Kommune 'K1 Ost', Ostberlin," unpublished radio broadcast manuscript for Deutschlandfunk-Radio, copy in possession of the author, p. 28; Ulrich Enzensberger, *Die Jahre der Kommune I: Berlin 1967–1969* (Cologne: Kiepenheuer & Witsch, 2004), p. 233; Dieter Kunzelmann, *Leisten Sie keinen Widerstand! Bilder aus meinem Leben* (Berlin: Transit, 1998), p. 91.

[33] Florian Havemann, interview with the author, Berlin, April 12, 2005.

[34] See Timothy S. Brown, "East Germany," in Martin Klimke and Joachim Scharloth, eds., *1968 in Europe: A History of Protest and Activism, 1956–1977* (London: Palgrave Macmillan, 2008), pp. 189–197. On the comparison of the East and West German "1968s," see the pieces in the special issue of *Aus Politik und Zeitgeschichte* (B 45/2003). See also Dietrich Mühlberg, "Wann war 68 im Osten? Oder: Wer waren die 68er im Osten?," in *Berliner Blätter: Ethnographische und ethnologische Beiträge* (Berlin: Institut für Europäische Ethnologie der Humboldt-Universität zu Berlin, 1999), pp. 44–58.

[35] Kaiser, "Kommune 'K1 Ost'," p. 21.

became all the more urgent. Practicing partner-swapping and antiauthoritarian child-rearing in their efforts to destroy the "bourgeois family," the communards attempted to overcome their social programming through group-therapy sessions on the West Berlin model. These attempts to revolutionize the private sphere were hardly private, however, for the founders were closely watched children of leading regime figures, a fact that accounts not only for the (relatively) light sentences they received in the wake of the protest action of fall 1968 but also for their ability to found the commune in the first place.[36]

The pressure of attempting to embrace Western styles of dress and music under a regime that tolerated neither, simultaneously bucking the conformity of social roles embraced by the overwhelming majority of the population, all the while living in a fishbowl of state security surveillance, took its toll. A more fundamental problem, however, lay in the impossibility of reconciling the cultural and political, fusing the youth revolution in appearance, music, and mores with new forms of political struggle. Increasingly, these two goals, more or less fused together in the Western Kommune I, came into conflict in the East. The attempt to find a way forward via the study of classic texts of Marxism–Leninism and support for the revolutions in the Third World, both poor means of opposition in the DDR when the government officially supported both, led toward a dead end. The ultimate moment of cognitive dissonance occurred when Fidel Castro, the Eastern communards' Third World hero, proclaimed his support for the Soviet crushing of the Prague Spring, thus cutting the ground out from under any attempt to fuse Third World revolution and Socialism with a Human Face.[37] Unable to forge a meaningful connection between internal and external space, between private and public revolution, the Eastern communards were doomed to impotence.

The failed East Berlin commune experience was but one of the more visible outcomes of broader patterns of exchange, both within and between the three "worlds." Opportunities for study and travel abroad in the 1960s, broadened by expanded international travel networks and increasing prosperity, resulted in increased contact between young people of different Western European countries and between those in Europe and North America.[38] From the second half of the 1950s, youth travel increased to locations such as Italy, southern France, Spain, and

---

[36] Kaiser, "Kommune 'K1 Ost'," p. 23.   [37] Brown, "1968 East and West," p. 93.

[38] See Axel Schildt, "Across the Border: West German Youth Travel to Western Europe," in Axel Schildt and Detlef Siegfried, eds., *Between Marx and Coca-Cola*, pp. 149–160.

Greece, an upsurge of mobility connected with a growing trend toward freethinking. Eastern Bloc students were on the move as well. The intelligence service of the East German state, the Stasi, noted extensive contacts between East German and Western students, estimating in 1968, for example, that 75 percent of students at the Technical University in Dresden had contacts with young people in the West. These contacts were established through chance meetings with Western students traveling in the DDR or other Eastern Bloc countries, through visits to West Berlin, or through the dissemination of pen-pal addresses by illegally received Western radio.[39] A new availability of Anglo-American (and European) cultural products – books, movies, music, and clothes – played a major role in the spread of a new life feeling that was central to the development of an antiauthoritarian youth consciousness on both sides of the Iron Curtain.[40]

Student-exchange programs helped facilitate the new interconnectedness. In particular, they were important in bringing Third World students to West Germany, where some of them, already highly politicized by experiences and conditions in their native countries, occupied a central position in the radicalization of the West German student movement. Their agitation took place in a favorable climate, for knowledge of Third World human-rights issues, transmitted by journalism, photos, and film, was becoming increasingly available in West Germany in the 1960s. This was true in both the mainstream and left-wing press; the leftist magazine *konkret* featured the face of the murdered Patrice Lumumba on its cover on the occasion of his death in 1961, and gruesome photographs of the fighting in the Congo (with an emphasis on the activity of German mercenaries) appeared in the illustrated *Stern* in November–December 1964 at the very moment of Tshombe's visit to West Germany.

The protest against Tshombe, indeed, marked one of the first and most visible moments when foreign students helped to synergize protest in West Germany. The Latin American Student League and the African Student League were co-organizers of the protests in Munich and Berlin.[41] Foreign students dogged Tshombe with shouts of "Murderer!" during his appearance before wealthy industrialists in Düsseldorf on December 17

[39] Armin Mitter and Stefan Wolle, *Untergang auf Raten: Unbekannte Kapitel der DDR-Geschichte* (Munich: Bertelsmann, 1993), pp. 380–381.
[40] See Michael Rauhut and Thomas Kochan, eds., *Bye Bye, Lübben City: Bluesfreaks, Tramps und Hippies in der DDR* (Berlin: Schwarzkopf & Schwarzkopf, 2004). See also Rebecca Menzel, *Jeans in der DDR: vom tieferen Sinn einer Freizeithose* (Berlin: Ch. Links Verlag, 2004).
[41] The *Argument-Klub* and the LSD were also co-organizers.

and made up some 150 of the 800 protesters in West Berlin the next day.[42] African students, marching shoulder to shoulder with Germans, appear prominently in photographs of the December 18 protest in West Berlin. These foreign students, noted Rudi Dutschke approvingly in his diary, helped turn what had originally been planned as a "silent demonstration" on December 18 into an assault on public order involving catcalls, thrown tomatoes, and scuffles with the police. "Our friends from the Third World stepped into the breach," he wrote afterwards, "and the Germans had to follow."[43]

Later actions, notably the protest against the showing of the racist exploitation film *Africa Addio* in August 1966, were also synergized by foreign exchange students concerned both with conditions in their homelands and with the portrayal of their ethnicities in the metropole. Directed by the Italian Gualtiero Jacopetti, *Africa Addio* was an exploit-ation film masquerading as a documentary. Employing footage shot in the Congo in 1964, shortly before Tshombe's visit to Berlin, it depicted gruesome scenes of mob violence, animal sacrifice, and execution. The all-too-obvious message, as the SDS and the African Student League put it, was "that the people of the African continent lack the ability to build civilization."[44] The inherent racism of the film's depiction of Africans was underlined by scenes in the film in which German mercenaries executed black prisoners, scenes that called to mind Gerd Heidemann's 1964 *Stern* series on mercenaries fighting with Tshombe in the Congo. This series profiled the activities of German mercenary Siegfried "Kongo" Müller, a former member of Hitler's Wehrmacht involved in atrocities against black prisoners and civilians.[45] *Africa Addio* presented a golden opportunity to protest against racism, against the persistence of colonial exploitation, and against the continuing presence of fascism. The protest kicked off when Fritz Teufel and Adekunle Ajala (head of the African Student League in

---

[42] "'Der Beginn unserer Kulturrevolution.' Vor 40 Jahren: Studentischer Protest gegen den Kongolesischen Staatspräsident Moise Tshombe," *So oder So!* 14 (fall 2004), p. 15.

[43] Dutschke, *Diaries*, undated entry, p. 23. See "Flughafen Tempelhof: Platz der Luftbrücke, Freitag 10.00 Uhr, Schweigedemonstration," reprinted in Frank Böckelmann and Herbert Nagel, eds., *Subversive Aktion: Der Sinn der Organisation ist ihr Scheitern* (Frankfurt: Verlag Neue Kritik, 1976), p. 279.

[44] Sozialistischer Deutscher Studentenbund, Afrikanischer Studentenbund, "Sehr geehrter Herr Kinobesitzer," undated, Archiv des Hamburger Instituts für Sozialforschung (hereafter HIS), 110/01.

[45] On Siegfried Müller, see Christian Bunnenberg, "'Kongo-Müller': Eine deutsche Söldnerkarriere," in Bernhard Chiari and Dieter H. Kollmer, eds., *Wegweiser zur Geschichte Demokratische Republik Kongo* (Paderborn: Militärgeschichtlichen Forschungsamtes, 2006), pp. 36–38. See also Otto Köhler, *Kongo-Müller oder Die Freiheit, die wir verteidigen* (Frankfurt: Bärmeier u. Nikel, 1966).

Figure 1.4 Protest against visit of Moïse Tshombe to West Berlin,
December 18, 1964. Landesarchiv Berlin.

West Berlin) pulled shut the curtains over the stage of the theater, perfectly symbolizing the internationalization of the student movement both
in terms of aims and personnel.[46]

The Tshombe and *Africa Addio* protests marked the confluence of the
Third World student diaspora with the nascent politics of West German
student revolt, highlighting, in particular, the importance of educational exchange networks that brought foreign students such as Ajala,
an exchange scholar with the Deutscher Akademischer Austauschdienst
(DAAD; German Academic Exchange Service), to West Germany.[47] Yet

[46] "'Africa addio' am Kurfürstendamm abgesetzt," *Die Welt*, August 6, 1966, p. 9. See the photo of
the protest in Michael Ruetz, *"Ihr müßt diesen Typen nur ins Gesicht sehen": APO Berlin, 1966–
1969* (Frankfurt: Zweitausendeins), p. 15. See also Jan-Frederik Bandel, "Das Malheur. Kongo-
Müller und die Proteste gegen 'Africa Addio,'" in *iz3w*, no. 287 (2005), pp. 37–41. On the protest
see Niels Seibert, "Proteste gegen den Film *Africa Addio*: Ein Beispiel fur Antirassismus in den
60er-Jarhen," in Interface, ed., *WiderstandsBewegungen: Antirassismus zwischen Alltag und Aktion*
(Berlin: Assoziation A, 2005).

[47] The DAAD weighed in on Ajala's behalf in the criminal proceedings against him on account
of the protest; DAAD, "An den Polizeipräsidenten von Berlin ... Betr.: Herrn Adekunle Ajala,
July 4, 1967"; HIS 110/01. The DAAD sponsored some 2,379 foreign students in West Germany
in 1968, including 472 from so-called developing nations. *DAAD Jahresbericht 1968*, p. 92, cited

the protests also marked the intersection of two related but competing conceptions of German identity. The *Africa Addio* protest, for example, stood at the heart of a bitter conflict between West and East Germany over the legacy of colonialism and fascism. "Kongo" Müller was the subject of a documentary film by the East German journalists Walter Heynowski and Gerhard Scheumann.[48] Intended to educate both First and Third World audiences about the persistence of colonialism and racism, the film was based in part on materials used in Gerd Heidemann's 1964 *Stern* series. The filmmakers were invited by the SDS to a screening and discussion of their film in West Berlin, an event that attracted a heavily multicultural audience.[49] Helping to shape the attitudes of the West German students protesting *Africa Addio*, the film represented a striking example of inter-German "dialogue," while illustrating both how German–German conflicts could be projected onto the Third World and how these same conflicts could reflect back into Germany.

It is unsurprising in this context that the Tshombe protest marked the first instance of open cooperation between the SDS and the official East German youth wing, the Freie Deutsche Jugend (FDJ; Free German Youth). A number of the African students in the protest, indeed, came over from East Berlin and can be seen in photographs bearing signs reading "Bonn = Enemy of the Congo, DDR = Friend of the Congo." The attempt of the FDJ to "cooperate" with Western student organizations, part of a larger strategy of infiltration and subversion against the West pursued by the Communist regime, bore a striking similarity to the United Front from Below strategy of the Weimar-era Communist Party, which had been aimed at stealing Social Democratic workers away from the SPD under the pretense of joint action against fascism.[50] Like the East German regime's other organizational initiatives – the Sozialistische Einheitspartei Deutschland's (SED; Socialist Unity Party) use of the reconstituted Weimar-era Kommunistische Partei Deutschland (KPD;

in Bjørn Pätzoldt, *Ausländerstudium in der BRD: Ein Beitrag zur Imperialismuskritik* (Cologne: Pahl-Rugenstein, 1972), p. 103. Ajala was later the author of a book on Pan-Africanism: Adekunle Ajala, *Pan-Africanism: Evolution, Progress and Prospects* (New York: St. Martin's Press, 1973).

[48] *Der lachende Mann*, dir. Walter Heynowski and Gerhard Scheumann, 1965–1966. A book based on the film was published as Walter Heynowski and Gerhard Scheumann, *Der lachende Mann: Bekenntnisse eines Mörders* (Berlin: Verlag Der Nation, 1966).

[49] Kristina M. Hagen, "Internationalism in Cold War Germany," doctoral dissertation, University of Washington, 2008, p. 200.

[50] On the "United Front from Below" strategy, see Timothy S. Brown, *Weimar Radicals: Nazis and Communists between Authenticity and Performance* (New York and Oxford: Berghahn Books, 2009).

Communist Party of Germany) as a wedge against the Federal Republic until its banning in 1956, or the founding, in 1962, of a Sozialistische Einheitspartei Westberlins (SEW; Socialist Unity Party West Berlin) out of the SED's West Berlin branch – this cooperation sought to straddle German–German boundaries in a way that proved awkward for all concerned.[51]

For the SDS, cooperation with the FDJ was both an act of defiance against the anti-Communist ideology of the Federal Republic and an attempt to weaken the hard and fast categories of the Cold War bloc system. The SDS demanded recognition of the DDR as the only rational response to existing realities. Contact with the FDJ was an attempt to work toward normalization from below. "Any attempt to come into conversation with youth in the DDR," the SDS argued,

comes up against the FDJ, [which organizes] a sizable portion of the youth who are critical to the foreseeable political development of the DDR … [The SDS] hopes through its contacts to improve the quality of the information available to each side about the other … and thereby above all to take some of the emotion out of [German–German] relations.[52]

Relations between the SDS and the FDJ were problematic, however, as they must necessarily have been given the FDJ's status as the youth wing of a dictatorial Communist party that saw "cooperation" as a welcome opportunity to meddle in the internal affairs of the Federal Republic.[53] The Tshombe protest had originally been organized as a *silent* demonstration, for example, because the FDJ objected to the proposed language of a joint communiqué that referred to "the tragedy of the wall."[54] Negotiations surrounding the proposed visit of an FDJ delegation to a joint seminar with

---

[51] See Thomas Klein, *SEW: Die Westberliner Einheitssozialisten – Eine "ostdeutsche" Partei als Stachel im Fleische der "Frontstadt"?* (Berlin: Ch. Links Verlag, 2009).

[52] "FDJ kommt nicht nach Frankfurt. Dokumente über Verhandlungen zwischen dem Bundesvorstand des SDS und dem Zentralrat der FDJ aus der Zeit vom 1.6.1964 bis zum 11.2.1965," BArch Koblenz, Zsg 153/8. "West German students, including the less radical, are inclined to think that such contacts serve to promote German unity," read a CIA report, "and that they can elude SED influence and indeed weaken the hold of the SED on its own youth. They are not in every case mistaken. But the SED apparently hopes to [establish] a network of intermediate-level control in student (as in other) organizations, and then to use these contacts to manipulate the organizations"; CIA Report, "Restless Youth," available online at www.faqs.org/cia/docs/64/0000518840/RESTLESS-YOUTH.html (accessed April 23, 2010).

[53] On the DDR's multiple connections inside the West German student movement see Hubertus Knabe, *Der diskrete Charme der DDR: Stasi und Westmedien* (Berlin: Propyläen, 2001), pp. 321–323, 361–363; see also Hubertus Knabe, *West-Arbeit des MfS: Das Zusammenspiel von "Aufklärung" und "Abwehr"* (Berlin: Ch. Links Verlag, 1999).

[54] In the published SDS account of these negotiations, blame was layed at the feet of the LSD; Bergmann et al., *Rebellion*, p. 63.

the SDS in Frankfurt dragged on from mid 1964 through the following year, made difficult by charges in the press of secret dealings between the organizations, in part due to an inability to reach agreement on the content of the program.[55] In the run-up to a combined SDS–FDJ seminar on the political problems of the day in East Berlin in July 1967, the FDJ worried about the political independence of the SDS, noting that its "Marxist-Leninist positions [were] only weakly developed."[56]

Attitudes toward the FDJ were more positive among the traditionalists in the SDS, a group whose power was curtailed when the pro-Eastern-Bloc faction in the SDS was expelled by the antiauthoritarians in the wake of the World Youth Festival in Bulgaria.[57] A supporter of contact between the FDJ and the SDS, writing in the Marxist journal *International Socialism*, noted that a hoped-for reduction of "anti-Communism" in the SDS was "not an attractive program for students." The "[equation of] socialism with the GDR (East Germany)," he concluded, "arouses little sympathy."[58] The gulf separating the FDJ and the SDS came out with special clarity in the aftermath of the Warsaw Pact invasion of Czechoslovakia in August 1968, a blow against aspirations for a democratic form of socialism that provoked demonstrations on both sides of the Iron Curtain.[59] "In this connection it is necessary to observe," noted an FDJ memorandum, "that the overwhelming majority of young workers and student organizations took a position against the measures of the allied socialist countries."[60]

Complaining about the influence of Trotskyism and Maoism in the SDS, the FDJ noted the worrying signs presented by "an array of anarchist and sectarian conceptions and actions of different functionaries and groups, as for example in an incorrect attitude toward West German trade unions, in a 'vanguard attitude,' and in commune-building at various universities in West Germany and West Berlin."[61] Obvious overlap in the issues of potential interest to two socialist organizations, such as questions of anti-imperialism and Third World national liberation, provided the formal grounds for attempts at joint action. Yet, for the FDJ, socialist youth

---

[55] "FDJ kommt nicht nach Frankfurt," p. 2.   [56] *Ibid.*

[57] Kurt L. Shell, "Extra-Parliamentary Opposition in Postwar Germany," *Comparative Politics*, 2 (4), Special Issue on the West German Election of 1969 (July 1970): 653–680, at p. 676.

[58] Manfred Buddeberg, "The Student Movement in West Germany," *International Socialism*, 33 (summer 1968): 27–34.

[59] See Brown, "1968 East and West."

[60] Compare this with the unfounded assertion of Tony Judt that "if Western youth looked beyond their borders at all, it was to exotic lands whose image floated free of the irritating constraints of familiarity or information"; Tony Judt, *Postwar: A History of Europe since 1945* (New York: Penguin, 2005), p. 421.

[61] *Ibid.*

politics were always, and above all, *regime* politics. For Rudi Dutschke, a chief exemplar of the "vanguard attitude" criticized by the FDJ, there was no question of defending the actions of the Warsaw Pact, nor of trying to protect socialism in the DDR. Reflecting on the moment at which demonstrators had stopped to purchase tomatoes to hurl at Tshombe, he wrote, "The women ... in the market screamed at us: 'just get out of here and go to the East.' But a lot of us just came from there!"[62]

ASSAULT(S) ON THE METROPOLE

On a map of 1968 in West Germany, the Tshombe and *Africa Addio* protests belong at that point at which Cold War-bloc politics intersected with German–German politics, cut across by a diasporic politics of Third World students in the metropole. These protests also have to be situated with respect to the indigenous streams of radicalism that fed into them and whose further development they helped to synergize; for the history of 1968 in West Germany is much less a history of organizations such as the SDS per se than it is of a series of *interventions* on the SDS by an activist avant-garde, more or less coterminous, in the early phase, with the group Subversive Aktion, whose members looked beyond West German borders for revolutionary raw material. Their intervention may be seen as an "assault on the metropole" in two senses: first, it sought to transplant the revolution of the Third World periphery into the heart of West Germany, linking the revolution at home to the revolution abroad; second, it sought to deploy the materials and modalities of an international cultural revolution – theories, protest repertoires, cultural products – in the space of Germany's cities and streets. Actively engaged in facilitating connections both conceptual and concrete, protagonists of what will be referred to in this study as the *active transnational*, these activists brought the world to West Germany even as they imagined West Germany into the world.

Almost as if in subconscious imitation of the peasant guerrilla armies whom they admired and later sought to emulate, they planned this twofold assault in the countryside: Our map of 1968 in West Germany, with its concentric circles of armed alliance spiraling down to the explosively packed space of West Berlin, must include a small village in upper Bavaria: Kochel am See. Bringing together two geographic factions, one from Berlin, one from Munich, the July 1966 meeting in Kochel am See marked a transition from the early phase of activism associated with Subversive

---

[61] Dutschke, *Diaries*, entry for December 1964, p. 24.

Aktion to the beginning of the radical phase of the (mass) student movement. The Munich contingent revolved around Dieter Kunzelmann, who, before founding Subversive Aktion, had been "chief theorist" to a Munich artists' collective known as the Gruppe Spur.[63] Operating in the legendary artists' enclave of Schwabing, Spur carried out a two-pronged assault on the institutionalized art world and the cultural and political consensus that supported it, aiming to transform the conditions of human existence by erasing the distinctions between art and daily life.

The Spur group was decisively influenced by its involvement with the Situationist International, a transnational anarchist avant-garde operating at the intersection of art and politics. Centered around the Parisian theorist Guy Debord, the Situationist International offered a radical, total critique of Western consumer capitalism and bureaucratic Eastern Communism. For Debord, modern society was dominated by the "spectacle" – an endless parade of images and commodified experiences that became a substitute for authentic existence.[64] The disruption of the spectacle through any means necessary became the political act par excellence. The Situationist concept of *détournement* (the deliberate subversion of the significance of an object or event to suggest the opposite of the meaning intended) underpinned Spur's "Bense-Happening" of January 1959, in which an audience invited to hear a lecture by the philosopher Max Bense was presented with a tape-recorded impersonation of Bense reading a hopelessly complex mishmash of theoretical claptrap. An astonished Bense only found out about his "appearance" when questioned about it afterward by reporters.[65]

In the summer of 1963, Kunzelmann helped found a more explicitly political (as opposed to artistic) group named Subversive Aktion.[66] Within a year, "microcells" had been established in cities around West Germany, including Munich, Hamburg, Nuremberg/Erlangen, Frankfurt, Tübingen, Stuttgart, and Berlin. Dutschke and Bernd Rabehl

---

[63] Founded in 1957, the group included the painters Hans-Peter Zimmer, Heimrad Prem, Helmut Sturm, and the sculptor Lothar Fischer. See Mia Lee, "Gruppe Spur: Art as a Revolutionary Medium during the Cold War," in Brown and Anton, eds., *Between the Avant-garde and the Everyday*, pp. 11–30.

[64] "The spectacle," Debord wrote, "is the ruling order's nonstop discourse about itself, its neverending monologue of self-praise, its self-portrait at the stage of totalitarian domination of all aspects of life"; Guy Debord, *The Society of the Spectacle* (Detroit, Mich.: Black and Red, 1983).

[65] Lee, "Gruppe Spur."

[66] Co-founders were Kunzelmann's brother-in-law Christofer Baldeney (aka Rudolf May), Rodolphe Gasché, Marion Steffel-Stergar, and Peter Pusch. The group was subsequently supplemented by the addition of Frank Böckelmann and Herbert Nagel.

joined Subversive Aktion at the beginning of 1964. They named their group Anschlag (Attack) after the title of the newspaper they printed in Berlin on behalf of the group. In contrast to the bohemian Kunzelmann, Dutschke and Rabehl were every bit the Marxist theoreticians, mutant offspring of the East German workers' state from which they had escaped.[67] Their heavily theoretical Marxist orientation sometimes left them at odds with their Munich counterparts. After the Anschlag group's inaugural provocation, an attempt to prevent a right-wing student fraternity from establishing itself at the Free University, Dutschke noted in his diary: "[A] comrade said to me: 'The SDS should take an example from this.' Was it really so exemplary? The arguments of the comrades from Munich aren't so easy to resist. But I was never a Situationist, in the DDR I didn't have the opportunity."[68]

The Munich and Berlin sections of Subversive Aktion were nevertheless united in a concern with the liberation of consciousness as a prerequisite to the liberation of society, an orientation reflected in the targets of their attacks: an advertising convention, a Catholic mass, a building owned by the Springer Press. This focus on the liberation of consciousness was heavily influenced by Frankfurt School thinkers such as Theodor W. Adorno and Max Horkheimer, whose *Dialectic of Enlightenment* became a key text within Subversive Aktion circles. Adorno, like Max Bense before him, became a target of Situationist impersonation when he unwittingly lent his name to the group's *Suchanzeige* (Want Ad) flyer of May 1964, prompting a lawsuit. The focus on the transformation of consciousness also extended into the realm of personal motivation, being explored in depth by group members in the psychological self-criticism meetings known as "Psychoamoks."

Present in the early actions of Subversive Aktion were all the elements that would ultimately find expression in West Berlin's First Commune, the Kommune I, as well as in the cultural productions of the antiauthoritarian revolt more generally:

- provocation – in the case of the Adorno incident, provocation of an unmistakably postmodern cast in which texts were appropriated and authorship erased or reassigned;
- the attack on the right of the media to monopolize public discourse, combined with the seizure of the (cultural) means of production (in

---

[67] Alexander Holmig, "'Wenn's der Wahrheits(er)findung dient': Wirken und Wirkung der Kommune I (1967–1969)," Magisterarbeit, Humboldt University, August 2004, p. 25.
[68] Dutschke, *Diaries*, undated entry (1964), p. 21.

the form of the Rotaprint machine used to create alternative printed material);

- the reliance on the media and the court system to amplify the effect of actions in a sort of "deviancy amplification" from below;
- political engagement on the terrain of transpersonal psychology; and
- an explicit attempt to break down boundaries between fun and politics.

The only remaining piece of the puzzle was the successful penetration of the SDS with the aim of turning its politics in a more explicitly revolutionary direction. Dieter Kunzelmann and Frank Böckelmann joined the Munich branch of the SDS in mid December 1964, although they were quickly kicked out. Dutschke and Rabehl, along with Subversive Aktion members Rodolphe Gasché and Herbert Nagel, joined the Berlin branch in January 1965. Dutschke and Nagel quickly won influence in the Project Group on Socialist Internationalism and the Third World, and by the end of February Dutschke had been elected to the Political Advisory Council of the Berlin SDS. Ultimately, in the wake of infighting and the dissolution of several branches, most Subversive Aktion members made their way into the SDS.

The intervention of the antiauthoritarian faction around Rudi Dutschke came at a time when the intertwined issues of university reform and the American war in Vietnam were reaching a fever pitch. The issue of freedom of speech at the Free University had crystallized during the 1965/1966 winter semester, driven by a series of incidents in which the University President issued politically colored decisions by fiat. These included the prohibition of a drive to collect funds for Algerian refugees (a previous campaign to aid East German students had caused no problem); the disinviting of the writer Erich Kuby from a speaking engagement at the university for the crime of having criticized it during a previous visit; and the firing of assistant professor Ekkehart Krippendorff, ostensibly for publishing incorrect information, more likely for having published the information in an article critical of the University President and of the Vietnam War. These incidents raised suspicions that the Free University was free only for those who supported the status quo.[69] Around the same time, the issue of the war in Vietnam began to generate increased interest among students and intellectuals, leading to a congress, "Vietnam: Analysis of an Example" in Frankfurt and to a series of resolutions condemning the war signed by students and leading intellectuals.

[69] Klimke, *The "Other Alliance,"* p. 61.

This politicization developed a head of steam at a moment when the possibility of party-political opposition to the status quo appeared to be foreclosed. The decision of the social-democratic SPD in 1966 to enter the so-called Grand Coalition with the conservative CDU, abandoning once and for all the last vestiges of its Marxism as the price for entry into the halls of power, caused widespread consternation on the left. Feelings toward this perceived betrayal were ably expressed by the writer Hans Magnus Enzensberger, publisher of leading New Left journal *Kursbuch*: "The sell-out was complete. Since then there has been no organized opposition in West Germany. The parliamentary form of government has completely become a façade hiding a power cartel that the constitutional sovereign, the people, can no longer do away with."[70] Rudi Dutschke was prompted, before an assembly of the SDS, to call for an "extraparliamentary opposition," a term that came to stand in for the collection of organizations and agendas aimed at opening up the authoritarian political culture of the Federal Republic in the 1960s, and which passed into general usage by its acronym APO (for *Ausserparlamentarische Opposition*).

The activist response to the foreclosure of the electoral road to change was direct action. Over the night of February 3–4, 1966, Dutschke and others distributed a flyer accusing the West German government of "murder" for its support of the US war in Vietnam. This so-called "poster action" had an incendiary effect in a West Berlin in which the overwhelming majority of the population as well as the authorities viewed the Americans as friends and protectors. The executive board of the SDS also challenged Dutschke's right to undertake actions on behalf of the SDS on which no vote had been taken. In response, Dutschke cited the example of Che Guevara, who had shown in Cuba that a small determined group could make a revolution. Che's so-called foco theory, which emphasized the importance of taking the initiative to create revolutionary conditions in a given local situation, was freely adapted by Dutschke as a theoretical model to be followed in the metropoles.[71] Influenced by Marcuse, Dutschke further argued that the industrial proletariat was no longer the motor force of history. The mass base of the revolution was to be, in Dutschke's words, the "underprivileged of the world."[72]

---

[70] Hans Magnus Enzensberger, "Klare Entscheidungen und trübe Aussichten," in Joachim Schickel, ed., *Über Hans Magnus Enzensberger* (Frankfurt: Suhrkamp, 1970), pp. 225–232, 230.

[71] Klimke, *The "Other Alliance,"* p. 67.

[72] Rudi Dutschke, "Die geschichtlichen Bedingungen für den internationalen Emanzipationskampf," in Rudolf Sievers, ed., *1968: Eine Enzyklopädie* (Frankfurt: Suhrkampf, 2004), p. 252.

The poster action announced the arrival of the new politics of spectacular direct action hatched by Subversive Aktion and signaled the victory of the antiauthoritarian faction in taking over the West Berlin SDS. It also signified the importance of the Third World, not only as a site of humanistic engagement but also as a source of solutions for the revolutionary problems of the metropole. According to the various accounts of the protagonists, this answer was crystallized, in a way very characteristic of 1968's blending of pop culture and radical politics, by a movie. Some time during the month of February 1966, Rudi Dutschke, Dieter Kunzelmann, and others attended a screening at the Zoopalast cinema in West Berlin of the Louis Malle film *Viva Maria!*[73] The movie starred Brigitte Bardot and Jeanne Moreau as two women, both named Maria, who used their cover as performers in a traveling circus to fight in the Mexican Revolution in the 1910s. This lighthearted revolutionary sex romp was imbued by its young viewers with deep significance. For Dutschke, the Marxist former East German, the two main characters were personifications of two important revolutionary streams: Jeanne Moreau's character embodied a theoretical but passive Marxism; Brigitte Bardot represented anarchism, full of passion but lacking in theory. Dutschke's inspiration was to combine the two. "Marxist theory," as his close collaborator Bernd Rabehl put it, "would make fruitful anarchism's will to revolt, its spontaneity, fantasy and passion."[74] For Kunzelmann, the movie reaffirmed a key concept: that the revolution must be fun.[75] The so-called Viva Maria Group founded in the wake of the film was meant, for Kunzelmann, as a provocation against what he called the "tie-wearing Marxists" in the SDS; but it was also the first attempt to bring the Third World home.[76] The Kochel am See meeting of July 1966 was an attempt to extend and concretize this idea.

When Dutschke arrived in Kochel am See with his American wife Gretchen Dutschke-Klotz, the two were only recently returned from a trip

---

[73] The group also included Dorothea Ridder and Ulrich Enzensberger, both later of Kommune I, and Hans-Joachim Hameister, the Vietnam specialist from SDS; Holmig, "Wenn's der Wahrheits(er)findung dient," p. 32.

[74] Bernd Rabehl, "Die Provokationselite: Aufbruch und Scheitern der subversiven Rebellion in den sechziger Jahren," in Siegward Lönnendonker, Bernd Rabehl, and Jochen Staadt, eds., *Die antiautoritäre Revolte: der Sozialistische Deutsche Studentenbund nach der Trennung von der SPD*, vol. 1: *1960–1967* (Opladen: Westdeutscher Verlag, 2002), p. 425. See also Bernd Rabehl, "Viva Maria und die Verknüpfung von Anarchismus und Marxismus innerhalb der neuen Linken," in *Kino*, Heft 1, Cologne, 1965.

[75] Kunzelmann, *Leisten Sie keinen Widerstand*, p. 51.

[76] *Ibid.*; Dreßen et al., *Nilpferd des höllischen Urwalds*, p. 194.

to Budapest to visit the Marxist philosopher Georg Lukács. Also present from the Berlin contingent was Dutschke's friend Bernd Rabehl, along with Eike Hemmer, Horst Kurnitzky, and Hans-Joachim Hameister. In between breakfasting, hiking, and watching West Germany lose the World Cup Final to England on television at a pub in a neighboring village, the group met to take stock of the past several years of radical agitation and to consider the problems and possibilities of further action. A cross between a conspiratorial council and a university seminar, the meeting featured lectures on topics of revolutionary history and tactics combined with discussions of key texts of current import. The latter included Frantz Fanon's *The Wretched of the Earth* and Herbert Marcuse's recently published *One-Dimensional Man*.

Explicitly synthetic in intention, the ten-day meeting was aimed at bringing together a set of influences drawn from European, American, and postcolonial sources. It was a meeting about how to realize the revolution in West Germany using materials drawn from the world – that is, a meeting designed to realize the revolutionary-global in the local. One important focus was the tradition of civil disobedience lifted from the American civil-rights movement, which had inspired the first "Sit-In" at the Free University in Berlin only the month before, surprising members of the Berlin faction with its effectiveness.[77] Another, even more important, was the wave of liberation movements in the Third World and the corresponding question of the role to be played by avant-garde groups in the metropole.[78]

Another model, closer to home, was provided by the Provos in Amsterdam. The Provos' smoke-bomb attack on the marriage of Queen Beatrix in March 1966 demonstrated in striking fashion the political possibilities of media scandal. The bombs provoked police into a frenzied and indiscriminate overreaction, captured in photographs, which were then placed on display in an exhibit about police violence at the royal wedding. The impact was amplified when police, in a perfect postmodern moment, assaulted the crowd outside the exhibit, prompting an official inquiry.[79] Dutschke and Kunzelmann had first learned about Provo

---

[77] "In contrast to Munich," writes Dieter Kunzelmann, "the anti-authoritarian nucleus in Berlin exerted already an enormous influence in SDS and the Sit-In had in fact competely surprised the SDS people who took part in showing that it was possible to get hundreds of people into action who were determined to practice passive resistance against the clearing out of university buildings by the police"; Kunzelmann, *Leisten Sie keinen Widerstand*, p. 47.

[78] Kunzelmann, *Leisten Sie keinen Widerstand*, p. 48.

[79] See Niek Pas, "In Pursuit of the Invisible Revolution: Sigma in the Netherlands, 1966–1968," in Brown and Anton, eds., *Between the Avant-garde and the Everyday*, pp. 31–43; see also Richard Kempton, *Provo: Amsterdam's Anarchist Revolt* (Southport: New Autonomy, 2007).

during a 1964 trip to Amsterdam and later established personal contacts. The December 1965 visit to West Berlin of the Dutch writer Leo Klatzer, a former left-Communist activist with ties to Provo, proved particularly inspirational.[80] Dutschke, as he would explain in an interview some years later, admired the Provos but questioned the extent to which their spontaneous, anarchistic form of activism could provide a model in the West German situation.[81] The influence on Kunzelmann, as subsequent events would demonstrate, was immense.

The concrete outcome of the Kochel meeting was the decision to found a commune that would help bring together the struggle abroad with the struggle at home, serving as a strongpoint from which to "attack the nerve-points of the imperialist war machine."[82] The fateful outcome of the Kochel meeting was the decision to found this commune at the urban epicenter of the Cold War. Berlin was chosen, writes Dieter Kunzelmann, because, "in contrast to Munich, [it represented] a practically ideal-typical paradise for provocateurs."[83] Whereas the Tshombe protest in Munich had hardly caused a stir, the one in Berlin had produced a violent, red-baiting response in the Springer Press.[84] For Kunzelmann, the possibility of evoking a resonance in the media trumped all other considerations: "Berlin," he wrote, was "ripe for a spectacle."[85]

The commune that Kunzelmann helped found after moving to Berlin in late 1966 – the so-called Kommune I – represented the crystallization of the fusion of the political (revisionist Marxist) and cultural (bohemian Situationist) strands that had marked the activities of Subversive Aktion. Ironically, the Kommune I was not actually the first commune but was preceded by a few weeks by the so-called SDS Kommune (later Kommune 2) co-founded by Kunzelmann's former Subversive Aktion colleague Marion Steffel-Stergar.[86] Established on February 4, 1967 as

[80] See Chaussy, *Die drei Leben des Rudi Dutschke*, pp. 152–153; Enzensberger, *Die Jahre der Kommune I*, pp. 49–53.

[81] "Because they haven't really yet organized themselves," he observed, "they are currently in danger of being integrated into society, [and thereby are unable] to carry forward the politicization process"; "rt-Gespräch mit Rudi Dutschke," *Der Rote Turm*, 2 (1967), Green Library, Stanford University, Germany. Extraparliamentary Opposition movement, 1967–1984 collection, box 87, folder 3.

[82] Kommune 2, *Versuch der Revolutionierung des bürgerlichen Individuums. Kollektives Leben mit politischer Arbeit verbinden* (Berlin: Oberbaumpresse, 1969), p. 365.

[83] Kunzelmann, *Leisten Sie keinen Widerstand*, p. 49.

[84] *Ibid.*   [85] *Ibid.*

[86] Other members of the Kommune 2 were Jan-Karl Raspe, Eberhard Schulz, Eike Hemmer, and Dagmar von Doetinchem.

an attempt within the SDS to deepen the organization's political work through experiments in communal living (literally in the SDS headquarters at Kurfürstendamm 140), the Kommune 2 came to focus heavily on personal and interpersonal psychology, the assault on repressive gender roles, and antiauthoritarian child-rearing. Like the Kommune I, the Kommune 2 was understood by its founders in terms derived from the growing identification with the national liberation struggles of the Third World as the primary locus of revolutionary action in the world. Both communes were conceived of by their founders as urban strongpoints for the importation of the revolutionary struggle of the Third World into the metropole.[87] "Reality is ripe for revolution," noted the Kommune 2; "[w]e no longer need to merely wait for the aftershocks of the revolutionary movements of the Third World."[88]

Rudi Dutschke declined to join in either of these two experiments in communal living, pledging instead with Rabehl to found a "Wissenschaftskommune" (scholarly scientific commune). The experiment never came to pass, probably because it was nothing more than a face-saving measure to begin with; Dutschke's and Rabehls's resistance to join in the commune experiment appears to have been mainly to do with the fact that they objected to Kunzelmann's demand that the commune be based on open sexual relationships.[89] Dutschke's wife Gretchen did not get along with Kunzelmann, who regarded her as a stick in the mud; Dutschke-Klotz, for her part, regarded Kunzelmann as a bully and a bore.[90]

In any case, Kommune I very quickly established itself as a preeminent vehicle for the escalating radicalism of the antiauthoritarian faction in the SDS. The commune was initially spread over several Berlin apartments, one of them belonging to the writer Uwe Johnson, another to Hans Magnus Enzensberger, older brother of the communard Ulrich Enzensberger. Alongside Kunzelmann and Enzensberger, the commune

[87] "Notizen zur Gründung revolutionärer Kommunen in den Metropolen," *Kommune I, Quellen zur Kommuneforschung,* November 1966, APO-Archiv Berlin.

[88] Kommune 2, *Versuch der Revolutionierung des bürgerlichen Individuums. Kollektives Leben mit politischer Arbeit verbinden* (Berlin: Oberbaumpresse, 1969). See also Kommune 2 (Christel Bookhagen, Eike Hemmer, Jan Raspe, Eberhard Schultz), "Kindererziehung in der Kommune," *Kursbuch,* 17 (1969), pp. 147–187; Hans-Eberhard Schulz, "Die 'Kommune 2': Was bleibt von dem antiautoritären Projekt im Rahmen des West-Berliner SDS 30 Jahre nach seiner Auflösung," *Kalaschnikow: Das Politmagazin,* 12 (1) 1999.

[89] Ute Kätzel, *Die 68erinnen: Portrait einer rebellischen Frauengeneration* (Berlin: Rowohlt, 2002), p. 206.

[90] Gretchen Dutschke, *Rudi Dutschke: Wir hatten ein barbarisches, schönes Leben* (Munich: Droemersche Verlagsanstalt Th. Knaur Nachf., GmbH & Co., 1998).

included Hans-Joachim Hameister, Dorothea Ridder, Dagmar Seehuber, Dagrun Enzensberger, and Fritz Teufel. Later, this group was joined by two defectors from Kommune 2, Antje Krüger and Rainer Langhans. After a short time, the communards were able to move together into a single apartment in the Stuttgarter Platz, in a red-light section of the Charlottenburg district. There they embarked on a program of agitation on parallel tracks: a series of Situationist-inspired provocations that helped transform the radical scene, and a push to uncover and uproot the psychological bases of personal behavior, a goal pursued through punishing group-psychology sessions that earned Kommune I a reputation as the "Psycho-" or "Horror-Commune."[91]

Unease with the latter aspect of the communards' program was by no means confined to the sensationalist editors of the Springer Press nor to the comparatively staid activists of the SDS; Gunther Langer, a member of the later Wielandstraße commune, explained years later:

I too moved into a commune; just not into the K1, where every night one had to lay one's soul bare. I took part in one of the preparatory meetings of the K1, but felt myself still too inexperienced. People like Dieter Kunzelmann could out-talk everybody else. I wouldn't have been able to stand up to him at that time.[92]

The situation was described less charitably by female activists writing in the underground newspaper *Die neue Scheiße*, around the time of the commune's disbanding. The paper's satirical "K1 Commandments" included injunctions such as "Be hard and brutal to your fellow man! Recognize immediately their psychological weaknesses and hit them swift and sure!"; "realize the idea of utopia today at any price, even if it costs the idea, or your life, or the lives of others."[93]

There is little doubt that this dynamic within the commune was heavily driven by Dieter Kunzelmann, a person operating very much in the mold of the classic avant-garde "artist-hero" for whom personal conflicts and abridged human relationships were legitimate means for the destruction of bourgeois mores and society. Unsurprising in this context is that, as the authors of the piece in *Die neue Scheiße* implied, the overwhelmingly male

---

[91] See Bergmann et al., *Rebellion*, p. 63.

[92] Gunther Langer, "'Meine Schüler finden es irre, dass ich Hippie war,'" *Die Tageszeitung*, April 14, 2008. Available online at www.taz.de/1/archiv/print-archiv/printressorts/digi-artikel/?ressort =bl&dig=2008%2F04%2F14%2Fa0120&cHash=81dc37d0ce (accessed March 5, 2011).

[93] "Everyone under 30 in Berlin," the authors sarcastically observed, "is K1 damaged"; *Die neue Scheiße*, 1 (March 1969). Green Library, Stanford University, Germany. Extraparliamentary Opposition movement, 1967–1984 collection, box 35.

commune reproduced patterns of male dominance characteristic of the European avant-garde tradition in both its artistic and military-political iterations. Inga Buhmann, a friend of Frank Böckelmann from the pre-commune Subversive Aktion, came quickly to note this dynamic in her dealings with Kunzelmann et al. The group was stamped, she wrote, by the "brutal authoritarian manner of a few guys who believed they had the right, because they possessed the truth about the world, who were allowed to destroy everyone who still had scruples or even simply just enormous difficulties. A sadism ruled there, especially against the women, that was unbelievable."[94] Subversive Aktion nevertheless represented for Buhmann a sphere of qualified female autonomy where it was at least possible for women to attempt new ways of relating to the world, a situation that carried over, despite the continued dominance of the male-theoretical voice, into Kommune I.[95]

Yet the situation for women in Kommune I could be far from ideal. Dagmar Przytula (née Seehuber) writes of the dominance of the men in the actions of the commune:

The flyers and above all the strongly aggressive character of the actions were mostly a male thing, although I have to say that I mostly adapted myself to this male style. Above all, I tried to keep up with the aggressive talk, which wasn't foreign to me ... I had had to aggressively verbally defend myself against my brother and father.[96]

On the sexual front, Przytula writes of the young girls who rotated through the commune for short periods, attracted by the aura of excitement around the male "stars" of the scene. "We regular commune women suffered too," she writes, "because the situation was impossible ... I remember the one day, as Dagrun [Enzensberger] lay wailing in bed. In the evening something had happened once again, and they had insulted us as 'touchy [*empfindliche*] hens.' I didn't sleep all night and Dagrun didn't either. She was certain the next day that she was going to leave."[97] Seehuber herself left a short time later after becoming pregnant by Kunzelmann and getting an (illegal) abortion. "I had the impression that I couldn't get a foothold in this commune, in which I had once believed," she writes; "there I would not be able to liberate myself as a woman. That had in fact been my illusion."[98] Antje Krüger, whose time at the commune

---

[94] Inga Buhmann, *Ich habe mir eine Geschichte geschrieben* (Frankfurt am Main: Zweitausendeins, 1983), p.88.
[95] Buhmann, *Ich habe mir eine Geschichte geschrieben*, pp. 142–143.
[96] Kätzel, *Die 68erinnen*, pp. 209–210.   [97] Kätzel, *Die 68erinnen*, pp. 208–209.
[98] Kätzel, *Die 68erinnen*, p. 211.

only partially overlapped with that of Seehuber and Enzensberger, takes a somewhat less dim view of matters, although she also recalls a tough environment: "One can say, it wasn't just fun and games."[99]

Whatever the case, the aura of "free love" that hung over the commune was more myth than reality. Incidents such as Kunzelmann's demand that his "orgasm difficulties" be relayed to the public, or the publication in *Der Spiegel* of the famous Thomas Hesterberg photograph of the naked communards up against the wall – a photograph meant to telegraph sexual freedom even as it played with the imagery of police repression or, according to some analyses, the Holocaust – combined with lurid reports in the boulevard press, helped cement a reputation for sexual experimentation that was out of step with reality.[100] The grueling psychological self-criticism sessions and the atmosphere of (often brutal) intellectual and rhetorical competition, not to mention the relative paucity of women in the commune – at its worst the male–female ratio was four to one – hardly appear to have been conducive to a spirit of generalized lovemaking.[101] Far from being a group of taboo-breaking libertines, Przytula recalls, the communards were an "uptight bunch."[102]

If the promise of overturning bourgeois personal relations ended up being less successful than first hoped, the communards' public actions were dramatically successful in shifting the tenor of demonstrations in West Berlin. Kunzelmann et al. had begun to probe the possibilities for provocation even before the founding of the commune. During a December 10, 1966, anti-Vietnam War demonstration on the busy Kurfürstendamm, West Berlin's premier shopping boulevard, the future communards set up a Christmas tree decorated with American flags and a sign reading "Petit Bourgeois of All Lands Unite." They then produced papier-mâché busts of American President Lyndon Johnson and East German Head of State Walter Ulbricht, which they proceeded to douse with kerosene and burn along with the tree.[103] A week later, they instigated a "strolling demonstration" in which protesters avoided direct confrontation with the police by mingling with Christmas shoppers along the Kurfürstendamm. Inevitably, as the communards undoubtedly

---

[99] Antje Krüger (Kommune I), interview with the author, Berlin, October 5, 2006.

[100] See Reimut Reiche, "Erinnerung an einen Mythos," in Lothar Baier, Wilfried Gottschalch, and Reimut Reiche, *Die Früchte der Revolte: Über die Veränderung der politischen Kultur durch die Studentenbewegung* (Berlin: Wagenbach, 1988), pp. 45–71.

[101] Baerbel Becker, ed., *Unbekannte Wesen: Frauen in den sechziger Jahren* (Berlin: Elefanten Press, 1987), p. 169.

[102] Kätzel, *Die 68erinnen*, p. 214.

[103] Holmig, "Wenn's der Wahrheits(er)findung dient," p. 37.

anticipated, innocent passersby were swept up in the police response, thereby exposing a non-student public to the reality of state power.

Subsequent provocations were more ambitious. In April 1967, a planned bomb attack on the motorcade of visiting American Vice President Hubert Humphrey was foiled by the police. It was quickly revealed that the communards' "bomb" was made of nothing more deadly than pudding, but not before the Springer Press had gleefully trumpeted the arrest of dangerous assassins armed with "explosives from Peking."[104] In the aftermath of this "pudding assassination," the communards became household names. Two months later, they again flirted with symbolic terror, this time in a series of satirical flyers produced in response to a tragic fire in the Belgian department store L'Innovation in which hundreds had been killed. Styling the fire "a new demonstration method" intended to introduce "American methods" (i.e. napalm) to a European audience, the communards posed an ominous rhetorical question: "When will the Berlin department stores burn?"[105]

Fritz Teufel and Rainer Langhans were arrested a month later and charged with incitement to arson. Less than a year later, in a telling example of life imitating art, the flyers were cited by real-life arsonists Andreas Baader and Gudrun Ensslin in justification for their attack on a Frankfurt department store. Langhans and Teufel were eventually acquitted, but not until they had made a mockery of the justice system through their unconventional behavior and refusal to defer to the rituals of authority. Languishing in jail on unrelated (trumped-up) charges of throwing a stone at police during the anti-Shah demonstration of June 2, 1967, Teufel became a cause célèbre, his release from jail in August of that year marked by a festive "happening" on the Kurfürstendamm. The latter event, which brought a momentary simulacrum of American hippie culture to the cramped confines of the Cold War Kurfürstendamm, both celebrated the act of resistance against the state and prefigured the role of the Kommune I in helping to foster the development of a West German counterculture.

Each of these actions and provocations was rich in symbolic content, and it is no surprise that scholars in linguistics and communication studies have paid much attention to the role of the Kommune I in the development of the new "communication style" that characterized

---

[104] Quoted in Thomas, *Protest Movements*, p. 100.
[105] Flugblatt 8, APO-Archiv Berlin, Ordner K I.

the antiauthoritarian revolt in West Germany.[106] The activities of the Kommune I also hold a central narrative significance, for during the peak period of 1967–1969 the actions that it initiated or in which it was involved mark out the stations of the antiauthoritarian revolt in West Germany.

From a theoretical-methodological perspective, the Kommune I holds an additional significance: as a product of the conspiratorial meeting in Kochel am See and the search for new revolutionary goals and tactics it initiated, the Kommune I highlights the key importance of the *active transnational* in 1968. Seeking out the ideas, traditions, and cultural products they believed to be necessary in their local context, the protagonists of the commune discussion group fused a diverse set of influences drawn largely from beyond the boundaries of West Germany: French and Scandinavian Situationism, Dutch Provo, American tactics of direct action and civil disobedience, a revised Eastern Bloc Marxism, international pop culture, central European traditions of psychoanalysis, and the revolutionary theory (and mythology) of the Third World. A paradigmatic example of the globalizing imagination at work, the Kommune I became a key nodal point in the set of global – local intersections that helped produce the West German 1968.

At the same time, the Kommune I created a space, both conceptual and concrete, around which could coalesce new revolutionary conceptions and actors. By establishing a base in the urban landscape where the revolution could be *lived* rather than just theorized, the communards sought to establish new possibilities of being in the human interior and new possibilities of action in the public spaces of the city. This "transformation of space," to borrow a term used by Kristin Ross to denote the link between physical space and discursive space behind the barricades of the Paris Commune of 1871, was connected with the development of the Kommune I into the centerpiece of a nonconformist imagined community with transregional and transnational reach.[107] The commune's foundational strategy, the use of the mainstream media as a giant amplifier for radical actions, helped turn the Kommune I into a sort of mirror in which were reflected the worse fears of the *Spießbürger* (the petit bourgeois) and the best hopes of young would-be radicals. Communards such as Fritz Teufel and Rainer Langhans, recipients of a voluminous fan mail

[106] See, for example, Joachim Scharloth, *1968: Eine Kommunikationsgeschichte* (Munich: Wilhelm Fink, 2010).
[107] Kristin Ross, *The Emergence of Social Space: Rimbaud and the Paris Commune* (Minneapolis, Minn.: University of Minnesota Press, 1988).

containing everything from expressions of adolescent affection to suggestions for future targets of provocation, became the equivalent of pop stars, fantasy figures of antiauthoritarian revolt with an appeal reaching out into the West German provinces far removed from the radical hotbed of West Berlin.[108]

Meanwhile, the apartments of the Kommune I provided a physical location in which members of the left-wing scene(s) could come together and cross-pollinate. In late summer 1968, the commune moved to the so-called "KI Fabrik," a large apartment in the Stephanstraße, decorated with aluminum foil in homage to Andy Warhol's New York City "Factory." There, the Kommune I became a sort of radical clearing house where student intellectuals and bohemian *Lebenskünstler* mingled with rockers and runaways, beautiful people of the "swinging sixties" set with future desperadoes of the militant underground. Many of the latter – above all the future members of the Hash Rebel group, who were shortly to go on to found their own very radical communes – were not middle-class students or professional provocateurs but young workers, whose radicalization stemmed from very different sources than that of the intellectual avant-gardists who founded the Kommune I.

INSURRECTIONARY SPACES

The radical potential of youth in the street that would be realized around the commune scene at the end of the 1960s had been foreshadowed in Dieter Kunzelmann's very own Munich neighborhood some five years before the founding of the Kommune I. The events that came to be known as the Schwabing Riots began on June 20 with an escalating series of interventions by police against small knots of young people gathered around street musicians.[109] On the evening of June 20, 1962, police broke up a group of 150 young people listening to street musicians on the Wedekindplatz. Official commands, grudgingly obeyed at first, began to be met with resistance. Late the next night, when police tried to disperse a crowd of listeners gathered around three guitarists on the Leopoldstraße, they were met with a hail of rocks and bottles. Crowds of young people physically interfered with police trying to make arrests, damaged police

---

[108] Collected in *Korrespondenz der Kommune I, 1967–1968*, HIS SAK 130.03.
[109] I am indebted to Herr Heinz Korderer for his painstaking reconstruction of the events; "Die 'Schwabinger Krawalle' vom Juni 1962: Eine kurze Chronologie der Ereignisse," APO-Archiv München, Sammlung "Schwabinger Krawalle" I.

vehicles, and attempted to stop and overturn passing cars.[110] Crowds taunted police with cries of "VoPo," "Gestapo," and "NS-Polizei."[111] Over the weekend and into the next week, hundreds of police fought running battles with crowds of demonstrators 4,000–6,000 strong.[112]

The riots left a deep impression in their aftermath. Newspaper accounts expressed outrage against the rioters, who in one particularly imaginative account were presented as a "half-organized mob out of the Munich underworld" that had succeeded in causing a disturbance "comparable only to the gangster battles of Chicago in the twenties."[113] Yet there was also widespread condemnation of the police, whose liberal use of truncheons against all and sundry could hardly be ignored. "This case must be investigated," ran a characteristic headline in the *Süddeutsche Zeitung*; "'The police beat me down.'"[114] Letters of complaint to city officials and depositions taken in the many post-riot legal proceedings painted a lurid picture of beatings randomly administered to rioters and passersby alike. In the wake of the riots, a "Munich Association for the Protection of Citizens' Rights" was formed to defend those charged and to bring charges against police who had used excessive force.[115] One hundred and forty charges were brought against police, although in the event only four officers were found guilty.[116]

Initial responses to the riot revolved less around the motivations of the young people involved than around the implications of the behavior of the police. The student council of the Ludwig Maximilian University in Munich "distanced itself" from the riots, while nevertheless criticizing police brutality.[117] The illegal Communist Party, banned by the West German government since 1956, distributed a flyer linking the riots to

---

[110] Winfried Martini, "Die Schwabinger Krawalle," in Gerhard Fürmetz and Thomas Kleinknecht, eds., *Schwabinger Krawalle: Protest, Polizei und Öffentlichkeit zu Beginn der 60er Jahre* (Essen: Klartext, 2006), p. 5.

[111] Martini, "Die Schwabinger Krawalle," p. 6.

[112] The Schwabing Riots are depicted in the second of the "Heimat" films, *Second Heimat*, 1992, dir. Edgar Reitz.

[113] "Wir haben Angst: Die Schwabinger klagen über den Terror," *8-Uhr Blatt*, June 26, 1962.

[114] *Süddeustche Zeitung*, June 25, 1962. "Rubber truncheons," ran another headline in the same issue, "flew like flails."

[115] Esther Arens, "Auf dem Weg zur Zivigesellschaft: Die 'Schwabinger Krawalle' von 1962 und die Münchner Interessengemeinschaft zur Wahrung der Bürgerrechte," Magisterarbeit, Ludwig-Maximilians-Universität München, 2002.

[116] Martin Winter, "Police Philosophy and Protest Policing in the Federal Republic of Germany, 1960–1990," in Donatella Della Porta and Herbert Reiter, eds., *Policing Protest: The Control of Mass Demonstrations in Western Democracies* (Minneapolis, Minn.: University of Minnesota Press, 1998), pp. 188–212, at p. 210.

[117] *Münchener Merkur*, June 26, 1962.

the debate about the Emergency Laws, which had already been going on for several years. "In the nights just past," it began, "we have seen in Schwabing what we can expect if the federal government gets its Emergency Law ... Students, youth, uninvolved persons, and women were beaten down without distinction ... That is the Emergency Law in action, in Schwabing it was tried out first."[118] The uproar over police actions also prompted a debate about the efficacy of, and rationale for, the police tactics used at the demonstration, and the problems and perils of their revision for such situations in the future.[119] Internal assessments of the Bavarian Interior Ministry concluded that the rioters were overwhelmingly unpolitical in orientation and that the violence had been prompted by police overreaction.[120] Nevertheless, the police journal *Die dritte Gewalt* drew the conclusion that no matter how harmless the events that launched it the riot showed that, despite sentiment to the contrary, an "internal emergency" was indeed possible in the Federal Republic.[121]

The perception that youth run riot represented a species of "internal emergency" was by no means new in 1962; the rise of a youth culture based around rock 'n' roll, with attendant conflicts over behavior, attitude, and appearance, was a striking feature of the post-1945 period on both sides of the Iron Curtain. Youth behavior quickly came to be politicized by both capitalist and Communist regimes, which saw in the new styles and behaviors a threat to socially prescribed behaviors, not least in the realm of gender.[122] The riot organized around the performance of popular music became a standard feature of the relationship between youth and the state in both halves of Germany from the mid

[118] "Notstandsgesetz in Aktion," Kommunistische Partei Deutschland: Gruppe Geschwister Scholl; "Betreff: Störungen der Öffentlichen Sicherfheit und Ornung in München, Stadtteil Schwabing, vom 20.6 mit 27.6.1962; hier politische Auswirkungen und Hintergrunde," Bay HStA, M Inn 97954. "Unrest," concluded a second flyer, "is the first duty of a citizen"; "Erklärung der Kommunistischen Partei Deutschlands/Stadtteil Schwabing zu den Schwabinger 'Kravallen'!," "Betreff: Störungen der Öffentlichen Sicherfheit und Ornung in München, Stadtteil Schwabing, vom 20.6 mit 27.6.1962; hier politische Auswirkungen und Hintergrunde," Bay HStA, M Inn 97954.

[119] This is ably discussed in Winter, "Police Philosophy."

[120] "Betreff: Störungen der Öffentlichen Sicherfheit und Ornung in München, Stadtteil Schwabing, vom 20.6 mit 27.6.1962; hier politische Auswirkungen und Hintergrunde," Bay HStA, M Inn 97954.

[121] *Die dritte Gewalt*, 13. JG., no. 14, July 30, 1962, APO-Archiv München, Sammlung "Schwabinger Krawalle" I.

[122] The East German government saw in the "Beat wave" of 1965 an "organized effort of enemy forces to demoralize a portion of the youth"; Magistrat von Groß-Berlin, Stadtrat G. Müller, Berlin, November 5, 1965, Zusammengefaßte Information, Landesarchiv Berlin, Rep. 120, no. 3869.

1950s onward. The protagonists of these riots, the so-called *Halbstarken*, prefigured in their style and attitude the rise of the "rocker," the leather-jacketed and blue-jeaned tough who would remain a fixture on the West German scene throughout the 1960s. Yet, insomuch as the *Halbstarken* (or the rockers) were political, they received their political gloss from above; states clearly perceived the danger inherent in conflict between young people and the police, even if the political meaning of such conflict was more implicit than explicit.[123]

The Schwabing Riots carried with them a vague but unmistakable sense of something different – a teenage riot in a new key. This was in part more a matter of timing than of content. As Detlef Siegfried has observed, the riots stood at the point of transition between two eras of protest: the 1950s era of Beat fans and youth riots and the 1960s era of politicized youth protest.[124] Contemporaries palpated this shift only imperfectly. Subversive Aktion member Frank Böckelmann, in his essay on the riots in the first number of *Anschlag*, seemed to miss the subversive significance of music fans run riot. Falling reflexively back onto a Frankfurt School-style critique of mass culture, he argued that the seeming rebellion of rock 'n' roll precluded other, more serious forms of rebellion.[125] The potential meaning of the riots surfaced more clearly in a comment attributed to the future terrorist Andreas Baader, a participant in the riots and later a regular at the Kommune I: "Mother, in a state where the police attack singing young people with rubber truncheons, something is not right."[126]

For the historian, the Schwabing Riots signal the new insurrectionary potential of youth in the city and thus may be seen as an early, exacerbated incidence of the conflict around youth "place roles" in the urban environment highlighted in the recent scholarship.[127] The conflict potential of a nascent youth culture, especially as it appeared in the spaces of

---

[123] Detlef Siegfried, "Unsere Woodstocks: Jugendkultur, Rockmusik und gesellschaftlicher Wandel um 1968," in *Rock! Jugend und Musik in Deutschland: Stiftung Haus der Geschichte der Bundesrepublik Deutschland. Zeitgeschichtliches Forum Leipzig* (Berlin, 1995), pp. 52–61, at p. 53.

[124] Detlef Siegfried's review of Fürmetz and Kleinknecht, eds., *Schwabinger Krawalle, in Sehepunkte, Rezensionsjournal für die Geschichtswissenschaften*, 7 (2) (2007).

[125] Frank Böckelmann, "Im Rythmus unser Zeit," *Anschlag*, 1 (August 1964), in Frank Böckelmann and Herbert Nagel, eds., *Subversive Aktion: Der Sinn der Organisation ist ihr Scheitern* (Frankfurt: Verlag Neue Kritik, 1976), pp. 181–184.

[126] Cited in Butz Peters, *RAF: Terrorismus in Deutschland* (Stuttgart: Deutsche Verlags Anstalt, 1991), p. 39.

[127] Axel Schildt and Detlef Siegfried have recently emphasized the importance of the urban environment as the space in which youth and youth subcultures confront authority; see Axel Schildt and Detlef Siegfried, "Introduction," in Axel Schildt and Detlef Siegfried, eds., *European Cities, Youth and the Public Sphere in the Twentieth Century* (Aldershot: Ashgate, 2005), pp. 1–7, at pp. 1–2.

the city, provided one key stream of the antiauthoritarian revolt. The other was represented by the activism of a subversive avant-garde that, at the time of the Schwabing Riots, as we have seen, was only just beginning to come into existence. The hallmark of the West German 1968 would be the dovetailing of these two fundamental disputes with authority, both of which, in calling into question the uses of public space, challenged the rules of social order.

The inchoate rebellion represented by young people revealed in the Schwabing Riots began to be supplanted from the beginning of the 1960s by a new type: the *Gammler*. The *Gammler* represented a new stage in the relationship of youth to public space, for, unlike the young people who congregated around some event such as a concert, and who, occasionally, rioted when provoked by police, *Gammler* represented, as it were, "professional" intruders into public space. To "gammeln" was to "bum around" from place to place (from space to space), settling temporarily in appealing outdoor hangouts – the area around West Berlin's Kaiser Wilhelm Memorial Church was one such well-known haunt – and spending time in particular *Gammler*-friendly pubs before moving on to other locations. *Gammler*-dom was connected with a culture of travel involving hitchhiking and foreign trips, including, from the end of the 1960s, visits to exotic Eastern locales (e.g. Afghanistan), where drugs were plentiful and living was cheap. "[*Gammler*] simply did not understand themselves as a political opposition," writes Wolfgang Seidel; "[t]he theme that ran through all their statements was simply: out, just out. Out of Germany. For on the outside waited a world that was different. Marrakesh and Paris."[128]

This "out" did not function exclusively in geographic terms; no mere analog for travel abroad, it was operative equally at home in the space of the city. In the act of sitting, lying, standing, or milling about in public space, space meant to be moved through by people on their way to work, the *Gammler* stood in living opposition to the socially constructed space of the urban environment organized in accordance with the needs and logics of capitalism. This refusal of the logic of capitalist space, as the French neo-Marxist philosopher Henri Lefebvre noted, was simultaneously a rejection of capitalist time; for time spent "hanging out" was time spent not working at a useful occupation, time "stolen," as it were, from the needs

---

[128] Wolfgang Seidel, "Berlin und die Linke in den 1960ern: Die Enstehung der Ton Steine *Scherben*," in Wolfgang Seidel, ed., *Scherben: Musik, Politik und Wirkung der Ton Steine Scherben* (Mainz: Ventil, 2006), pp. 25–50, at p. 33.

of capitalist society.[129] Either way, whether moving from place to place or inhabiting specific locations, the *Gammler* represented an escape from the spatial norms that were, simultaneously, social and political norms. Usually a middle-class male of between seventeen and twenty-five years in age, the *Gammler* signaled an uncomfortable extension of the delinquency traditionally associated with working-class youth. Not only did the style of the *Gammler* challenge bourgeois conceptions of cleanliness and order but the *Gammler*'s movement through, and occupation of, space, heralded a worrying "end to certainty about the social location of delinquency."[130]

For the authorities and the public, the *Gammler* was a nuisance or worse. In 1966, a year after their first significant appearance, "the debate about Gammler grew into a veritable culture war about the binding force of social norms."[131] In Munich, *Gammler* were widely regarded by city officials and conservative politicians as a public nuisance at best, a criminal threat at worst. "The city council yesterday called for an offensive against Gammler, prostitutes, and homosexuals," read an article in the *Süddeutsche Zeitung* in the fall of 1966, "above all against the long-haired dirty figures who linger around Schwabing."[132] The article cited the efforts of politicians from the conservative CSU to combat the *Gammler* problem and demanded stiffer legal measures from the police and city attorneys. The flavor of the piece can be gleaned from a subject-heading reading, in the clipped prose of newspaper headlines, "unfortunately no law against filthy human beings."[133]

The Munich police, in contrast to those in some other cities, were noted for their relatively liberal treatment of *Gammler*. *Polizeipräsident* Manfred Schreiber insisted that as long as they did not become involved in criminal activity, *Gammler* would be allowed to go their own way.[134]

---

[129] See Henri Lefebvre, *The Production of Space*, trans. Donald Nicholson-Smith (Oxford and Cambridge, Mass.: Blackwell, 1991).

[130] Klaus Weinhauer, "The End of Certainties: Drug Consumption and Youth Deliquency in West Germany," in Schildt and Siegfried, eds., *Between Marx and Coca-Cola*, pp. 376–397, at p. 390.

[131] Siegfried, *Time Is on My Side*, p. 401.

[132] "Der Gammlerfeldzug: nur eine Redeschlacht," *Süddeutsche Zeitung*, 222, September 16, 1966. Munich's spacious public park, the Englischer Garten, especially the areas around Monopteros and the Chinesischer Turm, were a main meeting point; Margret Kosel, *Gammler, Beatniks, Provos: die schleichende Revolution* (Frankfurt: Barmeier & Nickel, 1967), p. 5. Police also detected a lively drug trade in and around locales on the Leopoldstraße such as "Picnic," "Café Europa," and "Big Apple"; Staatsarchiv München, Polizeidirektion München 15631, "Polizeiamt Nord to Direktion der Schutzpolizei," March 22, 1971.

[133] "Der Gammlerfeldzug."

[134] "Eingeschritten wird nur, wenn es kriminell wird. Polizei: Laßt die Gammler in Frieden," *AZ*, March 13, 1968. "Even the citizens have gotten used to them," read a newspaper heading in March 1968; "Die Gammler: besser als ihr Ruf," *Süddeutsche Zeitung*, 63, March 13, 1968.

"The Munich police regard the Gammler with a broad-mindedness ... not to be found in other cities," wrote an informed observer in 1967; "[o]fficers who in the Schwabing Riots had vigorously employed their truncheons hold themselves back when it comes to the Gammler."[135] This restraint was in part a product of the so-called "Munich line" adopted in the wake of the Schwabing Riots, although it also reflected the generally more relaxed atmosphere in Munich as compared with other large German cities. Nevertheless, by the end of the decade, with anywhere from fifty to 1,000 *Gammler* estimated to be present in Schwabing alone on any given day, police expressed relief that the world press coverage had been insufficient to turn Munich into any more of a hippie destination than it already was.[136]

In West Berlin, a hotbed for the transformation of conflicts at the level of daily life into a geopolitical existential threat, *Gammler* were a hunted species, despite the fact that, as an article in *Der Spiegel* acknowledged in September 1966, most Germans had never seen one.[137] *Gammler* were indelibly associated with their chief hangout, the plaza around the Kaiser Wilhelm Memorial Church. Built in the 1890s, the church had been heavily damaged in a bombing raid in 1943. Known simply as the *Gedächtniskirche* – or, by its nickname, Der Hohle Zahn ("The Hollow Tooth"), the church was left in its partially ruined state after the war to loom over the capitalist playground of the Kurfürstendamm. Alex Gross, a visiting correspondent for the London-based *International Times*, profiled the scene around the *Gedächtniskirche* in a late 1966 essay entitled "Beatniks of Berlin."[138] Illustrated with a photograph of a well-dressed Berlin citizen punching a young Beatle-booted ne'er-do-well in the face, the essay featured an interview with the pastor of the *Gedächtniskirche*, Gunter Pohl. Although sympathetic to the young people milling around his church, the pastor had been unable to avoid becoming involved in the problems created by open marijuana use, "public displays of affection," and street hassles between *Gammler* and passersby. "The Gammlers [sic] were not really arrested," writes Gross; "[t]hey were merely taken down to

[135] Kosel, *Gammler, Beatniks, Provos*, p. 97.
[136] *Ibid*. Munich was enough of a destination for *Gammler* at the turn of the decade that they figured in the title of a satirical guidebook: Helmut Seitz, *Wie werde ich ein echter Münchener? Ein methodischer Leitfaden für Preußen, Franken, Schwaben (Schla)-Wiener, u.a. Österreicher, Gammler, Generaldirektoren sowie sonstige Zugereiste aller Art* (Munich: Süddeustscher Verlag, 1970).
[137] Weinhauer, "The End of Certainties," p. 380.
[138] Alex Gross, "Beatniks of Berlin," *International Times*, 4, November 28–December 11, 1966, p. 8.

the station for an 'inspection.' On what grounds, I asked. Disturbing the peace. And what constituted disturbing the peace? Any act which interrupted the normal rhythm of life."[139]

To the question of whether the *Gammler* "could possibly be the first wave of some new social alignment," Pastor Pohl remained silent.[140] Yet the question was on many lips. Herbert Marcuse, whose emphasis on the revolutionary importance of "marginal groups" was a major influence on the New Left and on Rudi Dutschke in particular, replied to it during a lecture appearance in West Berlin in 1967:

I am supposed to have asserted that what we in America call hippies and you call Gammler, Beatniks, are the new revolutionary class. Far be it from me to assert such a thing. What I was trying to show was that in fact today there are tendencies in society – anarchically unorganized, spontaneous tendencies – that herald a total break with the dominant needs of repressive society. The groups you have mentioned are characteristic of a state of disintegration within the system, which as a mere phenomenon has no revolutionary force whatsoever but which perhaps at some time will be able to play its role in connection with other, much stronger objective forces.[141]

Dutschke similarly recognized in the figure of the *Gammler* a certain subversive potential, even if, as a student-intellectual, he remained noncommittal about the political value of dropping out of society altogether. "We were also very interested in the Gammler-Beatniks along the Seine," he wrote to a friend in October 1966 after a trip to Paris;

For the most part they were school kids between 17 and 21 who, discontented with the pressure of home, school, and the factory, demonstrate their antiauthoritarian mindset at the level of everyday life [*ihre Anti-Autoritäts-Haltung lebendig demonstrieren*]. Not infrequently there were also left-wing students among them, for whom concepts such as the proletariat, the dictatorship of the proletariat, and class had become stale [*brüchig geworden sind*], and who felt they saw, in the emergence of *Gammlertum*, evidence of the historically changed situation of the revolutionary forces in "late-capitalist" society.[142]

[139] *Ibid*. A *Gammler* interviewed by the sympathetic author Margaret Kosel expressed wonderment that church staff had never tried to recruit the assembled hippies into their flock, since, after all, "Jesus was the first *Gammler*"; Kosel, *Gammler, Beatniks, Provos*.

[140] Gross, "Beatniks of Berlin."

[141] Herbert Marcuse, "The End of Utopia," in *Five Lectures: Psychoanalysis, Politics, and Utopia*, trans. Jeremy Shapiro and Shierry Weber (Boston, Mass.: Beacon, 1970), pp. 62–81.

[142] "Lieber Gábor, liebe: noch unbekannte – Margit!," Rudi Dutschke to Gábor Révai, October 30, 1966; Rudi Dutschke, Gábor Révai, "Briefwechsel 1966 bis 1971," *Eurozine*, available online at www.eurozine.com/articles/2009{hy}04{hy}23-dutschke-de.html#footNoteNUM1 (accessed February 2, 2010).

Figure 1.5 Photograph from the cover of *International Times*, no. 4,
November 28–December 11, 1966. IT Archive. www.internationaltimes.it/archive/

Others were not so sure. The Iranian exile writer Bahman Nirumand, a
significant force in the West German New Left, lumped *Gammler* along
with the other countercultural types, from lovers of jazz to aficionados of
Zen Buddhism, whose dangerous embrace of personal fulfillment over
political militancy threatened to derail attempts at systemic change.[143]
Such critiques would pick up force from 1968 on, as the gulf between the
"hedonistic" and "militant" left further widened.[144]

Nor were conventionally minded student-left types such as Nirumand
the only ones with a critique of the *Gammler*. Like the American Beatnik
movement that served as their model, the *Gammler* represented a rebellion against the "achievement society" (*Leistungsgesellschaft*) of duty, sobriety, and competition. Yet the *Gammler* as such offered little in the way of
an explicitly political program. By contrast, the Dutch Provo movement

---

[143] Bahman Nirumand, "Die harmlose Intelligenz: Über Gammler, Ostermarschierer, Adorniten
und andere Oppositionelle," *konkret*, no. 7, July 1967.

[144] Wilfried Mausbach, "'Burn, Warehouse, Burn!' Modernity, Counterculture, and the Vietnam
War in West Germany," in Schildt and Siegfried, eds., *Between Marx and Coca-Cola*, pp.
175–202, at p. 188.

sought to make the rebellion against the "achievement society" explicit, positing the notion of a "Provotariat" in which the placid working classes were supplanted by a new revolutionary subject:

What is the Provotariat? All Provos, Beatniks, bums, Halbstarken, teddy-boys, blouson noirs, Gammler, raggare, stiljagi, mangupi, students, artists, criminals, a-socials, anarchists, and the ban-the-bombers. Who don't want a career, don't want to endure a regular life ... Here, in the carbon-monoxide-polluted asphalt jungles of Amsterdam, London, Stockholm, Tokyo, Moscow, Paris, New York, Berlin, Milan; Warsaw, Chicago. The Provotariat is the last insurgent group in the welfare state.[145]

Inclusivity aside, the Provos emphasized the need for a politically con-sequent rejection of social norms. "A Gammler resists impulsively," they argued, "whereas the Provos deny themselves to the society consciously and rationally."[146]

The Provoclub Frankfurt, a West German group inspired by the Amsterdam original, took a similar tack. "The Gammler," they wrote,

were the first of our generation of youth to go over from reaction to provocation. While the Halbstarken represented an understandable yet fruitless rejection of the world of adults, the Gammler were something completely new. Their prov-ocation inhered not in their purposeless refusal, but in a radical turning away from the materialist values of the consumer society.[147]

Yet the rebellion of the *Gammler* was, they argued, ultimately a passive one: "We are making the transition from passivity into radical activity, into a provocation that has become conscious. Through provocation we will expose the weaknesses of this society."[148]

Analyses of this sort aside, the term *"Gammler"* hardly referred to any one readily defined social type. Detlef Siegfried has pointed out that the rapidly expanding estimates about the number of *Gammler* in West Germany and in Europe had in part to do with uncertainty about what exactly a *Gammler was*.[149] *"Gammler"* rather quickly became a catchall term for youthful nonconformists of whatever stripe, from runaways to

---

[145] Aufruf an das internationale Provotariat, from *Provokatie*, no. 8, reprinted in *Oberbaum Linkeck Almanach, 1965–1968*, available online at www.infopartisan.net/archive/1967/266718.html (accessed April 1, 2012). Provo's globalizing vision stands out strikingly in this passage's invoca-tion of groups such as "raggare" (Sweden), "stiljagi" (Soviet Union), and "mangupi" (Turkey).

[146] Saral Sarkar, *Green-Alternative Politics in West Germany*, vol. 1: *The New Social Movements* (New York, Paris, and Tokyo: United Nations University Press, 1993), p. 230.

[147] "Provoclub Frankfurt," *Der Rote Turm*, no. 2, Green Library, Stanford University, Germany. Extraparliamentary Opposition movement, 1967–1984 collection, box 87, folder 3.

[148] *Ibid.*   [149] Siegfried, *Time Is on My Side*, p. 401.

hippies to students with a little bit of hair over the ears. Rudi Dutschke and those like him became, in the Springer Press, *"Polit-Gammler"* or "academic Gammler" (while remaining, simultaneously, "Red Guards"), and the ideal-typical figure of the student (still relatively clean-cut in reality at this time, the mid 1960s) was portrayed in the cartoons printed in the *Bild Zeitung* as a cross between a crazed Beatnik and a Hells Angel (see Fig. 5.7). For Reinhard Lettau, writing in the pages of the left-wing literary journal *Kursbuch*, the portrayal of *Gammler* in the Springer Press was symptomatic of a broader demonization of the "other," which was intimately bound up with the repressive power of the state.[150] *Gammler*-dom became, in effect, a code concept for the crypto-political face of youth radicalism at the level of daily life.

To note that *"Gammler"* was a fluid social category is not to fail to recognize what the too-liberal use of the term concealed: that the "youth revolution" in West Germany was composed of a partly overlapping set of constituencies running the gamut from serious and relatively conventional student activists to artists and cultural provocateurs, to every stripe of rocker, hippie, and freak. If we think of 1968 not just as a product of a student movement but as a product of the convergence of these several and diverse sets of actors, then it becomes necessary to think in spatial terms. As we have seen, the various practices of unruly youth took place in certain types of public space, and certain types of space – coffee houses, pubs, and concert venues – became sites at which these various actors came into contact with each other. The convergence between students and (for example) *Gammler* took place typically not in organizations such as the SDS but in the enclaves and liminal zones of the urban environment and the subterranean spaces of an "underground" with both literal and figurative connotations.[151]

Space stood at the center of the deliberations of the group of left-wing intellectuals who founded one of the West German New Left's most important institutions: the Republican Club. The first Republican Club was established in West Berlin in April 1967. It was founded by a group of leading artists and left-wing intellectuals including Hans Magnus Enzensberger, Ossip K. Flechtheim, Ekkehart Krippendorff, and Wolfgang Neuss. The point of the Republican Club was to provide a meeting place for anyone interested in discussing the need for fundamental

---

[150] Reinhard Lettau, "Journalismus als Menschenjagd," *Kursbuch*, 7, 1966.
[151] Walter Hollstein, *Der Untergrund: Zur Soziologie jugendlicher Protestbewegungen* (Berlin and Neuwied: Luchterhand, 1969).

change. With 200 members at its founding, the club expanded rapidly. "The starting point for an understanding of the political strategy of the Republican Club," noted the club the following year, "is the fact that the over 800 members of the RC do not come from a homogeneous social stratum, as is the case with the student groups. The Republican Club is made up, much more, of those who work in the different professions and institutions, and who are fighting against the oppressiveness of this society in a host of different ways."[152]

The Republican Club was an attempt to establish physical space for the left that was simultaneously a discursive space. The idea spread rapidly. In Frankfurt, the club was known under the name Club Voltaire, in Düsseldorf as the Republican Center. Thirty clubs were founded in the first year. By 1969, some 20,000 persons were organized in some sixty Republican Clubs across West Germany.[153] Quickly transformed from "debate clubs for left-wing intellectuals" to sites of mobilization for various left-wing campaigns, Republican Clubs advised young people on issues such as how to avoid military service, and played a major role in the agitation against the Emergency Laws and the Springer Press.[154] The Republican Clubs were important precisely because of their open-ended orientation; providing the space and support for a range of initiatives stemming from diverse quarters of the antiauthoritarian movement, they helped provide the backbone for an otherwise ambiguously contoured social movement. The non-party character of the clubs corresponded to the spiritual content of the antiauthoritarian movement in its peak period, when common enemies and common goals, above all the fight against the Emergency Laws, pushed sources of division into the background.

On the other end of the spectrum, independent youth clubs played a key role in forging connections between the APO and the burgeoning youth culture based around rock 'n' roll. These clubs, founded from the mid 1960s, became sites where young workers, apprentices, school pupils, and white-collar employees, attracted by rock music and other subcultural interests, could come into contact with the ideas of the APO. One of the earliest such establishments was the Club Ça Ira in West Berlin.

---

[152] Republikanischer Club e.V. Berlin, *RC-Bulletin*, October 10, 1968.
[153] Quoted in *APO aktuell: Heft 3–Die APO und die Oberschulen aus wehrpolitischer Sicht*, (Sinzig: Boehlke, 1969), pp. 33–34. *Spontan* noted in 1969 that while orthodox Communists made up only 10–15 percent of the membership of the Republican Clubs, another 50 percent was composed of radical school pupils, apprentices and young workers, trade unionists, and a smattering of the free professions.
[154] *APO aktuell*, pp. 34–35.

Founded in 1966 by members of Die Falken (The Falcons, a youth organization still close to the SPD at the beginning of the 1960s but which moved away over the course of the decade), the club became a thriving venue for both rock concerts and political events. "They came here out of interest in the music," explained one of the organizers, "but through the other events they became more and more strongly interested in politics."[155] The situation was similar in other clubs such as the Lila Eule in Bremen. Offering mixed programs of left-wing politics, rock concerts, and other cultural events, the clubs helped break down the wall separating pop and politics. Rudi Dutschke spoke at both the Ça Ira and the Lila Eule, the latter in November 1967, just as a wave of protest centered in the city's secondary schools was beginning to take off. The club played a central role in this and later mobilizations, acting as a launching point for various actions.

Eventually, not only individual establishments but also entire neighborhoods became something resembling "liberated zones" where the writ of authority did not always run.[156] In West Berlin, from the Zodiak on the Halleschen Ufer in Berlin-Kreuzberg, to countercultural dives such as "Mr. Go" in the Yorckstraße in Berlin-Schöneberg, bars and music venues became incubators of rebellion. By the end of the 1960s they also became sites of pitched combat between police and countercultural militants fighting to preserve their rights to spatial autonomy in the urban environment.

WORLDS COLLIDE

This striking proclamation identifying the right to *occupy* space and the right to *move through* space as twin pillars of an antiauthoritarian praxis was both a fulfillment of the "promise" of the Schwabing Riots (a final stage in the politicization of youth in the street), a realization of the politicization of daily life sought by the Gruppe Spur and Subversive Aktion, and a harbinger of future battles over public space connected with the *Hausbesetzer* or squatter movement, one of the most significant near-term results of the antiauthoritarian movement in West Germany. At the same time, it was linked with the elaboration of a subcultural identity that, as

[155] Günter Soukup, quoted in Rolf Raasch and Markus Henning, *Neoanarchismus in Deutschland: Entstehung, Verlauf, Konfliktlinien* (Berlin: Oppo-Verlag, 2005).
[156] On "liberated zones," see Siegfried, *Sound der Revolte.*

Figure 1.6 June 2, 1967. The placard in the background reads "Murder!" See poster
of Farah Diba (right) and the collapsible metal baton in the hand of the
SAVAK agent (bottom left). Landesarchiv Berlin.

we shall see in subsequent chapters, was part of a broader and often bitter
conversation about the meaning of terms such as "subculture," "counterculture," and "underground." This conversation was in turn bound up
with one of the key antinomies of 1968: the tension between the desire to
act as a part of society to change it for the better and the desire to exist
apart from society in order to change oneself (the latter an act usually
freighted with the notion that to change oneself *was* to change society).[157]

For the SDS, the emphasis remained very much on changing society
by contesting the prerogatives of state power. From this perspective, the
move toward unconventional behavior and iconoclastic provocation pioneered by the Kommune I seemed an unwelcome intrusion into an otherwise responsible attempt at democratic left-wing politics. Ever-present in
the mass actions in favor of university reform or against the Vietnam War
was the threat that radical elements, acting alone, would push events in

[157] On this theme, see the essays in Davis et al., eds., *Changing the World*.

new, unexpected, and not necessarily favorable directions. In November 1966, activists led by Eike Hemmer, veteran of the Kochel am See meeting and soon-to-be co-founder of the Kommune 2, disrupted a forum on university reform, seizing the microphone and distributing a nonapproved flyer denouncing the faculty as *Fachidioten* ("expert idiots").[158] After the so-called "strolling demo" in December, police raided SDS headquarters and seized the organization's membership files. In March, students attending an anti-Vietnam War demonstration threw paint-filled eggs at the Amerikahaus, the American cultural center near the Zoo station, leading to fighting with police.

The elected leadership of the Berlin SDS finally tired of such antics when, in May 1967, the Kommune I mocked those willing to participate in the upcoming referendum at the Free University as "lame-asses [and] careerists."[159] The Kommune I was expelled from the SDS, the leadership observing, "It is not this or that form of action that is false; what is false is a form of politics [operating] not in the service of education, mobilization and organization, but rather in the service of self-representation, 'self liberation,' and elitist secluding away of individual persons."[160] Another declaration put it more succinctly: "Smoke bombs, eggs, and pudding are the means of an impotent rebellion."[161]

The visit of the Shah Mohammad Reza Pahlavi of Iran to West Berlin on June 2, 1967, demonstrated that the question of what would constitute a *potent* rebellion was not so easy to answer as this dismissive formulation would suggest. More importantly for our purposes, it demonstrated, again, the extent to which defining moments of the antiauthoritarian revolt in West Germany were shaped by exogenous influences or, more properly, by the interplay between these influences and the local conditions to which they were linked via supranational structures of alliance and transnational lines of influence. Like the anti-Tshombe protest of December 1964 and the protests surrounding the film *Africa Addio* in August 1966 and February 1967, the protest against the Shah of Iran in June 1967 arose out of the interaction of West German and foreign students.

The Iranian expatriate author Bahman Nirumand played a central role. Thirty-one years old at the time of the protest against the Shah,

[158] The flyer was composed by Bernd Rabehl and Hans-Joachim Hameister.
[159] Flugblatt 2, APO-Archiv Berlin, Ordner K I.
[160] *SDS-Korrespondenz*, no. 6, May 1967, Beschluß des BV des SDS vom 29/30 April 1967, BArch Koblenz, Zsg 153, Band 13.
[161] "Niederlage oder Erfolg der Protestaktion: Erklärung des SDS," HIS, FU Berlin, Flugblätter Diverses, 1966 ff.

Nirumand had been sent to Germany at the age of fourteen to study. After his return to Iran, while working as an instructor at the Goethe Institute in Tehran, Nirumand met Hans Magnus Enzensberger, who encouraged him to write about repressive conditions under the Shah.[162] Nirumand was a leading figure in the Confederation of Iranian Students (National Union), an organization with a particularly strong presence in West Germany.[163] By the time of the publication of his book in March 1967, *Persien: Modell eines Entwicklungslandes oder die Diktatur der freien Welt* (*Persia: A Model of a Developing Nation or the Dictatorship of the Free World*), Nirumand had been forced into exile in West Berlin. The book had sold 40,000 copies by the time of the Shah's visit to West Berlin at the beginning of June.[164]

The city administration's attempt to force the Free University to cancel an appearance by Nirumand scheduled for June 1, the day before the visit of the Shah to West Berlin, set off a fateful chain reaction of events. Nirumand approached the SDS about organizing a protest against the Shah but was allegedly rebuffed by SDS leaders Christian Semler and Rudi Dutschke, who worried that a protest against the Shah would be a distraction from the issue of Vietnam.[165] The members of the Kommune I, by contrast, were keen to participate. It was they who created the signature prop of the protest: paper masks of the Shah and his queen Farah Diba, part absurdist humor, part protection for Iranian students from the Shah's secret police.[166] The SDS joined in on preparations for the protest, and the General Student Committee of the Free University produced materials contrasting the democratic pretensions of the Shah ("We Persians are of the opinion that no price is too high to achieve the human values contained in a democracy") with the grim reality of a dictatorship

---

[162] Bahman Nirumand, interviewed by Jürgen Gottschlich, "Ein Attentat auf der Schah?" *Die Tageszeitung*, May 31, 1997.

[163] When the Shah's visit to West Germany began on May 27, the Confederation of Iranian Students (National Union) had already distributed 10,000 flyers around the country; Afshin Matin-Asgari, *Iranian Student Opposition to the Shah* (Costa Mesa, Calif.: Mazda, 2001), p. 97.

[164] Bahman Nirumand, *Persien: Modell eines Entwicklungslandes oder die Diktatur der freien Welt* (Reinbek: Rowohlt, 1967). Subsequently published in English as *Iran: The New Imperialism in Action* (New York: Monthly Review Press, 1969), the book became a best-seller and an important influence on the New Left internationally.

[165] The communards satirized the careful approach of the SDS in their flyer no. 12: "three podium discussions, the announcement of a demonstration (tactical maneuver), solidarity-telegram to the Vietcong, establishment of a sub-committee for the creation of Vietcong flags, paperwork. The Shah will be amazed!" *Kommune I*, Flugblatt no. 12, APO-Archiv, Ordner K I.

[166] The masks, fashioned out of paper bags stolen from supermarkets, were finished in the SDS headquarters; Antje Krüger (Kommune I) interview with the author, Berlin, October 5, 2006.

that tortured and murdered its own citizens.[167] Dutschke's antiauthoritarian faction produced a "wanted poster" for the Shah that cited specific instances of human-rights abuses ("The Shah Mohamed Reza Pahlawi is wanted for the torture and murder of the journalist Karimpour Schirazi") and called attention to the culpability of the West German government ("last seen in the company of the Federal President Heinrich Lübke").[168] That Lübke, like Federal Chancellor Kurt Georg Kiesinger, was a former member of the Nazi Party was lost on no one who read the flyer.

The events of June 2, 1967, have often been described in both the German and anglophone literature.[169] Early in the day, in front of the Rathaus Schöneberg, demonstrators were set upon jointly by police and undercover agents of the Shah's secret police, the SAVAK. The latter, posing as Iranian celebrants of the Shah's arrival, held aloft pictures of the Shah's queen Farah Diba on wooden poles. These *Jubelperser* ("celebrating Persians") – renamed afterward, with grim humor, *Prügel-Perser* ("beating Persians") – used their wooden poles, along with telescoping metal batons, to launch a vicious attack on the protesters. In the evening, before the Deutsche Oper, where the Shah was to attend a performance of Mozart's *The Magic Flute*, demonstrators found themselves hemmed by metal barricades into narrow spaces along each side of the street. Security police under the command of Hans Ulrich Werner, a veteran of the brutal campaign against "partisans" during World War II, joined in the attack. "What followed was some of the most uncontrolled mayhem I have ever had occasion to watch or participate in," writes Alex Gross; "[t]he police went after the students with a ferocity I have never seen equaled, with truncheons, the stocks of weapons, their bare hands."[170] They "boxed in the demonstrators," wrote the journalist Sebastian Haffner, "crowded them together and then, with uninhibited brutality, used their nightsticks and boots on the defenseless demonstrators as they stumbled and tripped over each other."[171]

In the ensuing melee, as police chased students into side streets and alleys, the student Benno Ohnesorg was shot in the back of the head by

---

[167] "Informationen über Persien und den Shah," HIS, FU Berlin, Flugblätter Diverses, 1966 ff.

[168] "Mord: Gesucht wird Schah Mohamed Reza Pahlawi," Flugblatt SDS, May 31, 1967, APO-Archiv, Ordner K I.

[169] Most recently in Soukup, *Wie starb Benno Ohnesorg?* See also the detailed account of the incident and its aftermath in Thomas, *Protest Movements*, pp. 107–126.

[170] Gross, *The Untold Sixties*, p. 223.

[171] Quoted in "1968 Revisited: The Truth about the Gunshot that Changed Germany," *Der Spiegel* online, May 28, 2009. Available at www.spiegel.de/international/germany/1968-revisited-the-truth-about-the-gunshot-that-changed-germany-a-627342.html (accessed July 1, 2010).

Figure 1.7 Shah masks in action, June 2, 1967. Landesarchiv Berlin.

undercover police officer (and Stasi agent) Karl-Heinz Kurras. The image
of a dying Ohnesorg cradled in the arms of a shocked young woman,
reprinted on the cover of the Free University's *FU Spiegel*, became the
iconic image of the West German 1968. The murder and its aftermath,
in which blame for the violence was laid on the students and the responsible parties left unpunished, helped spread the intense radicalism of the
West Berlin student milieu to the rest of the country. Fueling a fundamental break between the left milieu and the establishment, the murder
would lead, by the end of the decade, to the first instances of left-wing
terrorism.

It must be emphasized that this event, so central to the antiauthoritarian revolt in West Germany, arose out of the interaction of overlapping
fields of engagement: West German students protesting against the Shah
as a symbol of neocolonial oppression and Cold War anti-Communism,
and Iranian students protesting as members of a diaspora concerned as
much with national (Iranian) issues as with global ones. In both cases,
the issues were understood in global–local terms: There could be no democracy in one country without democracy in the other.

The revelation that the killer of Benno Ohnesorg was an "unofficial employee" of the East German Stasi has unsettled the hardened narratives that have governed the politics of memory in Germany for decades. There is no consensus – nor, in the absence of evidence, is there likely to be – on the question of whether Kurras's status as a Stasi agent played any role in his actions on June 2, 1967; Kurras has claimed variously that the shooting was in self-defense, an accident, or something he did "for fun."[172] It is a matter of historical record, however, that the West German authorities conspired to destroy evidence in the case, that Kurras was twice exonerated in West German courts (despite the failure of witnesses to corroborate his story), and that the Springer Press in West Berlin immediately blamed the victim and used the case to intensify its witch hunt against the student movement.[173]

It is also quite clear that the reductionist interpretations that transform 1968 in West Germany into a narrow product of June 2, 1967, an assumption that lies behind the recent attempts to paint the revelations about Kurras as necessitating a fundamental reinterpretation, is hopelessly overstated, especially where they are meant to imply that the antiauthoritarian revolt was somehow instigated by East Germany.[174] As we have seen, and as subsequent chapters will further demonstrate, the antiauthoritarian revolt began long before June 2, 1967. It encompassed a wide range of activities and actors, not just student activists but also bohemians and intellectuals, artists and musicians, dropouts and nonconformists, who were operating on projects of their own, for reasons of their own, constrained by Cold War structures while striving against Cold War taboos.

CONCLUSION

What the Ohnesorg killing did do, aside from spreading the revolt around the country, was to emphasize in a way that a thousand teachins could not the reality of state violence, and in this way it marked out a site of convergence between the aspirations of those who hoped to bring the Third World liberation struggles home to the metropole and the local conditions in which such aspirations had to operate. But the antiauthoritarian revolt was no product of a policeman's bullet;

---

[172] *Ibid.* [173] See Thomas, *Protest Movements*, p. 118.

[174] See, for example, S. F. Kellerhoff and U. Müller, "Historiker Horvath: 'SED und Stasi inszenierten die 68er-Revolte,'" Die Welt online, June 15, 2009. Available online at www.welt. de/kultur/article3926843/SED-und-Stasi-inszenierten-die-68er-Revolte.html (accessed July 5, 2010).

rather, it was a multifaceted response, extending over a decade, both to unique German–German Cold War conditions and to the pressures and opportunities presented by West Germany's imbrication in global flows and structures. It was both an act of the globalizing imagination that placed West Germany in the world and a response to the arrival of the world in West Germany, whether in the form of Third World students and dictators, in the form of pop culture (e.g. the *Viva Maria!* film), or in the form of the globally available forms of activism which, and here is the key point, did not just wash up somehow in West Germany but were sought out by activists looking for building blocks of a new form of activism suitable to the needs of the West German situation.

The spatial perspective embedded in this analysis – 1968 as a product of global – local exchanges with a strongly active component – is perhaps more relevant in West Germany than anywhere else, for, as we will see in the following chapters, activists in the Federal Republic experienced the need to import elements of their revolution in a way that seems to have few parallels, at least in the West. Yet, for all the importance of global imaginings and transnational exchanges, the antiauthoritarian revolt was also heavily conditioned by the topography, both concrete and imagined, of the local environment. This "local" was by no means a mere synonym for the national, moreover, for, as we have seen, the activism of 1968 typically unfolded amid small groups of protagonists operating within discrete spatial confines. These protagonists, rather than being members of a monolithic *movement*, are more properly understood as members of partially overlapping *scenes*. These communities of affinity were based around one or more shared commitments – to cultural provocation, neo-Marxism, rock music, dope-smoking, or any number of other more or less subversive activities – and rooted in shared spaces both semiprivate (music venues, pubs, and bars) and public (the street). As we have seen, these scenes, revolving around particular individuals, became key sites of the active transnational in 1968.

Simultaneously, both the key protagonists of the antiauthoritarian revolt and the wider activist circles to which they were connected belonged to transnational communities of affinity organized around cultural consumption (reading books, listening to music, consuming images). These communities – *publics*, to use the term increasingly being adopted by scholars as an alternative to the more static and bounded notion of the "public sphere" – stretched far beyond the borders of the nation-state to encompass distant sources of cultural production and international readerships, listenerships, and viewerships.[175] These publics became key vehicles of the transnational in 1968. Yet, as we will see in the next chapter, the antiauthoritarian revolt did not exist in a horizontal, ever-present now: just as activists struggled to make sense of their situation by responding to, and borrowing from, the global present, they simultaneously reached back into history, grappling with their own country's horrific past while retrieving lost traditions of subversion, emancipation, and resistance.

[175] On publics, see Thomas Olesen, "Transnational Publics: New Spaces of Social Movement Activism and the Problem of Global Long-Sightedness," *Current Sociology*, 53 (2005): 419–440. See also Laila Abu-Er-Rub, Jennifer Altehenger, and Sebastian Gehrig, "The Transcultural Travels of Trends: An Introductory Essay," *Transcultural Studies*, 2 (2011).

CHAPTER 2

Time

In October 1968, a little over a year after the killing of Benno Ohnesorg, four young defendants stood trial in Frankfurt for the crime of arson. The fires they were accused of setting in the Kaufhof and Schneider department stores in Frankfurt caused significant damage but no deaths or injuries, aside from the psychic injury to a badly frightened security guard confronted by a "wall of flame."[1] This crime against property, a symbolic blow against so-called "Consumerism Terror," which activists thought to see in West Germany's embrace of American-style consumer capitalism as well as a protest against the American war in Vietnam, was a direct outcome of the tense atmosphere in the Federal Republic in the wake of the killing of Benno Ohnesorg. One of the defendants, the twenty-eight-year-old Gudrun Ensslin, is alleged to have proclaimed in the aftermath of Ohnesorg's death: "This is the Auschwitz generation, and there's no arguing with them!"[2] Ensslin's co-defendant, Andreas Baader (twenty-five), had missed the events of June 2, being in jail at the time for stealing a motorcycle. A roguish troublemaker on the fringe of the SDS, and a frequent visitor to the Kommune I, Baader was, like his other two co-defendants, the would-be poet Thorwald Proll (twenty-seven) and the aspiring actor Horst Söhnlein (twenty-six), a regular participant in demonstrations of the APO.

During the trial, the defendants mocked the authority of the court in an even more forceful manner than had Fritz Teufel and Rainer Langhans in their just-concluded trial for incitement to arson in Berlin. Acting in the same satirical spirit but with a sharper edge than the fun-loving Teufel and Langhans, the defendants enjoyed themselves at the expense

---

[1] See Sara Hakemi and Thomas Hecken, "Die Warenhausbrandstifter," in Wolfgang Kraushaar, ed., *Die RAF und der linke Terrorismus*, 2 vols. (Hamburg: Hamburger Edition, 2006), vol. 1, pp. 317–331.

[2] The quote, possible apochryphal, is originally given in Stefan Aust, *Der Baader Meinhof Komplex* (Hamburg: Hoffmann & Campe, 1985), p. 54.

of presiding judge Gerhard Zoebe, sprawling in their chairs, smiling and laughing, Proll chomping on a cigar like Groucho Marx. Undermining the proceedings while turning the courtroom into a pulpit for their political views, the defendants highlighted the American war in Vietnam, which, they argued, obviated all moral comparisons with their puny act of violence. As Ensslin put it, "I'm not talking about burned foam mattresses; I'm talking about burned children in Vietnam."[3] The seriocomic tone of the trial was established right from the start in an exchange between Proll – pretending to be Baader until corrected by an officer of the court – and Judge Zoebe. Asked, in a routine ritual of court proceeding, to confirm the year of his birth, Proll replied, "1789."[4]

In referencing the French Revolution, Proll was playing the smart aleck, trying to disconcert the court while lending a veneer of historical gravitas to his and his co-defendants' hijinks. Yet his response was more than just a practiced piece of contempt for authority; it hinted at the historical consciousness that underpinned the defendants' performance in the courtroom. In his concluding remarks to the court, Proll left no doubt that he understood himself as an actor within an historical continuum. "We do not answer to a judiciary that sentences small murderers of Jews and lets the big murderers of Jews get away," he proclaimed;

We do not defend ourselves against a judiciary that delved into fascism unharmed in 1933 and similarly emerged from it in 1945. Furthermore, against a judiciary that has always imposed more severe punishments on people on the left (Ernst Niekisch, Ernst Toller) and been soft on people on the right (Adolf Hitler), that rewarded the murderers of Rosa Luxemburg and Karl Liebknecht (it shot them, too) with a mild sentence, we cannot defend ourselves. Comrades, we want to take a moment to remember Rosa Luxemburg and Karl Liebknecht – stand up! – the eye of the law sits in this court ... Against a judiciary that does not abolish its authoritarian structures but keeps on rebuilding them, we do not defend ourselves.[5]

This (mostly accurate) summary of the trajectory of the German judiciary failed to convince the judge, who sentenced the defendants to three years in prison each. Yet Proll's remarks highlighted the extent to which, both

[3] Quoted in Martin Klimke, "'We Are Not Going to Defend Ourselves before Such a Justice System': 1968 and the Courts," *German Law Journal*, 10 (3) (2009): 261–274, at p. 271.

[4] Thorwald Proll and Daniel Dubbe, *Wir kamen von anderen Stern: Über 1968, Andreas Baader und ein Kaufhaus* (Hamburg: Edition Nautilus, 2003); see also Gerhard Mauz, "Mit voller Geistekraft in ernster Sache," *Der Spiegel*, 43, October 21, 1968.

[5] Andreas Baader, Gudrun Ensslin, Thorwald Proll, and Horst Söhnlein, *Vor einer solchen Justiz verteidigen wir uns nicht: Schlußwort im Kaufhausbrandprozess* (Frankfurt: Edition Voltaire, 1968).

for the defendants themselves and for the movement more generally, past and present were deeply intertwined.

Indeed, in challenging the legitimacy of the court on *historical* grounds, Proll signaled a commitment to an analysis linking past and present that was central to the West German student movement. At the same time, in highlighting how the historical trajectory of the court was tied in not only with the Nazi past but also with the destruction of the German left, Proll touched on the dual erasure at the heart of the antiauthoritarian revolt; for, if silence about the Nazi past was a reigning characteristic of the West German "restoration," as activists argued it was, silence about the revolutionary past was equally prominent. The German left had been destroyed by the Nazis, its traditions, in some cases even the memory of those traditions, erased, their human bearers murdered or driven into exile. To be sure, the SPD, a bulwark of left-wing mobilization since the nineteenth century, returned from the catastrophe of National Socialism with renewed vigor; but at critical junctures – the Godesberg Program of 1959 in which the party officially rejected Marxism; the subsequent expulsion by the party of the SDS in 1961; and the entry in 1966 into the Grand Coalition under the former Nazi Kurt Georg Kiesinger – the SPD proved its incapability, from the left perspective, of mounting any significant challenge to the restorationist status quo. Thus, from the perspective of the young radicals of the 1960s, the left-wing past had been erased twice: once by the Nazis, and once by the left-wing parties themselves, as they either allowed themselves to be coopted (SPD) or transformed into irrelevant tools of Stalinist bureaucracy (KPD).

Thus did history become all the more a central pillar of the antiauthoritarian revolt; it provided the language, motifs, and analytical tools not only of activist elites but also of the extraparliamentary opposition as a whole. Notwithstanding the broken lines of continuity with the revolutionary past that some activists sought to repair, and the opacity of a National Socialist past that society seemed to wish to recover as little of as seemed respectable, activists displayed an easy facility with history, readily marshaling historical facts to make their arguments. It is not for nothing that the names of left-wing clubs such as the Republican Club and Ça Ira referenced the French Revolution, or that banners juxtaposed the date 1968 with earlier dates such as 1848 and 1933 (see Fig. 2.1); activists saw themselves as part of a tradition, punctuated by bitter defeats and moments of caesura and rupture but vital nonetheless, stretching back to that prototype of the modern revolution launched in 1789 and including all the moments of revolutionary possibility since. Acutely aware, by the

Figure 2.1 "State of Emergency 1848, 1933, 1968." Demonstration against the Emergency
Laws, Berlin Wedding, May 1968. Landesarchiv Berlin.

global crisis year of 1968, of their part in a world-historical moment, activists clothed themselves in the garb of revolutions past even as they groped toward a hoped-for revolutionary future. At the same time, recourse to historical facts and embrace of alternative interpretations provided a ready antidote to the act of forgetting that activists saw as the basis of the restorationist West German consensus.

This form of analysis provided material for a counter-consensus binding together the disparate strands of the APO in opposition to contemporary developments, on the basis of historical analogies. In the historical imaginary of the APO, the key turning points in German history marked the stations of political possibility: the revolution of 1848, in which liberals had dithered until the forces of reaction regathered their strength; the German Revolution of 1918, in which the radical possibilities of the solders', sailors', and workers' councils had been foreclosed by an SPD too willing to compromise with entrenched elites; the murder of the revolutionaries Rosa Luxemburg and Karl Liebknecht by right-wing Freikorps mercenaries employed by the government; the chicanery of conservative elites at the end of the Weimar Republic that allowed Hitler to come to power; the destruction of the left through

Hitler's terror – all provided ready material for the analysis of the present. Nor did these key concerns exhaust the list of historical topics on offer. The publications of the antiauthoritarian press regularly covered topics ranging from the Catholic Church's relationship to interwar fascism to the historical background to the Israeli–Palestinian conflict, the roots of current conflicts in the Third World to past revolutionary high points such as the Spanish Civil War.

From this perspective, recovery of the past was another form of the truth-telling central to the antiauthoritarian revolt. Investigation of the past was intimately connected to investigation of the present, a natural adjunct to the focus within the APO on documentation – as for example in the "documentary turn(s)" in literature, popular music, and filmmaking – and in the publicistic strategies of the student movement, which focused heavily on the reproduction of *primary documents* as ultimate sites of recourse in conflicts with the authorities.[6] The concern with history furthermore informed the self-conception of the antiauthoritarian movement, its analysis of its own course and prospects. The creation of a "generation" around the events of the year 1968 – or more properly, initially, around the events of 1967 – was itself an act of self-periodization, one that, by situating the West German protest wave as part of a global movement, drew a line underneath the "peculiarities" of German history.

The effort to define the movement in the present, and to understand where it had been in the recent past, was likewise an effort to place the movement in the long-term historical scheme of the revolutionary left. The impasse reached by the APO in the crisis year 1968 became the source of intensive debate about future directions, debate that was cast in terms of an intensive self-theorization and self-periodization. Activists in the nascent *K-Gruppen*, hard-line Communist groups formed beginning in 1968 with the aim of recovering the Marxist-Leninist tradition, drew a line between themselves and the just-passed "antiauthoritarian" phase. Having recourse once again to the writings of the "great men" of the revolutionary socialist tradition, they sought to position themselves in the trajectory of history outlined by Marx. Simultaneously, activists of the anarchist "Sponti " scene (after "spontaneous") – loose groupings of radicals influenced by anarchism who favored an "undogmatic" approach

---

[6] See, for example, the document collection published by the Verband Deutcher Studentenschaften on the events and aftermath of June 2, 1967, published the same year: Knut Nevermann and Verband Deutscher Studentschaften, eds., *Studenten zwischen Notstand und Demokratie: Dokumente zu den Ereignissen anläßlich des Schah-Besuchs* (Cologne: Pahl-Rugenstein Verlag, 1967).

to activism – drew on other, competing bodies of source material to argue for an alternative vision of the movement's post-1968 direction. In all cases, as we will see, history served as a battlefield on which the struggles of the present were fought.

The strong historical consciousness of the 68er generation was, on the one hand, part of a general trend according to which youth movements around the world sought to break out of Cold War stasis by reconstructing broken narratives and returning to first principles. In the USA, for example, Students for a Democratic Society responded to racism and the threat of nuclear destruction by referencing the principles enshrined in the US Constitution, whereas in France the protests against the Algerian War loomed as unfinished business, even as activists such as the Enragés deployed (indeed, named themselves after) symbolic references from France's revolutionary past. Everywhere, activists sought to undermine the easy assurances of power in the present by calling to life the ghosts of the past. In West Germany, this impulse took on a particular force not only because of the Nazi past, nor on account of the fractured nature of German history (the dates 1848, 1918, 1933, 1945 marking out key caesurae), but because of the country's Cold War position. The flow of history was stamped on the very topography of a divided Germany and a divided Berlin. In a landscape marked by wastelands and ruins, with a Nazi eagle adorning the façade over the door to the SDS headquarters at Kurfürstendamm 140, it was impossible for young West German radicals *not* to be historians. It was the results of their research, as much as any contemporary event, that helped light the fuse for the explosion of 1968 in West Germany.

ZERO HOUR?

The year 1945 is the most profound of the caesurae marking the history of modern Germany. The defeat of National Socialism with the attendant devastation of German cities and loss of territory; the moral crisis unleashed by the revelation of the extent of Nazism's crimes, above all the Final Solution; the partition of the Reich and the former capital Berlin among the four victorious powers, leading a few short years later to the establishment of two German states with their own (newly created) master narratives and legitimizing traditions: all seemed to suggest a break with the past so profound that it became possible to speak of a Stunde Null, or Zero Hour, at which the clock of German history was reset to begin ticking anew.[7]

[7] Peter Alter, "Nationalism and German Politics after 1945," in John Breuilly, ed., *The State of Germany: The National Idea in the Making, Unmaking, and Remaking of a Modern Nation-State* (London and New York: Longman, 1992), pp. 154–176, at p. 154.

The scholarship of recent decades has increasingly cast doubt on the extent to which 1945 marked a break with the past, emphasizing instead the many continuities with which German history after the war was marked. Certainly where the German left is concerned, the post-1945 period was characterized by both continuities and discontinuities. The Weimar-era Marxist mass parties – the remnants of the Old Left – attempted to reestablish themselves after 1945 in a radically altered situation that was in some ways hardly more favorable than it had been before 1945. Both the SPD and the KPD had been destroyed by the Nazis, beginning in January 1933. The KPD suffered especially heavily. Some 10,000 Communists were murdered, and another 10,000 forced to flee abroad.[8] Up to 50 percent of the KPD's 350,000 members suffered persecution of some kind.[9] The SPD and the various Marxist splinter parties were hit hard as well.[10] After the military defeat of the Nazi regime in the spring of 1945, the reformed SPD and KPD bounced back quickly, riding a postwar antifascist surge to once again become mass movements in the early postwar period.[11] Yet the two parties very quickly settled back into the relationship of antagonism they had enjoyed before 1933, not least because of the KPD's role in browbeating the Social Democrats into a merger in the Soviet Occupation Zone in April 1946. The organization thus formed, the SED, continued for decades afterward to harass the SPD in the West with calls for "unity of action" (*Aktionseinheit*) under Communist leadership, while controlling the rump KPD in the West as a sort of fifth column within the Federal Republic.[12]

From here the two Weimar-era parties set out on familiar trajectories: the SPD to a place in government (with revolutionary rhetoric and aspirations jettisoned on the way); the KPD once more into illegality, this time by dint of its close association with the Federal Republic's East German

[8] Richard Loss, "The Communist Party of Germany (KPD), 1956–1968," *Survey: A Journal of Soviet and East European Studies*, 14 (4) (1973): 66–85, at p. 72; Patrick Major, *The Death of the KPD: Communism and Anti-Communism in West Germany, 1945–1956* (Oxford: Clarendon Press, 1998), p. 24.

[9] Beatrix Herlemann, "Communist Resistance between Comintern Directives and Nazi Terror," in David E. Barclay and Eric D. Weitz, eds., *Between Reform and Revolution: German Socialism and Communism from 1840 to 1990* (New York and Oxford: Berghahn Books, 1998), pp. 357–371, at p. 359.

[10] See the essays and documents in Erich Matthias and Rudolf Morsey, eds., *Das Ende der Parteien 1933: Darstellungen und Dokumente* (Düsseldorf: Droste, 1960).

[11] Major, *The Death of the KPD*, p. 13. At the end of August 1945, the KPD had 150,000 members; this figure had risen to 250,000 by the end of October and to 624,000 by the end of April 1946; Werner Müller, "Kommunistische Partei Deutschlands (KPD)" in Martin Broszat, Hermann Weber, Gerhard Braas, eds., *SBZ Handbuch* (Munich: R. Oldenbourg Verlag, 1990), 440–459.

[12] Hilmar Hartig, "Die Entwicklung des Kommunismus in der Bundesrepublik," in Wolfgang Schneider and Jürgen Domes, eds., *Kommunismus international, 1950–1965: Probleme einer gespaltenen Welt* (Cologne: Verlag Wissenschaft und Politik, 1965), p. 91.

Cold War enemy. The government ban on the KPD in August 1956 represented a second major defeat for German Communism, one which it
took a second twelve years in the political wilderness to overturn, and
then to no great effect. The action against the KPD, which by the time of
the ban had already lost the bulk of its electoral support, was driven by
the intense anti-Communism of the Adenauer government. Communists
who attempted to continue their activity on behalf of the party, and to
agitate in favor of a lifting of the ban, were sentenced to jail terms, in
some cases by judges who had served under the Third Reich.[13] When the
Communist Party was finally able to reconstitute itself in late 1968 as the
Deutsche Kommunistische Partei (DKP; German Communist Party),
after a long and hard-fought campaign waged in part by Weimar-era
activists who had served prison sentences under both the Third Reich and
the Federal Republic, it attracted a respectable amount of initial support
but performed poorly in elections and rather quickly became insignificant
as a political force.[14]

The young left-wing radicals of the extraparliamentary opposition
often sympathized with the illegal KPD and sometimes also with the
SPD, but, in general, they relied on theorists who had been marginalized by the left-wing mass parties during the Weimar Republic. The
independent liberal and left-wing intelligentsia to which these thinkers
belonged had been decimated under Nazi rule. Theologians and academ-
ics such as Martin Buber, Paul Tillich, and Karl Mannheim were forced
into exile. The pacifist writer and publicist Carl von Ossietzky, editor of
the left-wing daily *Die Weltbühne*, died of an untreated illness in police
custody after a long imprisonment in a concentration camp. Members of
Frankfurt's Institute for Social Research were scattered into exile. Erich
Fromm, Theodor Adorno, Max Horkheimer, and Siegfried Kracauer emi-
grated to America. Wilhelm Reich ended up in America as well, where he
was hounded to death by the authorities for his unconventional views.[15]
Walter Benjamin, the literary and cultural critic, committed suicide as
a refugee on the Spanish–French border. The majority of the Frankfurt
School thrived in exile, but only Theodor Adorno and Max Horkheimer

[13] On the campaign to refound the Communist Party, see Timothy S. Brown, "Richard Scheringer,
    the KPD, and the Politics of Class and Nation in Germany: 1922–1969," *Contemporary European
    History*, 14 (1) (2005): 317–346.
[14] The DKP had a membership of some 23,000 at the end of 1969, rising to 30,000 by the end of
    the following year. Its youth organization, the Sozialistischen Deutschen Arbeiterjugend (SDAJ)
    had approximately 10,000 members in 1970; Jahresbericht des BfV für 1969/70 offene Fassung,
    November 24, 1971. BArch Koblenz, B106, Band 78917, p. 5.
[15] Reich died in police custody in November 1957.

ever returned to Germany, becoming important mentors to the nascent student movement.[16]

In addition to the work of intellectual forefathers such as Adorno and Horkheimer, young antiauthoritarians derived support from a set of influences rooted in the mobilizations of the previous decade. Indeed, both the student movement and the nascent underground scene grew to a significant extent out of earlier trends, personnel, and organizational initiatives. Among the most important of these were the mass protests of the 1950s, first against the re-establishment of the German army (Bundeswehr), later against the arming of that army with tactical nuclear weapons, and against nuclear weapons generally. Adenauer's announcement of a program of rearmament in August 1950, at a time when the rubble of World War II was still being cleared away in German cities, met with widespread consternation. The Ohne mich (Count Me Out) movement that arose in the wake of Adenauer's announcement was ultimately limited in its influence but did signal the potential for extraparliamentary protest initiatives to come. The government's move to arm the Bundeswehr with tactical nuclear weapons in 1958 gave rise to a more forceful wave of protest, with trade unions, pacifist groups, and the Protestant churches uniting under the nominal leadership of the SPD in the Kampf dem Atomtod (Fight Nuclear Death) movement. Despite launching a series of significant protests around the country, Kampf dem Atomtod failed to prevent the arming of the Bundeswehr with tactical nuclear weapons in 1959; its failure did, however, contribute to the decision of the SPD, faced with punishing attacks on its loyalty by the Adenauer administration, to reorient itself in a more establishment-friendly direction in Bad Godesberg.[17]

The wave of extraparliamentary protests that the SPD had helped to launch continued, however, in the Ostermarsch (Easter March) movement founded the following year. The Ostermarsch der Atomwaffengegner (Easter March of the Opponents of Nuclear Weapons) served as a rallying point for those who had no intention of letting the issue of nuclear weapons go simply because the SPD had decided for party-political reasons

---

[16] Fromm went on to co-found the William Alanson White Institute in New York. He would move to Mexico and to Switzerland before his death. Kracauer would work at the Museum of Modern Art in New York and in 1947 published *From Caligari to Hitler: A Psychological History of German Film*. Marcuse went on to teach philosophy and politics at Harvard University, Columbia University, and Brandeis University.

[17] Thomas, *Protest Movements*, pp. 31–36; Karl A. Otto, *Vom Ostermarsch zur APO: Geschichte der ausserparlamentarischen Opposition in der Bundesrepublik 1960–1970* (Frankfurt: Campus Verlag, 1977).

to take a more accommodating line. For its part, the SPD opposed and generally tried to hinder the movement, which it resented for continuing on where the SPD had decided not to tread.[18] Founded in Hamburg by the schoolteacher and journalist Hans-Konrad Temple, the movement was directly inspired by the Campaign for Nuclear Disarmament, which had begun two years earlier in Great Britain. Like Kampf dem Atomtod before it, but to an even greater degree, the Ostermarsch had wide social support. "The Ostermarsch movement was no left-wing movement," recalls Ingo Boxhammer, one of the founders of the movement in the Ruhr region;

> It stood in opposition to the politics of Adenauer, but to call it left is not to do it justice. It was a very broadly based movement. We had for example an endless supply of pastors – if you wanted to call them all "left," my God, then we'd still have nothing but left-wingers running around here.[19]

Rapidly becoming the centerpiece of the antinuclear movement in West Germany, with up to 100,000 marchers attending annually by 1963, the Ostermarsch became a key umbrella organization of the left-liberal opposition. Bringing together pacifists and religious activists, trade unionists, party activists, students, workers, and young people, partaking of a common activity in a serious but festive spirit, the Ostermarsch represented the coming together of the forces that would fuel the extraparliamentary opposition.

In the realm of culture, too, the antiauthoritarian movement drew on important antecedents. Most of the main trends of the antiauthoritarian movements in the sphere of culture – the search for new modes of expression, the attempt to press art into the service of politics, and the valorization of personal subjectivity as a site of politics in its own right – were prefigured in developments of the 1950s, in some cases of the Weimar Republic and even earlier. The early *Gammler*, for example, a sort of prepolitical opening act for the broader youth revolt of the later 1960s, were preceded by the so-called Halbstarke of the 1950s, whose deep engagement with American popular culture, above all the film stars James Dean and Marlon Brando and the rock 'n' roll with which they were indelibly associated, was experienced and treated as a political threat on both sides of the

---

[18] Thomas, *Protest Movements*, p. 37.

[19] Ingo Boxhammer, "Ingo Boxhammer: über den Pläne-Verlag in Dortmund, die Ostermarschbewegung im Ruhrgebiet und die Pflege des sozialistischen Erbes in der Bundesrepublik," available online at http://erinnerungsort.de/ingo-boxhammer-_485 (accessed September 30, 2011).

Figure 2.2 Ostermarsch, March 26, 1967. Note the legend "Sonny & Cher" on the back of the young woman's parka. Landesarchiv Berlin.

Iron Curtain.[20] Similarly, the counterculture of the 1960s was prefigured in the youth movement of the late nineteenth and early twentieth centuries, which rejected bourgeois values while searching for more authentic bases of existence. Personnel from the most significant of the Weimar -era youth groups, the Bündische Jugend – some of whom were experimenting with a mixture of Eastern philosophy and poetic youth-revolutionary

---

[20] See Michael Rauhut, *Beat in der Grauzone: DDR-Rock 1964 bis 1972 Politik und Alltag* (Berlin: Basisdruck, 1993); and Timothy Ryback, *Rock around the Bloc: A History of Rock Music in Eastern Europe and the Soviet Union* (Oxford University Press, 1990).

ideas as early as the late 1920s – survived to participate in the youth culture scene of the postwar period. Some of them were active in the founding of the annual Burg-Waldeck Festival in 1964, which became a major locus of the burgeoning folk- and protest-music scene as well as a key site in the development of a self-consciously political West German countercultural scene later in the decade.[21]

More significant were the intellectual and publicistic links between the initiatives of the 1950s and those of the 1960s. Intellectuals such as Wolfgang Abendroth, a leading Marxist theoretician expelled from the SDS in the wake of Bad Godesberg, became intellectual mentors to the generation of students coming of age in the mid 1960s. The journal *Das Argument*, founded by the Professor of Philosophy Wolfgang Fritz Haug in 1958, became an important bridge between the anti-remilitarization campaign of the 1950s and the student movement of the 1960s.[22] A corresponding Argument Group within the Berlin SDS became a key constituent of the growing protest movement within the universities. Das Argument and its associated working group Kritik der Faschismustheorien (Critique of Fascism Theory) became, in particular, important bulwarks in the student movement's attempts to retheorize fascism.

These links and alliances came to the fore in the campaign against the Emergency Laws. The conference Demokratie vor dem Notstand (Democracy Facing an Emergency), organized by the SPD in May 1965, marked a major step in the campaign against the laws. As in the earlier campaign against the nuclear rearmament of the Bundeswehr, however, the SPD's attempt to win a place for itself at the governmental table, in this case by becoming part of the Grand Coalition, placed limitations on the scope of its oppositional politics. The SPD did not drop out of the campaign against the laws and, indeed, helped organize major demonstrations against them, but its passage into government did help cede the field in this and other areas to the extraparliamentary movement. The campaign against the Emergency Laws, for example, was dominated by the Deutscher Gewerkschaftsbund (DGB; Confederation of German Trade Unions) and the Kampagne fur Abrustung (KfA; Campaign for Disarmament) – known from 1968 as the Campaign for Democracy and

---

[21] Karl Otto Paetel, a leading Bündisch intellectual forced to flee to America by the Nazis, embraced postwar bohemian culture, publishing one of the earliest anthologies of Beat writings in German: Karl O. Paetel, *Beat: Eine Anthologie* (Hamburg: Rowohlt, 1962).

[22] The first issue, published in May, was an elaboration of a flyer produced by the "Student Group against Atomic Weapons" at the Free University in Berlin; see http://blogs.taz.de/hausmeisterblog/2009/04/30/das_argument_wird_50 (accessed August 2, 2012).

Disarmament – while the SDS and other student groups contributed heavily to it from 1966 onward. The point here is that the antiauthoritarian revolt did not emerge from thin air but arose out of, and drew strength from, a wide-ranging movement with roots in the previous decade and, to an extent, in the period before the war.

About Nazism there was rather less silence than was once supposed, but only because many of its still-living perpetrators turned out to be hiding in plain sight. In the public schools in the Federal Republic, the history of Nazism was taught in only a very desultory way until the mid 1960s, the limited passages on National Socialism and the Holocaust shot through with exculpatory passages.[23] Primary source materials on the Holocaust – photographs, eyewitness accounts by victims – did not begin to appear in school textbooks until the mid 1960s. For the many young people in and around the SDS who were originally socialized and educated under Communism, the situation was no different. To be sure, the crimes of fascism, both historic (under the Nazis) and current (in the capitalist West), were a major topic in the discourse of the DDR; yet, assuming as it did the mantle of the anti-Nazi resistance passed down from the wartime Communist Party, the DDR had little need to educate its children in the details, particularly through continuities that, officially in the DDR, did not exist. The fascist past was, in any case, not really past; the forced transition to democracy after 1945 concealed persistent authoritarian attitudes.

The program of denazification launched by the Allied occupation powers was rather quickly abandoned. Demands for justice were weighed against the perceived need not only to stabilize West Germany as a bulwark against Communism but also to placate the forces of right-wing nationalism and widespread popular resistance to punishment of Germans for the crimes of the Nazi era.[24] Public discourse in 1950s West Germany was indeed notable for loud and vociferous demands for justice, but, as Norbert Frei points out, these were on behalf not of the *victims* of National Socialism but of the *perpetrators*.[25] Again and again, the public came out in vociferous opposition to punitive measures and in favor of leniency for condemned Nazi criminals.[26] This response was not entirely

---

[23] Falk Pingel, "National Socialism and the Holocaust in West German Schoolbooks," *Internationale Schulbuchforschung*, 22 (2000): 11–29.

[24] Norbert Frei, *Adenauer's Germany and the Nazi Past: The Politics of Amnesty and Integration* (New York: Columbia University Press, 2002), p. 309.

[25] *Ibid.*

[26] As Anthony D. Kauders shows, a narrative of German victimhood had already begun as early as 1941; Anthony D. Kauders, *Unmögliche Heimat: Eine deutsch-jüdische Geschichte der Bundesrepublik* (Munich: Deutsche Verlags-Anstalt, 2007).

coterminous with the persistence of Nazi attitudes but stemmed from a host of motivations: resentment against imputations of collective guilt, linked with the perception that the allies were exercising a victors' justice (a justice, moreover, that tended to punish the minor functionary while sparing the ringleader); desire for a clean break on the part both of the government and the population; and an understandable psychological need to achieve distance from a period of barbarity in which, whatever their responsibility in a more overarching sense, many had only nominally participated.[27]

Alongside such passive resistance, however, authoritarian-conservative attitudes, shading off toward outright neo-Nazism, continued to persist and to find open and often quite intransigent expression in the public sphere. In a 1953 opinion poll, 32 percent of West Germans thought that Hitler, although he had made mistakes, had been a great statesman, perhaps the greatest in German history. Five years later, 15 percent expressed their hypothetical willingness to vote for someone like Hitler.[28] Pressure groups dedicated to alleviating the suffering of various German "victims" abounded. Vocal demands were made for the release of imprisoned Nazis, and veterans' and other groups demanded a clean slate for the soldiers of the Wehrmacht, who were to be excused of any liability for war crimes committed on the Eastern Front or elsewhere under the Nazis. These demands were supported by the political parties of the center-right end of the spectrum (the Free Democrats, the Deutsche Partei, the CSU, and the ruling CDU).[29]

Right-wing extremist and neo-Nazi groups and parties were a significant presence in the early postwar period. The neo-Nazi Socialist Reich Party (SRP), founded in 1949, enjoyed among its luminaries Otto Ernst-Remer, the officer in charge of crushing the attempted coup in the wake of the failed bomb attempt on Hitler in July 1944. It had some 20,000 members and won over 10 percent of the vote in the Saxon Landtag elections of May 1951.[30] The government ban of the SRP in October 1952, on the basis of Article 21 of the West German Constitution, blunted the resurgence of neo-fascism at the polls, but right-wing extremist publicists

---

[27] See Robert Moeller, *War Stories: The Search for a Usable Past in the Federal Republic of Germany* (Berkeley, Calif.: University of California Press, 2003).

[28] Moeller, *War Stories*, p. 478.

[29] A. J. Nicholls, *The Bonn Republic: West German Democracy, 1945–1990* (London and New York: Longman, 1997), p. 111.

[30] Karl Dietrich Bracher, *The German Dictatorship: The Origins, Structure, and Effects of National Socialism* (New York: Praeger, 1970), p. 471.

continued to popularize their ideas. By the beginning of the 1960s, a new constellation of forces was in play that would lead to the founding of a new extremist party, the Nationaldemokratische Partei Deutschlands (NPD; National Democratic Party), in November 1964. Publications such as the *Soldatenzeitung* (later *Nationalzeitung*), published from 1960 by Gerhard Frey, helped keep the spirit of militarism and right-wing extremism alive for a younger generation. Just how influential such papers could be on young rightist fanatics would be experienced by Rudi Dutschke in April 1968: his would-be assassin, Josef Bachmann, was an avid reader of the *Nationalzeitung*. Self-justificatory memoirs by former Nazi military men – the Stuka dive-bomber pilot Hans-Ulrich Rudel's *Trotzdem* (*Despite Everything*) is a memorable entry – glorified the war experience and linked the Nazi fight against Bolshevism on behalf of European civilization to a resurgent Cold War anti-Communism.[31]

The persistence in Nazi-like attitudes was facilitated by a startling continuity in personnel between the Hitler dictatorship and the Adenauer administration. Much of the higher civil service remained intact from the Nazi period. The amnesty conducted under Article 131 of the Basic Law, which protected former members of the Nazi civil service and was extended even to some former members of the Waffen SS, gave the *coup de grâce* to the already dying process of denazification.[32] The Nazi judiciary went largely untouched. It was not until 1967 that the first Nazi judge, Hans Joachim Rehse, was convicted of crimes.[33] University faculties were full of former Nazis, particularly faculties of law and medicine. Many doctors who had participated in the infamous T-4 euthanasia program continued to practice medicine in the Federal Republic.

Leading figures in the West German establishment, including Kurt Georg Kiesinger, Franz-Josef Strauß, and Axel Springer, belonged to the Nationalsozialistisches Kraftfahrkorps (NSKK; National Socialist Motor Vehicle Corps), which, as recent scholarship has shown, was far from

[31] Hans-Ulrich Rudel, *Trotzdem* (Buenos Aires: Dürer-Verlag, 1949). The book was printed in Germany in 1953; a heavily edited version appeared in English as *Stuka Pilot* (New York: Ballantine Books, 1958). Rudel was a member of the right-wing extremist Deutsche Reichspartei from 1953 and helped to turn it in a more explicitly pro-Nazi direction.

[32] See Curt Garner, "Public Service Personnel in West Germany in the 1950s: Controversial Policy Decisions and Their Effects on Social Composition, Gender Structure, and the Role of Former Nazis," in Robert G. Moeller, ed., *West Germany under Construction: Politics, Society, and Culture in the Adenauer Era* (Ann Arbor, Mich.: University of Michigan Press, 1997), pp. 135–198, at pp. 157–158.

[33] "West Germany: Judging the Judges," *Time*, July 14, 1967.

the unpolitical automobile club portrayed by its apologists.[34] Adenauer's Minister of Transportation, Dr. Hans Christoph Seebohm – dubbed in a *Spiegel* profile of March 1960 as "the prototype of the eternal Nazi" – was active in the economic administration of occupied Czechoslovakia during the war.[35] Adenauer's adviser Hans Globke was notorious for having written the official commentary on the Nuremburg race laws of 1935 and for having mooted the expedient of having all male Jews adopt the given name Israel and all females Sarah.[36] Globke also had dealings during the war with Adolf Eichmann, one of the chief bureaucrats of the Final Solution.[37] Adenauer's successor as Chancellor, Kurt Georg Kiesinger, had been a Nazi Party member active in the radio propaganda section of the Nazi foreign office.[38]

Numerous commentators wrote of the failure of Germans to come adequately to grips with the crimes of Nazism in general and the horrors of the Final Solution in particular. For Theodor Adorno, Auschwitz marked a caesura so powerful that it challenged the forward direction of history.[39] Lamenting Germans' inability to "come to terms with the past," Adorno worried over the failure to root out the structures that had produced Auschwitz in the first place.[40] The psychologists Alexander and Margarete Mitscherlich located the problem in an "inability to mourn" that afflicted Germans unable to come to grips with the psychic burden of Nazism's crimes.[41]

Nevertheless, as early as the 1950s, visual and filmic evidence of Nazi atrocities played a key role in expanding consciousness of the Nazi past. Alain Resnais's shocking 1955 short film *Night and Fog*, the subject of a scandal at the 1956 Cannes Film Festival when the West German government protested its appearance, went on to evoke a strongly positive response in West Germany, appearing at film festivals and being shown

---

[34] See Dorothee Hochstetter, *Motorisierung und "Volksgemeinschaft": Das Nationalsozialistische Kraftfahrkorps (NSKK), 1931–1945* (Munich: R. Oldenbourg Verlag, 2005).

[35] *Der Spiegel*, March 23, 1960.

[36] On Globke, see Erik Lommatzsch, *Hans Globke (1898–1973): Beamter im Dritten Reich und Staatssekretär Adenauers* (Frankfurt and New York: Campus, 2009).

[37] *Der Spiegel*, September 28, 1960.

[38] On Kiesinger, see Philipp Gassert, *Kurt Georg Kiesinger, 1904–1988: Kanzler zwischen den Zeiten* (Munich: DVA, 2006).

[39] This assertion is from Theodor W. Adorno, *Negative Dialectics* (New York: The Seabury Press, 1973).

[40] Theodor W. Adorno, "What Does Coming to Terms with the Past Mean?," in Geoffrey H. Hartman, ed., *Bitburg in Moral and Political Perspective* (Bloomington, Ind.: Indiana University Press, 1986).

[41] Alexander Mitscherlich and Margarete Mitscherlich, *Die Unfähigkeit zu trauern: Grundlagen kollektiven Verhaltens* (Munich: R. Piper & Co., 1967).

by film clubs.[42] Gerhard Schoenberner's photo documentation *Der gelbe Stern* (1960), representing the first significant appearance of Holocaust imagery (aside from Resnais's film) since the Nuremburg trials, was both controversial and well received.[43] The Eichmann trial of 1961 and the Frankfurt Auschwitz trials of 1963–1965 became the occasions for more open discussion of Nazi crimes.

Yet, left-wing critics adduced in the wealth of fact and detail the traces of a new sort of forgetting. The Frankfurt trials were covered by Peter Weiss in the first issue of the journal *Kursbuch*, an issue that also included Martin Walser's essay "Our Auschwitz."[44] Walser worried that the trial's focus on the gruesome deeds of individual perpetrators would overshadow the system that had created Auschwitz, that ultimately Auschwitz would be erased as a meaningful antidote to future atrocities.[45] Peter Weiss turned his and other observations of the trial into a play, *The Investigation* (1965), in which both the deeds and the justifications of the perpetrators were presented in clinical and chilling detail.[46] The documentary conceit of the play – it was constructed out of the actual textual evidence of the trials – was an argument, in the spirit of Walser's essay, for the primacy of structure over individual agency. Underlying continuities, above all in the relationship of fascism and capitalism, came organically to life in the play's naming of the firms that had profited from the destruction of human life, in its dry but provocative cataloguing of the hours and wages of those condemned to work to death. As Weiss put it in a laconic notebook entry: "Capitalist society driven to the most extreme perversion – exploitation even of blood, bones, ashes."[47]

Throughout the period of the 1960s, the Nazi past continued to rear its head in ugly ways. The turn of the decade saw well-publicized incidents of cemetery and synagogue defacement. On Christmas Eve 1959,

[42] Andrew Hebard, "Disruptive Histories: Toward a Radical Politics of Remembrance in Alain Resnais's *Night and Fog*," *New German Critique*, 71 (spring – summer, 1997): 87–113.

[43] See Robert Sackett, "Visions of Atrocity: Public Discussion of *Der gelbe Stern* in Early 1960s West Germany," *German History*, 24 (winter 2006): 526–556. See also Habbo Knoch, *Die Tat als Bild: Photographien des Holocaust in der deutschen Erinnerungskultur* (Hamburg: Hamburger Edition, 2001), and Habbo Knoch, "The Return of the Images: Photographs of Nazi Crimes and the West German Public in the 'Long 1960s'," in Philipp Gassert and Alan E. Steinweis, eds., *Coping with the Nazi Past: West German Debates on Nazism and the Generational Conflict, 1955–1975* (New York: Berghahn Books, 2006), pp. 31–49.

[44] *Kursbuch*, no. 1, 1965.

[45] Martin Walser, "Our Auschwitz," *Kursbuch*, no. 1, 1965.

[46] Robert Cohen, "The Political Aesthetics of Holocaust Literature: Peter Weiss's *The Investigation* and Its Critics," *History and Memory*, 10 (2) (1998): 43–67.

[47] Robert Cohen, *Understanding Peter Weiss* (Columbia, S.C.: University of South Carolina Press, 1993), pp. 88–89.

swastikas were daubed on the walls of a freshly reinaugurated synagogue in Cologne, accompanied by the slogan "Germans demand Jews out."[48] The vandalism caused an international scandal and inspired a "swastika wave" of copycat vandalisms throughout West Germany and abroad.[49] The Zind case, in which a schoolteacher involved in a bar fight was prosecuted for telling his opponent that "the Nazis had not yet gassed enough Jews," gained nationwide notoriety, as did the high-profile publication by Friedrich Nieland of a pamphlet blaming "international Jewry" for the world wars.[50] In the latter case, presiding judge Nicholas Budde dropped charges against the defendant on the basis that "the passage was not directed 'against Jews generally' but 'only against a narrowly limited circle of Jews' responsible 'for the world historical events of recent decades.'"[51] The resulting scandal was such that Chancellor Konrad Adenauer saw fit to issue an apology from West Germany to the rest of the world.[52]

Protesters who transgressed acceptable means of political expression sometimes tasted at first hand the persistence of authoritarian and Nazi attitudes. In November 1967, students at the University of Hamburg, upset over the continued dominance of stuffy and outmoded pedagogy, disrupted the installation ceremony of the new rector by carrying a banner in the van of the procession reading "Under the academic gowns, the mildew of 1000 years." The allusion to the thousand years of Hitler's Reich was lost on no one involved. The Nazi past and student antiauthoritarianism intersected in many subsequent incidents involving conflicts between students and faculty members with Nazi pasts.[53] In one incident, students at Munich University entered a lecture hall dressed in police uniforms, offering to "protect" a professor – a former Nazi functionary who had authored the anti-Semitic book *Russian Jewish Policy* (1939) – from "Left radical elements."[54] These references to Nazism took on added significance in the tumult following the Hamburg incident when a professor, himself a former stormtrooper and Nazi Party member, remarked, "you all belong in concentration camps."[55]

---

[48] "Synagogen-Schändung: Die Nacht von Köln," *Der Spiegel*, January 6, 1960.
[49] "Die Publicity der Hakenkreuze," *Christ und Welt*, January 14, 1960, BArch Koblenz, B106, 15517.
[50] Robert Andrew Kahn, *Holocaust Denial and the Law: A Comparative Study* (New York: Palgrave Macmillan, 2004), p. 66.
[51] Kahn, *Holocaust Denial*, p. 67.
[52] *Ibid.*   [53] Thomas, *Protest Movements*, p. 133.
[54] Thomas, *Protest Movements*, pp. 133–134.   [55] *Der Spiegel*, November 20, 1967.

ARGUMENT BY ANALOGY IN THE FASCIST PRESENT

Coming to terms with the continued presence of the murderers and those who had facilitated them became one of the central organizing motifs of the SDS. As early as 1959, a student at the Free University named Reinhard Strecker organized an exhibit, "Unexpiated Nazi Justice," that highlighted the continuities between the judiciaries under National Socialism and in the Federal Republic. Some fifty judges and lawyers were featured, all of whom had continued their careers from one regime to the other.[56] By the late 1960s, the ever-increasing legal difficulties of the student movement made the political color of the judiciary a source of burning concern. The high-profile trials of Rainer Langhans, Fritz Teufel, Reinhard Wetter, Horst Mahler, and others were only a few of the some 10,000 proceedings opened against APO members in 1967–1969.[57] It was easy in this context to contrast the notorious leniency of Weimar-era courts toward right-wing defendants with their punitive posture toward Communists and Social Democrats, and difficult not to resent a situation in which judges who once condemned Communists were now condemning radical students. The "anti-Nazi campaign" organized in 1968 gave voice to this frustration:

Former Nazi judges want to pronounce "justice" over us. Of all things the Moabit district judge Gente – once a member of the Nazi Party – wants to "condemn" our comrades who protested against the fascist race-baiting film Africa Addio. But we have worse than this Gente: we even have a former Nazi propagandist as *Bundeskanzler*! Our patience must now come to an end: Let's put a stop to Nazi race-baiters, Slav-killers, socialist-slaughterers, the entire *Nazi-Scheiße* of yesteryear being able to bring their stench over our generation. Let's make up for what they failed to do in 1945: drive the Nazi plague out of the city. Let's finally do a real de-Nazification … Let's offer resistance to former Nazi-judges, Nazi attorneys, Nazi lawmakers of all colors, Nazi policemen, Nazi bureaucrats, Nazi protectors of the constitution, Nazi teachers, Nazi professors, Nazi pastors, Nazi journalists, Nazi propagandists, Nazi Chancellors, and not least against Nazi war profiteers, Nazi industrialists, and Nazi financiers.[58]

[56] Abromeit, "The Limits of Praxis," p. 20. See also Tilman Fichter and Siegward Lönnendonker, *Kleine Geschichte des SDS: Der Sozialistische Deutsche Studentenbund von 1946 bis zur Selbstauflösung* (Berlin: Rotbuch, 1977), p. 109.

[57] "Bloße Flanken," *Der Spiegel*, no. 45, November 3, 1969.

[58] Anti-Nazi-Kampagne, "Organisieren wir den Ungehorsam gegen die Nazi-Generation!," in Lutz Schulenburg, ed., *Das Leben ändern, die Welt verändern! 1968: Dokumente und Berichte* (Hamburg: Edition Nautilus, 1998), pp. 118–119.

This call to offer the resistance against fascism that a previous generation had failed to offer cut to the heart of the student movement's approach to the Nazi past. It represented a retroactive antifascism that would do what the Weimar-era left had been unable to do. As Peter Paul Zahl, sometime editor of the underground newspaper *Agit 883*, put it, "we didn't want it to be said about our generation that we were just as silent about [this] swinishness as our parents were about what happened in the Third Reich."[59]

If the factual basis of the 68ers' claims about the continuity of Nazi personnel and attitudes is indisputable, the fascism analysis of the 68ers, that is, their theoretical approach to the nature, causes, and meaning of fascism in general and National Socialism in particular, has not fared well in the scholarship.[60] Focusing on a model of continuity based on the alleged affinity between fascism and capitalism, it sometimes came uncomfortably close to the vulgar Marxist fascism theory of the Third International – passed down more or less intact to the DDR – which gave a simple answer ("capitalism") to complex questions about the nature, causes, and social basis of fascism and which tended to downplay Nazi anti-Semitism as a causal factor. The basic position, as it filtered into the ideological praxis of the APO, was expressed by Rudi Dutschke as follows: "The victory and the power of the NSDAP, the origins of the Second World War, cannot be separated from the alliance between the NSDAP and the rich (monopoly capitalism)."[61]

Yet, in widening the lens beyond Europe, activists could perceive precisely this sort of capitalism – fascism dynamic at work. In Latin America, for example, US-backed police regimes protected the most extreme forms of capitalist exploitation with brutal violence directed at trade unionists, students, and left-wing intellectuals. If these regimes were not fascist in the strict sense, they exerted enough fascist-like violence against the left for the comparison to make sense to student radicals in West Germany. These radicals were well aware of the historical fact that fascism and authoritarian nationalism, in the political practice of the Hitler, Mussolini, and other interwar authoritarian regimes, was, above all, a war

---

[59] Quoted in Gerd Conradt, *Starbuck: Holger Meins – Ein Porträt als Zeitbild* (Berlin: Espresso, 2001), p. 116.

[60] For a characteristic treatment, see Wolfgang Wippermann, "The Post-War German Left and Fascism," *Journal of Contemporary History*, 11 (4) (1976): 185–219 (Special Issue: Theories of Fascism).

[61] Rudi Dutschke, *Aufrecht gehen: Eine fragmentarische Autobiographie* (Frankfurt: Olle & Wolter, 1981), p. 34.

of annihilation against the left.[62] For the historian, by contrast, the salience of the National Socialist *past* in West Germany can make it easy to forget about the persistence of fascism in the global sixties *present*.

That present was marked by the existence of two long-standing fascist or authoritarian conservative regimes, one in Portugal, the other in Spain. The continued existence of the Franco regime, a throwback to the interwar era of authoritarian rule that had won its insurgent war against Spanish democracy with the material assistance of Italian and German fascism, was an affront to those who supposed that friends of Hitler and Mussolini had no right to rule in a democratic postwar Europe. Outside Europe, fascist/authoritarian-nationalist/military rule held sway in Guatemala (from 1954), Paraguay (from 1954), Brazil (from 1964), Bolivia (from 1964), Argentina (from 1966), and Chile (from 1973). It was lost on no informed West German observer that America, the same America that protected West Germany's democratic freedoms, was mentor and friend to these anti-Communist police regimes, as well as to anti-Communist Cold War police arrangements closer to home. Italy saw continued and robust activity from former and current fascists active in and around its intelligence services, aided and abetted by the CIA. The terror bombings associated with the "strategy of tension" designed to turn a frightened public to the right, begun in 1969, were only the most prominent of the actions carried out by these forces.[63] These operations received substantial support from the CIA's Operation Gladio, a secret stay-behind army that helped organize anti-Communist actions up to and including terror attacks on civilian targets across the length and breadth of the NATO lands.[64]

Closer to home, the USA protected former operatives of the Nazi intelligence service, putting them into service against the new Cold War enemy. The Organization Gehlen, under the leadership of former Wehrmacht

---

[62] This fact comes out unequivocally for both Italy and Germany in the accounts of contemporaries as well as in the subsequent scholarship. On Italy, see Gaetano Salvemini, *Italian Fascism* (London: Victor Gollancz, 1938); Angelo Tasca, *The Rise of Italian Fascism, 1918–1922* (New York: H. Fertig, 1966); Paul Corner, *Fascism in Ferrara, 1915–1925* (Oxford University Press, 1975). On Germany, see Rudolf Diels, *Lucifer ante Portas: Zwischen Severing und Heydrich* (Zurich: Interverlag, 1949); Detlev Peukert, *Die KPD in Widerstand: Verfolgung und Untergrundarbeit an Rhein und Ruhr 1933 bis 1945* (Wuppertal: Hammer, 1980).

[63] It is notable, as Dorothea Hauser points out, that in Italy there were *ten times* more attacks initiated by neo-fascists than by left-wing groups in the period 1969–1974; Dorothea Hauser, "Terrorism," in Martin Klimke and Joachim Scharloth, eds., *1968 in Europe: A History of Protest and Activism, 1956–1977* (London: Palgrave Macmillan, 2008), pp. 269–280, at p. 276.

[64] Daniele Ganser, *NATO's Secret Armies: Operation Gladio and Terrorism in Western Europe* (London and New York: Routledge, 2005).

general and head of intelligence on the Eastern Front during World War II Reinhard Gehlen, staffed by many former SS and Wehrmacht officers, ran an estimated 4,000 agents operating in West Germany and in various Eastern Bloc countries. Beginning in 1955, with the formal acceptance of the Federal Republic into the NATO alliance, the Organization Gehlen was recognized as the official intelligence apparatus of the Federal Republic.[65] The founding of the NPD in 1964, and its startling electoral surge in 1968 – 9.8 percent of the seats in the state elections in Baden-Württemberg in April of that year – suggested that even openly fascist parties were far from a dead letter even in Germany.

The military coup in Greece in April 1967 offered shocking proof of the possibility for a terroristic anti-left "national revolution" to once again spring up on European soil. Along with Turkey, Greece had joined NATO at the beginning of 1952 and made up an important strategic base of operations against a hypothetical Warsaw Pact attack. The coup was carried out by the Greek military using a NATO counterinsurgency plan code-named Prometheus, and despite the dubious nature of the undertaking the coup leaders thereafter enjoyed cordial relations with NATO officials as well as with the CIA.[66] The coup was brutal in the extreme, making extensive use of torture, which was widely reported upon in the Federal Republic in both the mainstream and left-wing press.[67] The situation in Greece was the focus of a special issue of the journal *Das Argument* published in August 1970.[68] The student Project Group Greece called attention to press reports, based on leaked NATO documents, indicating that plans like Prometheus existed for other European countries as well, making the parallel with the debate about West Germany's Emergency Laws impossible to miss: "That which has happened in Greece must not be seen as an isolated case, because it can be repeated in all the NATO countries, insofar as an Emergency Law exists. Oppose the Emergency Laws in the BRD if you don't want to have two … three … many Greece's in Europe."[69] As in the case of the

---

[65] On Gehlen see Mary Ellen Reese, *Organisation Gehlen: Der kalte Krieg und der Aufbau des Deutschen Geheimdienstes* (Berlin: Rowohlt, 1992); see also the relevant sections in Norbert Frei, ed., *Karrieren im Zwielicht: Hitlers Eliten seit 1945* (Frankfurt: Campus-Verlag, 2001); and Saskia Henze and Johann Knigge, *Stets zu Diensten: Der BND zwischen faschistischen Wurzeln und neuer Weltordnung* (Hamburg: Unrast-Verlag, 1997).

[66] Sean Kay, *NATO and the Future of European Security* (Oxford: Rowman & Littlefield, 1998), p. 51.

[67] James Becket, *Barbarism in Greece: A Young American Lawyer's Inquiry into the Use of Torture in Contemporary Greece, with Case Histories and Documents* (New York: Walker, 1970).

[68] *Das Argument*, no. 57: "Revolution und Konterrevolution in Griechenland," 1970.

[69] Projektgruppe Griechenland, Sozialistischer Deutscher Studentenbund – Sozialistischer Hochschulbund, "Zwei … drei … viele Griechenland?," in Schulenburg, ed., *Das Leben ändern*, pp. 154–155.

anti-Tshombe and anti-Shah demonstrations, foreign students, especially Greek ones, played a key role in publicizing events and mobilizing protests against them.[70]

Another US intervention by proxy, the 1973 coup against democratically elected Chilean prime minister Salvadore Allende, provided a further example of the potential for Cold War anti-Communism to blossom into a regime of anti-leftist terror. The coup was the subject of fierce protests in the Federal Republic. US involvement in the coup, as well as in the subsequent transnational terror campaign organized by Pinochet's Chile (Operation Condor) provided ready evidence for lines of analysis that sought to link capitalism, Cold War anti-Communism, and a resurgence of anti-leftist terror regimes that, if not technically fascist, looked close enough to the original for activists to label them as such. Far from being the focal point of some sort of German psychodrama in which young people proved incapable of distinguishing between liberal democracy and fascist dictatorship – although, as we will see, that sometimes happened too – fascism analysis was a response to contemporary, Europe-wide and worldwide realities. The postwar epoch was not one in which fascism could be safely consigned to the past but, in a fundamental sense, an era of fascist/right-radical resurgence.

The existence of contemporary terror regimes, whether in Europe or in Latin America, was interpreted in terms drawn from Germany's own fascist past. Fascism was a key motif linking the global and the local in the left-wing imaginary. The connection between the local past and the global present was expressed in the visual iconography of student protest culture. Symbols drawn from the Nazi past provided a language that enabled protesters to draw analogies between Germany's fascist past and the present. One of the most common of these was the deployment of the runic "s" from the Nazi SS. In Fig. 2.3, a runic "s" replaces the "s" in "USA," likening US counterinsurgency warfare in Vietnam to Nazi atrocities.

Viewed through this broader lens, it is not too difficult to see how the course of events in the Federal Republic could seem to offer worrying evidence that analogies drawn from the Nazi past and the global present threatened to come together in sinister fashion. All the nascent issues animating the APO – the growing conflict with the establishment, sharpened by battles in the street with the police and the killing of Benno

---

[70] See the photos in Ruetz, *"Ihr müßt diesen Typen nur ins Gesicht sehen,"* pp. 76–77.

Figure 2.3 Anti-Vietnam War demonstration, Wittenbergplatz,
October 21, 1967. Landesarchiv Berlin.

Ohnesorg, as well as the escalating battle with the Springer Press –
became increasingly inseparable from the conviction that the destruction of the left enacted by the Nazis at the end of the Weimar Republic
(with the significant assistance before the fact of the press baron Alfred
Hugenberg, various industrialists, high army officers, and other conservative fellow travelers) was happening a second time. The parallels between
the Emergency Laws, which could be used to suspend civil liberties in
the event of an invasion, natural disaster, or general strike, and the use of
Article 48 of the Weimar Constitution to effectively end the first German

democracy even before Adolf Hitler came to power in January 1933, were difficult to ignore. Theodor Adorno was prominent in giving voice to this interpretation, citing Article 48 of the Weimar Constitution – and, as a more recent precedent, the Spiegel Affair of 1962 – as evidence that it could be dangerous to give the government such powers. "The appetite," he warned, "grows with the eating."[71]

The establishment, too, had ready recourse to analogies from the German past. After the Springer Tribunal of February 1968, the Springer tabloid *Bild* warned that Germany was now leaving the "twenties" and moving into the "thirties," a clear reference to the transition from increasingly radical rhetoric to an intensification of political violence in the late Weimar Republic.[72] Elsewhere, the Springer Press likened young protesters to Hitler's street-fighting *Sturmabteilung* (SA) toughs. These historical analogies easily articulated with the lines of a moral panic in which the discourse of moral corruption that had allegedly doomed Weimar (and, implicitly, needed correcting by the Nazis) was applied to the youth revolt of the 1960s. At the same time, the increasingly radical activism of the student movement provoked real fears on the part of a generation of intellectuals who were old enough to remember, or at least to be deeply aware of, how Nazi students had disrupted the universities of the Weimar Republic.

Many of these "45ers" supported the student movement's demands for democratic reform and criticized the harshness of the establishment's response; yet many were also repelled by what they saw as demagogic and anti-democratic privileging of action and emotion over rational debate and democratic process. The philosopher and Frankfurt professor Jürgen Habermas gave voice to some of these fears in June 1967 when, in response to Rudi Dutschke's call for the establishment of a countrywide network of "action centers" to facilitate student mobilization, he charged that students were playing "a game with terror, with fascistic implications."[73] This statement elicited a fierce response from the student movement and its allies, and Habermas later retracted his statement, but the incident further exposed the extent to which, across the political spectrum, the German past remained unfinished business.

[71] Theodor W. Adorno, "Gegen die Notstandsgesetze," in Sievers, ed., *1968: Eine Enzyklopädie*, p. 389. For the Spiegel Affair, see below.
[72] Stuart J. Hilwig, "The Revolt against the Establishment: Students versus the Press in West Germany and Italy," in Carole Fink, Philipp Gassert, and Detlef Junker, eds., *1968: The World Transformed* (Cambridge University Press, 1998), pp. 321–349, at p. 331.
[73] Matthew G. Specter, *Habermas: An Intellectual Biography* (Cambridge University Press, 2010), pp. 114–115.

"ONE DOESN'T MAKE THE SAME REVOLUTION TWICE": THE HISTORICAL IMAGINATION OF 1968

"One doesn't make the same revolution twice": thus observed the widow of the Spanish anarchist Buenaventura Durruti at the end of Hans Magnus Enzensberger's 1972 historical novel *The Short Summer of Anarchy: Life and Death of Buenaventura Durruti*. A documentary-historical treatment of the life of a legendary anarchist hero of the Spanish Revolution (not as well known then as he would later become, in part through Enzensberger's efforts), the novel was a meditation on themes of utopia, longing, and nostalgia, which juxtaposed the lost revolutionary moment of the 1930s against recently past events in the Federal Republic. The dead anarchist, a victim in the struggle against the fascist/radical conservative uprising that would turn Spain into Europe's longest-running dictatorship, represented a haunting reminder of the recurrent moment of utopian possibility in European history, a moment of which 1968 seemed to have offered yet another example. The widow's final lines expressed both resignation and hope, leaving open the possibility that a future such utopian moment was possible; but nostalgia for the last revolution, it seemed to suggest, was a dead end.[74]

Enzensberger's choice of topic was suggestive of the extent to which the revolutionary past still figured in the present. By the time of the publication of the novel, the high period of 1968 was already being treated by its protagonists as a phenomenon of a bygone age. But even as activists searched for answers, the allure of the revolutionary past became ever stronger, seeming to hold out the promise of new directions and insights for the future. The anarchist Spain of Enzensberger's novel was a staple of the libertarian-left imaginary. Already as early as 1964, rebel Spanish anarchists figured in a characteristic piece of Situationist détournement in which a nude woman, lounging by the pool, declared, "There's nothing better than fucking an Asturian miner!"[75] Books on the Spanish Revolution appeared prominently in the advertisements in West German left-wing periodicals. The Spanish Civil War was even deployed as a key

---

[74] Thomas J. A. Krüger, "From the 'Death of Literature' to the 'New Subjectivity': Examining the Interaction of Utopia and Nostalgia in Peter Schneider's *Lenz*, Hans Magnus Enzensberger's *Der Kurze Sommer der Anarchie*, and Bernward Vesper's *Die Reise*," Ph.D. thesis, McGill University, 2008, p. 182.

[75] A reference to the anarchist miners who had fought in the Civil War and who continued to rebel against Franco into the 1950s and 1960s. See "España en el corazón," *International Situationist*, July 1964, International Institute for Social History, Amsterdam.

analogy by the SDS, which made "Vietnam is the Spain of the present day" a slogan at the February 1968 International Vietnam Congress. The failure to combat fascism when it first appeared in Spain in the form of Franco's insurgency, the argument went, represented a piece of liberal-democratic cowardice that ensured the forward march of Franco's friends Hitler and Mussolini.

The attempt to uncover a "usable past," a left-wing past that the experience of fascist dictatorship and world war had helped to bury, went back to the earliest days of the antiauthoritarian revolt. Indeed, for activists of the antiauthoritarian movement, the project of making a revolution in the present was inseparable from the project of coming to terms with the past. The movement was marked, in a way that no other radical movement in history had been or has been since, by the attempt to historicize and theorize itself in real time. This was in no small part a product of the salience of rupture in German history; broken links with the past demanded historical-analytic work if the antiauthoritarian project was not to go blindly into the future, and theoretical work if the present was to be understood in a way that enabled meaningful action. But it also had to do with the unresolved contradictions at the heart of the left-revolutionary project: exactly which traditions needed to be recovered and which kinds of politics did they actually make possible?

In the beginning, contradictions within the antiauthoritarian movement did not matter as much as they would later come to. The large issues driving the APO, above all the Springer Press monopoly and the Emergency Laws, were issues of broad concern that could fit within both liberal and self-consciously socialist rubrics, uniting intellectuals, confessional and trade-union groups, as well as students. They were, in short, uniting rather than dividing issues. For the activist avant-garde, questions of revolutionary strategy and tactics could take a back seat as long as one seemed to be a member in a broadly based revolutionary movement, a citizens' movement with revolutionary connotations in which an increasingly large and more radical segment of the population (secondary-school pupils, apprentices, and young workers) were being integrated, and which was unfolding in the context of a global revolution of which West Germany was only one of the smallest and by no means the most significant parts. When this movement failed to produce fundamental change, however (both the anti-Springer and anti-Emergency Law campaigns had run out of gas by the summer of 1968), the problem of what steps to take next, and how such steps were to be theoretically grounded, took center stage.

For a variety of reasons, from 1968 on, the SDS no longer served as an adequate vehicle for the antiauthoritarian revolt. At the World Festival of Youth in Sofia, Bulgaria, at the beginning of August 1968, relations between the antiauthoritarians and the traditionalists in the SDS, uneasy at the best of times, exploded into open conflict. While the former attempted to demonstrate against the Vietnam War in front of the American embassy, the latter, incensed at this "insult" to their hosts, assisted the Bulgarian secret police in beating them up.[76] A few weeks later, the invasion of Czechoslovakia by the "people's armies" of the Warsaw Pact fractured the APO coalition and intensified divisions within the SDS. The Republican Clubs split on the invasion, a majority coming out in favor of condemning it and in many cases refusing any further cooperation with the pro-Soviet minority.[77] While the traditionalists in the SDS quietly prepared their exit to the DKP or other more agreeable destinations, the bulk of the antiauthoritarian movement organized rallies condemning the Stalinist blow against the attempt to create a Socialism with a Human Face. The following month, at the Twenty-Third Delegate Congress of the SDS in Frankfurt, the organization's loss of direction (not to mention its patriarchal power structure) was painfully placed on the agenda by representatives of the nascent women's movement. A further congress in November in Hanover ended without any consensus about the SDS's further direction. At this point, the dissolution of the SDS by a rump congress in March 1970 was a foregone conclusion.

The crushing of the Prague Spring exposed the false unity of the APO, making it clear that common short-term objectives notwithstanding, grave differences existed both in terms of goals and methods. That a significant minority of the APO (e.g. in the Republican Clubs) could support the Warsaw Pact invasion not only undercut the humanistic claims that underpinned the student movement but also underlined the extent to which the New Left in Germany, even at its supposed high point in 1968, had failed to break with the categories and concepts of the Old Left. Indeed, it exposed a dichotomy at the heart of the APO's rejection of the conceptual categories of the Cold War, for if, on the one hand, this rejection meant that activists resisted the false choice of Communism or anti-Communism, it also meant that it could easily provide space for activists who wanted to believe in the East German experiment to continue to see

---

[76] Subsequently, five members of the traditionalist faction were branded "Stalinists" and kicked out of the organization; Henning and Raasch, *Neoanarchismus*, p. 115.

[77] Raasch and Henning, *Neoanarchismus*, p. 115.

Figure 2.4 Anti-Vietnam demonstration, Kurfürstendamm, February 18, 1968.
Note the images of Rosa Luxemburg among those of Che Guevara and
Ho Chi Minh. Landesarchiv Berlin.

themselves as having common cause with those who rejected state social-
ism altogether. This was true not least because the teleological nature of
Marxist orthodoxy made it possible for them to hope that states such as the
DDR would some day advance to a fuller realization of Communism.

For the small group of activists who helped launch the antiauthoritarian wing of the SDS and the commune experiments that accompanied it,
the attempt to mine the past for revolutionary source material occupied
center stage. In the Kochel am See meeting of July 1966, for example,
Dieter Kunzelmann spoke on the nineteenth-century utopian socialist
experiments of Charles Fourier and Robert Owen, Dutschke on the Paris
Commune of 1871, and Bernd Rabehl on the early libertarian socialist
experiments in Bolshevik Russia. Dutschke was highly active in pursuing
friendships with surviving members of the older-generation international
Marxist intelligentsia and counted among his friends and correspondents
Herbert Marcuse, Ernst Bloch, and Georg Lukács. The circle around
Kunzelmann, too, derived inspiration from relationships with an older
generation of artists and self-conscious engagement (positive or negative)
with the legacy of politicized art from Dada to surrealism.

Rudi Dutschke's *Bibliography of Revolutionary Socialism*, published in
October 1966 as a special issue of *SDS-Korrespondenz*, aimed to codify

the historical source material underpinning the extraparliamentary opposition. By no means a value-neutral attempt to present texts of the revolutionary past, the bibliography was rather an attempt to define and justify the activity of the antiauthoritarian faction in the SDS. In particular, the *Bibliography* represented an attempt, as against the state-socialist traditionalist tendency, to reassess the importance of anarchism.[78] In an interview with the journalist Hans Kundnani, Bernd Rabehl remembers having encountered Dutschke sitting in a student café in Charlottenburg with a pile of books by Lenin piled on the table before him. To Rabehl's suggestion that the time for Lenin was past, Dutschke replied, "No, now is exactly the time we need to study it all over again."[79]

Not everyone agreed on the need to study the history of the working-class movement; indeed, as Mia Lee has shown, the value of history and, in particular, of historical materialism as a tool of analysis (Rudi Dutschke and Bernd Rabehl insisted upon it, Kunzelmann and the Munich faction rejected it) was a primary source of disagreement in Subversive Aktion. Nevertheless, for the APO as a whole, history remained central. Typical was the announcement in July 1968 by the Republican Club in West Berlin of the formation of working groups on the theme "50 Years of Counterrevolution Are Enough." Topics included "the role of the SPD and the trade unions in the workers' movement in the last 50 years," "the revolutionary situation of 1918/19," and, tellingly, the "workers' participation [*Mitbestimmung*] discussion from 1918 to 1968; the situation of the factory councils in society."[80]

Such discussions necessitated a reassessment of the relationship between the three great strands of socialism generated between the beginning of the nineteenth century and the end of the First World War: socialism, communism, and anarchism. They also entailed an analysis of the revolutionary situations – France (1871), Russia (1905 and 1917–1921), Germany (1848 and 1918–1919), and Spain (1936–1939) – in which they were put into practice. This historical vetting process, one that critically analyzed the claims of Bolshevism while attempting to recover what Bolshevism had tried to destroy and suppress, was but another front in the fight against the ossified Cold War impasse central to 1968.

---

[78] Rudi Dutschke, *Ausgewählte und kommentierte Bibliographie des revolutionären Sozialismus von K. Marx bis in die Gegenwart* (Heidelberg-Frankfurt-Hanover-Berlin: Druck- und Verlagskooperative HFHB, 1969), p. 4.

[79] Quoted in Hans Kundnani *Utopia or Auschwitz: Germany's 1968 Generation and the Holocaust* (London: Hurst, 2010), p. 35.

[80] "Republikanischer Club: Acht Arbeitskreise Konstituiert," *Berliner Extra-Dienst*, July 27, 1968, p. 3.

In the battles about the direction of the antiauthoritarian movement that began to heat up from 1968 onward, any hope of a monolithic revolutionary past upon which it was possible to unproblematically draw went by the wayside; activists of the radical underground increasingly had recourse to the history and theory of anarchism, while the Marxist-Leninist *K-Gruppen* founded in the wake of the attack on Dutschke returned evermore single-mindedly to the words and deeds of the great men of the socialist-revolutionary tradition. The historical consciousness of the *K-Gruppen* extended to their own self-periodization, a strict line being drawn between the "new" phase of building a base in the proletariat and the antiauthoritarian moment through which they had just lived.

For the French-German activist Daniel Cohn-Bendit, a leading figure in the events of May 1968 in France and subsequently a leader of the Sponti scene in Frankfurt, the French May was an object lesson for anyone concerned with the historical and contemporary problems of left organization. From the antidogmatic perspective, the French Communist Party had played a pernicious role in the French May, attempting at every juncture to smear student protesters as bourgeois dilettantes and to steer workers organized in Communist-affiliated trade unions away from the course of open confrontation with the state.[81] The actual rebellion in the universities adhered more closely to the spirit of the Situationists, whose (implicitly anarchist) writings influenced the so-called "Enragés" of the Nanterre campus who helped kick off the revolt. The wildcat strikes by workers at Renault, Sud-Aviation, and other concerns took place in spite of, not because of, the leadership of the Communist and Socialist parties.

Cohn-Bendit addressed this situation in a work of historical-political polemic written with his brother Gabriel: *Obsolete Communism: The Left-Wing Alternative*. The title of the work referred to Vladimir Ilyich Lenin's *Left-Wing Communism: An Infantile Disorder*, an attack on the Bolsheviks' left-wing critics published in 1920. In *Obsolete Communism*, the Cohn-Bendit brothers argued that the vanguard-party model of Bolshevism had been flawed from the start, the "deformation" of Communism in the Soviet Union beginning not with Stalin but with the party's founders. In the French May, the Cohn-Bendits argued, the Communist Party and trade unions had lagged consistently behind the masses, just as they had done in

---

[81] See confirmation of this claim in Richard Wolin's recent book on French Maoism; Richard Wolin, *The Wind from the East: French Intellectuals, the Cultural Revolution, and the Legacy of the 1960s* (Princeton University Press, 2010).

Russia half a decade earlier.[82] In the German context, the implication was that far from being a model that should be revived, as the *K-Gruppen* were attempting to do, Leninist vanguardism needed to be rejected in favor of the spontaneous unfolding of the revolutionary energy of students and workers. Via Cohn-Bendit, the lessons of the French May, and the historical debates with which it was connected, informed the activism of the Sponti scene in Frankfurt and elsewhere in the Federal Republic.

Reevaluation of the Russian Revolution and assessment of its implications for contemporary activism were important staples of debates in which the undogmatic left tried to distance itself from the theory and practice of the *K-Gruppen*. Of particular importance in the historical-theoretical contest with the dogmatic left was the Kronstadt Uprising of 1921, in which revolutionary sailors in the Baltic Sea fortress had rebelled against the brutal and oppressive strictures of Bolshevik "War Communism."[83] The demands of the rebels, which centered on a restoration of the non-party status previously enjoyed by the Soviets ("councils"), a status that had allowed them to serve as sensitive instruments of the popular will, resonated strongly in the context of the attempt to lift the dead hand of Leninism off the shoulder of the antiauthoritarian revolt. In *Agit 883*, along with *Radikal* and *InfoBUG*, among the most important of the journals serving the Sponti scene, coverage of the Kronstadt Uprising correlated with a shift in the makeup of the editorial staff in the direction of the Sponti scene and away from uncritical acceptance of the assumptions of Marxism-Leninism. A "Kronstadt Congress," organized in May 1971 at the Technical University in West Berlin, publicized the revolt further, as did the publication of a fifty-year-anniversary documentary collection on Kronstadt in the "historische Reihe" series of the Anarchist Union Wilhelmshaven.[84] This volume, *The Rebellion of the Kronstadt Sailors: Completion and Liquidation of the Russian Revolution*, contained a foreword by imprisoned militant Fritz Teufel, writing from Stadelheim prison, thus linking the revolutionary struggles of the past with those of the present.

By the beginning of the 1970s, engagement with the European revolutionary past dominated the output of left-wing publishers, even as

---

[82] Daniel Cohn-Bendit and Gabriel Cohn-Bendit, *Obsolete Communism: The Left-Wing Alternative* (London: AK Press, 2000).

[83] During his stop in Leningrad in April 1965, Dutschke wondered in his diary: "Where does Kronstadt actually lie, seen from here, and what is happening there?" Dutschke, *Diaries*, entry for April 20, 1965.

[84] "Materialheft zum Kronstadt Kongreß, Berlin 11 Mai 71 (TU)," Archiv Peter Hein, Berlin.

contemporary struggles in the Third World continued to figure prominently. Presses such as the Karin Kramer Verlag and Verlag Roter Stern published works on or by figures such as the anarchist Gustav Landauer in the German Revolution of 1918–1919 or the German Marxist Clara Zetkin alongside treatments of the Communist youth organizations of the Weimar Republic or the trade-union struggles of twentieth-century England.[85] In its "Learn: Subversive" series, Verlag Roter Stern published ring-bound volumes of material on "Amerikkka" and on the Weimar Republic, offering alternative left-wing histories of key periods of labor militancy and social unrest. The publication of such texts, alongside works on contemporary feminism, child care, social pedagogy, and so on, helped create a knowledge sphere mirroring the concerns of an increasingly fractured left in which the search for models, drawn from the local past or the global present, continued with even more urgency than during the mid to late 1960s high period.

As much as it could be a source of revolutionary lessons and source material, the past could not itself be the source of forward progress. The ransacking of the past for clues to the present – the search for revolutionary source material, analogies, counter-histories – coexisted and ran in parallel with a turning away from the *German* past toward a future constructed out of non-German materials. For the antiauthoritarian faction in the SDS, the sought-after revolution was to be created in dialogue not just with the European revolutionary past but also with the contemporary anticolonial present. At the countercultural end of the left spectrum, by contrast, the future lay less in the national liberation struggles of the Third World and more in the vistas of countercultural artistic possibility represented by London, New York, and San Francisco, sites that promised an escape from the dead end of a German history marked by authoritarianism, war, and genocide. The future lay in the escape from everything "*bieder*" (a term used by activists in reference to the Biedermeier style and sensibility associated with the post-1815 period of reaction in Europe) toward the cosmopolitan modernity of Western capitals marked by experimentation in the arts and in lifestyles.[86]

At the same time, the SDS and the nascent counterculture represented initially by the Kommune I marked two different approaches to the future. Whereas the activity of the former was predicated on a

---

[85] Karin Kramer Verlag, *Bücher-Info*, no. 6, June–July 1973; *Verlag Roter Stern Almanach '72*. MO613, box 55, Stanford APO.

[86] See, for example, the usage in Inga Buhmann, "Frankfurt, der SDS und vieles, was weh tut," in Carsten Seibold, ed., *Die 68er: Das Fest der Rebellion* (Munich: Droemer Knaur, 1988), p. 312.

Figure 2.5 The Kronstadt Uprising in *Agit 883*. Hamburg Institute for Social Research.

revolution that would happen in the future, the latter was based on the idea of making the revolution now. The Hash Rebel Michael "Bommi" Baumann noted this in his memoir, observing that his attraction to the Kommune I lay precisely in the fact that, in contrast to the SDS, with its highly theoretical talk of a revolution to come, the commune offered a chance to live the revolution every day. Similarly, Kommune I member Dagmar von Doetinchem remembers that the most important outcome for her of her time in the commune was the break with the past.[87] In this context, the change in personal appearance that accompanied the rise of the counterculture – long hair on men, shabby and often second-hand mix-and-match clothing, with a prominence of denim, corduroy, and leather – signaled the embrace of personal fulfillment in the present moment as opposed to self-abnegation in pursuit of a theoretical millennium. It is no accident that the Maoist *K-Gruppen* rejected youth fashion, pressuring its members to dress like "regular workers"; here fashion was sublimated to the needs of the historical dialectic according to which the working class, and the working class alone, would be the motor of historical change. The goal of restoring the broken continuity of the Marxian socialist narrative required not "do your own thing" fulfillment in the present but discipline in the present in service of victory in the future.

Yet the countercultural violation of bourgeois dress codes signaled a break with a second teleological narrative: that of technocratic capitalist rationality. In this respect, *Gammler*-dom was not merely a spatial intervention but a temporal one. The shaggy beards, loose blouses, and sandals affected by communards such as Dieter Kunzelmann and Fritz Teufel possessed a distinctly premodern aspect, an impression reinforced by stunts such as the one in which Teufel, dressed in a white penitent's gown, had himself paraded chained into a rolling cart before a Berlin courthouse. Later, with the development of a more fully fledged West German counterculture, complete with American-style "back to the land" movement, this rural premodern ploy would take on even greater weight as both marker of difference and temporal intervention.

CONCLUSION

The historiographical practice of the antiauthoritarian revolt mirrored the split at its heart. Prior to the assassination attempt against Rudi Dutschke

---

[87] Quoted in Becker, *Unbekannte Wesen*, p. 174.

and the culmination of the anti-Emergency Law and anti-Springer campaigns, these differences could remain concealed; thereafter, they came increasingly into the open. It was a characteristic feature of the anti-authoritarian revolt that, because it was cobbled together from disparate sources for sometimes disparate aims, there could be no unanimity of direction. The feeling of revolutionary upsurge that accompanied the movement as it approached its apogee helped conceal the fact that no one in the movement, neither leaders nor rank and file, understood where they were going next. The basic teleology at the heart of the Marxist conception of history, according to which, at some point, socialism would arise out of capitalism, had to serve where more precise predictions could only be lacking. The notion that "the revolution" was out there waiting to be reborn, implicit not only in Marxist but also in anarchist conceptions, lent structure to activism composed of ad hoc initiatives and responses to constantly evolving situations.

The SDS and the APO were part of a *new* left; that is, part of a constellation of forces organized around opposition to the Cold War, against the Stalinist/capitalist anti-Communist binary with its threat of nuclear destruction, and in favor of democratization, free expression, and liberalization of social mores. In West Germany, the latter concerns in particular resonated with the need to overcome traditions of authoritarianism associated with Germany's late and troubled path to democracy. Yet, rather than something wholly new, the antiauthoritarian revolt was an unstable mixture of new and old elements. This was true of the New Left everywhere to an extent but especially so in Germany, where the fractured nature of the country, both in terms of its division and in terms of its historical narrative, left key issues unresolved. The weight of this fracturing would be fully exposed after the high-water mark of the APO, when significant numbers of SDS members would be sucked into the orbit of the DDR via the newly founded DKP, with others joining the Communist *K-Gruppen* seeking to take up the mantle of the interwar Communist Party.

Simultaneously, the "hedonistic" left, that portion of the radical milieu whose members privileged personal fulfillment at the expense of (or, ideally, as an adjunct to) a future revolution, would come increasingly into conflict with those radicals who, in ransacking the past for revolutionary models and lighting afresh upon the Marxist-Leninist "vanguard party," sought to impose a new dogmatism in the service of the future. Their differing conceptions, as we will see, provided much of the substance for a long-running debate about what the "revolution" actually entailed. Was a revolution of lifestyle itself revolutionary? Or did the radicalization of personal subjectivity amount to nothing more than a personal rebellion of no consequence for the unfolding of the revolution predicted by Marx? These and other questions would inform the debates not only within the political movement itself but also in the intersection between politics and the spheres of cultural production.

CHAPTER 3

Word

In September 1968, the twentieth annual *Frankfurter Buchmesse* (Frankfurt Book Fair) took place. Featuring over 3,000 publishers from some fifty-seven countries, the *Buchmesse* was a symbol both of the vibrancy of German publishing and of the growing internationalization of West Germany.[1] It was a symbol also of the extent to which the ideas of the New Left and the student movement had begun to penetrate the world of mainstream publishing. Prominent among the exhibitors were publishers such as Rowohlt, Suhrkamp, and Kiepenheuer & Witsch, all of whom offered well-developed lines of revolutionary history and theory that were becoming increasingly central to the left-liberal reading milieu. Not far away, in the basement of a Frankfurt student house in the Jügelstrasse, activist-publishers of the alternative press staged an Anti-Book Fair (*Gegenbuchmesse*). Presenting systematically for one of the first times the vibrant energy and eclecticism of the underground press, with some seventy foreign and domestic publishers and newspapers in attendance, the event was explicitly conceived as a response to the success of the mainstream publishers in cornering the revolutionary market: "Don't let yourselves be sold by the Rowohlts, comrades. Organize yourselves!"[2]

While the publicistic forces of a new underground alternative milieu marshaled themselves in the basement of the student center, a riot raged overhead in and around the exhibition halls. The catalyst was the decision of the German Publishers and Booksellers Association to bestow the annual Peace Prize of the German Book Trade on the Senegalese Head

---

[1] Hellmuth Karasek, Petra Kipphoff, Rudolf Walter Leonhardt, and Dieter K. Zimmer, "Getrennt von Buch und Bors," *Die Zeit*, no. 39, September 27, 1968. Some 3,048 exhibitors took part in the book fair: 845 from the Federal Republic, forty-five from East Germany, and 2,158 from foreign countries; Peter Weidhaas, *Zur Geschichte der Frankfurter Buchmesse* (Frankfurt: Suhrkamp, 2003), p. 233.

[2] Thomas Daum, *Die 2 Kultur: Alternativliteratur in der Bundesrepublik* (Mainz: NewLit Verlag, 1981), p. 62.

Figure 3.1 Rainer Langhans of the Kommune I at the printing press.
Photo courtesy of Archiv Rainer Langhans.

of State Léopold Senghor. A poet and intellectual known for elaborating the concept of *Négritude*, a theoretical vehicle for the protection of African cultural identity in the face of colonialism, Senghor served as leader of Senegal beginning with independence in 1960. In contrast to many postcolonial African leaders who sought to steer clear of cooperation with their former colonial masters, Senghor was a strong advocate of continued relations with France under a commonwealth. A member of the French National Assembly from 1946 to 1958, he saw no contradiction between the requirements of independent African identity and the concept of France as a "motherland." This assimilationist orientation placed Senghor at odds with student radicals, who, if they needed to bolster their instinctive dislike of an African statesman who remained on friendly terms with former colonial masters, could point to, among other facts, that 80 percent of Senegalese industry remained in the hands of French companies.[3]

A more immediate issue, however, was that less than five months before, in the direct aftermath of the May events in Paris, Senghor had unleashed his troops on striking students and workers at the University of Dakar. One student was killed, hundreds arrested, and the university (which Senghor had helped to found) closed.[4] The fact that the Senegalese students had been inspired to strike by the May events in Paris was lost on no one involved in the protest, least of all Daniel Cohn-Bendit, who had fled France in the wake of the May events and who was now, as a member of the Frankfurt SDS, helping to organize the *Buchmesse* protest. The French May events, in a way wholly characteristic of 1968, had found their way quickly to Dakar, and now Dakar had found its way to Frankfurt. In this context, it was easy to see Senghor not just as a neocolonial figurehead but as the African face of Gaullist reaction.[5]

Although the previous year's *Buchmesse* had seen student protests against both the Axel Springer Verlag and the recently established military dictatorship in Greece (as well as the long-standing dictatorship in

[3] See the discussion in Niels Seibert, *Vergessene Proteste: Internationalismus und Antirassismus, 1964–1983* (Münster: Unrast Verlag, 2008).

[4] See Amadou Lamine Sarr, "Mai 68 im Senegal: Fortsetzung des Unabhängigkeitsprozesses in Afrika?" in Jena Kastner and David Mayer, eds., *Weltwende 1968? Ein Jahr aus globalgeschichtlicher Perspektive* (Vienna: Mandelbaum, 2008), pp. 130–142.

[5] Sozialistischer Deutscher Studentenbund, "Wer ist Senghor?" in Schulenburg, ed., *Das Leben ändern, die Welt verändern!* pp. 313–315; see also Wolfgang Kraushaar, ed., *Frankfurter Schule und Studentenbewegung: Von der Flaschenpost zum Molotowcocktail, 1946–1995*, vol. 1: *Chronik* (Hamburg: Rogner & Bernhard, 1998), p. 468.

Spain and the Apartheid state in South Africa – targets that, in the consanguinating imagination of student radicals, were seen as inextricably linked together), the 1968 protests were of a different order of magnitude altogether.[6] Two main actions were planned. The first, on September 21, was a Teach-In in Exhibition Hall 6 in front of the stand of Senghor's publisher, the Diederichs Verlag. The second, scheduled for the following day, was the occupation of the Paulskirche with the aim of physically preventing the awarding of the prize to Senghor. "We will block the way into the Paulskirche of the philosophizing character mask of French imperialism," read an SDS announcement, "who with Goethe in his head and a machine gun in his hand, oppresses the exploited masses of his people."[7]

The teach-in on the 21st resulted in an initial victory for the SDS. The convention organizers attempted to prevent the teach-in by closing the hall to protesters and visitors alike, prompting a number of the exhibitors to close their stalls and to walk out in protest. The organizers had no choice but to relent, allowing the teach-in to go ahead. The featured speakers from the Frankfurt SDS were Hans-Jürgen Krahl, Günter Amendt, and Daniel Cohn-Bendit. A lone voice of dissent in the proceedings was provided by Senghor's translator, the Senegalese consul Jan-Heinz Jahn. Jahn's protestations were drowned out by others' condemnation of Senghor's dictatorial actions and of his concept of *Négritude*, which, it was argued, was mere ideological cover for the continuation of colonial domination. Not content to protest the decision to award the peace prize to Senghor, the organizers of the teach-in considered an alternative list of prize recipients composed of Third World and African-American revolutionaries. Out of a list including Patrice Lumumba, Frantz Fanon, Malcolm X, and Stokely Carmichael, the assembly settled on the Guinean anticolonial theorist and guerrilla fighter Amílcar Cabral.

The next morning saw some 2,000 demonstrators face off against 800 police in front of the Paulskirche. Attempts to stop the motorcade conveying dignitaries to the event were thwarted by the police. Three hundred students, arms linked, attempted to storm through police lines but were repelled. Forty-two demonstrators, including Daniel Cohn-Bendit and K. D. Wolff, were arrested. Protesters attempted to overturn the broadcasting vans of the Hessische Rundfunk, which, in the event, proved too

[6] Weidhaas, *Zur Geschichte der Frankfurter Buchmesse*, pp. 230–231.
[7] Quoted in Seibert, *Vergessene Proteste*, p. 61.

heavy. Students bombarded both attacking police and the windows and doors of the Paulskirche with bottles and paving stones. Among the victims of police truncheons were student leaders Hans-Jürgen Krahl and Joschka Fischer.[8] A running battle ensued, with police employing tear gas and water cannons. Students built barricades out of fence posts and rubbish bins before melting away to attack, in turn, the headquarters of the German Publishers and Booksellers Association and the Frankfurter Hof hotel where Senghor and guests were staying. In protest against the arrest of Cohn-Bendit, demonstrators returned to the exhibition hall. Once again it was shut down, the doors barricaded by the police. Frustration with the situation spilled over from the protesters to the exhibitors and visitors. Amid shouts of "Büchermesse: Zuchthausmesse" ("Book Fair: Jail Fair"), over three dozen German and foreign exhibitors shut down their stands, releasing a joint statement demanding free passage through the exhibition hall. By the time the organizers finally relented, the exhibition hall had been shut for the better part of eight hours.[9]

The salience of the figure of Senghor in these events makes it easy to see the *Frankfurter Buchmesse* protest of 1968, along with the visit of Moïse Tshombe in December 1964 and of the Shah of Iran in June 1967, as one in a series of critical moments in which the concrete intrusion of the Third World into the First opened up the occasion to protest neo-colonialism while striking a blow against authoritarianism at home. As in the earlier protests, the transnational – in the form of foreign leaders and foreign students – played a key role; in this case, the Senegalese student union distributed information about Senghor's crackdown at Dakar University, and an African student agitated in favor of a demonstration at the Frankfurt SDS congress in the second week of September. The SDS operated in solidarity, fusing the concerns of their African fellow students with their own, drawing connections between oppression abroad and oppression at home. In this sense, the anti-Senghor protest at the 1968 *Frankfurter Buchmesse* represents the 68er protest par excellence.

Yet the anti-Senghor protest was, in fact, the least important of the left-wing initiatives launched in connection with the Frankfurt Book Fair of 1968. While the battle over physical space raged between students and the police, a much more important battle was being waged over the means and conditions of cultural production. The theoretical and practical concerns

---

[8] Kraushaar, *Frankfurter Schule und Studentenbewegung*, p. 359.
[9] Many of the closed stands bore the legend "Closed due to fascist methods"; Kraushaar, *Frankfurter Schule und Studentenbewegung*, p. 360.

of the insurgents, saliently expressed in the staging of the Anti-Book Fair but also introduced into the *Buchmesse* proper through a number of channels, represented an intervention of far greater long-term significance, one in which were mirrored central themes of the antiauthoritarian revolt in West Germany. The critique of the decision to award the peace prize to Senghor was, to begin with, less a critique of Senghor per se than a challenge to the implicit authoritarianism of the Book Fair as an institution. This challenge intersected with the *Ur* antinomy at the heart of the 68er movement's battle with the establishment: the dichotomy between a fierce anti-Communism that effectively criminalized any contact with, or benign assessment of, the East German *other*, and a disturbing toleration for the persistence of radical right-wing views and personnel. To be sure, the *Buchmesse* was a site of inter-German contact; there were, for example, some thirty-eight DDR booths at the 1967 fair.[10] Yet the confiscation that year of the so-called "Brown Book," published by the DDR to expose former Nazis in high places in West Germany, accompanied by the shutting down of the stands of East German publishers, exposed the limitations of this contact.[11]

More fundamentally, the politicization of the *Buchmesse* challenged the right of cultural authorities to monopolize the terrain of meaning in society, questioning their authority to determine what was true and what was false. This authority, it was argued, was often little more than a thinly veiled attempt to buttress the claims of power. Protests within the *Buchmesse* – against the Springer Press monopoly and in favor of greater participatory decision-making power for authors and editors – were aimed at democratization of the public sphere; but they also posited the notion of an "alternative public sphere" (*Gegenöffentlichkeit*), which was to be the repository of alternative claims to knowledge and truth. The notion of a *Gegenöffentlichkeit* was inextricably connected to the student movement's revolutionary claims, for it struck at the heart of the narrative power supporting existing social relations. Yet it also helped create a *Gegenmilieu* connecting the student movement with the counterculture and the arts (and concerned particularly, in the case of the *Buchmesse*, with debates about the meaning and status of literature). The Frankfurter *Buchmesse* of 1968 thus held a fourfold significance: it was (1) a site of articulation between the political movement and the counterculture; (2) a site where

---

[10] "Was möglich ist," *Der Spiegel*, no. 44, October 23, 1967.

[11] Seibert, *Vergessene Proteste*; *Brown Book: War and Nazi Criminals in West Germany* (Dresden: Verlag Zeit im Bild, 1965). The Federal Republic responded with its own exposé: Olaf Kappelt, *Braunbuch DDR: Nazis in der DDR* (Berlin: E. Reichmann, 1981).

rights of free movement were seen to be inextricably linked with rights of free expression; (3) a site for the channeling of transnational connections and influences; and (4) a site where the claims of student radicals and avant-garde artists spilled over into other parts of society.

The term *Gegenöffentlichkeit* came into use sometime in 1966–1967, in the course of the escalation of the conflict in West Berlin between the SDS and the Springer Press. Connected with the perceived need to combat the distorted picture of the student movement presented in the Springer papers – and all with which it was seen to be connected – the concept of *Gegenöffentlichkeit* relied heavily on the critique of mass-media manipulation put forward by Frankfurt School thinkers such as Adorno, Horkheimer, and Marcuse. The latter, in his emphasis on the role played by control of public opinion in systems of rule, was particularly influential in this regard. The critique of Springer also stretched across into the literary sphere, Hans Magnus Enzensberger having taken up this theme some years before in his essay collection *Einzelheiten* (1962). Borrowing from Adorno and Horkheimer's idea of a "culture industry," Enzensberger developed the concept of a *"consciousness* industry," a term suggestive of a more thoroughgoing conditioning of consciousness via, especially, the press and mass media. The problem of press concentration appeared regularly in Enzensberger's journal *Kursbuch* from its founding in 1965.

The concept of *Gegenöffentlichkeit* was codified in the anti-Springer campaign launched at the annual SDS convention in Frankfurt in September 1967. "Enlightened *Gegenöffentlichkeit*," argued Rudi Dutschke, Jürgen Krahl, and others in the campaign's founding resolution, was the only antidote to the "dictatorship of the manipulators."[12] Echoing Marcuse, the authors argued that monopolistic mass media created "[p]ublicistic forms of psychological pressure" that reduced its objects to the status of slaves. "[Turning] the fundamental right of freedom of information and opinion into the exclusive preserve of private publishers," the Springer Press created a "feudalized" public sphere. According to this analysis, the role of mass media was not merely one among other aspects of capitalist domination; in its means as well as in its effects, it was absolutely central. The anti-Springer campaign was thus nothing less than an assault on the very foundations of capitalism: "Our struggle against Springer is … a struggle against the late-capitalist system of rule itself."[13]

[12] Elmar Altvater, Bernhard Blanke, Rudi Dutschke, Hans-Jürgen Krahl, and Helmut Schauer, "Die demokratische Öffentlichkeit ist zerstört," in Bernd Kramer, ed., *Gefundene Fragmente, 1967–1980* (Berlin: Karin Kramer Verlag, 2004), vol. I, pp. 63–66.
[13] Altvater et al., "Die demokratische Öffentlichkeit ist zerstört."

Criticism of the Springer Press was by no means limited to the student movement. The sheer extent of Axel Springer's empire, combined with the widespread perception that he allowed his personal hatred of Communism to become a substitute for objective journalism, was widely condemned. The extent of the Springer monopoly is ably summed up by Nick Thomas:

[I]n 1964 the [Springer] group controlled 31 per cent of the daily newspaper market, along with 89 per cent of regional and 85 percent of Sunday newspaper sales. In Berlin 67 per cent of daily newspapers, and in Hamburg 69 per cent, came from the Springer stable. In 1968 the tabloid *Bild-Zeitung* had a circulation of 4,094,884 copies per day, with a further 2,319,192 copies of *Bild am Sonntag*, making it by far the largest newspaper in Germany. *Die Welt*, Springer's largest broadsheet title, with sales of 225,886 newspapers every day, was approximately equivalent in size to its main non-Springer rivals such as *Die Zeit*, *Frankfurter Allgemeine Zeitung*, and *Süddeutsche Zeitung*. In Berlin, *BZ* and the *Berliner Morgenpost* sold more than a half a million copies between them every day.[14]

That the concentration of so much power in the hands of one man posed a problem in a democracy dedicated to a plurality of opinion was a matter of wide consensus, shared by trade unions, liberal news journals such as *Stern* and *Spiegel*, and many writers, intellectuals, and pastors.

THE NEW CRITICAL JOURNALISM

The extraparliamentary opposition was marked by an intensive engagement with, and instrumentalization of, the printed word. This held true not only for the student movement, for which the printed handbill and the slogan-bearing placard were primary means of communication, but for publicists active in a wider communicative field ranging from journalism to the underground press to the worlds of literature and publishing. This vast outpouring of speech was rooted in a set of diverse but complementary motivations: the attempt to bring to light previously hidden information and to open up new areas of inquiry (particularly where they impacted on the state's claims of confidentiality, or on the individual's right to live outside conventional social parameters); the attempt to establish the right to intervene in the creation of social meaning through the disputation of official narratives and the creation of counter-narratives; and the attempt to establish direct access to important texts, both those from abroad in need of importation or translation, and, in particular,

---

[14] Thomas, *Protest Movements*, p. 165.

those lost as a result of Nazism's attempted erasure of humanist and revolutionary traditions. This project was by no means limited to a putative group of young student 68ers but spanned generations and cut across the artificial lines often drawn between the student movement, the counterculture, and the establishment.[15]

The journalistic forebearers and fellow travelers of the student movement represented, in particular, part of an attempt to question the state's monopoly on information, especially in connection with plans for West German rearmament. The potential for conflict between the state's need to keep secrets and the rights of an informed citizenry to be aware of them came explosively to light in October 1962, when the West German news magazine *Der Spiegel* published an article detailing plans for an increase in the strength of the West German army. In response, the government carried out illegal searches of the offices of *Der Spiegel*, as well as the homes of four senior staff members. Spiegel publisher Rudolf Augstein was detained and held until the following February. The resulting public scandal led to the resignation of several government officials, including Defense Minister Josef Strauß, and precipitated the dissolution of Adenauer's coalition government in November 1962.

This so-called Spiegel Affair was only one in a series of clashes between the government and the print media that signaled a new journalistic vitality in the Federal Republic. The Spiegel Affair, argues Christina von Hodenberg,

was neither a singular incident nor the "big bang" that brought about a democratized public sphere. Rather, as the climax of a long series of conflicts, it mirrored tensions that had built up since the late fifties in the form of the strained relations between government and mass media, the increasing polarization of the media spectrum and the growing influence of younger journalists who had discovered critical political reporting to be a formula for success.[16]

The emergence of these young journalists – "45ers" born around the end of World War II–signaled the shift in West Germany from a "consensus journalism" to a "new critical journalism."[17] The former had been rooted

---

[15] On this theme, see Mia Lee, "Art and Revolution in West Germany: The Cultural Roots of 1968," Ph.D. dissertation, University of Michigan, 2007.

[16] Christina von Hodenberg, "Mass Media and the Generation of Conflict: West Germany's Long Sixties and the Formation of a Critical Public Sphere," *Contemporary European History*, 15 (2006): 367–395, at p. 378.

[17] Von Hodenberg, "Mass Media and the Generation of Conflict." On the effects and meaning of the Spiegel Affair, see Nicholls, *The Bonn Republic*, p. 177; Daniela Münkel, "Die Medienpolitik von Konrad Adenauer und Willy Brandt," *Archiv für Sozialgeschichte*, 41 (2001): 297–316, at p. 310.

in the attempt to solidify a still-nascent West German statehood, linked on the one hand to a desire to avoid the contentiousness of the Weimar past and, on the other, the unease over the threat posed to German *Kultur* by America generally and by American journalism in particular. In practice, this focus represented a default capitulation to the requirements of the state in the spheres of rearmament and Western integration. The latter, by contrast, enthusiastically embraced Anglo-American journalistic practices and models, and was less interested in policing Cold War boundaries than in exposing the claims of authority to harsh scrutiny.[18]

The spirit and personnel of the new critical journalism was carried forward in particular by muckraking left-wing magazines such as *konkret* and *Pardon*. The former, founded by Klaus Rainer Röhl in 1955 at the University of Hamburg under the name *Studenten-Kurier* and established officially as *konkret* two years later, was established with the explicit purpose of politicizing the pacifist movement, of which the campaign against West German nuclear armament was a major constituent. *konkret* served as a journalistic bridge between the pacifist movement of the 1950s and the extraparliamentary opposition of the 1960s, combining articles on new social trends (e.g. the advent of the pill) with hard-hitting photojournalism, including some of the earliest (very graphic) photographic reportage on the American war in Vietnam. The discomfiture of the West German establishment effected by *konkret* was a boon to the East German regime, which secretly funded the journal from 1955 to 1964.[19] After the SED's withdrawal of support (for the journal's failure to fire an author supportive of the opposition in Communist Czechoslovakia), Röhl spruced up the magazine's sales through a pornographic turn, which fit in well enough with the rather undifferentiated notion of the sexual revolution then current (see Chapter 7) as to seem, if not necessarily progressive, then at least somehow hip.[20]

konkret was notable for launching the career of Ulrike Meinhof, a major journalistic voice of the extraparliamentary opposition before achieving infamy at the beginning of the 1970s for other reasons.[21] Meinhof joined the SDS in the late 1950s as a student at the University of Münster, becoming deeply involved in the movement against the West German

[18] Von Hodenberg, "Mass Media and the Generation of Conflict," p. 379.
[19] Siegfried, *Time Is on My Side*, pp. 294–297.
[20] The relationship between *konkret* and the DDR was not made public by Röhl until 1974. On the role of the DDR in the publication of *konkret* see Knabe, *Der diskrete Charme der DDR*, pp. 321–326.
[21] See Chapter 8.

government's attempt to obtain nuclear weapons. "To what end will come a state," she asked in an early article, "in which the measure of the integrity of a party member is not a democratic ethos, not the relationship to the German past, but rather the willingness to agree to ... nuclear armament and the acquisition of means of mass annihilation?"[22] Part of a group of new, young politically oriented editors, Meinhof became the periodical's foreign editor in 1959, served as editor-in-chief of the entire production from 1961 to 1965, and continued to write for the magazine for several years afterward. Meinhof's essays condemning state criminality in its various forms, particularly West German support for the American war in Vietnam, became an important part of the extraparliamentary opposition.[23]

Pardon, founded in Frankfurt in 1962 by Erich Bärmeier and Hans A. Nikel, presented a cocktail of prurience and critical intelligence similar to that offered by *konkret*. Bärmeier was a registered Social Democrat, Nikel a radical pacifist who was active in leftist scenes in Cologne and Frankfurt throughout the 1950s and 1960s. Nikel was also, with Hans Hermann, a co-founder of *Twen*, a magazine that, although nominally aimed at a teenage readership, contained much of the same sort of content as *Pardon*. Indeed, many of the same writers – Otto Koehler (also an editor at *Pardon*), Erich Kuby, Robert Neumann, Günter Wallraff, and Gerhard Zwerenz – contributed regularly to *Twen* and to *konkret* as well as to *Pardon*.[24] Acting as a watchdog against resurgent militarism, with the object lessons of the recent Nazi past applied to a host of contemporary situations, the satirical monthly exposed the machinations of the military-industrial establishment and mocked patriotic and religious pieties, all the while presenting the 1960s youth revolution in a favorable if irreverent light.[25]

In its focus on alternative truths, and in its combativeness, the "new critical journalism" paved the way for the journalistic practices of the extraparliamentary opposition. Magazines such as *Spiegel, Stern, Pardon, konkret*, and *Twen* contributed to the creation of a sphere in which a set of overlapping actors and concerns – writers and journalists of the 45er

---

[22] Quoted in Mario Krebs, *Ulrike Meinhof: Ein Leben im Widerspruch* (Reinbek: Rowohlt, 1988), p. 52.
[23] See the essays collected in Ulrike Meinhof, *Die Würde des Menschen ist antastbar: Aufsätze und Polemiken* (Berlin: Wagenbach, 1994).
[24] See Siegfried, *Time Is on My Side*, pp. 294–297.
[25] For an interesting contemporary discussion of *konkret* and *Pardon*, see H. J. Gieseler, *APO Rebellion Mai 68* (Munich: G. Rosenberger, 1968), pp. 141–149.

generation, youth revolution and popular culture, sexual provocation and political critiques of postcolonial warfare – mediated the concerns of radical political actors out to a broader audience. Simultaneously, they helped to legitimize the arguments of the SDS by establishing a critical sphere in which the claims of authority were open to question. Efforts to expose official lies and to reveal state secrets, from the Spiegel Affair to the pages of *konkret* and *Twen*, were simultaneously attempts to breach the permissible, to push back the boundary of what one was allowed to say, and to challenge Cold War boundaries. The left-leaning journals, in particular, perfected an arch, irony-laced style that resonated in the rhetorical approach of the student movement and was taken up with abandon and elaborated upon in the underground press starting around 1968.

BOOTLEG PUBLISHING AND THE UNDERGROUND PRESS

The new critical journalism, the printed output of the student movement, and the underground press, despite their obvious differences in political orientation, journalistic standards, and style, were connected by a strong internal continuity; all three challenged the claims of cultural authorities to absolute truth; each asserted the act of speech as a fundamental right; and each took as its aim the exposure of secrets and the telling of hidden truths. The assertion of the right to speech became, in the left-radical milieu, intimately bound up with the possession of the cultural means of production – that is, with the possession of the printing press. Here, the Rotaprint printing machine became the indispensable technological tool of the antiauthoritarian rebellion in West Germany. The Rotaprint machine not only allowed young radicals to create flyers and alternative newspapers but also to print *Raubdrucke* (bootleg publications) that made available long-lost texts of revolutionary theory and history, thus dramatically expanding the parameters of political discussion.

"The whole history of the Communist and working-class movement was reinvented [by the bootleg publishers]" remembers former SDS Chairman Karl Dietrich Wolff, founder of the Roter Stern publishing house,

so all kinds of texts from the working-class movement from the Marxist movements were found, reprinted, edited. It was a kind of reception from the early sixties to the middle of the seventies that was really wide and in a certain way historically unprecedented because the whole history came back to Germany. Of course, some people reprinted Stalin and Trotsky and stuff like that but mostly much more interesting stuff on the verges, on the fringe of the movement. For instance, the Dutch Council Communists were reprinted. Texts from the early twenties that had not been read for fifty years.[26]

Bootleg publishers produced an astonishing array of titles, including works by Karl Marx, Leon Trotsky, Max Horkheimer, Theodor Adorno, Erich Fromm, Herbert Marcuse, Jürgen Habermas, Otto Rühle, Rosa Luxemburg, Georg Lukács, G. Dimitroff, Karl Korsch, Isaac Deutscher, Michael Bakunin, Henryk Grossman, Joseph Stalin, Siegfried Krakauer, Mao Zedong, and Hans Magnus Enzensberger.[27] Providing access to lost knowledge and perspectives, bootleg publishing became a key element in the cultural-political recovery project of resuscitating the lost history of German leftism and a means of creating a new oppositional culture from below.

The Kommune I was one of the pioneers of bootleg publishing in West Germany. Running off hundreds of copies on cheap colored paper, the communards of the Kommune I produced and sold copies of lost classics of Marxism and psychoanalysis – Reich's *The Function of the Orgasm* was an important title – alongside their own writings. Antje Krüger of the Kommune I recalls:

We had also a room with a print machine ... and did all kinds of work; I ... mailed out our publications and reprints to the bookstores, and I also went to the bookstores in person and sold them, and sold them at the university ... [I] also did the mailing to West Germany, to bookstores in Frankfurt and in München and ... Bamberg ... and elsewhere. I was always carrying on correspondence with people.[28]

These sales provided a not-insubstantial source of income for the commune.

Alongside bootleg publishing, the underground press became a key site of the cultural-political revolution in West Germany. Combining new and vibrant forms of visual and rhetorical expression with hard-hitting political

---

[26] K. D. Wolff, interview with the author, Frankfurt, February 21, 2010.

[27] The leading authority on the bootleg publishing movement is Götz von Olenhusen; see Albrecht Götz von Olenhusen and Christa Gnirss, *Handbuch der Raubdrucke: Verlag Dokumentation Pullach bei* (Freiburg im Breisgau: Raubdruck-Archiv, 2002); Albrecht Götz von Olenhusen, "Entwicklung und Stand der Raubdruckbewegung," in Heinz Ludwig Arnold, ed., *Literaturbetrieb in der Bundesrepublik Deutschland: ein kritisches Handbuch* (Munich: Edition Text u. Kritik, 1981), pp. 164–172; Götz von Olenhusen, Schwarze Kunst, and Rote Bücher, "Zur Produktion von Raubdrucken in der Bundesrepublik," in Hans Widmann, ed., *Gutenberg Jahrbuch 1972* (Mainz: Verlag der Gutenberg-Gesellschaft, 1972); Götz von Olenhusen, "'Lasst 1000 Raubdrucke blühen!' Copyright und Copywrong," in Werner Pieper, ed., *Alles schien möglich ... Die Aktiven der 60er werden 60: Was trieb sie damals um, was machen sie heute? Rückschau und Bestandsaufnahme einer Generation die nach vorne schaute* (Löhrbach: Der Grüne Zweig, 2007).

[28] Antje Krüger, interview with the author, Berlin, February 21, 2010.

Figure 3.2 Cover of the June/July 1968 issue of the Berlin underground newspaper *Charlie Kaputt*. Note the image from the recently released American science-fiction epic *Planet of the Apes*. Hamburg Institute for Social Research.

content, the underground press challenged the dominant social narrative, contesting the cultural hegemony that propped up the West German Cold War consensus.[29] One of the earliest underground newspapers was *Linkeck*, founded by Hartmut Sander and Bernd Kramer. *Linkeck* was produced by the Oberbaum Press, one of the first left-wing self-publishing establishments in West Germany. Established by the twenty-six-year-old Hartmut Sander and the twenty-four-year-old Martin Dürschlag in 1964, the "press" was little more than an old, beat-up Rotaprint machine set up in a former shoemaker's shop at Oberbaumstraße 5 in Kreuzberg, on Oberbaum Bridge over the river Spree marking the boundary between East and West Berlin. The original conception of the press was not political per se, but cultural; its earliest supporters were the "new" writers Peter Handke, Peter O. Chotjewitz, and Rolf Dieter Brinkmann, and its early catalogue consisted primarily of "Pop und Provo-Poems."[30]

The press become more explicitly political in parallel with the overall politicization of 1966/1967. In particular, the arrival of the philosophy student and SDS member Gerd Petermann helped transform Oberbaum into an "APO press." In connection with the visit of the Shah of Iran in June 1967, the press printed the notorious "wanted poster," charging the Shah of Iran with murder, and the first number of its underground newspaper *Oberbaumblatt*, which contained a satirical essay entitled "The Shah Is Dead: Farah Violated!"[31]

The *Oberbaumblatt* pioneered the style taken up shortly afterward by *Linkeck*. The first issue of *Linkeck* appeared in late 1967. There were nine subsequent issues at irregular intervals over the course of 1968/1969, in print runs of between 4,000 and 8,500. Edited by Hartmut Sander and Bernd Kramer, the paper was published in cooperation with the Linkeck Commune in the Bülowstraße. Presenting political analysis alongside film and music reviews, cartoons, and pornography, *Linkeck* tweaked both mainstream and student-leftist sensibilities with verve and irony. From the scatological cover of its first issue, which accused West German society of wishing to "Gas the Commune" – a characteristic double entendre linking the establishment's hatred of the Kommune I with the

---

[29] Sabine Von Dirke, *"All Power to the Imagination!": The West German Counterculture from the Student Movement to the Greens* (Lincoln, Nebr.: University of Nebraska Press, 1997), p. 4.

[30] *Der Spiegel*, no. 30, July 22, 1968. "The name of the press is lovely," wrote Brinkmann to Sander; "(OBERBAUM-PRESS because it's in the Oberbaumstrasse, good, good)"; Rolf Dieter Brinkmann to Hartmut Sander, Cologne, April 16, 1966, reprinted in Kramer, ed., *Gefundene Fragmente*, vol. I, p. 52.

[31] *Der Spiegel*, no. 30, July 22, 1968.

Nazis' destruction of the Communist Party (referred to by the Nazis as "the commune") and the Jews (by gas) – *Linkeck* attempted to provoke authority along as many lines of attack as possible, wherever possible by breaking sexual taboos. Unsurprisingly, each of the first six issues was almost immediately confiscated by the authorities.[32] The newspaper and the commune lasted through 1969, after which Bernd Kramer went on to found the Karin Kramer Verlag, whose first publication, unsurprisingly given the increasing popularity of anarchism in West Berlin, was a new edition of the Russian anarchist Mikhail Bakunin's *State and Anarchy*.[33]

The most well known of the underground newspapers was *Agit 883*, published from 1969 to 1972, with its home in the Uhlandstrasse in West Berlin. *Agit 883*, later simply *883*, functioned as the chief organ of the post-SDS West Berlin radical scene.[34] Produced by a local collective in Berlin, and selling for 50 *pfennig* in left-wing bars and hangouts, *883* sensitively reflected the changing currents within the left-wing scene on a weekly basis. *883* and papers like it (*Fizz, Love, Berliner Anzünder, Hundert Blumen*, and many more) prefigured an unprecedented explosion of underground creativity that would characterize the 1970s and 1980s. Many of them also became key disseminators of propaganda for the left-wing terror groups launched at the end of the 1960s.

SUBCULTURE TRANSNATIONAL

The West German underground press that came into existence in West Germany circa 1968 was decisively influenced in its initial stages by the American underground press, which had emerged some years previously and which was assigned an almost mythological status by Germans – like the American counterculture generally. Early attempts to publicize the rise of the underground press in West Germany were very much transnational affairs, with the output of the American underground press, as well as that of the pan-European literary and countercultural avant-garde,

[32] See Robert Halbach, ed., *Linkeck: Erste antiautoritäre Zeitung – Jedes Urteil wissenschaftlicher Kritik ist mir willkommen* (Berlin-Neukölln: Kramer-Verlag, 1987).
[33] The printing establishment in the Oberbaumstraße fell into the hands of the newly founded KPD(AO) (on which more below).
[34] See Knud Andersen, Markus Mohr, and Hartmut Rübner, "Aus der Kneipe Kreuzberger Vereinshaus (dröhnte) die Internationale oder 'Der Osten ist rot.' Ein paar Schlaglichter zur Geschichte der Zeitschrift Agit 883 (1969 bis 1972)," in Bernd Hüttner, ed., *Verzeichnis der Alternativ Medien 2006/2007* (Berlin: Edition ID-Archiv, 1991); see also Rotaprint 25, eds., *Agit 883: Bewegung Revolte Underground in Westberlin, 1969–1972* (Berlin: Assoziation A, 2006).

featuring prominently. A key event in this connection was the *Literarische Messe* (Literary Fair) that took place in Frankfurt in the spring of 1968, a few months before the *Frankfurter Buchmesse* and the *Gegenbuchmesse* of September. The *Literarische Messe* had its roots in the *Literarische Pfingstmessen* organized in 1963 and 1964 by the writer and publisher Victor Otto Stomps and nominally made up a third entry in the series.[35] Organized by the writer and publisher Horst Bingel, the *Literarische Messe* featured a who's who of the American Beat and countercultural scene (Allen Ginsberg, Gary Snyder, Alan Watts, Timothy Leary), a section on "Prague Happenings" (featuring the work of Czech artists and writers whose manifestations were deemed superior to those of the New York scene in terms of spontaneity and political content), and a range of "books, newspapers, object-poems, year books, calendars, flyers, maps ... manifestos, poems" drawn from Belgium, Argentina, Hungary, India, Uganda, England, and elsewhere.[36]

The *Literarische Messe* was explicitly conceived by its organizers as an antidote to the perceived poverty of the German literary scene. "Does Germany have a literary consciousness? Do writers matter?" asked Bingel in the introduction to the exhibit catalogue; "They don't matter, and there is no literary consciousness ... Nothing has changed since Heine: the writer is a figurehead if docile before the state, a Don Quixote if he expresses revolutionary views."[37] Tracing the significance of the *Literarische Messe* back to the first of the events put on by V. O. Stomps, Bingel expressly identified the political content at the heart of the literary-publicistic enterprise:

Initiative counts. For that reason, the impulse of the organizer of the 1st Literarische Pfingstmesse is to be welcomed. [That event] presented over ninety domestic and foreign journals and presses, that take up the élan of the young, make it visible, show that there is a young generation that mistrusts the culture business the world over. We cannot have enough small presses! If we had them, in every street, in every house we would be immune to every dictatorship for all time ... A salute to the new journals and presses![38]

The *Literarische Messe* drew no distinction between the worlds of literature and the underground press, seeing both as part of a continuum dedicated

---

[35] See Horst Bingel, ed., *Zeitschriften, Pressen und progressive Literatur* (Frankfurt: Affenpresse, 1963). There were no entries in the series for 1965–1967.

[36] Horst Bingel, ed., *Literarische Messe 1968: Handpressen, Flugblätter, Zeitschriften der Avant-garde* (Frankfurt: Metopen-Verlag, 1968), pp. 12, 39.

[37] Bingel, *Literarische Messe 1968*, p. 7.

[38] Bingel, *Literarische Messe 1968*, p. 9.

to new forms of expression from below. Similarly, for the publishers of the underground newspapers, there was, initially at least, no clear distinction between the alternative-literary world and the world of countercultural-political newspapers. The latter were seen, as Thomas Daum points out, as an antipode to the big publishers, in which form, content, and production methods were of a piece.[39]

The underground press was one of the primary places in which the counterculture theorized itself, working through partially contradictory and overlapping concepts such as "underground," "subculture," and "counterculture." The debate about subculture/underground was launched in *Song*, one of the earliest German underground magazines. Founded in 1966, and edited by Reinhard Hippen, Rolf Gekeler, and Tom Schroeder, *Song* (its full name was *Song. Chanson. Folklore Bänkelsang*) began as a folk-oriented magazine associated with the annual Burg Waldeck Festivals. Its assessment of subculture was intimately bound up with an assessment of the value and worth of popular culture, an analysis that, as we will see in the next chapter, was tied in turn to reflections on the merits of specific musical genres. More generally, however, *Song* played an early and continuing role in distinguishing between the negative content associated with subculture – ascribed to an undifferentiated hippie-like hedonism, linked with the consumption of markers of identity already recuperated by capitalism – and its positive content, associated with a critical stance involving both aesthetic and political parameters. This critical stance was reflected in a series of name changes intended to better capture the magazine's evolving mission. The change of the magazine's subtitle in 1969 from *German Underground Journal* to *Journal for Progressive Subculture* was meant to reflect a more discerning approach to the question of subculture.[40]

A leading voice in the attempt to theorize subculture was the Austrian actor, singer, songwriter, and author Rolf Schwendter. In an essay published in *Song* in 1968, Schwendter wrote:

The hippies and Beatniks, the Gammler and the Provos, the students (virtually throughout the world) and the schoolchildren, the peace marchers, protest singers and intellectuals of the underground newspapers, also the negroes and the Puerto Ricans [a reference to the Young Lords, a Puerto Rican nationalist street gang active in New York City and Chicago]: a whole multitude is

---

[39] Daum, *Die 2 Kultur*, p. 75.
[40] Thomas and Bullivant, *Literature in Upheaval*, p. 167.

increasingly, visibly, articulating their resistance against a conformist, profit-seeking, bureaucratically frozen society.[41]

Citing approvingly Rudi Dutschke's use of the terms "subculture" and "oppositional milieu" (*Gegenmilieu*) during his 1967 television interview with Günter Gaus, Schwendter offered subcultures as a living example of Herbert Marcuse's "great refusal." Refuting those who dismissed youth nonconformism as a distraction from urgent political tasks, Schwendter insisted on its value. He quoted at length a (rather entertaining) passage of Adorno's:

The apartment of ... a young bohemian corresponds to his spiritual household. On the wall, the illusory [but] true-to-the-original color print of the famous Van Gogh ... on the bookshelf, a distillation of socialism and psychoanalysis, a little sexual lore for the uninhibited with inhibitions. Also the Random House edition of Proust ... classiness at cut-rate prices ... a couple of loud jazz records, with which one can feel simultaneously collective, adventurous, and comfortable. Every opinion is automatically agreed upon by friends, they know all the arguments ahead of time ... The outsiderness of the initiated is illusion and mere idleness.

In response to this passage, astonishingly elitist even by the standards of Adorno, with his legendary contempt for popular culture, Schwendter wrote, "Here as well the historical situation has overtaken the analysis ... next to Proust stands Barbarella, next to Jazz the Rolling Stones. Agreed-upon opinions, even about critical theory ... have become rare."[42]

Schwendter's 1971 book *Theory of Subculture* expanded forward on these ideas, arguing that, in order to be valid, subcultures must hold an emancipatory content. In contrast to "retrogressive" subcultures – among which Schwendter included both nineteenth-century bohemia and twentieth-century pop – "progressive" subcultures held within themselves the positive potential to contribute to the remaking of society along new lines. A corollary was that in order to avoid being recuperated into the dominant culture, subculture must involve political action. Here, Schwendter came close to articulating a model of counterculture that echoed that proposed by the editors of *Song*. The latter argued that "a subculture is only a counterculture, firstly, when it strives for a fundamental change of society, aimed at its humanization and emancipation, and secondly, when it cannot be easily integrated or made to conform."[43] The underground press was

---

[41] Rolf Schwendter, "Zur Theorie der Subkultur," *Song: Deutsche Underground-Zeitschrift*, no. 8, 1968.
[42] Schwendter, "Zur Theorie der Subkultur."
[43] Quoted in Thomas and Bullivant, *Literature in Upheaval*, pp. 167–168.

important, Schwendter had argued in the *Song* essay, precisely because it was difficult for capitalism to assimilate.[44]

Such concerns about recuperation were central to the protests at the *Frankfurter Buchmesse* of 1968 and provided the conceptual basis for the *Gegenbuchmesse* as well. The latter was no mere publicistic event but a literary analog to a multifaceted anti-milieu encompassing the underground press, the art scene, and the counterculture. This anti-milieu, like the international counterculture of which it was an expression, was a product of transnational connections, a fact reflected in both the *Buchmesse* and the *Gegenbuchmesse*. One of the attendees at the former was Jörg Schröder, a former head of press and advertising for Kiepenheuer & Witsch in Cologne, now editor for the Joseph Melzer Verlag in Darmstadt. Billing itself as a "conscious opposition-movement [*Gegenbewegung*] against the standards-machines [*Niveauwalze*] of the book factories," Melzer specialized in presenting the work of the young generation of international authors including the American Leroi Jones and the Dutchman Hans Tuynman.[45] Tuynman's book, *Ich bin ein Provo: Das permanente Happening* (*I Am a Provo: The Permanent Happening*) had appeared with Melzer the previous year. Schröder invited Tuynman and his friends to attend the book fair. "Just imagine this group of Provos," he recalled; "[Herman] Ysebaert with a silver top-hat, his friend wearing a tall bishop's mitre; with them these colorful 'Dollen Minas' [Dutch anarcho-feminists] with their round granny glasses; and then Hans Tuynman and his clique."[46] The Provos lent flair to the already-harried proceedings at the book fair, with Ysebaert, to Schröder's dismay, contributing to an anti-Springer protest by taking out his penis and urinating all over the carpet.[47]

[44] Schwendter, "Zur Theorie der Subkultur."
[45] "Erfolg der Erfolgs. Melzers Frühjahrsprogramm," *Frankfurter Rundshau*, no. 93, April 20, 1968.
[46] See www.buchmesse.de/staticpages/jubilaeum/de/jubilaeum/zeitzeugen/00687/index.html (accessed July 17, 2011). See Hans Tuynman, *Ich bin ein Provo: Das permanente Happening* (Melzer: Darmstadt, 1967).
[47] Tuynman, *Ich bin ein Provo.* "Ysebaert didn't shout," recalls Schröder, "more like said three times loudly: 'Piss on Springer! Piss on Springer! Piss on Springer!' into the stunned silence of the protesters. He pissed alone, we just laughed a little, 'ha! ha! ha!' Siegfried Unseld was as if paralysed, standing at a suitable distance and then, when he'd pulled himself together, he said, 'This is outrageous! It's outrageous! No, that's definitely going too far!' But Ysebaert just kept on pissing. I was also a bit taken aback myself, I hadn't expected it, that hadn't been discussed, but from the concept point of view, of course I thought it was right and I pulled myself together. Actually, in circumstances like that you want the ground to swallow you up, you would rather be in a blue suit and be able to say, 'This is outrageous!' The really good performance is precisely the one you wish you weren't part of when it happens, even if you are joining in the performance yourself, you sometimes wish you weren't in it."

Schröder had for some time been preparing to establish his own publishing house aimed at bringing new cultural, literary, and political currents from England, the Netherlands, and the USA to West Germany. Around the time of the *Buchmesse*, Schröder was busily engaged in translating American Beat poetry into German with his friends Ralf-Rainer Rygulla and Rolf Dieter Brinkmann. Born in 1940, Brinkmann grew up in Vechta near Bremen, which he characterized as a "Catholic small town milieu, enormously sexually repressive."[48] He later moved to Cologne, on the river Rhine, a city with a thriving underground scene.[49] A man of many talents – novelist, essayist, short-story writer, travel writer, radio dramatist, aficionado of film and photography, amateur Super 8 experimental/documentary filmographer–Brinkmann was a seminal figure in the importation of the international underground into West Germany as well as a key participant in debates about the nature and value of subculture.

Brinkmann was fundamentally influenced by his contact with the city of London. In 1965, the year of Brinkmann's first visit, London was rapidly being transformed into the capital of the international youth revolution. With bands such as The Rolling Stones, The Beatles, The Kinks, and The Small Faces, the amphetamine-fueled mod subculture in transition to the flowery acid-drenched groovyness of "Swinging London," alternative newspapers such as *Oz* and the *International Times*, vibrant scenes around clubs such as Ufo and Middle Earth, the London Free School, the Arts Lab, and the Scottish-Italian Beat poet Alexander Trocchi's Project Sigma, London was a center for the intersection of fashion, music, drugs, and sexuality that formed the international counterculture.[50]

The *International Times* correspondent Alex Gross, a frequent visitor to West Berlin in his capacity as playwriting fellow, translator of Peter Weiss's *The Investigation* for the London stage, and friend to members of the Kommune I, writes strikingly of the "counterculture gap" separating London and Berlin at this time. In addition to being a major site of countercultural creativity in its own right, London was also a window to the breezes blowing in from America, the output of the American underground newspapers such as the *East Village Other*, the *Los Angeles Free Press*, the *San Francisco Oracle*, and the Detroit-based *Fifth Estate* readily

[48] "So im Gange," *Der Spiegel*, no. 25, June 17, 1968.
[49] Sibylle Spath, *Rolf Dieter Brinkmann* (Stuttgart: Metzler, 1989).
[50] On the London scene, see Joe Boyd, *White Bicycles: Making Music in the 1960s* (London: Serpent's Tail, 2007); Jonathan Green, *Days in the Life: Voices from the English Underground, 1961–71* (London: Pimlico, 1998).

Figure 3.3 Rolf Dieter Brinkmann in Cologne with Super 8 camera. Photo: Jens Hagen.

available to Gross at the legendary Indica Bookshop in Mason's Yard. Gross inevitably arrived in Berlin bearing the latest underground titles, which he pressed on friends and acquaintances as examples of how things should be done. Among other things, he advised Heinrich Guggomos, publisher of the rather staid *Berlin Extra-Blatt* (later *Extra-Dienst*) to spice things up with "far-out sex, lots more photos and graphics, and a style that ridiculed the enemy instead of boring one's friends."[51]

For Brinkmann in Cologne, Gross's prescription was made to order and London was the place to get it filled. "Memories of the revolt [of 1968], of sweat-filled rock concerts, of the times of ACID and Fuck You, are intimately bound up with London," recalls a friend with whom Brinkmann spent a lot of time in London in the early 1970s.[52] In Brinkmann's "pop novel" *Keiner weiß mehr* (*Nobody Knows Anymore*, 1968), a bestseller praised by *Die Zeit* as "remarkable and obscene," London represents a major presence, and the city appears repeatedly in his subsequent writings.[53] More importantly, London represented a major node in the transnational network through which Brinkmann imported key texts of the international youth revolution into West Germany. It was through his friends Ralf-Rainer Rygulla and Rolf Eckart John, working in London as booksellers, that Brinkmann first came into contact with the English and American underground press, small underground magazines, and the literary output of the nascent American counterculture. When he returned to Cologne from his first trip to London in 1965, Brinkmann carried works by the New York poets Frank O'Hara and Ted Berrigan in his suitcase. He subsequently continued to receive regular shipments from Rygulla.

The Cologne to which Brinkmann returned was in the process of becoming a major bastion of the West German counterculture. The Cologne scene of the 1960s has received virtually no attention from historians, with West Berlin (and to a lesser extent Frankfurt), sucking up most of the historiographic oxygen. Yet Cologne experienced its own, extraordinarily vibrant 1968.[54] Well before the murder of Benno Ohnesorg – marked in Cologne by a procession of some 6,000 students and professors though the city center

---

[51] Gross, *The Untold Sixties*, p. 193.

[52] Jürgen Theobaldy, "Bevor die Musik vorbei ist: Zu Rolf Dieter Brinkmann," *Literaturmagazin*, 15 (April 1985), p. 18.

[53] Anthony Waine, "Fatal Attractions: Rolf Dieter Brinkmann and British Life and Culture," *The Modern Language Review*, 87 (2) (1992): 376–392.

[54] See Kurt Holl and Claudia Glunz, *1968 am Rhein: Satisfaction und Ruhender Verkehr* (Cologne: Verlag Schmidt von Schwind, 1998).

bearing placards reading "Peace and order proceed over corpses!?" – and well before the events of May 1968 in Paris, which also registered strongly in the city, Cologne was already the center of a thriving literary and artistic avant-garde scene. The cultural-political awakening of Cologne from 1967 onward was captured and documented by the photographer and author Jens Hagen, who contributed to the periodicals *konkret*, *Spontan*, and *Underground* before going on to found the alternative Cologne newspaper *ANA&BELA*, which ran from 1969 through 1972. "Although Adenauer was from Cologne and was mayor here for a long time," recalls Hagen, "Cologne was for me the city that was least 'Adenauer era'-like. I experienced in Cologne very little that was Adenauer-ish, even though naturally the whole structure of politics and society was exactly the same as elsewhere."[55]

Cologne was home to numerous small presses and bootleg publishing operations, such as Die Waffe der Kritik (The Weapon of Criticism) press, operated by a certain Peter S. out of his garage from 1965, as well as the political cabaret-cum-rock group Floh de Cologne, which achieved a good deal of notoriety as one of the more explicitly political groups in West Germany.[56] The Cologne scene was entirely characteristic of 1968 in a number of ways: in its breaking down of boundaries (between different areas of the arts and between the arts and the counterculture); in the radical-democratic, "do-it-yourself" ethos that governed its activities; in its demonstration that the "political" lay not just within the realm of student activism but in the total effect of a multifaceted assault on the strictures governing artistic and personal expression; in its demonstration that the *Gegenöffentlichkeit* posited by student activists as an antidote to the deforming power of the mass media was no mere publicistic phenomenon but encompassed the entire range of cultural activities associated with the New Left and the counterculture; and, finally, in its demonstration that cultural activism at the local level was intimately bound up with (indeed, fueled by) attempts to obtain the globally available, whether in the American avant-garde films screened by local collective X-Screen, the Anglo-American rock influences channeled by Floh de Cologne, or the Beat literature imported by Rolf Dieter Brinkmann.

For Brinkmann, Beat literature corresponded to deep personal and aesthetic-artistic longings, bound up with his love for the city of London and, via London, the American underground. Yet here the global was

[55] Jens Hagen, quoted in Benedikt Geulen and Peter Graf, *Mach mal bitte platz, wir müssen hier stürmen: Als der Beat nach Deutschland kam. Fotografien von Jens Hagen* (Cologne: M7 Verlag, 2007), p. 72.
[56] See the profiles in Holl and Glunz, *1968 am Rhein*.

very much prescribed by the needs of the local. The foreign was, for Brinkmann, an answer to the impasse in which the artist found himself at home. In contrast to the situation in West Germany where, Brinkmann complained, even small presses operated from "outdated and rotten notions of literature handed down to them by the editors of the large publishing-houses," the literature of the "new American scene" represented something truly fresh and new. "I say, the Beat Scene is better in every regard!" he wrote to his friend Hartmut Sander; "It is truly rich! What rare value! Rare, not just because the notebooks or booklets are handmade. No. I'll be very sad if you can find anything comparable."[57]

The year after the tumult at the *Frankfurter Buchmesse*, Brinkmann and Rygulla published two anthologies that were to play a crucial role in introducing American Beat literature to a German reading public. Rygulla and Schröder had already introduced some of the Beat poets the previous year in the anthology *Fuck You(!) Underground Poems*, published with the Melzer Verlag. The first publication of Schröder's own März Verlag, founded in March 1969, was Brinkmann and Rygulla's *ACID: Neue amerikanische Szene*. Presenting the work of writers such as William S. Burroughs, Diane di Prima, Marshall McLuhan, and Charles Bukowski, all translated into German by Schröder, Rygulla, and Brinkmann in the winter of 1968/1969, the volume aimed to present "a total picture of a unitary sensibility encompassing the realm of the trivial to the realm of high culture, for which the concepts Pop or Subculture are inadequate."[58]

A second anthology, published by Brinkmann the same year, was *Silverscreen: Jüngste amerikanische Lyrik*. The introduction, writes Anthony Waine, consisted of

[s]eventy-five random observations on the poets featured in the anthology, their backgrounds, the influence of the Beat Generation, differences between German and American culture, and the Poetry Project at the St. Mark's Church in the Bowery in New York ... images taken from film, adverts for cars, boots, eye make-up, breast enlargements, pin-ups of Elvis and Jim Morrison and from porn mags ... and a close-up of an enticingly sensual woman's open mouth with a contraceptive pill (or is it an LSD tablet?!) on the tip of the tongue about to be swallowed.[59]

[57] "Rolf Dieter Brinkmann an Hartmut Sander: Briefe," in Kramer, ed., *Gefundene Fragmente*, vol. I, p. 51.

[58] Rolf Dieter Brinkmann and Ralf-Rainer Rygulla, eds., *ACID: Neue amerikanische Szene* (Darmstadt: März Verlag, 1969), p. 99.

[59] Anthony Waine, *Changing Cultural Tastes: Writers and the Popular in Modern Germany* (New York and Oxford: Berghahn, 2007), p. 94.

Both works attempted, in their collage-style juxtaposition of words and images, to capture the interpenetration of diverse elements that Brinkmann and others sought to meld into a new and life-affirming attack on the staid high-cultural thrust of West German letters.

This project would have been impossible without – indeed, was inseparable from – the fusion of global and local that characterized the entire West German 1968. "Growing up in an age in which technology, commerce, and the communications industry had already placed most forms of culture into a global marketplace," writes Anthony Waine, "Brinkmann ... was able to choose freely from the goods on offer, especially those originating in Britain and America. Moreover, the proximity of Britain to Germany also meant that he could experience at first hand the life and spirit of the people."[60] Brinkmann's project depended on the increased mobility of people and ideas in the 1960s. He was profoundly influenced, for example, by the talk on postmodernism given by the American literary critic Leslie Fiedler at Freiberg University in June 1968. Fiedler's lecture, "Cross the Border, Close the Gap: The Case for Postmodernism," argued in favor of erasing the artificial distinctions between "high culture" and "pop culture," a theme very dear to Brinkmann's heart.[61] Needless to say, this conception of art ran in direct opposition to Adorno's influential critique, and would prove to be a major bone of contention in West German debates about the political potential of literature.

LITERATURE AND REVOLUTION

Fiedler's talk sparked off a fierce debate in West German literary circles in which were reflected some of the themes that would be prominent in the *Frankfurter Buchmesse* a few months later. After the publication of Fiedler's talk in the weekly *Christ und Welt* – the second essay was entitled, tellingly, "Indians, Science Fiction, and Pornography: The Future of the Novel Has Already Begun" – the newspaper launched a series of "Fiedler Discussions" in which various well-known writers and critics weighed in on the significance of Fiedler's intervention.[62] Fiedler had been

---

[60] Waine, "Fatal Attractions."

[61] Leslie Fiedler, "Cross the Border, Close the Gap," *Playboy* (December 1969). The talk was published in German as "Das Neue Zeitalter der neuen Literatur," *Christ und Welt*, September 13 and 20, 1968.

[62] The contributions are collected in Uwe Wittstock, ed., *Roman oder Leben: Postmoderne in der deutschen Literatur* (Leipzig: Reclam, 1994). On the Fiedler controversy, see Gregory Divers, *The Image and Influence of America in German Poetry since 1945* (Rochester, NY: Camden House,

challenged during his talk by audience members who worried that his call for a literature of "myth, irrationality, dream, and ecstasy" was misguided for reasons peculiar to the West German situation.[63] "Only we who have again and again to wrestle with the phenomenon of National Socialism," the poet Hilde Domin told Fiedler, "can actually grasp, how dangerous is what you have to say."[64] The novelist Martin Walser spoke in a similar vein, charging Fiedler's talk with being "against enlightenment in the worst sense."[65] In the forum in *Christ und Welt*, in which the writer Peter O. Chotjewitz denounced Fiedler as a "counterrevolutionary," Walser called for a "democratic, myth-destroying, courage-giving, writing."[66] Unsurprisingly, Rolf Dieter Brinkmann vigorously defended Fiedler in his contribution to the forum, an essay provocatively entitled "Attack on the Monopoly: I Hate All Writers."[67]

The battle lines drawn in this debate cut across the entire field of the antiauthoritarian revolt in West Germany. The question of whether the turn to an exacerbated form of personal subjectivity and the embrace and deployment of the images of popular culture represented a legitimate form of engagement, or whether it represented any sort of engagement at all, was of central importance to the subsequent development not only of literature and alternative publishing but of the antiauthoritarian political struggle itself. The terms of this debate were highlighted by Martin Walser, perhaps the sharpest critic of the pop-cultural turn heralded by Leslie Fiedler and his West German acolytes. For Walser, the literature produced by Fiedler's West German admirers, above all Rolf Dieter Brinkmann, was merely "narcissistic posturing."[68] Elaborating on his earlier charges against Fiedler in a revised version of his *Christ und Welt* piece published in *Kursbuch*, Walser warned of the dangers of what he dubbed the "latest mood in the West."[69] With its juxtaposition of cultural motifs lifted out of their context as items of indoctrination or consumption, pop literature and its companions, drugs, rock music, new religions,

2002), p. 124; see also Danny Walther, "Die 'Fiedler-Debatte' oder Kleiner Versuch, die 'Chiffre 1968' von links ein wenig auf-zuschreiben," Magisterarbeit, University of Leipzig, 2007.

[63] Walther, "Die 'Fiedler-Debatte,'" p. 33.

[64] Tagungsprotokoll, Part I, p. 7, cited in Walther, "Die 'Fiedler-Debatte.'"

[65] Tagungsprotokoll, Part I, p. 5.

[66] *Christ und Welt*, October 18, 1968, pp. 21, 17.

[67] Rolf Dieter Brinkmann, "Angriff aufs Monopol: Ich hasse alte Dichter," *Christ und Welt*, November 15, 1968; later reprinted in Wittstock, ed., *Roman oder Leben*, p. 71.

[68] "Über die Neueste Stimmung im Westen," *Kursbuch*, no. 20, 1970, p. 36.

[69] *Ibid.*

and Hermann Hesse, reneged on the imperative to demand change in the world. "I hold it possible," he wrote, "that in these latest moods are being created the spiritual concoctions [*Bewußtseinspräparate*] for the latest form of fascism."[70]

It is worth noting that this distinctly West German firestorm was entirely a response to the penetration into the Federal Republic of influences from the USA. The primary culprits in Walser's *Kursbuch* piece, countercultural prophets such as Tuli Kupferberg, William S. Burroughs, and Marshall McLuhan, were American; imitators such as Brinkmann, Helmut Heißenbüttel, and Peter Handke, whatever their artistic shortcomings, were guilty primarily of the crime of trying to import the *wrong* America. Walser believed – incorrectly, as it happens – that the counterculture and the political "movement" in the USA were separate phenomena; in fact, they cut across each other in significant ways.[71] Indeed, as Thomas Daum points out, the American literary underground played a critical role in helping prepare the way for the rise of the generational revolt that underpinned the student movement.[72] It is also important to note, as Rolf Dieter Brinkmann and Ralf-Rainer Rygulla pointed out in the afterword to *ACID*, that the literary output of the American underground was posed precisely against the market forces that otherwise conspired to push quality into the background.

In the same month that the Fiedler debate was raging in the pages of *Christ und Welt*, Hans Magnus Enzensberger opened up another front in the war over the status of literature, in a seminal issue of *Kursbuch*. Famous for Enzensberger's much-cited (and much misunderstood) announcement of the "death of literature," the issue also contained an essay by Karl Markus Michel who, in contrast to Martin Walser, claimed to detect the traces of a new literary praxis in "pop and happenings and many forms of the subculture" and in the wall slogans and placards of the insurrectionary students in the recently passed Paris May.[73] Of greater impact in the debate was Enzensberger's essay in the volume, which called into question the very usefulness of literature (of any type). Diagnosing a situation in which literature had developed a function as a "safety valve" that decreased rather than increased the impetus toward political action,

[70] *Ibid.*
[71] See the essays in Peter Braunstein and Michael William Doyle, eds., *Imagine Nation: The American Counterculture of the 1960s and 70s* (London and New York: Routledge, 2002).
[72] Daum, *Die 2 Kultur*, p. 68.
[73] K. M. Michel, "Ein Kranz fiir die Literatur," *Kursbuch*, no. 15, November 1968.

Enzensberger claimed that literature had lost the social or political relevance it once held.[74]

Enzensberger's provocative remarks came at a time when literary practice was already changing to accommodate the perceived need for greater social relevance. The advent into literature of the "68er generation" (actually a misnomer since the new left literary project was very much a multigenerational affair), was marked by a rejection of earlier models of politicization. Or perhaps it is better to say that earlier models of politicization came to seem increasingly out of step in the overall climate of radicalization from the mid 1960s. This trend played out in pronounced form around one of the primary vehicles of political writing in the postwar period, the legendary Gruppe 47. An informal writing circle whose membership included a veritable who's who of postwar German letters associated with the radical turn, the Gruppe 47 played host to Hans Magnus Enzensberger, Uwe Johnson, Peter Handke, and Reinhard Lettau among others. Yet the group itself, and, in particular, the iconoclastic author Günter Grass, increasingly came under attack from those who advocated a more thoroughgoing politicization of literature. Ulrike Meinhof's well-known piece in *konkret* that accused the group of having been left behind in its politics to the extent that it had become a tool of the ruling class helped lend weight to the critical tone.[75]

The push toward a politicization of literature was connected with the rise of new literary forms, of which the so-called "documentary turn" was of particular importance. Linked with a shift in the emphasis of literature from the past to the present, the documentary turn focused on the revealing facts of social existence seen to be absent both in the rarified sphere of high-cultural literature and in the reportage of the bourgeois press.[76] Literary productions of the documentary turn frequently relied on evidence drawn from public hearings, recontextualized in order to reflect deeper truths about contemporary society. Peter Weiss's 1965 *Die Ermittlung* (*The Investigation*), drawing on transcripts of the Frankfurt Auschwitz trials, and Hans Magnus Enzensberger's 1970 *Das Verhör von Habana* (*The Havana Inquiry*), utilizing transcripts of public hearings in the aftermath of the Bay of Pigs invasion in Cuba, were both outstanding examples of the genre.

More explicit attempts to deploy artistically the raw materials of social oppression were present in the works of writers such as F. C. Delius and

---

[74] Hans Magnus Enzensberger, "Gemeinplätze, die Neueste Literatur betreffend," *Kursbuch*, no. 15, November 1968.

[75] Ulrike Meinhof, "Gruppe 47," *konkret*, no. 10, 1967, pp. 2–3.

[76] Thomas and Bullivant, *Literature in Upheaval*, p. 109.

Günter Wallraff. Delius's 1965 *Wir Unternehmer* (*We Employers*), billing itself as a "documentary polemic," used language from transcripts of the 1965 Economic Conference of the CDU/CSU to build up an overwhelming impression of a conservative worldview in which private property is the fundament of social existence.[77] Wallraff, by contrast, used a method of first-person social reportage to recapitulate information gathered in undercover forays into industry and the establishment. In *Wir brauchen Dich* (*We Need You*) (1966), and *13 unerwünschte Reportagen* (*13 Undesired Reports*) (1969), he exposes, respectively, the exploitation of workers and the (revealing) attitudes of a range of establishment figures.[78] Here, the documentary turn had much in common with the new critical journalism in that it sought to uncover the machinations of power and to reveal hidden truths that lay under the façade of bourgeois democracy. As Wallraff put it, "the individual's strong line of defense against an organization is his chance of bringing things to the attention of the public."[79]

Attempts to stake out new vistas of social relevance for literature came up against the hard reality that literary production took place within the larger sphere of capitalist production, a fact that rendered problematic any claims for a revolutionary literature. Enzensberger had highlighted this problem in his essay in *Kursbuch* 15, which emphasized the ever-growing ability of modern capitalism to commodify art and to destroy its revolutionary potential. "Through industrial detours, via advertising and styling," he wrote, "[literary interventions] wind up sooner or later, mostly sooner, in the consumer sphere."[80]

Almost simultaneously, the "Culture and Revolution" working group in the Berlin SDS weighed into the debate with a piece in the leading daily *Die Zeit*. Entitled "Art as a Commodity of the Consciousness Industry," the essay elaborated on the questions posed by the status of the literary product as an item of capitalist consumption.[81] A central theme had to do with the role played by production and distribution; if the goal

---

[77] F. C. Delius, *Wir Unternehmer: Über Arbeitgeber, Pinscher und das Volksganze–Eine Dokumentar-Polemik anhand der Protokolle des Wirtschaftstages der CDU/CSU 1965 in Düsseldorf* (Berlin: Wagenbach, 1966).

[78] Günter Wallraff, *Wir brauchen Dich: Als Arbeiter in deutschen Industriebetrieben* (Munich: Rütten und Loenig, 1966); Günter Wallraff, *13 unerwünschte Reportagen* (Cologne: Kiepenheuer & Witsch, 1969).

[79] Quoted in Thomas and Bullivant, *Literature in Upheaval*, p. 115.

[80] Enzensberger, "Gemeinplätze, die Neueste Literatur betreffend." *Kursbuch*, no. 15.

[81] "Kunst als Ware der Bewußtseinsindustrie," *Die Zeit*, no. 48, November 29, 1968. See the response to the "Kultur und Revolution" piece by Peter Handke, one of the writers criticized by Martin Walser; Peter Handke, "Totgeborene Sätze," *Die Zeit*, no. 49, December 6, 1968.

of left-wing authors and publishers alike was to develop a "revolutionary" literature ("literature" understood here more broadly to encompass both fiction and nonfiction productions) there was also a general recognition that capitalist relations had embedded themselves in the very production of literature itself.

ALTERNATIVE PUBLISHING

Writing in the introduction to the 1969 edition of his *Bibliography of Revolutionary Socialism*, Rudi Dutschke observed:

A large number of the titles collected [in the 1966 edition] were difficult to access. The situation has partly improved since then, above all through anarchist bootleg-production, and through the activity of the presses that have been integrated into, or created by, the movement itself, but also through the bourgeois publishers hoping to enlarge their market.[82]

Dutschke's "bourgeois publishers" played a major role in expanding the left-literary sphere in West Germany, maintaining their preeminence until, and to an extent after, the advent of the radical left's own presses toward the end of the decade. Major presses such as Suhrkamp and Rowohlt were quick to develop specialty imprints aimed at a left-student audience. Dutschke himself was published in Rowohlt's "rororo-aktuell" paperback series, as was student leader Daniel Cohn-Bendit. Publishers such as Fischer, Kiepenheuer & Witsch, Melzer, Europäische Verlagsanstalt, Deutsche Taschenbuch Verlag, and Luchterhand, were all involved in publishing for a student-left audience.[83] A glance at the titles available in the crisis year of 1968 – texts by the major Third World revolutionaries (Che Guevara, Frantz Fanon, Ho Chi Minh), major New Left thinkers such as Marcuse, up-to-the-moment works on the student unrest in France, treatments of the controversy around the Springer Press monopoly and on the student movement itself – indicates the heavy involvement of the major presses in helping to create the left publicistic sphere in West Germany.[84]

---

[82] Dutschke, *Ausgewählte und kommentierte Bibliographie.*
[83] The last years of the decade saw the creation of new lines aimed at a left-youth readership. Europäische Verlagsanstalt launched its "res novae provokativ" imprint in 1968, followed two years later by its "basis-reihe." Deutsche Taschenbuch Verlag started its "dtv report" series in 1968, and Luchterhand created its "Sammlung Luchterhand" in 1970.
[84] Hans Dieter Müller, *Der Springer-Konzern: Eine Kritische Studie* (Munich: R. Piper & Co. Verlag, 1968); Ulrich Sonnemann, *Institutionalismus und studentische Opposition: Thesen zur Ausbreitung des Ungehorsams in Deutschland* (Frankfurt: Suhrkamp Verlag, 1968); Peter Berger

This wide availability of texts was a double-edged sword, however, for many saw in the pronounced role of the mainstream press an act of capitalist recuperation that sold the left back its own ideas, robbing them of their subversive potential in the process. In terms both of content and style, the publishing programs of the major houses were seen as incursions into the territory of the antiauthoritarian movement. As Götz von Olenhusen put it in an essay of 1971: "The new Luchterhand typescript, the Sammlung Luchterhand, the low-priced Basis books of the Europäische Verlagsanstalt, countless paperback editions from Suhrkamp or the Rowohlt paperback texts of socialism and anarchism, are all examples of borrowing from the programs of the bootleg publishers."[85] For authors possessing the opportunity, publishing with the large presses offered many advantages, not least the promise of money and the possibility of reaching a large audience. Yet, as Rudi Dutschke experienced when he had to defend himself against charges that he had "sold out" by publishing with Rowohlt, the struggle over who had the right to speak for the left cut to the heart of the antiauthoritarian revolt. As the Ça Ira press put it:

> What is being communicated (our criticism) is more and more determined by the means of communication. We can be "revolutionary," print, write, talk, whatever we want: the machine (the bourgeois publishers, marketing organizations, printers etc.) absorbs everything, makes it into [mere] decoration, quickly exploits it: our words must mean something in practice! That means, that we must switch over to *self-organization*, if we don't want our critical stance to become just a higher form of nonsense.[86]

This question of self-organization, one of the key motifs of the entire 68er project, was central to the initiatives enacted in the wake of the *Frankfurter Buchmesse* of 1968. It had been taken up at the *Buchmesse* by a group calling itself the Literaturproduzenten (Literature Producers). Founded by Jörg Schröder, Frank Benseler, Walter Boehlich, and Lothar Pinkal, the group took its inspiration from Walter Benjamin's famous essay "Der Autor als Produzent" ("The Author as Producer"). In that essay, accessible now only some thirty years after its genesis in a talk of Benjamin's in Paris, the Marxist philosopher problematized the notion of

---

and Richard Neuhaus, *Protestbewegung und Revolution oder die Verantwortung der Radikalen* (Frankfurt: S. Fischer Verlag, 1982).

[85] Götz von Olenhusen, "Entwicklung und Stand der Raubdruckbewegung.

[86] Ça Ira Presse Berlin to "Kollegen und Genossen," September 5, 1968, in Hartmut Sander and Ulrich Christians, eds., *Subkultur Berlin: Selbstdarstellung, Text-, Ton-Bilddokumente, Esoterik der Kommunen, Rocker, subversiven Gruppen* (Darmstadt: März Verlag, 1969).

literature as a value-free sphere of knowledge, arguing that it was capable of "assimilating, indeed of propagating, an astonishing amount of revolutionary themes without putting into question its own continued existence or that of the class which owns it."[87] In this spirit, the *Literaturproduzenten* demanded a democratization of the administration of the *Buchmesse* and mooted plans to organize a *Messerat* or "Convention Soviet."[88]

In the aftermath of the *Buchmesse*, calls for democratization and self-management were met by the establishment of "authors' advisory committees" at Luchterhand, Suhrkamp, and other publishing houses, while at Bertelsmann authors and editors founded the so-called Autoren Edition (Authors' Edition), a line of publications run democratically and collectively by the authors and editors themselves.[89] The founding of the Verlag der Autoren (Authors' Press) in March 1969 by editors at Suhrkamp who felt themselves no longer able to reconcile the discrepancy between the content of the publications and the capitalist relations that governed their production represented a logical extension of the push toward self-management.[90] These initiatives took place alongside a wave of press-foundings that, by the end of the 1960s, accompanied the establishment of a vibrant and partly self-contained left-publicistic milieu with its own instrumentalities of production, distribution, and sales.

The founding of new left-oriented presses and experimentation with models of self-management predated the post-1968 wave. An early model of the latter was the Wagenbach Verlag, founded by Klaus Wagenbach in West Berlin in 1964. Organized along collective principles, officially codified (after some dissent) in 1969, the press was notable for its attempt to overcome the East–West divide by publishing texts of both East and West German authors. Wagenbach established its own *Rotbücher* (Red Books) series in 1968 – predecessor of the Rotbuch Verlag founded in 1973 – and later came into conflict with the authorities by publishing texts associated with the RAF. Another important press founded in West Berlin in the same year as Wagenbach was the Voltaire Verlag (later Edition Voltaire). The "Voltaire Flugschriften" paperback series presided over by Bernward

---

[87] Walter Benjamin, "The Author as Producer," in Victor Burgin, ed., *Thinking Photography* (Basingstoke: Macmillan, 1992), pp. 15–31.

[88] Daum, *Die 2 Kultur*, p. 62.

[89] Stephan Füssel, ed., *Die Politisierung des Buchmarkts: 1968 als Branchenereignis* (Wiesbaden: Harrassowitz, 2007), p. 8.

[90] See Peter Urban, *Das Buch vom Verlag der Autoren 1969–1989: Beschreibung eines Modells und seiner Entwicklung – Zusammengestellt von Peter Urban* (Frankfurt: Verlag der Autoren, 1989).

Vesper was both influential and successful, publishing an impressive range of titles on topics of history and cultural and political criticism.

The intense politicization of 1967–1968 and the battles over the meaning of literature taken up in a number of major fora added fuel to attempts to seize the cultural means of production and further to open up the literary-productive sphere to new voices and perspectives. Some of the new presses, such as Jörg Schröder's März Verlag (a press whose democratic credentials were subsequently called into question by participants unhappy with the inequitable distribution of income), focused on widening the West German bridgehead of the "latest mood from the West." Others, such as the Roter Stern Verlag, founded by Schröder's associate K. D. Wolff after his departure from März, catered to the explicitly political texts prized by the left-student milieu. All of these presses, among them Trikont, Linkeck, Oberbaum, Ça Ira, Peter Paul Zahl Verlag and many others, were founded on the principle that the left should have its own media rather than simply relying on the market-based decisions of the big publishers.[91]

From the end of the decade and into the 1970s, attempts accelerated to create an alternative (underground) public sphere aimed less at storming the commanding media heights, as in the SDS campaign to "expropriate" Axel Springer, than in creating access to the grassroots publications that exploded out of the antiauthoritarian revolt and took it in new and interesting directions from 1968 on. This turn was marked by the rise of so-called "info" services seeking to draw together small local publishing initiatives into a network with regional, national, and international reach. One of the most important of these was the "Non-Conformist Literary Information Center" (*Ulcus Molle Infodienst*) established by Josef Wintjes in November 1969. A computer specialist for Krupp, an aspiring poet, and, like Rolf Dieter Brinkmann, a great fan of American Beat literature, Wintjes found a calling in the effort to collect and publicize the output of the countless new small presses and bedroom publishing operations. These so-called "Minipressen" were featured in a number of conventions, the most successful and influential of which took place in Mainz in September 1970. Displaying a wide selection of experimental pop-art books and examples of the international underground press, the convention also featured lively debates about the meaning of subculture in general (Rolf Schwendter was one of the invited speakers) and the significance of Minipressen in particular.[92]

---

[91] Daum, *Die 2 Kultur*, p. 60.
[92] Daum, *Die 2 Kultur*, p. 77.

These debates informed the pages of *Ulcus Molle Infodienst*, which, alongside publication notices and mail-order listings, contained Wintjes's stream-of-consciousness musings on the state of the underground and short pieces by guest publishers discussing the philosophy behind their work. Billing itself as "a mouthpiece of the alternative press," *Ulcus Molle Infodienst* sought to connect young authors with publishers while advertising the latest underground publications of every type: "internat[ional] Underground-newspapers, political writings, bootleg publications, newly published poetry, bibliophile editions, spoken word." Wintjes's aim was to encourage communication on the widest possible basis while helping to crystallize a burgeoning underground "literary TOTAL SCENE." Just how extensive in range and diverse in interests was this "total scene" at the end of the 1960s comes across clearly in the pages of Wintjes's publication, which featured periodicals such as *Aktion* ("class struggle porno-facts left-engaged underground APO-info"), *Edelgammler* ("poetry-satire-prose" from Bavaria), *Hotcha* ("authentic underground design, internationally-oriented"), *Ex-Libris* ("independent press Nuremberg/politics/music-literature"), and a hundred others blending the hard-political, subcultural, and literary-bohemian left(s).[93]

In 1971, Wintjes and his co-editor Frank Göhre launched a series of "Scene Readers" designed to capture the eclecticism of the alternative publishing milieu. With the "Project Ulcus Molle Scene Reader 72" (the scholarly scientific imperative hard at work in the term "project"), the journal launched an extended discussion of its own publishing program and of the scene generally. The project aimed at collecting contributions for publication in concert with the 1972 Frankfurt Book Fair. "We want ideas and constructive contributions to the self-understanding of the German scene," wrote Wintjes and Göhre, "that is, we want theoretical critiques of the actual circumstances of that which can be lumped under the category of progressive subculture. We want protocols and studies based upon practical rank and file work that can demonstrate meaningful learning-processes within the counterculture."[94]

Not everyone approved of the transnational nature of Wintjes's "total scene," nor of the fractured and politically impotent scenes that fed into it. Wintjes published a critique of the previous year's "Scene Reader 71" by the literature critic and Rowohlt editor Jürgen Manthey, who criticized

[93] *Ulcus Molle Infodienst*, no. 8, July/August 1970, reprinted in J. Wintjes and J. Gehret, eds., *Ulcus Molle Infodienst: Jahrgaenge, 1969–1974* (Amsterdam: Azid Presse, 1979), p. 18.
[94] "Project Ulcus Molle Scene Reader 72," in *Ulcus Molle Infodienst*, no. 10, 1971.

the reader concept in terms familiar to participants in the debates about the worth of subculture generally and the value of American-imported underground culture in particular. "Such a scene-mirror on the American model doesn't translate to the German context," Manthey wrote, adding that the desire to take "the international trip" propagated by the likes of Rolf Ulrich Kaiser was not a ticket, but an "undeliverable telegram." The impulses capable of actually changing society, Manthey argued, were coming not from the "'Provo-POP-Porno'-Revolt," but from the universities.[95]

The following year, Wintjes launched an explicit discussion of the "scene" concept in the pages of *Ulcus Molle Infodienst*. The anarchist and underground publisher Peter Paul Zahl, writing from prison where he was serving a sentence of four years for shooting at a police officer (later changed into a sentence of fifteen years for attempted murder) observed,

it seems to me that it must be clarified who or what the SCENE is. and/or whether it actually exists? The "polit[ical]-scene' – is there one? The macro[biotic]-scene. the yippie-scene. The drug scene. The jesus-, -allah, -buddha, -maharishi, – hare krishna, – etc. scene. who or what is SCENE?... is scene [an] import good made in uSSa like bubblegum, western[s], levy's [sic]?

Referring to the common practice of adopting terms and phrases of the American counterculture – "cool," "dig it," and "shit" (for drugs) – Zahl wrote, "[I]s it in and of itself logical when the scene as a symbol of the great refusal is adopted on the basis of expressions adapted from the language of the occupier?"[96]

For Wintjes, as for Rolf Dieter Brinkmann, the vitality and inspiration coming into Germany from abroad trumped these concerns, not least because, as Wintjes liked to point out, the originality and individualism of the alternative scene offered a necessary antidote to the "stereotypical (publishing) programs" of the increasingly monopolistic large publishers.[97] Referring to his enterprise with dry but literal wit as "the experiment of a single individual without any capital," Wintjes assumed the role of an alternative Robin Hood, fighting for the creative and political worth of the underground against the large publishers. These he often called out by name ("Peter Melzer I'm waiting for an answer!") in humorous

---

[95] *Ibid.*

[96] "Underground," *Ulcus Molle Infodienst*, nos. 9/10, 1973, p. 424.

[97] "Eil-nachricht an alle buchhandlungen. THEMA: alternativepresse & underground literatur" Literarisches Informationszentrum, July 1, 1971, in *Ulcus Molle Infodienst*, no. 8, July/August 1970.

but pointed diatribes against recuperative intentions and exploitive prices ("Where are the bootleg publishers?"). Wintjes's up-to-the-minute commentary on forthcoming publications – "When you become happy, is that already revolutionary?????" (in a blurb about a forthcoming issue of the countercultural commune-newspaper *Pääng*) – serve as a useful barometer of the kinds of questions that were being asked *circa* 1968 and afterward. In every case, Wintjes's comments were informed by a concern with *authenticity* as the ultimate arbiter of aesthetic, political, or spiritual worth, a concept that played a key role in other aspects of the antiauthoritarian revolt as well.

The listings and commentary in *Ulcus Molle Infodienst* read like a series of dialectic snapshots of the antiauthoritarian revolt in its moment of transition from a narrowly defined student movement to the more complex and diffuse interplay of initiatives and voices characteristic of the fractured "alternative" culture(s) of the post-1968 period. Yet the central questions being posed on the cusp of the 1970s – about the possibilities of working within the framework of capitalism, about recuperation, about the ownership of the cultural means of production, about the merit and content of cultural versus strictly political means of rebellion, about the value of working to change society from within versus attempting to leave it behind – cut through the entire antiauthoritarian revolt almost from its inception. The sheer number of publications produced beginning *c.* 1967–68, as well as their wide geographic distribution both within West Germany and beyond, indicates the extent to which the antiauthoritarian revolt in West Germany was a product of the desire to express hidden or inchoate ideas and perspectives. Any account of 1968 in West Germany, thus, that focuses narrowly on the student movement, at the expense of the sphere of "literary" production, or that implies the autonomy of the overall left project from the broader society of which it was a part (when, as this chapter has shown, the two cut across each other in key ways, provoking many of the most fundamental debates in the left publicistic sphere), misses one of the aspects of 1968 of the greatest contemporary and long-term significance.

CONCLUSION

Student/countercultural politics and alternative publishing were intimately connected. This is true not only because, as we saw in the case of the *Frankfurter Buchmesse* of 1968, the struggle over the meaning and content of the literary-publicistic sphere was inseparable from the struggle over access to public space, one of the key arenas of conflict with the authorities, but also because in the antiauthoritarian revolt, political action was inseparable from the production of knowledge. This is hardly surprising since in key revolutionary moments of the modern era – 1789, 1848, 1905/1917–surges in publicistic activity and surges in revolutionary activity went hand in hand. Arguably more than in any of the previous moments – owing in part to the wider availability of the cultural means of production (e.g. the Rotaprint printing press), in part to the more widespread literacy accompanying what was in its first movements a student revolt heavily supported by the literary and journalistic intelligentsia, 1968 in West Germany was a revolt of texts.

Key works such as Reich's *Function of the Orgasm*, or Mao's Red Book supplied a shared theoretical and symbolic repertoire that allowed activists to communicate with each other; it also allowed them, by referencing this shared repertoire, to perform (i.e. read, write, cite) their opposition to the system. It was not necessary in this context to have *read* a particular book in question; rather, books represented badges of membership in one or more of the radical transnational publics that helped constitute 1968. At the same time, texts provided one of the central vehicles through which activists of varying orientations tried to import *their* version of the "world" into West Germany. For the bohemian-literary-countercultural left, this meant the work of the American Beats and the underground press out of London, New York, and San Francisco; for the hard-political left it meant the works of Third World revolutionaries such as Che, Fanon, and Mao, American Black Power writers such as Stokely Carmichael and Angela Davis, and reports on the student unrest in France.

Characteristic is that in almost every case the necessary raw materials were seen to lie *outside* the Federal Republic. This was partly a result of the legacy of fascism, as we saw in the last chapter, which had erased indigenous traditions that then had to be painstakingly recovered by young activists trying to make sense of their current situation; but it was also a product of a globalizing, syncretic imagination that looked out in search of the newest and best on offer in a Europe and a world of increasing interconnectedness. This imagination helped drive an active transnationalism that strove to bring into the Federal Republic the work of writers, whether Che Guevara or Jack Kerouac, seen to be necessary in the West German situation.

Both aspects of the 68er publication program, the appropriation of existing texts from without and the creation of new texts from below, functioned as vehicles for the claim to the right to intervene in the production of meaning in society. In this sense, the cultural productions of bootleggers and alternative publishers resonated with a larger project, stretching across from the essays of the new critical journalism to the placards and handbills of the student movement, of challenging and proposing alternatives to the narrative claims of authority. The underground press, especially, became the publicistic analog to a radical democratic explosion in which a range of personal/political alternatives were thrown open for debate. If, as one scholar has observed, politics – especially grassroots politics – is the assertion of the right to speak, then the publicistic explosion became one of the primary sites in which the antiauthoritarian revolt in West Germany found its voice.[98] Yet the literary-publicistic sphere was only one area in which this speech was carried out; indeed, the antiauthoritarian revolt found expression across a range of communicative practices encompassing the visual arts, film, music, and personal style. These practices, as the following two chapters will demonstrate, were shot through with the same contradictions and dilemmas affecting literature.

[98] Ronald Grigor Suny, "Back and Beyond: Reversing the Cultural Turn?" *American Historical Review*, 107 (5) (December 2002): 1494–1495.

CHAPTER 4

Sound

In September 1968, the Ruhr Valley city of Essen hosted a cultural spectacle the likes of which Europe had never seen before. At the Internationale Essener Songtage (IEST; International Essen Song Days), dozens of musical acts from all over the world performed over a five-day period to an audience estimated at upward of 40,000 people. With light shows, experimental films, open-mic sessions and a psychedelic happening, the festival put on display for a European audience all the exciting new wares of the 1960s cultural revolution. Billed as "Europe's first great festival of folklore, folksong, chanson and good popular music" (note the distinction regarding popular music), the Songtage were explicitly conceived of as a European answer to the Monterey Pop Festival, which had taken place in California only a little over a year before.[1] At Monterey, where Jimi Hendrix concluded his sexually charged performance by setting fire to his Fender Stratocaster guitar, beckoning to the flames as feedback moaned through stacks of Marshall amplifiers, the link between the new youth culture and the revolutionary potential of popular music was solidified for a mass audience. In importing this revolution to West Germany, the organizers of The Essener Songtage bridged not only continents and cultures but also musical and artistic genres. Top American acts such as The Mothers of Invention and the Fugs shared billing with well-known figures of German political song such as Franz Josef Degenhardt and Dieter Süverkrüp; English performers such as Julie Driscoll with jazz musicians such as Gunter Hampel and Peter Brötzmann. Most strikingly of all, the festival showcased the new crop of German experimental rock bands, Amon Düül, Can, Tangerine Dream, and others, marking the breakout of German performers onto the world stage. Showcasing both international and local performers, attended by fans from throughout

---

[1] Internationale Essener Song Tage (IEST 68) veranstaltet (press release, English version), Sammlung Uwe Husslein, Cologne; *Information Nr 1*, Sammlung Uwe Husslein, Cologne.

Figure 4.1 Uschi Obermaier performs with Amon Düül at the Internationale Essener Songtage, September 1968. Photo: Jens Hagen.

Europe and beyond, the festival represented a key transnational moment of the late 1960s, signaling the birth of an international youth culture with popular music as its soundtrack. At the same time, the festival represented the dovetailing of the new youth culture with the new politics associated with the student left. Conceived by its organizers, and received by its establishment detractors, as an explicitly political event, the festival was rooted in confident assumptions about the fundamental symmetry between pop and politics.

Yet the left-wing extraparliamentary opposition in West Germany and the new popular music were by no means natural bedfellows. The student movement in 1960s West Germany exhibited little official interest in popular music. This was in part a matter of timing: the high period of the SDS mostly predated the massive politicization of popular music that was just getting started toward the end of the decade of the 1960s.[2] More fundamentally, however, the serious and highly theoretical orientation of the movement's leaders left little room for a consideration of the

---

[2] See Wolfgang Seidel, "Scherben ..." in Seidel, ed., *Scherben*, pp. 69–114.

potential emancipatory power of rock 'n' roll.[3] This was due in part to the influence of the Frankfurt School critique of popular culture, which held popular music, in particular, to be a debased product of the culture industry. Theodor Adorno, who worried in an early essay that the repetitive rhythms of popular music threatened to turn human beings into "insects," continued to vehemently insist, even at the height of the student movement, that popular music possessed no emancipatory potential whatsoever, admitting, in an interview on West German television, that he found the idea of "protest music" – in this case the protest songs of the American folksinger Joan Baez – "unbearable."[4]

The student intelligentsia did not, of course, hold such draconian views; there was wide acceptance of the notion that popular music conveyed a new life feeling that was antiauthoritarian both in intention and effect. Even the relatively straight-laced Rudi Dutschke could praise The Rolling Stones and Aretha Franklin as important harbingers of revolution alongside Malcolm X and Frantz Fanon.[5] Yet Dutschke does not seem to have had any deep understanding of the appeal of popular music. "We were ... in Hyde Park, wanted to listen to the 'Rolling Stones,'" he wrote in a diary entry of July 1969;

it was relatively boring[;] however it is a permanent phenomenon, that these "musicians" of the "young generation" are in the position, without any politically-defined "evaluations" of the societal situation, to bring 70,000 ... [people] out on "their" side, [whereas] the "left," working mostly with concepts and content of "tradition," are simply not in the position to find something in [Marx] that will ... capture the "new generation."[6]

Popular music, functioning as it did primarily at an emotional-visceral level, simply did not fit easily into Dutschke's serious student-Marxist paradigm.

---

[3] "In the Socialist German Student League," writes Detlef Siegfried, "Beat Music as mass culture was looked at skeptically, because, as Theodor Adorno postulated in connection with the Beatles, it 'represented in its objective form something backward'." Detlef Siegfried, "Unsere Woodstocks," p. 53.

[4] Where jazz is concerned, Adorno was almost wholly ignorant of that about which he wrote; for the historian Eric Hobsbawm, an avid jazz fan and critic, Adorno's writings on jazz represented "some of the stupidest pages ever written about jazz"; Eric Hobsbawm, *The Jazz Scene* (New York: Pantheon, 1993), p. 300.

[5] Dutschke, "Die geschichtlichen Bedingungen für den internationalen Emanzipationskampf," p. 260.

[6] Dutschke, *Diaries*, entry for July 5, 1969. "[Dutschke] no doubt failed to understand this enthusiasm," writes Wolfgang Seidel, "because there was a social disparity, but also a difference in age, between he (and the protagonists of SDS) and the young workers who were suddenly turning the demonstrations into mass events"; Seidel, "Berlin und die Linke in den 1960ern," p. 44.

Whatever the attitudes of middle-class German students, many of whom in any case retained high-cultural tastes in music, even if they embraced pop music as well, it was among young workers that popular music evoked its greatest resonance. The insurrectionary potential of young rock fans was demonstrated in spectacular terms in September 1965 when a concert by the English group The Rolling Stones in West Berlin's Waldbühne degenerated into a pitched battle between young fans and police. The protagonists, many of them rockers from Berlin's working-class Märkisches Viertel, had earlier in the day burst through police lines to enter the concert grounds without tickets.[7] After the Stones' performance of "Satisfaction," the short concert came abruptly to an end. "[P]eople stood up and wanted an encore," recalls Ralf Reinders, "[at which] point the organizer simply turned out the lights. And in a flash, total chaos broke out in the Waldbühne."[8] A pitched battle developed between the police and concert-goers, the former making liberal use of truncheons and water cannons, the latter tearing apart the stadium stands and pelting police with the debris. The battle continued on the S-Bahn. In the wake of the hours-long melee, seventeen city train cars were destroyed, four so badly that they had to be taken permanently out of service.[9]

At around the same time, youth in East Berlin were also rioting in connection with Beat music. Preliminary attempts of young East Germans to create their own Beat groups on the Western model, which produced a brief flowering of home-grown activity in the early 1960s, were halted by the crackdown initiated by the Eleventh Plenum of the Central Committee of the Socialist Unity Party (ZK der SED) in December 1965.

---

[7] Wolfgang Kraushaar, "Berliner Subkultur: Blues, Umherschweifende Haschrebellen, Tupamaros und Bewegung 2 Juni," in Martin Klimke and Joachim Scharloth, eds., *1968: Handbuch zur Kultur- und Mediengeschichte der Studentenbewegung* (Stuttgart: J. B. Metzler, 2007), pp. 261–275, at p. 262.

[8] See Ralf Reinders and Ronald Fritsch, *Die Bewegung 2 Juni: Gespräche über Haschrebellen, Lorenzentführung, Knast* (Berlin and Amsterdam: Edition ID-Archiv, 1995), pp. 14–15. See also Michael Baumann, *How It All Began* (Vancouver: Arsenal Pulp Press, 1977). Reinders's memory appears to fail him in his contention that the tickets for the 1965 show cost 20 deutsche marks, as pictures of the tickets posted on *Spiegel* online indicate that the ticket price was only 6 deutsche marks. It appears that the 20-deutsche-mark figure comes from the Stones' show at the Berliner Deutschlandhalle in September 1970, which also saw fans storm through barricades to enter the hall for free; see the comments by Fabian Wurm (July 11, 2012), available online at http://einestages.spiegel.de/s/td/25170/rolling-stones-konzert-in-der-waldbuehne.html (accessed November 5, 2012).

[9] "On the next day," writes Wolfgang Kraushaar, "the balance-sheet read: 87 injured, among them 26 police; 61 first-aid interventions of the Red Cross; 85 arrests; an injured police horse; a demolished loudspeaker truck; [and] countless overturned and damaged cars." The damages were estimated at 300,000 to 400,000 deutsche marks; Kraushaar, "Berliner Subkultur," p. 262.

Figure 4.2 Scenes from the Waldbühne, September 15, 1965. Bill Wyman (left), Brian Jones, Mick Jagger. Bildarchiv Preußischer Kulturbesitz. Photo: Alexander Enger.

Figure 4.3 Scenes from the Waldbühne, September 15, 1965. Bildarchiv Preußischer Kulturbesitz. Photo: Alexander Enger.

Figure 4.4 Scenes from the Waldbühne, September 15, 1965. Bildarchiv Preußischer Kulturbesitz. Photo: Alexander Enger.

Thereafter, both bands and fans could count on brutal suppression of any attempt to continue in the spirit of the Western bands they admired. Young music fans angered by the crackdown subsequently engaged in the largest protests since the workers' uprising of July 1953. The protests, in Leipzig in October 1965, were brutally repressed by police with water cannons, truncheons, and attack dogs. This assault established a pattern in the state's relationship with nonconformist youth culture that would persist, with occasional breaks, through the 1970s.[10]

Whereas in the East the space in which music-based youth protest could unfold was restricted at best, in the West, with its generally more relaxed attitude toward youth nonconformism, it could form the basis of a more thoroughgoing resistance. Ralf Reinders, like a number of the other concert-crashers a soon-to-be infamous member of the hard core of West

---

[10] A few years later, in October 1969, The Rolling Stones caused a riot again, this time in East Berlin, where young people attracted by the rumor that the Stones would be playing on the roof of the Axel Springer building on the Kochstraße overlooking the wall, were dispersed by riot police yielding truncheons and water cannons. Characteristically, in terms of the often-overlooked degree of cross-border communication, the rumor about The Rolling Stones' performance is supposed to have originated with an announcer on the American Cold War radio broadcaster RIAS (Radio in the American Sector).

Berlin's radicalized subcultural scene, the "Blues," cited the Waldbühne riot as a decisive first moment of politicization. "A mood developed there on this night," he recalls,

where for the first time I saw otherwise totally unpolitical people [develop] a maniacal hatred and frustration against the cops ... The battle raged for four, five hours, also on the surrounding streets. There for the first time I saw people lose it and really attack the cops. I had never known that to happen before.[11]

The battle, noted Reinders, produced "a little bit of community, a community feeling." Echoing Rudi Dutschke's assessment of the charge through police lines during the anti-Tshombe protests of a year before, Reinders saw that with the Waldbühne riot a psychological Rubicon had been crossed: "In 1965 the Stones came for the first time to Berlin. And for many of us came also a small breakthrough."[12]

The Waldbühne riot, like the Schwabing Riots three years earlier (or the West Berlin Bill Haley riots of 1958, the Leipzig riots of October 1965, or a host of other incidents on both sides of the Iron Curtain), showed the extent to which the performance of popular music could provide an arena for conflict with authority.[13] But it also indicated the capacity of popular music to serve as a vehicle for antiauthoritarian longings that could easily find concrete expression. That the riot took place at a Rolling Stones concert is entirely appropriate, indeed, for The Rolling Stones were accorded a political import far out of proportion with their actual political engagement. Their oppositional charge, as Detlef Siegfried has pointed out with respect to popular music more generally, came less from any explicit content than from the projections of their opponents, proponents, and fans.[14] The music of the Stones became a powerful vehicle for a feeling of rebellion that became connected, in the minds of both protagonists and commentators, with left-wing politics, even if this rebellion transcended the critical categories of student Marxism.[15] "The Stones criticized their impoverishment in illusionary consumption," wrote Peter Mosler, "the

[11] Reinders and Fritsch, *Die Bewegung 2 Juni*, p. 15.   [12] *Ibid.*

[13] On Bill Haley, see Uta Poiger, *Jazz, Rock, and Rebels: Cold War Politics and American Culture in a Divided Germany* (Berkeley, Calif.: University of California Press, 2000), pp. 91, 187. On the Leipzig riots, see Dorothee Wierling, "Beat heißt schlagen: Die Leipziger Beatdemonstration in Oktober 1965 und die Jugendpolitik der SED," in Rolf Geserick, ed., *Unsere Medien, Unsere Republik 2: 1965 – Warten auf den Frühling*, vol. IV (Marl: Deutschen Volkshochschul-Verbandes, 1993).

[14] Siegfried, "Unsere Woodstocks."

[15] Detlef Siegfried, "Music and Protest in 1960s Europe," in Klimke and Scharloth, *1968 in Europe*, pp. 57–70, at p. 59.

duping [of people with the idea of the] attainment of happiness through commodities. The Marxist-Leninists ... only ever criticized *capitalism.*"[16]

Songs such as "Satisfaction" – the big hit of the summer of 1965 – captured an inchoate sense of rebellion that was arguably the more powerful for its lack of specific target.[17] The song became "a type of anthem for the antiauthoritarians," recalls the Cologne photographer Jens Hagen;

> There's definitely a difference whether one listens to [The Beatles'] "Yellow Submarine," where it's about a nice old man in a fairytale world telling beautiful stories, or whether [in "Satisfaction"] you don't want to be hassled by some ... advertising man. Leave me alone with your shit! And with a rhythm that goes into your bones – music to riot by.[18]

The Stones derived their oppositional charge from their deep stylistic connection with the blues and from their perceived "proletarian" qualities. "There was a reason that it was the Stones and not the Beatles," writes Wolfgang Seidel; "whereas the sonic antecedents of the Beatles lay only partly in rock 'n' roll, and their sound was otherwise marked by a conventional European easy listening music [*Unterhaltungsmusik*], the Stones, with their rooting in the Blues, were, to the German ear, something very much like messengers from another world."[19]

Indeed, it was the otherness, the "not-German-ness" of popular music that marked it out as a vehicle of the utopian imagination; opening up new vistas beyond the often-grim realities of day-to-day life, music transmitted *possibility.* "Berlin was ... the place in Europe where one could hear the best music," remembers Antje Krüger of the Kommune I,

> and that was because [of], first of all, the [Armed Forces Radio], one of the best ... stations in the world. They were really fantastic. They played things here that weren't even allowed in the States ... You could listen right through from early in the morning ... to the end of the day. I never in my life had such an education. When [I] came home from school in the afternoon I would turn on the radio, and I would hear [some blues] or some crazy Hillbilly broadcast. And that was so foreign to me. And I wanted to understand it.[20]

The thrill of the forbidden foreign took on a special urgency in Germany, where indigenous musical traditions had been crushed, driven

[16] Peter Mosler, "Die Revolte frißt ihre Väter," originally published in *Diskus*, 6/75 8, in K. Kreuzer, R. Maroldt, P. Kopp, eds., *Die Mythen knacken. Materialien wider ein Tabu*, (Frankfurt: Linke Liste, 1987), 51–57.

[17] Jens Renner, *1968* (Hamburg: Europäische Verlagsanstalt/Rotbuch Verlag, 2001).

[18] Jens Hagen, quoted in Geulen and Graf, *Mach mal bitte platz*, p. 80.

[19] Seidel, "Berlin und die Linke in den 1960ern," p. 39.

[20] Antje Krüger, interview with the author, Berlin, September 2006.

underground or into exile.[21] The Nazi regime had banned jazz and blues as racially degenerate "nigger music."[22] Leading lights of the interwar music scene such as Marlene Dietrich and Kurt Weill disappeared to the USA. German cabaret performers with critical sensibilities had been driven from the stage, as had classical performers and conductors who refused to collaborate with the Nazis. "In musical terms," writes Wolfgang Seidel, "Berlin was a wasteland … A new music *had* to come here. And because the old had thoroughly disqualified itself, [this music] had automatically to come from outside – this 'outside' meant jazz, rock 'n' roll, and Beat."[23] The originally African-American provenance of this music only increased its subversive power.

That the new music came from outside West Germany was, moreover, a simple fact of a postwar cultural landscape in which Anglo-American cultural forms, and the technologies and channels of dissemination for distributing them, achieved an unparalleled preeminence; a landscape in which to be European was, for good or ill, to be on the receiving end of a cultural pipeline through which flowed the latest innovations of Hollywood and Detroit, London and Liverpool. Popular music was by far the most explosive of these imports.[24] The spread of new styles to Germany and elsewhere in Continental Europe began with the "Beat wave" of 1962. The new music was disseminated through multiple channels. The legendary residency of The Beatles at the Star-Club in Hamburg, as well as the later set of engagements by The Monks – a group of American GIs stationed in Germany who had remained after their discharge to pursue a musical career – helped solidify local music subcultures and spread the popularity of the new music.[25]

Specific new innovations in television and radio programming made the new music, as well as the American blues and soul music from which the British Invasion was largely derived, available to an even wider young audience. Military radio programming on the Armed Forces Network

---

[21] Reinhold Brinkmann and Christoph Wolff, *Driven into Paradise: The Musical Migration from Nazi Germany to the United States* (Berkeley, Calif.: University of California Press, 1999).

[22] See Michael H. Kater, *Different Drummers: Jazz in the Culture of Nazi Germany* (Oxford University Press, 2003).

[23] Seidel, "Berlin und die Linke in den 1960ern," pp. 27–28.

[24] See Mark Fenemore, *Sex, Thugs and Rock 'n' Roll: Teenage Rebels in Cold-War East Germany* (New York and Oxford: Berghahn Books, 2007); Poiger, *Jazz, Rock, and Rebels*; Ryback, *Rock around the Bloc*.

[25] The Monks are the subject of a recent documentary film, *Monks: The Transatlantic Feedback* (Dietmar Post and Lucia Palacios, 2006).

(AFN) and the British Forces Broadcasting Service (BFBS) had substantial civilian listenerships in Europe. Pirate radio stations such as
Radio Veronica in the Netherlands (broadcasting from 1960) and Radio
Nord (broadcasting from a ship anchored in international waters off
the coast of Sweden from March 1961) made new music available irre-
spective of local radio programming formats. Radio London and Radio
Caroline both began broadcasting all-pop formats from ships moored
in the English Channel beginning in 1964.[26] Starting the following year,
the latest British and American pop sensations were beamed directly
into West German homes by the German television program *Beat Club*.
Modeled on British programs such as *Top of the Pops* and *Ready, Steady,
Go!*, the Bremen-based program had a viewership of 75 million people
by 1968.[27]

"THE GERMANS MEET THE UNDERGROUND": THE ESSENER SONGTAGE OF 1968

The Essener Songtage of 1968 was meant to make explicit what had before
been merely implicit: to codify the centrality of popular music for the
youth revolution and to express its fundamental connectedness with other
emancipatory forms of cultural expression. In a way typical of an era of
high expectations and boundless optimism, and in keeping with the
scholarly scientific imperative according to which cultural activity needed
to be theorized and legitimated, the organizers of the Essener Songtage
conceived of their project in grandiose terms. The festival was to be "the
greatest thing of its kind that has ever existed in Europe," a total event
bridging musical and artistic genres while staking a claim for the political and social relevance of popular culture.[28] The leading light of the
festival was a twenty-five-year-old music journalist from Cologne named
Rolf Ulrich Kaiser. A pop-cultural renaissance man who first came to
appreciate the social significance of popular music in connection with the
annual folk-song festivals at Burg Waldeck, Kaiser played a role in the
debates around the political function of the festival during the mid 1960s.
Like Rolf Dieter Brinkmann, he looked abroad for sources of inspiration,
reaching out to bring the best of the world into West Germany even as he
sought to place West German innovations into the world. For Kaiser as

[26] Siegfried, "Music and Protest," p. 61.   [27] *Ibid.*
[28] IEST 68 press release. See the photos and press excerpts on the festival in Holl and Glunz, *1968
am Rhein.*

well, America and Britain were the twin lodestars. In 1967, he published a book on the international folk scene featuring interviews with leading American figures such as Joan Baez and Pete Seeger. Two years later he co-founded the Ohr record label, which became home to many of the new experimental German rock groups who appeared at the Songtage. With his hand in radio, production, promotion, and publishing – he wrote some dozen books on popular music and underground culture between 1967 and 1972 – Kaiser was an indispensable organizational and intellectual talent behind the rise of the nascent German rock scene for which British music journalists coined the term "Krautrock."[29]

The rise of this new German scene was connected with a reevaluation of the import of popular music. No longer simply entertainment directed at teenagers, no longer just "Beat music," as the music associated with the original British invasion was known in Germany, popular music was now to be recognized as a serious artistic and social force in its own right. This reevaluation was carried forward in the new West German music periodicals such as *Sound* and *Song*. The decision of the latter in 1967 to begin covering pop and rock as "serious music" alongside jazz and folk was indicative of the new direction.[30] It is easy to forget that, until the late 1960s, it was folk and avant-garde jazz that represented, for the young intelligentsia, the primary font of musical innovation. A key goal of the organizers of the Essener Songtage, which included, alongside Kaiser, Martin Degenhardt (brother of the singer Josef) and Thomas Schroeder, was to transmit this new evaluation of the worth of pop music to a mass audience.

The assertion of worth, regarding not just popular music but also the broader culture of lifestyle and artistic experimentation with which it was connected, was expressed by the organizers of the Songtage through the idea of the "underground," a term gaining a new currency in the 1960s as it was applied to aspects of the cultural explosion (e.g. "underground film"). The Songtage marked one of the first times that the idea of "the

[29] Uwe Husslein, "'Heidi Loves You!' in Knallgelb – oder: Pyschedelia in Germania," in *Summer of Love: Art of the Psychedelic Era* (Stuttgart, 2006). Kaiser's books include *Protestfibel: Formen einer neuen Kultur – Mit einem lexikographischen Anhang von Rolf-Ulrich Kaiser* (Bern: Scherz Verlag, 1968); *Zapzapzappa: Das Buch der Mothers of Invention* (Cologne: Kinder der Geburtstagpresse, 1969); *B ist doch ein Scheißer: Das Beste aus der deutschen Untergrundpresse* (Düsseldorf: Econ-Verlag, 1969); *Das Buch der Neuen Pop-Musik* (Düsseldorf: Econ-Verlag, 1969); *Underground? Pop? Nein! Gegenkultur!* (Cologne: Kiepenheuer & Witsch, 1970). The term "Krautrock" retains currency to the present day. For a treatment of Krautrock in English, see Julian Cope, *Krautrocksampler: One Head's Guide to the Great Kosmische Musik – 1968 Onwards* (Yatesbury: Head Heritage, 1995).

[30] Husslein, "'Heidi Loves You!'"

underground" was systematically propagated as an antidote to the artistic and spiritual deficiencies of the "mainstream." "One person shivers or makes the sign of the cross," read the festival's press release,

> another smells subversive intentions, many think of the metro, a few on the revolution, most don't even know where to begin with the idea: underground. What that it, underground or *Untergrund*, will be shown by the Internationalen Essener Song Tage, IEST '68, from the 25th to the 29th of September. IEST '68 will not only be Europe's biggest festival of Folklore, Chanson, Folksong und popular music, but also a mammoth underground party, a celebration of what astute thinkers from McLuhan to Scheuch have designated subculture.[31]

The use of terms such as "subculture" and "underground" and the reference to scholars such as Marshall McLuhan and Erwin Scheuch were part of an attempt to legitimize the festival and the youth revolution it claimed to represent. This focus was evident in the organizers' trumpeting of the "Brain Trust" of experts involved in choosing acts and the inclusion of panels and seminars during the festival to discuss the social significance of popular music.[32] "[The] choice of artists," argued the organizers, "shows that this festival does not shut out [popular music], but ... makes a definite [distinction] between tearjerkers and hit-songs."[33]

The assertion of popular music's artistic merit complemented the attempt to establish its political credentials. The two were intimately linked, indeed, for the claim to rock music's artistic significance (and the attempt to connect rock music with a lineage embracing folk, jazz, and political song) were part of a larger attempt to establish and legitimize a sphere of cultural activity autonomous from traditional spheres and producers of culture.[34] This autonomous sphere of culture, the "underground," was not a sphere of "conspiracy and criminality," argued the organizers, but rather a sphere in which it was possible "to produce ... without worrying about the commercial potential, that which is fun, which corresponds to one's own convictions, which the established producers can't and don't want to do, and which is therefore not available in the [mainstream] market."[35] The idea of the underground was linked,

---

[31] Internationale Essener Song Tage (IEST 68) veranstaltet (press release: German version), Sammlung Uwe Husslein, Cologne.

[32] Each day of the festival included a morning seminar on "The Song as a Means of Expression in Our Time" (IEST 68 English press release).

[33] *Information Nr 1*, Sammlung Uwe Husslein, Cologne.

[34] Frank Gingeleit, "The 'Progressive Seventies' in South Western Germany: Rock in the Rhein-Neckar Area – Nine Days' Wonder, Kin Ping Meh, Twenty Sixty Six and Then, Tritonus," *Aural Innovations*, 21 (2002).

[35] IEST 68 German press release.

in short, with the right to produce an alternative culture from below, a right linked with the assertion of artistic and social worth; the goal was "to advance and expand [through] ownership of the means of production, that which is created with the intention, not to entertain, but to enlighten, to agitate, to provoke, to develop awareness."[36]

Many of the performers at the festival were, accordingly, chosen both for artistic and political merit. The political aspects of performers such as The Mothers of Invention and The Fugs, the German agit-rock group Floh de Cologne and political singer-songwriters such as Wolf Biermann (an East German) were emphasized in the festival's press releases. One entire segment of the festival – "Seht Euch diese Typen an!" (Look at These Guys) – was dedicated to protest singers.[37] Mocking overheated comments by SPD politician Klaus Schütz ("You have to look at these guys. You have to look them right in the face. Then you will know that for them, it all revolves around destroying our free constitutional order"), the title of the segment clearly aimed at solidifying the link between underground culture and New Left politics.[38] Acts such as Floh de Cologne and The Fugs did not disappoint, the latter parading a porcine presidential candidate on stage during a performance featuring Vietcong flags and posters likening American Vice President Hubert Humphrey to Adolf Hitler.[39] Such provocations had the desired effect of scandalizing West German opinion, but such explicit political displays represented only one face of the link between politics and music in the Essener Songtage.

As important as the explicit antiauthoritarianism of many of the new performers was the perceived consonance between the experimental thrust of much of the new music – freer form, longer compositions, more eclectic instrumentation, the use of the new sonic possibilities offered by electronic amplification in general and the electronically amplified guitar in particular – which differentiated it from the more or less blues-based, more or less derivative compositions of Beat music. In marking out "German Rock as a musical-political-psychedelic experimentation field," the Songtage helped to solidify a new linkage between musical experimentation and cultural-political experimentation.[40] This linkage

---

[36] *Ibid.*

[37] The concert took place on Thursday afternoon in the large hall of the Essen youth center (the Youth Welfare Office of Essen was a co-sponsor of the event) and was repeated the following day in a different venue; "Diese Typen," Sammlung Uwe Husslein, Cologne.

[38] "Diese Typen," *Der Spiegel*, no. 8, February 11, 1968.

[39] "Sex Show mit Vietkong Fahne," *Hellweger Anzeiger*, September 27, 1968.

[40] Gingeleit, "The 'Progressive Seventies'"; Siegfried, "Unsere Woodstocks," p. 55.

was carried forward in the festival's attempt to recreate, on West German soil, the psychedelic happenings of San Francisco and New York. The Saturday night blow-out in Essen's Grugahalle, entitled "Take a Trip to Asnidi" (or as festival co-organizer Thomas Schroeder preferred to call it, "Take a Trip to *Hash*nidi"), accomplished this in grand style.[41] With 10,000 fans in attendance, light and strobe effects, continuously running underground films, musical performances on two stages (often simultaneously) and Frank Zappa of The Mothers of Invention shouting "freak out" to the stoned masses, the event was meant to signal the full-scale arrival of the psychedelic revolution in West Germany.[42]

This unwelcome prospect was received with predictable alarm by the establishment. Press accounts of the festival, although not uniformly negative, emphasized its chaotic aspects while questioning its claims of political and social relevance. The condescending and sarcastic tone of much of the coverage was in part a product of the unprecedented tensions of the previous few years between members of the extraparliamentary opposition and defenders of the status quo, but it also reflected an attempt by the establishment to come to grips with the way in which the two previously more or less separate foes of pop music and political protest seemed to be dovetailing together and evolving into some new as yet poorly understood but vaguely dangerous animal. The impression of a "revolutionary" popular culture, and the conflation of the rhetoric of left-wing extremism with the rhetoric of youth cultural revolution, was a product not just of the festival organizers' grand pronouncements, but also, as Detlef Siegfried has shown, heavily reinforced in the music advertising of the period.[43] The link between pop and revolution forged by the Kommune I also played a role, and, indeed, numerous press reports before the event speculated that members of the commune were traveling from Berlin to take part in the festivities.[44] In the aftermath of the festival, journalists deplored the "dirty hippies" who had descended on Essen. Many papers expressed dismay at the "obscene" performances by groups such as Floh de Cologne and The Fugs. Special outrage – and much coverage – was reserved for an incident in which Mayor Wilhelm

[41] *Song-Magazine der IEST*; The Saturday night "happening" at the Grugahalle figures in a recent novel by Bernd Cailloux; see Bernd Cailloux, *Das Geschäftsjahr 1968/69* (Frankfurt: Suhrkamp, 2005).

[42] Husslein, "'Heidi Loves You!'"

[43] Siegfried, "Unsere Woodstocks," p. 55. See also Siegfried, *Time Is on My Side*.

[44] "Kommune auch dabei," in *Siegener Zeitung*, September 26, 1968. See also Peter W. Schröder, "Auch ohne Teufel war der Teufel los," *Wormser Zeitung*, September 26, 1968.

Nieswandt was jeered and pelted with beer coasters by "members of the extraparliamentary opposition."[45]

Significantly, some of the most biting criticism was reserved for the intellectual and political claims of the festival organizers. A number of writers juxtaposed the intellectual claims of West Germany's "critical youth" – based in a commitment to the Critical Theory of the Frankfurt School and exemplified in the founding of a "Critical University" in West Berlin in late 1966 – with the politics of cultural provocation on display at the festival.[46] One writer concluded that young people who applauded an "obscene" performance by Floh de Cologne renounced any claim to possessing a critical intelligence: "Twenty minutes of stage time were filled up with … the showing of obscene pictures [accompanied by] bestial cries. [The performers] were assured of applause all the same."[47] Glee over the alleged failure of young smart alecks to live up to their bold rhetoric – "critical youth asleep in Essen" was a fairly typical putdown – fairly leaps off the pages of the press coverage of the festival.[48] The concept of the "underground" – as in "culture bums from the underground" – was the object of sarcastic attention.[49] In a piece published even before the festival had begun, "New Magical Formula for the Uninhibited? The Germans meet the Underground," the *Bayernkurier* worried about what Germany should expect from an "underground" imported from the USA, a leading "hotbed of new religions for the frustrated neurotic."[50] With rather more sophistication, *Die Zeit* put its finger on the paradox of an "underground" placed on sale for mass consumption. "Entry into the underground," the paper wryly observed, "was not free."[51]

"WHAT WE HAVE DONE, EVERYONE CAN DO": TON STEINE SCHERBEN AND THE POLITICS OF (SUB)CULTURAL PRODUCTION

Such criticisms hardly detracted from the success of the festival, which even many of its critics grudgingly acknowledged, but they did identify an unresolved tension at the heart of the festival's attempt to combine

---

45 Peter W. Schroeder, "Den OB machen wir fertig," *Augsberger Allgemeine*, October 6, 1968.
46 On the critical university, see Fichter and Lönnendonker, *Kleine Geschichte des SDS*, pp. 112–114.
47 Rudiger Knott, "Auch Revoluzzer mögen Mußestunden," *Neckar und Enzbote*, September 30, 1968.
48 "*Die kritische Jugend schlief in Essen*," *Rheinische-Merkur*, October 1, 1968.
49 Kurt Unold, "Unter-, vorder-, hintergründig: 'Kultur Bums' aus dem Untergrund bei 'Essener-Song Tagen,'" *5-Uhr Blatt*, October 1, 1968.
50 "Neue Zauberformel für Hemmungslose?" *Bayernkurier*, September 9, 1968.
51 Manfred Sack, "Underground an der Oberfläche," *Die Zeit*, no. 40, October 4, 1968, p. 14.

music with politics and art with commerce, a tension that would become more pronounced in the years to follow. In the aftermath of the Songtage, Rolf Ulrich Kaiser answered charges that the festival had failed in its aims by underlining the vital link between culture and politics. He argued that by "present[ing], in all its diversity, the other culture that until now lived [only] in the underground," the festival had helped prepare the way for the elimination of taboos in television, radio, and the recording industry. This emancipatory impulse, he argued, could not but have positive political consequences.[52] Yet the idea of subculture connected with the festival, and the easy relationship between consumerism and revolution it assumed, became a point of heated contention as the psychedelic hippie era of optimistic experimentation began to turn, in West Germany, into a highly politicized and bitter struggle between denizens of the subculture and the rest of society. Even as consumer capitalism became more adept at commodifying youthful rebellion, rock music became more and more an explicit vehicle for radical politics.

The Essener Songtage had featured two openly "political" bands, the American Fugs and the Cologne-based Floh de Cologne, both of whom, as we have seen, succeeded in scandalizing mainstream observers. Floh de Cologne were prominent members of the same Cologne countercultural scene as Rolf Dieter Brinkmann, although their politics tended eventually toward the DKP, a position that countercultural activists such as Brinkmann tended to abhor. Another noteworthy radical group, not yet together at the time of the Songtage, was Ton Steine Scherben. A band of enduring significance, not only because of the subsequent rock-star career of its lead singer Rio Reiser but also because of the emotional force and staying power of political anthems such as "Keine Macht für Niemand" ("No Power for Anyone") and "Macht kaputt was euch kaputt macht" ("Destroy What Destroys You"), Ton Steine Scherben continues to be remembered as the band that supplied the "soundtrack for the revolt of a generation." More importantly, Ton Steine Scherben were deeply involved in the radical scene in West Berlin at the end of the 1960s, and their history and the history of the radicalized West Berlin counterculture *c.* 1970 are largely inseparable.[53]

The West Berlin scene at the end of the 1960s was rife with musical experimentation. Many of the new West German groups featured at the

---

[52] "Songtage waren Hoffnung für die 'Kultur aus dem Untergrund,'" *Westdeutsche Allgemeine Zeitung*, no. 229, October 1, 1968.
[53] See Timothy S. Brown, "Music as a Weapon? Ton Steine Scherben and the Politics of Rock in Cold War Berlin," *German Studies Review*, 32 (1) (2009): 1–22.

Figure 4.5 Ton Steine Scherben performing their first single "Macht kaputt was euch kaputt macht," 1971. Pictured are bassist Kai Sichtermann and drummer Wolfgang Seidel. Photo: Jutta Matthess.

Essener Songtage, groups such as Tangerine Dream and Agitation Free, came from West Berlin. A center of the nascent "Krautrock" scene was the Zodiak Free Arts Lab, opened in 1968 by Conrad Schnitzler. A sound and video artist with roots in the Fluxus movement, Schnitzler was assisted in the undertaking by members of his bands Geräusche ("Noises"), Human Being, and Kluster (later Cluster).[54] Like his mentor, the iconoclastic artist Joseph Beuys (see Chapter 5), Schnitzler adhered to a concept of art aimed at breaking down the boundaries between performer and audience. "[When] we started the Zodiak," he recalls,

it was basically a hippy hangout and I didn't want that. I wanted it cool, like black and white and nothing [else]. So we put in lots of pinball machines – that's

normal – but also lots of music boxes, five or six, and a bunch of radios ... So
the audience could play! ... So we would turn all the radios on and the pinball
machines would be going and the notice board had all these messages on them
like, "I'm looking for a girl" or "I'm following Mao," whatever, it was amaz-
ing ... It was a fantastic space and we played there for a year or so and everyone
did shows there, Ash Ra Temple, Tangerine Dream, Klaus Schulze. It was then
that we started Eruption, the whole concept of which was based around the idea
of always breaking out, breaking out from everything, erupting![55]

The Zodiak was a hot spot for both free jazz and experimental electronic music, and a major scene hangout. In the smoky strobe-lit bowels
of the Zodiak, distinctions between culture and politics, thin at all times
in the West Berlin of 1968, melted away to nothing. Members of the nascent Blues scene, veterans of the 1965 Rolling Stones riot such as Michael
Bommi Baumann and Ralf Reinders, were regulars at the Zodiak, as
were art students and cultural provocateurs such as Antje Krüger of
the Kommune I.[56] Students, workers, and young bohemians mingled
together in the Zodiak in a common flight into subcultural utopia.

By the time Ton Steine Scherben were founded in the summer of 1970,
sharing a rehearsal space on the Adelbertstraße in Berlin-Kreuzberg
with Zodiak regulars Tangerine Dream, the Zodiak had been closed
by police, but the scene that had coalesced at the Zodiak continued to
exist, and the Scherben were at the heart of it. Their roots lay in radical
street theater. The group's direct precursor, Hoffmann's Comic Teater
(Berliner Volkstheater), was a creative alliance between three brothers,
Gert, Peter, and Ralph Möbius (the future Rio Reiser).[57] Wearing colorful costumes and fanciful masks, accompanied by a live band for which
Ralph wrote the songs, the brothers performed on the streets and in the
youth homes of West Berlin beginning in 1969. Their aim was to create
an art that would liberate consciousness and thereby lead to political
action. To this end they developed a dozen or so pieces depicting the
conflicts of daily life, several of which would later supply the basis of
Ton Steine Scherben songs.

---

[55] Conrad Schnitzler, in *The Wire*, no. 267 (May 2006).
[56] When the Kommune I moved to its new Warhol-inspired "factory" in the Stephanstraße in late
summer 1968, Schnitzler's band Geräusche rehearsed in a space on the ground floor; "Everyone
who looked in the door, whether they could play an instrument or not, got involved"; Wolfgang
Seidel, "Freie Kunst," *Jungle World*, May 12, 2004.
[57] The troupe was named after the eighteenth-century poet and dramatist E. T. A. Hoffmann; see
"Informationen: Hoffmanns Comic Teater. Prospekt Programm," Rio-Reiser-Archiv, Berlin.

The flagship among these was the piece *Rita and Paul*, which was performed for the first time at a youth center in the Naunynstraße in Berlin-Kreuzberg in the fall of 1969.[58] The piece represented the centerpiece of the troupe's attempt to create a politically effective art: "The first goal of the theater group is to turn the theater into a practical and transferable weapon. The musical Rita und Paul is the first product of this work." The piece was a sort of Romeo and Juliet tale revolving around a young worker, Paul (portrayed by Ralf Möbius), and Rita, the daughter of a factory owner. In one scene a frustrated Paul sees the face of a conservative commentator on his TV screen. "At that point," writes Gert Möbius, "Paul, in biblical pose, grabbed the television and with burning rage smashed it to the ground."[59] The scene was followed by the performance of a song with a soon-to-be legendary refrain: "Macht kaputt was euch kaputt macht."[60] An iconic expression of rage and violent resistance against the multiple oppressions of daily life, the song would be recorded a year later as Ton Steine Scherben's first single.[61]

Audience participation was a critical element in the performances of Hoffmann's Comic Teater: Masks were laid out on a table, and young workers were invited onto the stage to play out scenes from their own lives.[62] Central to Hoffmann's Comic Teater's conception of theater was that the boundary between performer and spectator must be broken down and that the contribution of the latter was equal to, if not more important than, that of the former. "The predominant cultural and political consciousness of the audience member," read point no. 1 of the group's guidelines, "is the starting point for the planning and realization of the play."[63] A group of young apprentices who first appeared on the evening in the Naunynstraße performed with such verve and assurance that they were

---

[58] Kai Sichtermann, Jens Johler, and Christian Stahl, *Keine Macht für Niemand: Die Geschichte der "Ton Steine Scherben"* (Berlin: Schwarzkopf & Schwarzkopf, 2000), p. 16.

[59] Gert Möbius, "Hoffmanns Comic Teater, Rote Steine, Ton Steine Scherben, 1969–1971," *Kreuzberger Hefte*, no. 6, *Ton Steine Scherben: Geschichten, Noten, Texten und Photos au 15 Jahren* (Berlin: Dirk Nishen Verlag in Kreuzberg, 1985).

[60] The lyrics to the song were written by Norbert Krause.

[61] For a first-hand account by a member of Hoffmann's Comic Teatre, see Achim Müller, "Eisen erzieht," in Seidel, ed., *Scherben: Musik, Politik und Wirkung der Ton Steine Scherben*, pp. 115–124. See video of the band performing "Macht kaputt was euch kaputt macht" at www.youtube.com/watch?v=UwE8dlRnsio (accessed December 1, 2008).

[62] "Informationen."

[63] "Informationen," p. 15. Point no. 2 continues, "There should in the play be no unknown premises [*Voraussetzungen*], that is, no premises that are known to the actor, but not the audience member" (p. 16).

invited into a creative alliance with the members of Hoffmann's Comic Teater. In early 1970, the group split off to perform on their own as the Rote Steine, Proletarisches Lehrlingstheater.[64] Ralph and Gert Möbius continued to perform with the Rote Steine, while Peter Möbius – along with Kai Sichtermann and R. P. S. Lanrue, both later founding members of Ton Steine Scherben – remained with Hoffmann's Comic Teater. Like Hoffmann's Comic Teater, the Rote Steine tried to foster political consciousness through audience participation. "We attempt through our performances," stated the group in a manifesto,

to get young people to ponder their situation. The scenes are improvised. The performance is very simple, because a person plays a situation with which he is familiar. We play with masks, which at the end of the performance are distributed among the audience. In this way we attempt to get the spectator to play along … We see the basic task as the building of more theater groups. When more groups are built, more young people will ponder their situation and the more there are, the stronger we will be. Only when we are strong can we change our situation![65]

Rooted in lived experience, the engaged theater of the Rote Steine mirrored a key theme of the 1960s revolution in West Germany, that of self-liberation through action. In speaking the previously unspeakable, making visible previously taken-for-granted authoritarian relationships (between boss and worker, teacher and student, parent and child), Hoffmann's Comic Teater and the Rote Steine penetrated to the heart of the New Left understanding of locating the political in the everyday.[66]

At the same time, the Rote Steine were part of a transformation in the nature of left-wing politics in West Germany at the end of the 1960s, which began to include new actors motivated by new concerns. This shift was marked by a new focus on workers in general and young workers in particular, a particular focus of the emerging Marxist-Leninist and/or Maoist *K-Gruppen*. Alongside these were the *Basisgruppen* ("rank-and-file groups"), which represented a sort of "going to the people" on the part of the young left-wing intelligentsia, linked with a new focus on mobilizing working-class youth. At the same time, the countercultural stream of

---

[64] Sichtermann et al., *Keine Macht für Niemand.*

[65] See a slightly different version of the founding of the Rote Steine in Möbius, "Hoffmanns Comic Teater, Rote Steine, Ton Steine Scherben, 1969–1971."

[66] Hoffmann's Comic Teatre also became involved in working with children, a characteristic concern of the West German New Left. See the piece by Peter Möbius based on the group's experience in the Spielclub Kulmerstraße, a project of the Arbeitsgemeinschaft Spielumwelt in der Berliner Neuen Gesellschaft für bildende Kunst; Peter Möbius, *Kursbuch*, no. 34, December 1973, pp. 25–48.

Figure 4.6 The Rote Steine, Berlin-Kreuzberg. Photo: Jutta Matthess.

the 68er movement, which had begun to crystallize around the commune scene in 1968–1969, became increasingly autonomous and radical. Out of this stream arose the West Berlin Blues, a prototerrorist scene of anarchist hippies blending countercultural style with militant opposition to the state.[67] Both the Blues scene and the *Basisgruppen* represented a new privileging of the local. Their retreat into the neighborhood, the *Kiez*, was an attempt both to transform society by focusing on concrete local struggles and to escape from society by forming autonomous enclaves. It is with the most important of these enclaves – Berlin-Kreuzberg – that the name Ton Steine Scherben is indelibly linked.

Relegated by the building of the Berlin Wall to the margins of the city, with cheap rents, Kreuzberg was a major destination for would-be Bohemians in West Germany in the late 1960s and 1970s. For the leader

[67] A classic description of this scene is to be found in Baumann, *How It All Began*. See also Reinders and Fritsch, *Die Bewegung 2 Juni*.

of Ton Steine Scherben, Ralph Möbius, the district was attractive for a number of reasons. A Christian with a deep concern for social justice (although not a self-advertising one in a largely areligious left-wing milieu), an avid reader of the adventure stories of Karl May, and a homosexual (not openly until 1976), Reiser was an outsider with a powerful commitment to the weak and the marginalized. With its population of young workers, retirees, and Turkish immigrants, Kreuzberg was a perfect field of engagement for his populist romanticism. The band that would give expression to this romanticism was founded in August 1970 in a room off the Adalbertstraße in the heart of "Kreuzberg 36." It included, alongside Rio Reiser, drummer Wolfgang Seidel, guitarist R. P. S. Lanrue, and bassist Kai Sichtermann. The name Ton Steine Scherben was suggested by Reiser. "It sound[ed] socialist," writes bassist Kai Sichtermann, "or at least trade-union-like." But it also represented "a secret greeting to the band that was for us the greatest model: The Rolling Stones."[68]

The group's populist orientation asserted itself in a number of ways, not least in its musical innovations. One of these had to do with language. Ton Steine Scherben was the first German rock group to sing in German, a highly unusual step in an era when rock performers in Continental Europe tended to ape Anglo-American models right down to the language.[69] Using German was not a nationalist statement but a localist one; it was meant to allow the group to connect as intimately as possible with its target audience, the apprentices and young workers of Kreuzberg. Communicating in a rough proletarian vernacular, alternately sung, spoken, and shouted, Rio Reiser achieved a truer and more sophisticated level of artistic expression. But he also made a political point: that the needs of everyday people, the realities of daily life, trumped norms and standards imposed from the outside. "There are often real conversations that happen on the street, in pubs, or in the workplace," noted the band in an interview in early 1971; "[w]e just had to write them down."[70]

---

[68] Part of the appeal of the Stones lay, tellingly, in that they seemed "proletarian"; Sichtermann et al., *Keine Macht für Niemand*, p. 14. The name Ton Steine Scherben echoed the name of the trade union Bau Steine Erden; Sichtermann et al., *Keine Macht für Niemand*, p. 11. A further connotation, of "stones" breaking glass into "shards," is obvious.

[69] Hartmut El Kurdi, *Schwarzrote Pop-Perlen: Keine Macht für Niemand – Ton Steine Scherben, The Essence of Rock*, vol. II (Hannover: Wehrhanverlag, 2001). Singer Udo Lindenberg is often mistakenly given credit for being the first German-language rock performer.

[70] Peter Winkler, "Aggressiv, kritisch und unverschleiert: die Berliner 'Ton Steine Scherben,'" *Berliner Zeitung*, February 16, 1971.

This method influenced not only the language in which the songs were sung but also the themes with which they dealt. The title of the group's first album, *Warum geht es mir so dreckig* (1971), captured perfectly their concern with exploring the subjectivity and psychology of oppression rooted in the experience of daily life. The first single "Macht kaputt was euch kaputt macht," captured in a rough clipped prose the frustration of man caught in a world of inexorable and impersonal forces. The first stanza – "radios play, records play, films play, TVs play, buy vacations, buy cars, buy houses, buy furniture, what for?" – expressed a deep skepticism about consumer capitalist society and the happiness that possessions were supposed to bring.[71] Both a collective refusal and a call to arms, the refrain "Macht kaputt was euch kaputt macht" ("Destroy what destroys you") was expressive of the new level of combativeness with which this critique was being pursued at the beginning of the 1970s.[72]

In musical terms, the Scherben offered a raw, stripped-down sound, blues-based, with distorted guitars and sing-along refrains. While the influence of English "Beat groups" such as The Rolling Stones and The Kinks is obvious, the Scherben occupied a transitional space among the genres. Like their American contemporaries the MC-5 – a group also known for its association with radical politics and with whom they toured Europe in 1972 – the Scherben anticipated the punk rock of the late 1970s. They can be placed alongside other "proto-punk" groups such as the New York Dolls and The Stooges, bands that helped forge a link between the rock music of the 1960s and 1970s and the more stripped-down punk variant of the late 1970s and 1980s. In the case of the Scherben, however, there was a more fundamental link with punk that lay less in the realm of music per se than in the conditions of its production and distribution. Like many of the punk, post-punk and hardcore bands of the 1980s, the Scherben sought to bypass capitalist means of production and distribution, releasing their music on their own record label and distributing it through nontraditional channels. In embracing what would later be called a DIY aesthetic, the Scherben bridged the gap between the independent cultural practice of the 1960s and the explosion of independent bands, labels, and publishers accompanying the rise of punk from the end of the 1970s.

---

[71] "Macht kaputt was euch kaputt macht," *Warum geht es mir so dreckig* (David Volksmund, 1971).

[72] For a detailed analysis of the lyrics of "Macht kaputt was euch kaputt macht," see Werner Faulstich, *Zwischen Glitter und Punk: Tübinger Vorlesungen zur Rockgeschichte Teil III, 1972–1982* (Rothernburg-Oberdorf: Wissenschaftler Verlag, 1986), Chapter 22.

In the hands of Ton Steine Scherben, this cultural innovation functioned in explicitly political terms. The name of the band's record label, David Volksmund, combined a reference to the biblical story of David and Goliath (complete with slingshot logo) with the idea of the "people's voice," perfectly capturing the essence of the group's project. The idea of an artist-run record label was highly novel at a time when the official culture industry administered almost every aspect of the process of production and distribution of music. Very frequently, the industry controlled even the act of composition itself. Here, too, the Scherben went against the grain by writing their own compositions and singing them in German. The band's debut single and album did brisk business in the left-wing bookstore circuit. The band reported selling 10,000 copies of the "Macht kaputt was euch kaputt macht" single, and a similar number of the *Warum geht es mir so dreckig* (*Why Am I So Miserable?*) LP.[73] By the end of the decade, the Scherben had sold 300,000 copies of their own albums with no advertising and next to no radio airplay.[74] The Scherben were also precocious in publishing their own "fanzine," *Guten Morgen*. Reproducing lyrics, photos, and commentary in a vivid cut-and-paste style, the magazine combined a concern with local, neighborhood issues with issues drawn from the broader world, such as women's and gay liberation, Black Power and the American Indian Movement, and the armed guerrilla struggle in West Germany. The main message of the fanzine – of the group's entire project – was expressed in the introduction to *Guten Morgen*: "What we have done, everyone can do."[75]

This emphasis on self-management, both artistic and political, bled over into Ton Steine Scherben's more public commitments. It was symbolized most strongly by the band's role in the creation of West Berlin's legendary squat, the Georg von Rauch Haus. The background to the creation of the Rauch Haus lay in a project of urban renewal begun by mayor Willy Brandt in 1963. According to the initiative, Kreuzberg was to be used as a giant canvas for modern urban planning. The plan, which envisioned the tearing down of buildings containing some 16,000 individual living spaces, was put into action in 1968–1969.[76] The politicization of this issue – of the issue of what was to become of the buildings

[73] *Guten Morgen*, Rio-Reiser-Archiv, Berlin, p. 45.
[74] Albert Koch, *Angriff auf's Schlaraffenland: 20 Jahre deutschsprachige Popmusik* (Frankfurt: Ullstein Verlag, 1987), p. 53.
[75] *Guten Morgen*, p. 1.
[76] Hasso Spode, "Zur Sozial- und Siedlungsgeschichte Kreuzbergs," in Helmut Engel, Stefi Jersch-Wenzel, and Wilhelm Treue, eds., *Kreuzberg* (Berlin: Nicolai, 1994), pp. xi – xxix.

of the district – crystallized around the question of the status of the Bethanien hospital complex on the Mariannenplatz. The Bethanien had been important in the nineteenth century for taking care of the poor from the surrounding district; it stood empty when the issue of urban renewal brought matters to a head in 1970.

The seizure of what would become the Georg von Rauch Haus at the end of 1971 was actually the second of two building seizures with which the Scherben were connected. The first took place in July after a concert in the Mensa of the Technical University. The concert, which also featured performances by the bands Agitation Free and Ash Ra Temple, was part of an informational event organized by Peter Paul Zahl, editor of the leading Berlin radical organ *Agit 883*, in cooperation with the Rote Hilfe West Berlin ("Red Help West Berlin," the name taken from the Weimar-era organization of the KPD). The Rote Steine were present, along with a contingent of young workers, students, and radicals from the West Berlin anarchist scene. The activist Lothar Binger intended to use the concert as a jumping-off point for the seizure of an empty building in Kreuzberg, to be used for the creation of a self-organized youth center. After the Scherben's performance, as agreed ahead of time with Binger, Rio Reiser called upon the crowd to go into action. The result, the seizure of an empty factory building at Mariannenstraße 13, was the first such building seizure in West Berlin. By the end of the decade, more than 300 buildings in West Berlin were under the control of squatters.[77]

The Scherben's performance was recorded by Klaus Freudigmann and later made up the live Side 1 of the group's first album.[78] But the events of July 3 were merely a prelude to a more spectacular event, one with which the name Ton Steine Scherben would become indelibly associated. By the end of 1971, tensions between the radical milieu and the state were coming to a head. The RAF militant Petra Schelm had been killed in Hamburg in July, only a couple of weeks after the Mariannenstraße building seizure, leading to terrorist reprisals. On December 4, the anarchist militant Georg von Rauch was killed in Berlin in a shoot-out with police. The "murder" (as the radical left understood it) of Rauch symbolized the increasingly pitiless struggle between terrorists and the state and lent even greater urgency to the struggle over urban space in West Berlin. A teach-in scheduled at the Technical University on December 8 was to

---

[77] Kai Sichtermann raises the possibility that there might have been an earlier Hausbesetzung in another city; see Sichtermann et al., *Keine Macht für Niemand*, p. 54.

[78] Sichtermann et al., *Keine Macht für Niemand*, p. 52.

deal with the issue of the Bethanien, specifically the Martha-Maria-Haus, the former nurses' dormitory on the northwest side of the complex, facing the Berlin Wall.

Rio Reiser and his friend Anne Reiche, a leading figure in the Blues scene and shortly to be a member of the Bewegung 2 Juni (the Movement 2 June), the anarchist counterpart to the RAF, envisioned the seizure of the Martha-Maria-Haus as the prelude to a seizure of the entire hospital complex, forming the basis of a "Freie Republik Bethanien."[79] Fueled by anger over the death of Georg von Rauch, the teach-in on December 8 resulted in quick and decisive action. After the Scherben's performance, and accompanied by massive flyering and public announcements, some 600 militant youth descended on the Bethanien by automobile and subway. "I remember the performance of Ton Steine Scherben in the Audimax of the TU," recalls Christina Perincioli, women's activist and filmmaker,

where between the songs ever shorter political texts were read. That was new and great; until then, rock music had spoken only to the gut. But the crowning event came when the entire demonstration suddenly took off and we seized the Bethanien. That still has the power to inspire me today, the channeling of a cultural event into political action.[80]

The Martha-Maria-Haus, seized by young workers, apprentices, and runaways, aided and abetted by members of a local Basisgruppe and radicals from the Blues milieu, was quickly renamed the "Georg von Rauch Haus." The house became a major scene location, not only for runaways and drug users but also for members of the prototerrorist groups. Police raided the house on April 19, 1972, on information that Michael "Bommi" Baumann, a friend of the deceased Georg von Rauch, member of the Blues scene and later the Movement 2 June, was hanging out there.[81] The purported discovery of a "bomb laboratory" in the house was reported on with relish by the conservative *Bild Zeitung*, and the CDU agitated, without success, for the house's closure.[82] The seizure represented an initial blow in the struggle over urban space in Berlin, giving rise to a battle

---

[79] Rio Reiser, *König von Deutschland: Erinnerungen an Ton Steine Scherben und mehr – Erzählt von ihm selbst und Hannes Eyber* (Berlin: Möbius Rekords, 2001), p. 239.

[80] Quoted in Sichtermann et al., *Keine Macht für Niemand*, p. 72.

[81] See "Terror-Zentrale ausgehoben: Bei 'Bethanien' eingerückt," *Der Abend*, April 19, 1972. See also D. Discher, "Bethanien: Terrorzentrum oder Experimentierfeld mit Fehlern? Bei Razzia in Wohnkollektiv Materialien für Attentate gefunden," *Berliner Morgenpost*, April 20, 1972.

[82] Evelyn Köhler, "Kontroversen um Bethanien: CDU löste heftige Debatte aus," *Berliner Zeitung*, January 7, 1972.

between squatters and authorities that raged in the 1980s and continues in less spectacular form today.[83]

The seizure of the Rauch Haus was allowed to stand largely in no small part through the sympathy of the left-wing Social Democratic city councilor Erwin Beck, without whom the police might have cleared the building on the first day. Here, official liberal-mindedness transcended measured judgment to become something resembling cooperative radicalism. Yet, it is also clear that the authorities feared making a mistake that would further galvanize the radical left. So united was the left around the idea of the Rauch Haus, recalls Gert Möbius, that police "would have had to come with bombs" had they attempted to storm the house.[84] Nor were members of the radical scene alone in their support for the seizure. The "youths ... involved ... came for the most part from Kreuzberg," Möbius points out,

and they had families, and they stood on our side too. That is, the parents were not against us. And that was a decisive point; if they had tried to clear us out, they would have been placing themselves against the Kreuzberg population.[85] [I]t was a great signal, and was also a sign for the student left, that you didn't have to just do [agitation] in the factories ... that you could change things.[86]

MUSIC AS A WEAPON?

Ton Steine Scherben immortalized the seizure in its famous "Rauch Haus Song," a song that appeared on its second LP, *Keine Macht für Niemand*, released in October 1972. But the unity among antiauthoritarians celebrated in the song was far from a reality: At the very time at which the song was being recorded, with residents from the house invited to sing on the rousing chorus: "Das ist unser Haus – Ihr kriegt uns hier nicht raus" ("This is our house – You won't get us out of here"), the members of Ton Steine Scherben were on far from friendly terms with the people in control of the Rauch Haus. Accused of having written a song that, as Rio Reiser paraphrased it, had "nothing to do with reality," the group was prohibited by the leaders of the Rauch Haus from appearing at a teach-in against a threatened eviction in March 1972.[87]

---

[83] Spode, "Zur Sozial- und Siedlungsgeschichte Kreuzbergs," pp. xi – xxix, xxvii.

[84] Gert Möbius, interview with the author, Berlin, February 2005.

[85] *Ibid.* [86] *Ibid.*

[87] Reiser, *König von Deutschland*, p. 246. "This didn't hamper the same people," recalls the Scherben's bass player Kai Sichtermann bitterly, "from showing up two months later in Klaus Freudigmann's studio in the Admiralstraße to chant along as the song was being recorded for the

This falling out between the Scherben and the people in control of the Rauch Haus was emblematic of a more fundamental conflict between the band's anarchist-bohemian orientation and the dogmatic authoritarianism of many of its fellow leftists. Rio Reiser, for one, was repelled by the theoretical jargon of the student movement. "I had problems with the students," he writes. "I found what they said and how they said it boring. The flyers, the language, it was all Greek to me. The revolutionizing of the *Lehrbetriebe*. That always smelled a little too much like school."[88] The conflict between the Scherben and what Reiser called the "political managers" had already reared its head in the wake of the Scherben's gig preceding the seizure of the Mariannenstraße 13 property in July 1971. According to Rio Reiser, it was his co-conspirator Lothar Binger ("Lothar X" in Reiser's account) who, after instigating the seizure, called the police to make sure that a conflict with the authorities would ensue.[89] Here, Reiser observed, "ice cold Leninism had shown its face."[90]

The Scherben confronted a more fundamental problem, one that had to do with the relationship between art and politics. The intimate association between the Scherben and the radical-left milieu of West Berlin in the early 1970s was only in part a product of the band's own commitments; it was also a product of the place and moment in which the band first rose to prominence. The Scherben's first major gig took place at the beginning of September 1970. The occasion was the "Festival der Liebe" (Festival of Love), a major open-air rock concert on the Baltic Sea island of Fehmarn. Sponsored by the sex-shop magnate Beate Uhse and billed as the "German Woodstock," the festival featured performances by big names such as Rod Stewart and the Faces, Canned Heat, and (in the final performance before his death) Jimi Hendrix.[91] Rain, sound problems, and violence by biker hoodlums contributed to an atmosphere of frustration, which was ready to burst into the open by the time the Scherben performed. When the band took the stage, late on the third day of the festival, it was with the knowledge that the festival organizers had already departed with the receipts, news that not only angered the band but capped off the growing frustration of the 500 or so festival volunteers.

LP"; Sichtermann et al., *Keine Macht für Niemand*, p. 87. On the leadership factions within the house, see J. Grabowsky, "Die drei Interessengruppen waren zu keinen Kompromissen bereit," *Berliner Morgenpost*, December 15, 1971.

[88] Reiser, *König von Deutschland*, p. 114.
[89] Reiser, *König von Deutschland*, p. 221.
[90] Quoted in Sichtermann et al., *Keine Macht für Niemand*, p. 54.
[91] Hendrix died on September 18, 1970, in London.

In the telling of bass player Kai Sichtermann, the Scherben's performance lit the fuse of the crowd's frustration, setting off a riot that saw the festival facilities go up in flames.[92]

Sichtermann's account no doubt represents a bit of self-mythologization, but the group's performance at the festival nevertheless helped to cement an association between Ton Steine Scherben and radical action that subsequent events did little to disrupt. Just a few weeks later, the song "Keine Macht für Niemand" was used in the television documentary on the West German left: *Fünf Finger sind eine Faust* (*Five Fingers Make a Fist*).[93] In the wake of the broadcast, the station was besieged by some 1,000 cards and letters asking whether it was possible to buy the song on record.[94] The band swiftly pressed the song as its debut single, which appeared in August.[95] The widespread perception that rock and revolution were natural bedfellows, combined with the ever-widening conflict between the radical left and the state, contributed to making Ton Steine Scherben a focal point for efforts at political enlightenment and political mobilization. The band's performances were often accompanied by spontaneous discussions involving both audience and band.[96] The band's music, when not the band itself, was a presence across West Germany, accompanying building seizures in other cities, and appearing wherever radical activists came into conflict with the state. On tour in October 1970, the band were expelled from Switzerland after their final concert in Basel developed into a political demonstration.[97]

The tendency of young people to place their political aspirations onto Ton Steine Scherben dovetailed with the growing imbrication of the band in the radical scene. In September 1971, members of the band relocated to a large eight-room *Altbau* at Tempelhofer Ufer 32 on the Landwehrkanal in Berlin-Kreuzberg. They did so at the invitation of Jorg Schlotterer, anarchist man-about-town, erstwhile secretary of the executive board of the SDS, and former member of the Kommune 2. Moving in with one of the "stars" of the extraparliamentary opposition – whose former roommate was none other than the RAF fugitive

[92] Sichtermann et al., *Keine Macht für Niemand*, pp. 20–25.
[93] The film, by the director Michael Böhme, was broadcast on September 28, 1970.
[94] Koch, *Angriff auf's Schlaraffenland*, p. 53.
[95] The cover was pressed on the Rotaprint machine owned by Gert Möbius, which had previously belonged to West Berlin's Kommune I.
[96] Winkler, "Aggressiv, kritisch und unverschleiert."
[97] Sichtermann et al., *Keine Macht für Niemand*, p. 47.

Holger Meins – the band moved a step closer to the heart of the radical scene in West Berlin. Schlotterer became involved musically with the band, playing flute and helping to organize concerts and record distribution. But his real importance lay elsewhere. Appointed "spiritual adviser" to the band, in tongue-and-cheek reference to the American group MC-5's relationship with its manager/political guru John Sinclair, Schlotterer served as a bridge between the band and the student political scene. "Ideological adviser would have been more correct," Kai Sichtermann writes.[98] "Through his knowledge and his speaking abilities, the Scherben were now, at concerts with a large student audience, better armed against verbal attacks."[99]

The Scherben's stage presentation, which had begun to incorporate multimedia elements such as images projected on the wall behind the band, evolved to include more explicit political references. Performing under a banner bearing a slogan by the nineteenth-century humanist dramatist Georg Büchner – *"Friede den Hütten! Krieg den Palästen!"* – Rio Reiser sometimes read excerpts from Chairman Mao's Little Red Book between songs. Other band members joined in.[100] Yet the ideal nature of the relationship between music and politics was not easy to establish. A manifesto published in *Agit 883* in December 1970 attempted to codify it. Entitled "Music Is a Weapon" (an obvious appropriation of the Communist dramatist Friedrich Wolf's Weimar-era "Art as a Weapon" concept), the piece sought to cast the creation of music in essentially political terms, as a key component of the political struggle:

Music can become a collective weapon when you stand on the side of the people for whom you are making music! When you say something with your lyrics, describe a situation that everyone recognizes, but about which each eats themselves up inside about in isolation, then everyone will hear that they are not [alone] and you can demonstrate the possibility for change. Music can also become a weapon when you recognize the causes of your aggression. We want that you do not internalize your rage, that you are clear about where your discontent and your doubt come from.[101]

---

[98] Sichtermann et al., *Keine Macht für Niemand*, p. 62.

[99] *Ibid.*

[100] "This glorification of Mao at that time was terrible," Kai Sichtermann remembers. "We were naïve and starry-eyed"; Sichtermann et al., *Keine Macht für Niemand*, pp. 50–51. The Büchner slogan was used by the Rauch Haus Kollektiv as well; see Georg-von-Rauch-Haus-Kollektiv, *Frieden den Hütten, Krieg den Palästen: 6 Jahre Selbstorganisation* (Berlin: Selbstverlag, 1977).

[101] "Musik ist eine Waffe," *883*, December 24, 1970. The piece was republished in *Schwarze Protokolle*, no. 1, July 1, 1972. A very different piece under the same heading appeared in 1972 in the group's fanzine *Guten Morgen*, p. 23.

It continues:

Our public are the people of our generation: apprentices, Rockers, young workers, "criminals," people in and out of group homes. Our songs deal with their situation. Songs exist to be sung together. A song has impact when a group of people can sing it. Our songs are simple, so that many can sing along.[102]

It concludes:

We don't need any aesthetic; our aesthetic lies in political effectiveness. Our public is the measure, and not some flipped-out poet. We have learned to make songs from our public, only from them can we learn in the future how to write songs for the people. We belong to no party and to no tendency. We support every action that serves the class struggle, no matter which group organizes it.[103]

This understanding of the role of music, in its collectivism and in its privileging of political effectiveness over aesthetics (or in its attempt to elide the distinction between the two) was not new; it would not have been very out of place, indeed, in the mouth of Bertolt Brecht. Yet it was also very clearly the product of a distinct conjuncture marked by the collectivist claims associated with the anti-imperialist struggles of the Third World and the intense politicization of every sphere of life in the West Berlin left milieu.

Art and politics did not fit together so nicely as the "Music Is a Weapon" manifesto implied. For one thing, the deployment of the Scherben on the political front(s) involved a bottomless pit of commitments. After the release of the *Warum geht es mir so dreckig* album, the sleeve of which bore the band's phone number,

the telephone at the T-Ufer was never silent. Twenty-four hours a day. Most of the calls had to do with requests for the Scherben to appear in connection with a school strike, a college strike, to help prevent an announced increase in public transit fares, for planned building seizures, Knasthilfe, Rote Hilfe, Schwarze Hilfe, or in connection with a student government election. In between all that there were offers to perform at discothèques, youth homes, [for] Catholic or Evangelical youth groups, Falken, Jusos, the SDAJ.[104]

Pressure for the band to make its presence felt on the political scene came especially from Reiser's friend Anne Reiche. "We were to become the rock and roll fighting battalion," writes Reiser, "and to make music that would bring people 'shouting into the streets.'"[105]

---

[102] "Musik ist eine Waffe." [103] *Ibid.*
[104] Reiser, *König von Deutschland*, p. 244. [105] *Ibid.*

To this end, Reiche commissioned Reiser to write a fight song for the movement. The result – "Keine Macht für Niemand" – became one of the group's best-known songs. Challenging ideological and Cold War bloc boundaries ("Im Süden, im Osten, im Norden, im Westen, es sind überall die dieselben, die uns erpressen" ["In the South, the East, the North, the West, it's always the same ones who oppress us"]); calling for the destruction of walls both literal figurative ("Reißen wir die Mauern ein, die uns trennen. Kommt zusammen, Leute. Lernt euch kennen" ["Tear down the walls that separate us, come together people, get to know each other"]); repeating again and again a refrain rejecting authority in all its forms ("Keine Macht für Niemand!" ["No power for no one"]), the song was an antiauthoritarian statement of singular power. However, its anarchist sentiments were not universally appreciated on the left; it was rejected, for example, by the leadership of the RAF as "useless for the anti-imperialist struggle."[106]

The tension between the band's bohemian anarchism and the left-wing cadres stretched back to the earliest performances of Hoffmann's Comic Teater. "The revolutionary cadres rejected the review out of hand," writes Gert Möbius, "because in ideological terms it ended too resignedly ... [But] who can say what 'resigned' is? Who? Was not Goethe's *Sorrows of Young Werther* also resigned, but also revolutionary?"[107] Gradually members of the band began to see the relentless politicization of their music within the scene as stifling. "Playing at a teach-in was all but a duty," complained Rio Reiser; "we were required [to do it], it was like in the DDR ... That was happening even before *Keine Macht für Niemand* came out."[108]

The tension between art and politics, which in the eyes of the Scherben had become a tension between fun and sterile dogmatism, came increasingly to expression in the group's live performances. Whether harassed for adding "good time" rock 'n' roll standards to their set;[109] called out for strewing glitter across the stage ("we threw glitter over the revolutionary masses," writes Kai Sichtermann);[110] or challenged for engaging female background singers who committed the sin of dancing on stage

---

[106] See El Kurdi, *Schwarzrote Pop-Perlen*, p. 37.
[107] Möbius, "Hoffmanns Comic Teater, Rote Steine, Ton Steine Scherben, 1969–1971."
[108] Quoted in Sichtermann et al., *Keine Macht für Niemand*, p. 87.
[109] This took place at another Rauch Haus teach-in, in March 1972; Sichtermann et al., *Keine Macht für Niemand*, p. 97.
[110] This was the infamous (in the band's lore) "glitter gig" of April 1974; Sichtermann et al., *Keine Macht für Niemand*, p. 124.

(inspiring a heated discussion with audience members about the role of women),[111] the Scherben increasingly found themselves the focal point of highly politicized and emotive debates. "The Scherben were expected to be politically correct," writes Kai Sichtermann, "and it was the others who decided what politically correct was. The Scherben were [seen as] the *Hochkapelle* of the left, and so everyone believed they had the right to have a say in what the Scherben did."[112] It is unsurprising that the Scherben ultimately decided to escape this environment, fleeing to a band commune in the countryside in the early 1970s.

Ton Steine Scherben's contemporaries, the Cologne-based cabaret group-cum-rock band Floh de Cologne, enjoyed a somewhat less fraught relationship with the radical left, adhering as they did to a more thoroughly instrumental approach to the relationship between art and politics. Formed in 1966, Floh de Cologne was, from the beginning, an even more explicitly political band than Ton Steine Scherben. The band's founding members – Jürgen Alleff, Udo Weinberger, Britta Baltruschat, Markus Schmid, and Gerd Wollschon – were theater students at the University of Cologne. Members of the student APO scene, they represented a self-confident, theoretical, and didactic brand of politics. The group's first album, *Vietnam* (1968) directly took on the American war, while subsequent works focused heavily on capitalism's colonization of daily life. Like the Scherben, Floh de Cologne had its roots in radical theater, an influence that it never fully abandoned. While the Scherben always functioned very much like a rock band, throughout its career Floh de Cologne felt like something closer to an electrified cabaret act.

Like the Scherben and the Rote Steine before them, Floh de Cologne emphasized the importance of singing in German and forcefully took up the cause of young workers and apprentices. The band collected accounts of abuses and indignities suffered by apprentices – Employer: "An artist-mane (Beatle haircut), big sideburns, or a so-called philosopher's beard [goatee], are not worth of a fresh and lively apprentice and therefore cannot be allowed" – publishing them in a collection of lyrics and other writings.[113] Reaching out to young members of the proletariat was part of a larger project of supplementing the class struggle by the means to which the group was best suited. Declaring its intention of highlighting the

---

[111] Joachim Hentschel, "Spur der Steine," *Rolling Stone*, March 2005.

[112] Sichtermann et al., *Keine Macht für Niemand*, p. 124.

[113] Floh de Cologne, *Profitgeier und andere Vögel: Agitationstexte, Lieder, Berichte* (Berlin: Wagenbach, 1971), p. 7. The passage was quoted by the band out of a Spiegel article; "Jugend Lehrlinge: Dampf machen," *Der Spiegel*, no. 12, March 17, 1969.

Figure 4.7 Floh de Cologne. Photo: Jens Hagen.

conflict between "exploited and exploiter," the group nevertheless noted that young workers and apprentices required a different approach than their parents. Because "[y]oung workers and apprentices have little interest in theater and cabaret, but ... do have interest in music," a manifesto declared, "we use pop music as a transfer-instrument for our political texts. We take this to be more effective than, for example, lectures."[114]

Unlike the Scherben, who attempted to marry art and political conception in a way that enhanced both, Floh de Cologne sublimated the former to the latter, embracing music as a adjunct to politics rather than as an end in its own right. To be sure, the Scherben had made forays in this direction with their "Music Is a Weapon" manifesto, but they never really followed the inherent logic of the position to its extreme. By contrast, Floh de Cologne placed politics at the center of their musical interventions in a very thoroughgoing way.

This basic difference in orientation resonated with the style both of the group's politics and of its music. If Ton Steine Scherben were the voice of the undogmatic, anarchist left, Floh de Cologne supplied the soundtrack for a more staunchly Marxist, heavily didactic leftism, precisely the sort of leftism that irritated the Scherben.[115] Floh de Cologne's support for the East German-oriented DKP – it played many concerts for the party in conjunction with the DKPs' youth organization (Sozialistischen Deutschen Arbeiterjugend; SDAJ), and the individual band members actually joined the party in the early 1970s – cemented its position as Lenin to the Scherben's Bakunin. Yet Floh de Cologne were definitely the more avant-garde of the two groups, owing in part to their continued adherence to the forms of cabaret (even as they distanced themselves from cabaret's more conservative conventions), in part to their greater reliance on cultural provocation and shock tactics.[116] Floh's performances tended to feature fewer "songs" per se than political rants spoken or shouted over musical grooves. Pieces frequently contained didactic exchanges reminiscent of the work of the Rote Steine. In "Die Luft gehort denen, die sie atmen" ("The Air Belongs to Those Who Breathe It"), a series of populist political declarations were accompanied by a call-and-response exchange between "employer" and "employee." In "Fliessbandbaby" ("Assembly-Line Baby"), a domineering interlocutor berated the protagonist over a hypnotic groove with the claim "Arbeit macht Spaß" ("Work is fun"). "Overtime is double fun. Holidays are triple fun!" Floh readily employed obscenity as a means of shocking bourgeois sensibilities, a goal they achieved very successfully, as we have seen, at the Essener Songtage of

---

[114] Floh de Cologne, *Profitgeier und andere Vogel*.

[115] It is also notable, as Detlef Siegfried points out, that the members of Floh de Cologne were a decade older than the Scherben and had a correspondingly different relationship to pop music as a result (Siegfried, *Time Is on My Side*, p. 701).

[116] Guy von Auer, "Dreck und Schmutz aus Köln," *konkret*, no. 21, October 2, 1969.

1968. Unsurprisingly, the group had regularly to reckon with the threat of censorship.[117]

The activist impulses of groups such as Ton Steine Scherben and Floh de Cologne unfolded in the context of a widespread belief in the revolutionary power of rock music. This was fueled, as Detlef Siegfried has shown, not by the music's lyrical content (the explicit politics of groups such as Ton Steine Scherben and Floh de Cologne being an exception to the rule) but by the qualities ascribed to the music by listeners.[118] Even for the Scherben, as we have seen, revolutionary spirit was as much imputed by fans as it was embodied by the band itself. Belief in the emancipatory power of rock music dovetailed with warnings of capitalist recuperation, the underground press treating bands according to the seriousness with which they were believed to represent the interests of "the revolution."[119] The American group Grand Funk Railroad, for example, was dismissed as "the prototype of a capitalist pop group," while other performers such as Jimi Hendrix, the American radical rock band MC-5, and Ton Steine Scherben were held up as praiseworthy examples of radical art.[120] Meanwhile, the music industry was criticized for the exploitation of bands and fans.[121] The revolutionary power ascribed to rock music was symbolized visually by the frequent juxtaposition of the guitar and the gun as dual instruments of revolution (functioning simultaneously, in Detlef Siegfried's words, as "insignia of liberation in the technological ensemble of modernity").[122] In this depiction, the rock musician represented a parallel insurgent, making up the cultural wing of a two-pronged guerrilla assault on capitalism and all its works.

CONCLUSION

The revolutionary valence of rock music as a whole aside, political rock was itself an inherently unstable category. As an art form expressing individualism and extreme subjectivity, rock music sat uneasily with the more

---

[117] Numerous examples are listed in Floh de Cologne, *Profitgeier und andere Vogel*, pp. 24–32.

[118] Siegfried, "Music and Protest in 1960s Europe."

[119] Klaus Weinhauer, "Der Westberliner 'Underground': Kneipen, Drogen und Musik," in Rotaprint 25, eds., *Agit 883*, pp. 73–84, at p. 81.

[120] *Fizz*, no.1, reprinted in *Fizz Re-Print 1–10* (Berlin: Anti-Quariat Reprint Verlag, 1989); "Ton Steine Scherben," *883*, no. 73, December 24, 1970; "Scherben machen auch Musik," 883, no. 83, July 3, 1971.

[121] See "Stones, Spooky-Tooth, Broughton etc.: Macht Schluss mit der Ausbeutung der Veranstalter!," *Agit 883*, no. 71, October 15, 1970.

[122] Siegfried, *Time Is on My Side*, p. 693.

objectively dogmatic demands of revolutionary Marxism. Yet, as this chapter has shown, even when it was not serving as a vehicle for explicit politics, popular music played a critical and multifaceted role in the elaboration of left-wing identity in the West German 1968. The sonic qualities of the new music (discordance, volume, rhythmic allure) and the personal appearance of musicians and fans (long hair, unconventional clothing) marked out popular music as a site of symbolic challenges to the existing order, prior to any explicit politicization. These symbolic challenges could, under the right circumstances, be transformed into a manifest threat to order, whether in the propensity of music-oriented subcultures to gather in public spaces, or in those moments, such as the riot in the Waldbühne, when popular music brought masses of young people face to face with the authority of the state in the presence of police.

Popular music served, furthermore, as a vehicle for the construction of hybrid spaces in which music scenes and political scenes interacted and became mixed together. "Scene" bars and venues such as the Zodiak, organized around music appreciation and performance, provided a bridge across class divides, bringing together student Marxists and working-class anarchists, artists and avant-garde theorists, creating subcultural complexes that became a key site of the overlap between politics and culture characteristic of 1968. At the same time, music was an essential part of the same alternative public sphere to which, for example, the underground press examined in the last chapter also belonged.[123]

Music, moreover, became a site for key imperatives at the heart of the antiauthoritarian revolt. First, from radical rock bands to the organizers of festivals, music was seen as a key means of, or venue for, communication. This was closely linked, in the hands of figures such as Rolf Ulrich Kaiser and the other organizers of the Essener Songtage, with the desire to engage on the scholarly scientific terrain over which values about the worth of popular culture were fought. A hip capitalist such as Rolf Ulrich Kaiser wanted not only to make money but also to create and foster a scene, a "subculture" or "underground" – an enterprise that had to be intellectualized and theorized, justified, in short (in the spirit of the time) using the language of sociologists, cultural analysts, and youth pedagogues. At the same time, cultural-organizational work of this sort, such as the activities of bands like Ton Steine Scherben and Floh de Cologne, represented the self-organization imperative in action; that is, they marked attempts to create culture, and meaning, outside of, or in

---

[123] Seidel, "Berlin und die Linke in den 1960ern," p. 28.

some cases in opposition to, official channels. That considerable distance existed between the conceptions of someone like Rolf Ulrich Kaiser and a band like Ton Steine Scherben illustrates the wide ambit in which the self-organizational concept could be operative.

Music was, finally, a key site of the transnational in 1968. The Burg Waldeck Festivals, and later the Essener Songtage, became nodal points where extra-German musical sources and conditions helped synergize local developments. In Burg Waldeck, above all, the American and international folk movements, and in the Essener Songtage, folk, jazz, and the emerging new Anglo-American rock music of the high 1960s, articulated with, and helped to inform the subsequent development of indigenous musical forms. In a similar way, rock groups such as Ton Steine Scherben and Floh de Cologne, as well as a host of other less obviously political bands, were key in channeling the influence of Anglo-American Beat music in the creation of a German-language variant, one attuned to German cultural and political requirements. Music was thus by no means just a field for projections and vague longings, a vehicle for the transfer of style codes and mores, or a shaper of left-wing habitus; it was an active field of engagement in which young West Germans connected themselves to a world outside West Germany, even as they brought the best of the world home. By acting both as a focus of subcultural activism and a vehicle for the elaboration of radical identity, popular music became a critical component of the West German 1968.

CHAPTER 5

Vision

On February 1, 1968, in the Auditorium Maximum of the Technical University in Berlin, 1,500 attendees at the Springer Tribunal, organized to protest the press monopoly of Axel Springer, took a break from speeches full of incendiary rhetoric to view a short film. In the three-minute silent film, entitled *The Making of a Molotov Cocktail*, a pair of female hands add oil and benzene to an empty wine bottle, insert a rag, and set it alight. The device is thrown against a car, which burns. In a following montage, Molotov cocktails pass, hand to hand, from one furtive figure to the next. A box of matches is shown sitting on top of a book (Regis Debray's *Revolution in the Revolution*). In the final scene appears an image of the Springer Press headquarters in the Kochstraße. The audience erupted in cheers. Shocked by the apparent effect of his film, the young filmmaker, a twenty-seven-year-old film student named Holger Meins, took the film away and tried to erase his tracks. The organizers of the event were furious. That night, as if in answer to the film's call for exemplary violence, the windows of Springer-owned buildings across Berlin were smashed by unknown vandals.[1]

The Springer Tribunal had been carefully organized and meticulously prepared. Its goal, according to Peter Schneider, who had been called upon by Hans Magnus Enzensberger, Rudi Dutschke, and Gaston Salvatore to oversee the event, was to present the findings of the various working groups in the SDS, which had painstakingly documented the ways in which the Springer Press monopoly subverted the democratic potential of the mass media. Central was the contention that, by feeding the anti-Communist hysteria in West Berlin and squeezing out alternative voices, the newspaper chain contributed to the maintenance of a false consciousness that prevented any challenge to regimes of domination in

---

[1] The richest set of accounts of the film and the context of its showing is to be found in Conradt, *Starbuck*.

Figure 5.1 The scene outside the Kaiser Wilhelm Memorial Church, Berlin Charlottenburg, April 1971. Landesarchiv Berlin.

West German society. Concern over the effects of the Springer monopoly was by no means confined to the most radical circles in the SDS: like the campaign against the Emergency Laws, opposition to the Springer monopoly was a matter of wide left-liberal consensus.

For Schneider, who had organized much of the support for the tribunal, the showing of the Meins film was "a catastrophe."[2]

It was clear that it wasn't just about the making of the Molotov cocktail, but that there was also an address for it. On the same night, seven, eight, nine, ten plate-glass windows at Springer affiliates were smashed with stones, which were wrapped in flyers reading "EXPROPRIATE SPRINGER!" [Because of this], all those I had been cultivating for months, from whom I had got promises and money, immediately cancelled. This was the end of the "legal arm" of the anti-Springer campaign.[3]

[2] "At the event I had just given a speech and suddenly," recalls Schneider, "without my knowing anything about it, this film was shown. I didn't know where they got the projector or the projection screen. At the time it wasn't unusual, that someone would break in on the action and say: 'Hello, I'm here, may I have the microphone?,' or show a film. We were the last people who would have tried to prohibit something like that." Peter Schneider, "Wer springt durch den Feuerring?" in Conradt, *Starbuck*, p. 74.

[3] Schneider, "Wer springt durch den Feuerring?" p. 74.

The Springer Press trumpeted the deed the next day under headlines reading "Stones against Free Opinion."[4] A week later, a frustrated Schneider, in a perverse act of resignation, went and threw a stone through a Springer window himself.[5]

The showing of Meins's film and its aftermath illustrate the extent to which single individuals or groups of individuals, acting outside of or within formal mass organizations, could exercise disproportionate influence on the course of a movement that was by nature diffuse and nonhierarchical. But, even more strikingly, it demonstrates the power of images in 1968. The upheavals of the 1960s took place in a period of rapid expansion and democratization of the possibilities of mass media. The school attended by Meins, the Deutsche Film- und Fernsehakademie Berlin (DFFB; German Film and Television Academy Berlin), was established in 1966 on precisely these grounds. The media explosion of the decade is inseparable from the other trends that produced the 1960s cultural revolution. Moreover, the antiauthoritarian movement itself consciously used media to project its message, relying on those protest forms that were most shocking and photogenic. Through dress and hairstyle, through disguise and pageantry, through appropriation, recontextualization, and juxtaposition of symbols, the antiauthoritarian movement placed images in the foreground of its political practice. Thus, as much as the antiauthoritarian movement (especially the logocentric theoreticians of the SDS) could be dominated by words – by key texts, by oratory, by Marxist and scene vocabulary – it was dominated all the more by the visual image. And images, as Meins's *The Making of a Molotov Cocktail* showed, often held the power to trump words.

"BREAK THE POWER OF THE MANIPULATORS"

The power of the visual was, for the activists of the SDS, both a blessing and a curse. We have already seen how the film *Viva Maria!* helped crystallize for Rudi Dutschke and others the idea of a Third World–First World rebel alliance, one that, tellingly, involved comic depictions of a fun revolution steeped in the sexuality of bombshell French actresses. To be sure, free association of this sort came more easily to the circle around Dutschke and Kunzelmann, who were much more likely to allow themselves to be swept away by such images than the official position of the

4 *BZ*, February 3, 1978.
5 Schneider, "Wer springt durch den Feuerring?" p. 74.

SDS, informed by the Frankfurt School's suspicion of the visual, would typically allow. The striking absence of visual images in the materials produced by the SDS, in part the product of technical limitations in the production of flyers and so on, had at least as much to do with a sense that it was through words, and not images, that political ideas based in rational analysis were best conveyed. The pranks of the Kommune I helped to change this orientation, although, as we have seen, their interventions were ill received by the SDS for precisely the reasons just stated.

At the same time, SDS activists recognized the power of the image to shape consciousness and were alert to the potential of images to carry politically retrograde messages, as demonstrated in the protests against the film *Africa Addio* in August 1966.[6] The student movement itself deployed images of the Third World Other, as Quinn Slobodian has pointed out, not in order to inculcate a sense of Western superiority over savages but to confront the viewer with a moral choice; images of mutilated Vietnamese peasants, the burns of napalm victims, or torture-scarred Iranian journalists were meant not only to offer incontrovertible documentary evidence of the movement's claims about the crimes of the forces of repression but to make clear the real-world consequences of political decisions such as support for the American war in Vietnam.[7] The visual here represented a form of information designed both to *supplement* words – that is, to bolster the student movement's written and verbal claims about state violence – and to *trump* words, by revealing the horrible reality behind high-sounding establishment talk about the "free world" and "defending democracy."

A belief in the documentary power of images also underpinned the new style of activist filmmaking that grew up in conjunction with the antiauthoritarian revolt. The DFFB became a hotbed of cinematic agitation, its student-directors both documenting and egging on the protests that enveloped West Berlin in 1967 and 1968. Founded in September 1966, with an incoming class of thirty-four students, the DFFB was West Germany's first film college.[8] The school was characterized by conflict

---

[6] "'Africa addio' am Kurfürstendamm abgesetzt," *Die Welt*, no. 181, August 6, 1966, p. 9.

[7] To be sure, as Slobodian points out, the visual intervention was ambiguous in both execution and effect, since it asserted the right to revisit atrocity and instrumentalize human suffering in the interest of political edification, often with indifferent effect; see Quinn Slobodian, "Corpse Polemics: The Third World and the Politics of Gore in 1960s West Germany," in Brown and Anton, eds., *Between the Avant-Garde and the Everyday*, pp. 58–73.

[8] Some 800 students applied, including Rainer Werner Fassbinder, who failed the admissions test and was rejected; Volker Pantenburg, "Die Rote Fahne: Deutsche Film- und Fernsehakademie, 1966–1968," in Klimke and Scharloth, eds., *1968: Handbuch zur Kultur- und Mediengeschichte der Studentenbewegung*, pp. 199–206, at p. 200.

between students and professors from the beginning, first over students' unhappiness with inadequate technical facilities, later over professors' concerns about the emerging political content of student films. In May 1968, during the climactic protests against the Emergency Laws, the academy was occupied for three days. A group of students renamed the school the Dziga Vertov Akademie (after the Soviet director) and hung a red flag out the window.[9]

Films produced by students at the DFFB documented the main events of student protest. Harun Farocki's *Die Worte des Vorsitzenden* (*The Words of the Chairman*, 1967) employed the Shah and Farah Dibah masks used in the protests of June 2, 1967. Thomas Giefer's *Terror auch im Westen* (*Terror Also in the West*) dealt with the Vietnam Congress of February 1968, while his *Berlin, 2 Juni 1967* (with Hans-Rüdiger Minow) thematized the fateful visit of the Shah of Iran. The latter film was a documentary employing footage shot on the day of the protest, as well as footage of policemen (identified from photographs of the protest) being confronted about their role. Such films were seen by their makers as necessary interventions to fight against the false view of reality being propagated by the mass media. "A true documentary film," argued Giefer in a flyer, "has to agitate in order to result in what it is showing being changed. Provocation and destruction are legitimate means against the large-scale consolidation [*Gleichschaltungs-*] campaign of the counterrevolution. 'Axel, we're coming!' – armed to the teeth with purposeful, directed, and telling agitation."[10] The central conceit behind the films coming out of the DFFB, that film represented a vehicle for fighting the manipulation of consciousness by the powers that be, was well expressed in the title of student Helke Sander's 1967 film on the Springer Press monopoly: *Break the Power of the Manipulators!*[11]

This heavily didactic style of filmmaking represented only one facet of cinematic engagement in 1968. The ever-growing proliferation of the pop-cultural image sphere, the example of cutting-edge cinema from America and elsewhere, and new technologies of cultural production such as the Super 8 camera (introduced by Kodak in 1965), contributed to a democratization of the moving image with both artistic and political implications. The poet Rolf Dieter Brinkmann was only one of the well-known figures to embrace the new Super 8 camera, using it in his perambulations around

---

[9] Pantenburg, "Die Rote Fahne," p. 200.
[10] Quoted in Pantenburg, "Die Rote Fahne," p. 203.
[11] See also the documentary on the Hamburg Film-Coop, *Die kritische Masse: Film im Underground Hamburg '68* (dir. Christian Bau, 1998).

Cologne to document the cinematic face of the everyday. His poetry, and poetry collections such as *Silverscreen* (1969), were heavily cinematic in orientation. Important contemporaries of Brinkmann's in the avant-garde art scene in Cologne were the activists of the film troupe X-Screen, whose explicit aim was to introduce Cologne to the world of international avant-garde film, including the films of the American avant-garde (Kenneth Anger, Andy Warhol, and Bruce Connor) and the experimental film of the Vienna Actionists. "X-Screen was an avant-garde film troupe that really engaged with all the very latest stuff in the world," recalls the photographer Jens Hagen;

> They were totally unpolitical actually – political only in the sense that they wanted to do something new artistically that would have an impact on society. But not in the sense of – how shall I say it – wanting "the revolution" or something like that. And they lurched as it were into the – I still refer to this way– "revolt." Yes, it was a kind of revolt. That is, they suddenly realized that what they were doing, although they hadn't meant it that way, was political.[12]

As in so much of 1968, the cultural and the political, for X-Screen, intersected over the terrain of sexuality. "They wanted to provoke, naturally," recalls Hagen; "in the erotic, bodily arena [they] were definitely provocative."[13] The police raid on a showing of one of X-Screen's underground pornographic films, exposing what activists saw as the authoritarianism lurking just under the placid surface of the everyday, was a defining moment in the group's politicization.[14]

Also important in the visual end of the Cologne counterculture was the art collective EXIT Bildermacher, founded in 1969 by a group of artists who knew each other from the University of Basel. The group, which included Thomas Hornemann, Berndt Hoppener, and Hennig John von Freyend, worked out of a common apartment in Cologne until its dissolution in 1971. Operating under the slogan "Art is not just there for the rich," the group specialized in the democratization of visual imagery, founding the "Neumarkt der Künste" (New Market for the Arts) to provide a space for the dissemination of the products of small publishers and graphics houses outside of the mainstream channels of distribution.[15] Brinkmann and Rygulla worked closely with EXIT on a number of projects during the winter of 1969/1970. EXIT contributed illustrations to

---

[12] Jens Hagen, quoted in Geulen and Graf, *Mach mal bitte platz*, p. 83.
[13] *Ibid.*
[14] See *X-Screen: Materialien über den Underground-Film* (Cologne: Phaidon, 1971).
[15] Uwe Husslein, "Außerordentlich und obszön: Rolf Dieter Brinkmann und die POP-Literatur," in the catalog for the exhibit of the same name, Cologne, September–November 2006.

Der Gummibaum, the literary journal founded by Brinkmann and Rolf-Eckart John, and Brinkmann and Rygulla contributed texts to the EXIT art book *Erwin's*, which, in a manner congenial to Brinkmann, represented a collage of words and images.

These developments were part of a general politicization of the arts in the 1960s in which the boundaries between the art world, the counterculture, and the political movement became blurred or erased. This shift in the political potentiality of art was reflected in a turn away from art as a matter of *objects* toward art as a matter of *action*. On one level, this shift was a response to a more and more intensively mediated society marked by overlap between different communicative forms, but it also reflected an implicit, and sometimes explicit, critique of the work of art as a commodity in bourgeois society, a critique connected with a growing awareness of art as a potential field of political engagement.[16] New performance-oriented directions in the art of the 1960s – action-art, happenings, Fluxus, pop art – influenced the political praxis of the antiauthoritarian revolt on multiple levels. On the one hand, artists began to see the universities as fields of action and students as a "critical mass" for their artistic experiments; on the other hand, the student movement adopted elements drawn from action-art – humor, surprise, and "calculated disobedience"– combining them with the techniques of strike and demonstration passed down from the traditional working-class movement.[17]

The new directions were international in provenance and orientation. The "happening" was a phenomenon of the New York gallery scene, being first introduced by the American Allan Kaprow at the Reuben Gallery in October 1959. It was transmitted into West Germany by Wolf Vostell, video-art pioneer and co-founder of the Fluxus movement. Vostell and his fellow professor at the Düsseldorf Art Academy, Joseph Beuys, staged events across the Rhineland and beyond. The happening was characterized by the juxtaposition of different types of media (e.g. painting and music), by a performative aspect in which the process of making the art became part of the artwork itself, and by audience participation. In revealing the role of the artist in this way, and in involving spectators in the previously closed process of creation, the happening held political implications even where the content of the artwork at hand was not explicitly political. In any case, the happening quickly jumped the tracks of the art

[16] Martin Papenbrock, "Happening, Fluxus, Performance: Aktionskünste in den 1960er Jahren," in Klimke and Scharloth, eds., *1968: Handbuch zur Kultur- und Mediengeschichte der Studentenbewegung*, pp. 137–149.
[17] Papenbrock, "Happening, Fluxus, Performance," p. 138.

world to become a standard part of the repertoire of the cultural underground operating at the intersection of art, politics, and popular culture.
In this sense it became less an art category than something new, a gathering aimed at creating a space outside of bourgeois norms of behavior.

These goals were embodied in the group Fluxus, to which both Vostell
and Beuys belonged. A central figure in the development of Fluxus was
the Lithuanian-born American artist George Maciunas. A habitué of
the New York gallery scene, Maciunas was the organizer of numerous
events. Fluxus aimed at breaking out of a static conception of art focusing on "artworks" as such. "NON-ART – AMUSEMENT," Maciunas
proclaimed, "forgoes distinction between art and non-art, forgoes artists' indispensability, exclusiveness, individuality, ambition, forgoes all
pretension toward significance, rarity, inspiration, skill, complexity, profundity, greatness, institutional and commodity value."[18]

In 1962, Maciunas came to West Germany to work as a civilian con-
tractor at the US Air Force base in Wiesbaden. The West Germany to
which Maciunas arrived was already a primary center for happenings, new music, and performance art in Europe, as well as a key site
of the transnational exchanges that characterized the international artistic avant-garde. Important centers were Darmstadt (home to the Keller
Group, the Darmstadt Circle of dynamic theater and concrete poetry,
and the Ferienkurse für Neue Musik [International Summer Courses for
New Music] where John Cage had taught), Cologne (where Karlheinz
Stockhausen ran the Westdeutscher Rundfunk [West German Radio]),
and Düsseldorf (where both Wolf Vostell and Joseph Beuys taught). With
his connections on both sides of the Atlantic, Maciunas played a key role
in forging the connections that created Fluxus. While still in New York,
Maciunas began to correspond with the Korean-born artist Nam June
Paik, whose performance of his composition *Hommage à John Cage* in
1959 marked the first Fluxus event in Germany.[19]

Arriving with scores, tapes, and other Fluxus materials, Maciunas set
about trying to solidify Fluxus into a movement. Continuing with plans
for a Fluxus magazine already begun in New York, he set about organizing
a Fluxus festival, the "Fluxus Internationale Festspiele Neuester Musik"
(Fluxus International Festival for the Newest Music), which took place in
Wiesbaden in September 1962. At the festival, performing Philip Corner's

[18] Lee, "Gruppe Spur," pp. 21–22.
[19] Owen F. Smith, *Fluxus: The History of an Attitude* (San Diego, Calif.: San Diego State University Press, 1998), pp. 42–45.

Piano Activities, Maciunas, Vostell, Paik, and others destroyed the piano (on purpose), producing a satisfying minor scandal. "The press recounted this piece numerous times," writes Owen F. Smith, "often commenting on the destruction of a piano belonging to the museum and how the director would be shocked about the hooliganism 'when he returned from his vacation.'"[20] Pieces of the destroyed piano were auctioned off to the shocked audience. The performance was filmed for West German television and shown four times. "Wiesbaden was shocked," Maciunas wrote to a friend; "the mayor almost had to flee the town for giving us the hall."[21]

Fluxus artists subsequently proved adept at shaking up assumptions about the boundaries between art and life, with potentially explosive results. The most famous Fluxus artist, Joseph Beuys, excelled at exploiting conflict for artistic purposes with a political connotation. A legendary performance at the Technische Hochschule in Aachen on July 20, 1964, succeeded in provoking the audience probably beyond even Beuys's own expectations. Invited by the student council to perform at a Festival of New Art, Beuys conceived his performance as an alternative celebration of the twenty-year anniversary of the attempted assassination of Adolf Hitler. The performance by Beuys and his group began with a reading of a passage from Joseph Goebbels's famous "total war" speech of February 18, 1943, with its question: "Do you want total war?"[22] Beuys pounded at a piano filled with laundry detergent, while yellow powder was poured over the stage; performers danced amid shrill noises; and a bulldog was led through the aisles on a leash. Finally, a group of students rushed the stage, and in the ensuing fray Beuys was punched in the face. A photo of Beuys, blood streaming from his nose, one hand clutching a broken crucifix, the other raised in a Roman salute, turned him into "a symbol for everything shocking and provocative," cementing his reputation as the enfant terrible of the West German art scene.[23]

Artists such as Beuys pioneered a performative approach to art that would inform the political praxis of the student movement; staging his own life as an artistic event, and presenting himself in images meant to shock, Beuys prefigured the sort of self-depiction that would be central to the political practice of groups such as the Kommune I and the counterculture they helped give birth to. "[P]erformance," writes Mike Sell,

[20] In reality, the piano belonged to Maciunas, who had purchased it for $5 for the concert; Smith, *Fluxus*, p. 75.
[21] Maciunas, quoted in Smith, *Fluxus*, p. 76.
[22] "Ein Professor wurde geschlagen ...," *Die Zeit*, no. 31, July 31, 1964.
[23] See the account in Heiner Stachelhaus, *Joseph Beuys* (New York: Abbeville Press, 1991).

Figure 5.2 Joseph Beuys at the Festival of New Art, Aachen Technical University, July 20, 1964. Photo: Heinrich Riebesehl.

was a method that allowed radicals to devise actions that could address simultaneously the structures of language, economics, politics, social institutions, cultural history, and the body. As both practice and discourse, countercultural performance addressed the need (1) to identify and disrupt existing social, cultural, and economic boundaries, (2) to systematically challenge existing discourses of experience, everyday life, and the politics of culture, (3) to produce new ways of thinking and acting that effectively valued aspects of experience, everyday life, and culture systematically excluded from the mainstream, and (4) to ground all of this in specific social and cultural situations.[24]

Performance of given themes in the symbolic presentations accompanying public actions, from the choreography of marches, to personal appearance, to more explicitly performative actions such as street theater, or in the visual iconography employed in printed matter, the student movement and the counterculture, exemplified an active cultural practice. Provocation was a key ingredient of these cultural-productive strategies, precisely because, as Jan Verwoert observes, it was capable of "forcefully bringing about a debate over the legitimation of authority."[25]

The wall containing happenings within their artistic context was easily breached. The whole point of the happening was to erase the distinction between art and daily life, yet this easily bled over into projects even more firmly rooted in the politicization of the latter. The Viennese artist Otto Mühl, founder of Actionism, a doctrine similar to Fluxus in its emphasis on "action-art," took the happening to its logical conclusion, founding a commune blending principles of avant-garde art and psychoanalysis. Called "Action-Analytical Organization" (AAO), the Austrian commune and its German offshoots fused the commune idea with concepts and practices out of the nascent human potential movement. Initiates to the commune had to perform an introductory *Selbstdarstellung* (self-portrayal) in which they lay aside their "character armor" to reveal the person beneath. With shaved heads (for both men and women), owning no property, AAO members seemed less communards than victims of a cult, and the project was heavily criticized within the counterculture.[26]

One of the AAO's critics was John Joachim Trettin of the Horla Commune in Cologne, another offshoot of the action-art scene. The Horla Commune developed out of the POL theater group at the University of Cologne, which first came to prominence at a theater festival in Birmingham, England, as part of Otto Mühl's action theater.[27] Inspired by the Living Theater, which toured Europe in the mid 1960s,

[24] Mike Sell, *Avant-Garde Performance and the Limits of Criticism: Approaching the Living Theatre, Happenings, Fluxus, and the Black Arts Movement* (Ann Arbor, Mich.: University of Michigan Press, 2005), p. 16.

[25] Jan Verwoert, "The Boss: On the Unresolved Question of Authority in Joseph Beuys' Oeuvre and Public Image," *e-flux journal*, available online at www.e-flux.com/journal/view/12 (accessed April 18, 2012).

[26] On these practices, see the various issues of "AA Nachrichten" collected at the Hamburger Institut für Sozialforschung.

[27] "Die Horla Kommune," available online at www.trettin-tv.de/orgon/horla.htm (accessed October 30, 2011).

the POL group aspired to form a theater commune. In the event, members of the group went on to form the Horla Commune, a group that delved into Reichian child-sexuality work and became heavily involved in the psychedelic world of LSD.[28] Hamburg's Ablassgesellschaft commune also had connections to the theater scene, focusing less on psychoterror and the revolutionizing of private life than on art, parties, and happenings. The group put on plays, one member ran a photography studio out of the commune, and they published an underground newspaper.[29]

These examples illustrate the extent to which concepts and actors from the arts, based on or employing visual and performative artifacts and tropes, simultaneously infiltrated the practices of the counterculture, informing the new style of activism associated with the antiauthoritarians in and around the SDS. These impulses sat uneasily together. From a rationalist-political perspective, images could function both as lies (as in the *Africa Addio* film) or as truths when deployed on the posters of the SDS to enlighten or to shame supporters of the Vietnam War. On the artistic-political end of the spectrum, images were potent precisely because they provoked ambiguous, multivalent associations that nevertheless functioned politically, either because of their power to uncover hidden relationships and to challenge power hierarchies or because of their ability to call into being new ways of living. Characteristically, the line separating these two approaches was often ill defined. Both, however, represented responses to an ever-more-heavily mediated environment, overflowing with images and rife with the possibility of creating yet more.

THE SUBVERSIVE IMAGE

By the late 1960s, the world of action-art and the antiauthoritarian revolt spearheaded by the student movement and the counterculture had grown together in significant ways. Not only had the field of the arts become more politicized, as the discussion of literature in Chapter 3 illustrates, but the student movement had adopted iconography and approaches from the

---

[28] "Die Horla Kommune." Also on the Horla Commune, see Rolf Ulrich Kaiser, *Fabrikbewohner* (Düsseldorf: Droste Verlag, 1970).

[29] "While AG's members renounce personal property, share a common eating/dining room with grand table and also share a room for 'psychedelic fun,'" noted a report in *konkret*, "there is no common dormitory. Members tend to have their own bedrooms – some personal space to call their own. While no one 'owns' their own room per se, the commune does believe: 'Having a little space to yourself is a healthy thing'." Willi Koehler, "Die Ehe ist tot: Wohin treibt die Familie?" *Pardon* (1969), pp. 36, 40.

world of the arts. The blending of the two is exemplified in the anthology *Aktionen* published by Wolf Vostell in 1970. Its cover adorned by the famous nude *Spiegel* photo of the Kommune I, featuring the target image of the "Expropriate Springer" badge on its second page, the volume fused the names of activists, artists, and theorists: "Vostell, HSK, LIDL, Teufel, Langhans ... Cohn-Bendit ... Marcuse ... Christo, Ginsburg, guerrilla art ... Kunstmart, Akademien, Kriwet, Dutschke" in a way that erased the distinction between art and politics.[30]

Just as action-art in general and Fluxus in particular supplied a link between the gesture of the artist and the gesture of the activist, contemporaneous developments in pop art supplied a ready fund of iconography. Like action-art founded toward the end of the 1950s, pop art carried out an assault on the bourgeois bastion of high art from a different direction. Drawing on the artifacts of mass-produced culture and borrowing freely from "low" forms such as comic books and advertising – existing, indeed, in a symbiotic relationship with the latter – pop art trafficked in the ironic and parodic modes that underpinned the visual practice of 1968. Panels from artists such as Roy Lichtenstein, with their mocking commentary on the cultural norms of American consumer capitalism, were a regular feature in the West German left-liberal press, and pop art was an unmistakable presence in the visual culture of the antiauthoritarian movement.

The Expropriate Springer badge highlighted in Vostell's *Aktionen* anthology drew clearly on the new visual iconography coming out of London. The red, white, and blue roundel, originally derived from the insignia on British Royal Air Force aircraft, entered popular culture in the early 1960s, appearing in the paintings of Jasper Johns, and, most famously, in the clothes worn by the British rock group The Who, who, under the guidance of manager Kit Lambert, consciously adopted pop-art iconography into their look. "One of the first flecks of color in my life was the blue-white-red target on the t-shirt of Keith Moon, the drummer of the Who," recalls Wolfgang Seidel, the drummer of the Berlin band Ton Steine Scherben; "[i]n some unexplained way we saw these colors, even though Beat Club at this time was still broadcast in black and white."[31] The Expropriate Springer badge, created by the graphic designer and (future) filmmaker Helga Reidemeister, replaced the red, white, and blue of the British model with the red, white, and black of the imperial

---

[30] Wolf Vostell, *Aktionen: Happenings und Demonstrationen seit 1965* (Reinbek bei Hamburg: Rowohlt, 1970).
[31] Seidel, "Berlin und die Linke in den 1960ern," p. 31.

German flag, adding text in *Bild Zeitung* font. The stylized logo appeared everywhere, on buttons, posters, and in print, becoming a sort of symbolic stand-in for the extraparliamentary opposition (see, for example, the deployment of the image in advertising in Fig. 5.10).

The incorporation of images drawn from the arts and from pop culture into the visual productions of the antiauthoritarian movement occupied a space at the intersection of the spheres of art, consumption, and mass culture and political subversion, agitation, and mobilization. The global sixties were image-rich in two ways. Not only was there a greater profusion of available images than ever before, supplied by the ever-expanding possibilities of mass media, but also activists explicitly deployed images for political purposes. The antiauthoritarian revolt operated across the entire range of artistic productions: film, music, literature, theater, and the visual arts. It produced a rich visual culture spanning the student movement to the counterculture, expressed not only in the underground press but also in private photo collections, drawings, and other media of self-representation. Thus, alongside the media images of the antiauthoritarian revolt available as a result of its very public profile, we have the images the revolt created of itself, with all the opportunities for self-representation they presented.

We have already observed that the great explosion of images in the antiauthoritarian revolt occurred not within the student movement itself but on its margins, that is, in the underground press, the counterculture, and the more underground radical groups that began to emerge with the eclipse of the SDS. These groups could draw on an international visual language of "Leftist signs" (Rupert Goldsworthy), employing a fund of imagery drawn from the history of the international workers' movements and other radical groups.[32] These easily reproducible images – the star (red or black), the hammer and sickle, representations of the globe, of weapons, and more – were used to graphically represent a range of radical political identities, sometimes discrete, more often overlapping and ambiguous. These images depended for their force not only on their historic associations (susceptible to multiple meanings in any case) but also on the way that they were juxtaposed with other images to create new sets of associations. The gun and the red star in the logo of the RAF, or the gun and the globe in the logo of the Movement 2 June, are only two of the more well known of such juxtapositions.

---

[32] Rupert Goldsworthy, "Revolt into Style: Images of 1970s West German 'Terrorists'," Doctoral dissertation, New York University, 2007, p. 58.

As the latter example suggests, visual representation was a key site of the transnational in 1968, a site where the global and the local could be seamlessly fused together. This visual-discursive maneuver was particularly notable in the widespread deployment of images of political "heroes" such as Che Guevara, Mao Zedong, and Ho Chi Minh. As Jeremy Prestholdt has shown with regards to Che, these images played a key role in the elaboration of a "transnational imagination" linking struggles at home with struggles abroad. Images of Che, Mao, and Ho provided material for a "politics of heroes," according to which specific struggles, or aspects of struggle generally, were personified. These heroes stood in for qualities of the ideal revolutionary – resolute, far-seeing, wise, and (in Che's case at least), handsome and masculine – but they simultaneously served as arguments: living justifications for revolutionary action in general and for particular revolutionary strategies in particular. As Prestholdt puts it:

Heroes were profound symbols of shared ideals and transnational solidarity because they condensed multiple virtues in a single, extraordinary human life. As symbols of individual vision and courage, heroes added flesh to the bones of radical rhetoric. They stood at the center of an inspirational horizon as practically superhuman backdrops onto which radicals projected their hopes and dreams.[33]

Hero images, like the books discussed in Chapter 3 or the music discussed in Chapter 4, did not magically appear in their diverse locations but arrived via concrete routes. Prestholdt has reconstructed the path of the famous Che image, based on the 1960 photograph "Heroic Guerrilla" taken by the Cuban fashion photographer-turned-journalist Alberto "Korda" Diaz Gutiérrez. In 1967, Gutiérrez presented the photograph to the radical Italian publisher Giangiacomo Feltrinelli, who had thousands of posters made in the period before and after Che's death in October 1967. The same year, the image was given to the Irish artist Jim Fitzpatrick by members of the Dutch Provos. Fitzpatrick placed Che's image against the red backdrop well-known today, rendering the martyred revolutionary "into an easily reproducible work of pop art."[34] Appearing in countless demonstrations across Europe, Latin America, the USA, and the Middle East, the image symbolized and was accompanied by the embrace of Che's ideas. In West Germany, as we have seen, Che's foco theory was a

---

[33] Jeremy Prestholdt, "Resurrecting Che: Radicalism, the Transnational Imagination, and the Politics of Heroes," *Journal of Global History*, 7 (3) (2012): 506–526.
[34] Prestholdt, "Resurrecting Che."

key bridge to the actionist orientation of the antiauthoritarian faction in the SDS.

Perhaps even more ubiquitous and arguably even more fraught with meaning than the image of Che was that of Mao Zedong. As leader of the world's most populous Communist country, a legitimate heir to the revolutionary tradition of Marxism-Leninism who was seemingly free of association with the negative features of "deformed" Soviet and satellite Communism, Mao was a natural reference point for Western radicals looking for a third way between the Cold War blocs. For Western radicals, the Chinese Cultural Revolution launched by Mao in 1966 seemed to signal something truly new and exciting, a living example of the revolutionizing of everyday life sought by the New Left.[35] Mao's far-seeing visage seemed to exude wisdom, benevolence, and mystery, making him a perfect candidate for orientalist projections. For many young West Germans, Mao represented, in the words of the filmmaker Hellmuth Costard, a fellow student of Holger Meins at the DFFB, "a modern Buddha, an Enlightened one."[36]

Images made up a significant component of the Mao cult constructed over the course of the 1950s and 1960s. A series of fairly similar photographs were pressed into service, all clearly patterned on the socialist realist portrayals of Stalin encountered by Mao on a visit to Moscow in 1950.[37] In contrast to images of other dictators such as Hitler and Stalin, who were typically presented in uniform and engaged in activities of some kind, the Mao images depicted "an ageless father figure," removed from any signal of rank. The result was to highlight the "preternatural, quasi-divine capabilities of the 'great Chairman,' whose will and strength [stood] in the middle point of the depiction."[38] The most famous Mao image was the 1966 photograph taken by Wang Guodong, widely adopted for use in demonstrations in West Germany and elsewhere. The image was exploited by a number of artists, including Andy Warhol, who used it for his early 1970s series of Mao paintings. The German artist Thomas Bayrle used a late-1950s photograph of Mao as the basis for a series of kinetic art pieces realized between 1964 and 1966, in which motorized wooden panels, in

---

[35] See Richard Wolin, *The Wind from the East: May '68, French Intellectuals, and the Chinese Cultural Revolution* (Princeton University Press, 2010).

[36] Hellmuth Costard, "Das ist die Angst des Tonmanns," in Conradt, *Starbuck*, pp. 44–49, at p. 45.

[37] Gerhard Paul, "Das Mao-Porträt. Herrscherbild, Protestsymbol und Kunstikone," *Zeithistorische Forschungen/Studies in Contemporary History*, 6 (2009), available online at www.zeithistorische-forschungen.de/site/40208920/default.aspx (accessed June 30, 2012).

[38] Paul, "Das Mao-Porträt."

a way reminiscent of the mass choreography of Chinese parades, rotated to reveal the image of Mao. Joseph Beuys's students Sigmar Polke and Gerhard Richter produced images of Mao, as did artists such as K. P. Brehmer, Eugen Schönebeck, and Jörg Immendorff. The latter did so in his capacity as propagandist for the Maoist Kommunistische Partei Deutschlands-Aufbauorganisation (KPD[AO]), explicitly connecting his artistic project with Mao and Maoism.[39]

Nearly as important in its symbolic power as the image of Mao himself was Mao's Red Book. Carrying a talismanic power far out of proportion to its actual content, the "Mao bible" became a staple prop of the antiauthoritarian revolt. Available in German in a Chinese Foreign Language Press edition from 1966, the Red Book was published by the West German Fischer Verlag in a 1967 edition that quickly sold 75,000 copies.[40] The Kommune I and the Frankfurt Provos did good business selling the book (as did, by the way, the Black Panthers in the USA). The communards stocked up on the book at the Chinese embassy in East Berlin and sold it at the Free University. The Provos took delivery of a truckload, which they resold at a handsome profit.[41] The Red Book, as Tilemann Grimm of Fischer argued in his introduction to an edition of the book, represented a readily visible icon in the hands of the young, a symbol linking together "a billion service-ready revolutionaries."[42] For the activist Thorwald Proll, the Red Book had something "fairy tale-like about it," its simple aphorisms telegraphing a deeper wisdom even when not immediately understood.[43] Less important as a piece of literature than as a prop symbolizing revolutionary commitment and access to esoteric knowledge, the Red Book was the propaganda accessory par excellence.

Tellingly, the deployment of Maoist iconography had less to do with "Mao Zedong thought" per se than with the symbolic charge assigned to the icons themselves. As Sebastian Gehrig points out, Maoism, at least in the early days before the *K-Gruppen* began to assign literal importance to the Great Helmsman's words, was more a matter of performance than anything else.[44] Although the ground for the popular deployment of Maoism was prepared by intellectuals, above all in a series of essays

[39] Sebastian Gehrig, "(Re-)Configuring Mao: Trajectories of a Culturo-Political Trend in West Germany," *Transcultural Studies*, no. 2 (2011): 189–231.
[40] Koenen, *Das rote Jahrzehnt*, p. 147.
[41] Siegfried, *Time Is on My Side*, p. 425.
[42] Koenen, *Das rote Jahrzehnt*, p. 147.
[43] Proll and Dubbe, *Wir kamen vom anderen Stern*.
[44] Gehrig, "(Re-)Configuring Mao."

in the pages of *Kursbuch* that helped establish Maoism as an intellectually legitimate and timely phenomenon, it was the provocations of the Kommune I that introduced Maoism into the antiauthoritarian revolt.[45] Wearing Mao buttons at protests, hurling Red Books from the top of the Kaiser Wilhelm Memorial Church, or reading from the Red Book in front of the judiciary bench, communards deployed Maoism as a symbolic weapon against authority.[46] At the SDS delegate conference in West Berlin in September 1967, activists from the Kommune I pulled out the full panoply of Maoist symbols, donning Red Guard uniforms, playing Chinese Army marches and revolutionary songs, and passing out Red Books and other propaganda materials.[47]

These interventions represented a multivalent provocation, simultaneously attacking the establishment, challenging the legitimacy of Eastern Bloc Communism, and tweaking the sensibilities of more serious-minded SDS activists. For its part, the establishment was all too happy to play along with the charade, dubbing students "FU Chinese" and "Mao youth." In the SDS, however, the satirical nature of the Kommune I's deployment of Maoist iconography was cause for irritation. As Reimut Reiche complained in the journal *Neue Kritik*:

As recently as a half-year ago no one would have ventured to invoke Mao with a citation at an SDS assembly, today it happens on a regular basis, but accompanied by smirking laughter from the readers and the listeners ... Now we have to learn to read him correctly: to learn from the revolution of the Third World.[48]

Rudi Dutschke was characteristically quick to extract what he saw as the positive ideological content of Maoism, emphasizing the value of its insistence on the primacy of practice over theory.[49] Other activists sought to turn the Kommune I's performances into reality, forming "Red Guards" affiliated with the Schülerbewegung (the School Pupils' Movement, discussed below) that would eventually become the youth wing of the nascent Kommunistische Partei Deutschlands/Marxisten-Leninisten (KPD–ML;

---

[45] Sebastian Haffner, "Der neue Krieg," Introduction to Mao Zedong, *Theorie des Guerillakrieges oder Strategie der Dritten Welt* (Reinbek: Rowohlt, 1966), pp. 5–34, reprinted in Kraushaar, ed., *Die RAF und der linke Terrorismus*, vol. 1, pp. 157–181.

[46] On Rainer Langhans reading from the Red Book in court, see Joachim Scharloth, "Ritualkritik und Rituale des Protest: Die Entdeckung des Performativen in der Studentenbewegung der 1960er Jahre," in Klimke and Scharloth, eds., *1968: Handbuch zur Kultur- und Mediengeschichte der Studentenbewegung*, pp. 75–87, at p. 79.

[47] Gehrig, "(Re-)Configuring Mao."

[48] Reimut Reiche, "Worte des Vorsitzenden Mao," *Neue Kritik*, 41 (8) (1967): 9.

[49] Gehrig, "(Re-)Configuring Mao."

Communist Party of Germany–Marxists–Leninists). By the end of the decade, with the ascent of the *K-Gruppen*, Maoism would be taken in deadly earnest, not as a symbolic weapon to attack entrenched forces of whatever kind but as a source of solutions to West Germany's problems.[50]

The symbolic deployment of "heroes" such as Che and Mao enfolded a basic dichotomy at the heart of the antiauthoritarian revolt. Keen to adopt models that could inspire and legitimize, activists uncritically adopted "father figures" whose status as antiauthoritarian icons belied their actual authoritarianism. The reliance above all on *images* intensified this dichotomy, since the images themselves were empty of any inherent meaning. As Gerhard Paul has pointed out with respect to Mao, the status of the Mao image as an instrument of domination (*Herrshaftspraxis*) in China was fundamentally at odds with its status as a field for antiauthoritarian projection in West Germany.[51] This mirrored, more broadly, the dichotomy at the heart of the reception of the Cultural Revolution, a complicated picture of radicalism that was simultaneously "top down" and "bottom up," in which an upsurge of radicalism cynically unleashed by Mao as a means of bolstering his position was interpreted simplistically as radical-democratic rank-and-file activism. This take on Maoism was a product of the fact that the transnational reception of images was driven less by the meaning imputed to images or cultural products at their point of origin than at the point of their reception.

Hero images of the transnational imagination (and objects/texts such as the Mao bible) collapsed space, erasing the distance, both literal and figurative, between the viewer and the image/object. Simultaneously, they provided ritual objects for revolutionary performances, allowing activists to transplant the mass choreography of Third World revolutionary movements into the streets of West Berlin or Frankfurt. Placards carried at demonstrations were not just means of provocation or of signifying affiliation: they were props intended both to confer authenticity and to convey the appearance of a mass revolutionary base that extended beyond the confines of West Berlin or West Germany. In this way, hero images and objects served as a bridge between the global and the local.

But hero images also served as a bridge between past and present. By juxtaposing the faces of Third World heroes with those of heroes from the German past, activists fused the spatial and the temporal, connecting long-standing local issues and struggles with the struggles of the postcolonial present. The German radicals Rosa Luxemburg and Karl

[50] *Ibid.*   [51] Paul, "Das Mao-Porträt."

Liebknecht, murdered by right-wing mercenaries in the revolutionary events following the First World War, regularly appeared on placards alongside contemporary heroes of the Third World such as Che, Mao, and Ho. Luxemburg and Liebknecht were important on multiple levels. German revolutionaries who predated (and were thus free of association with) the "deformations" of Soviet and German Communism under Stalinism, they were also symbols of the perceived treason of social democracy, both in the German Revolution of 1918–1919 (when the SPD paid the right-wing mercenaries who murdered them) and, contemporaneously, as a party that had renounced Marxism, allied itself with conservatives as part of the Grand Coalition, and sought to enact the Emergency Laws. The death of Luxemburg and Liebknecht also represented the lengths to which the ruling class was willing to go when threatened. The "silencing" of Luxemburg and Liebknecht provided a perfect metaphor for the silencing of radical speech in the Federal Republic, either through censorship against radical publications or through judicial measures against well-known leftists. This angle was captured on the cover of one issue of *Radikalinski*, a *Schülerzeitung* (school newspaper) close to the Red Guards of West Berlin. The cover featured images of Luxemburg and Liebknecht alongside the legend "Free speech now, before it's again too late."[52]

This cover reveals the dichotomies inherent in the deployment of hero images. Underneath Luxemburg and Liebknecht appear another more ambiguous set of revolutionary heroes: Marx, Engels, Lenin, Stalin, and Mao. This ubiquitous "masthead" image of socialist eminences appeared throughout the cultural productions of the antiauthoritarian revolt, differing from location to location. In its famous iteration on the SDS poster "Everyone talks about the weather – not us," it was composed of Marx, Engels, and Lenin. Frequently Mao appeared, sometimes Stalin. The use of the "full-house" configuration of Marx, Engels, Lenin, Stalin, and Mao by *Radikalinski* telegraphed no particular ideological content beyond Marxism, but that is precisely the point. Symbolizing "revolution" in general, the deployment of these heroes was a visual shorthand, as likely to be tongue in cheek as ideologically principled. Appearing next to the legend "free speech," the image sent a message that would have been decidedly mixed had it formed the basis of a written or verbal discussion instead of an image. As it was, the unresolved dilemma at the heart of the juxtaposition of Lenin and Stalin – both notorious opponents of political pluralism, not least for their left-wing allies – and "free speech"

[52] *Radikalinski*, no. 4, January 1969, APO-Archiv Berlin.

Figure 5.3 "Free Speech, before it's again too late." *Radikalinski*, no. 4. Hamburg
Institute for Social Research.

elided the fundamental disagreement, cutting right through the heart of the antiauthoritarian movement, about the value of competing traditions of socialism, about antiauthoritarian versus authoritarian socialism, about top-down versus bottom-up.[53]

This ambiguity was in some respects a predictable outcome of the collage style characteristic of the underground press. But the collage style was no simple outcome of the (relatively) easy access to new reprographic technologies, nor was it simply an aesthetic choice, even if the links to contemporaneous developments in the arts are clear; rather, it was an attempt, if only a partly conscious one, to grapple with the overwhelming profusion of images exploding out of an increasingly saturated media landscape. At the same time, it represented an effort to come to grips with an ill-defined set of "revolutions" that seemed to be engulfing the entire world. The collage-style juxtaposition of a range of images – of sex organs and sex acts; of the socialist "great men" (and occasionally, women); of a whole host of images, by turns comic and shocking, drawn from popular culture and the mainstream press – sought to capture the intense ferment of a moment in which all roads seemed open and all signs pointed to "revolution."

Collage was, simply, a visual representation of a world youth revolution with too many facets to be captured in one image at a time. Ranging across the globally available image field, the antiauthoritarian gaze blurred the distinction between culture and politics at the same time that it erased the distance between space and place, between global and local. But, as we have just seen, the collage technique also allowed the juxtaposition of images that, while they might seem to fit together, were in fact distinctly at odds. Visual metaphors could and did help paper over fundamental disagreements that, in the course of the late 1960s, would lead to the splintering of the antiauthoritarian movement. One picture was worth more than a thousand words.

In this environment, it is no surprise that visual-discursive play became a site of ideological warfare within the antiauthoritarian revolt itself. With the rise of the *K-Gruppen*, images of the great men of socialist history, like the sayings of Chairman Mao collected in the Red Book, became transformed from playful citations into deadly serious totems of worship.

[53] On Lenin's suppression of left-wing political allies, see Grigori Maximov, *The Guillotine at Work in Russia* (Chicago, Ill.: Berkman Fund, 1940); see also Harold Goldberg, "Goldman and Berkman View the Bolshevik Regime," *Slavic and East European Review*, 53 (131) (1975): 272–276.

In reaction to this hardening of visual-discursive boundaries, activists of the Sponti scene sought to disrupt the integrity of the masthead, injecting spontaneity and contingency in place of certainty and rigidity. Turning the busts on their heads, or replacing them with their own faces, the editorial collectives of journals of the undogmatic left such as *Schwarze Protokolle* and *Carlo Sponti* displaced the "great men" of socialist history to the margins, putting themselves at the center. The *Schwarze Protokolle* replaced the socialist great men with an ever-evolving lineup of everyday men, women, children, and cartoon characters. On the cover of one issue, a crowd conveys the busts of Stalin et al. to the "ashbin of history."[54] The Heidelberg Sponti journal *Carlo Sponti* (the title a play on the name of the Italian film producer Carlo Ponti) went so far as to replace Stalin and Mao with another set of eminences dear to the hearts of West German radicals: the Marx brothers.[55]

The introduction of the comic element, both in the replacement of the figures in the masthead and in the choice of replacements, symbolized the turn away from the dogmatism, dour emotions, and "revolutionary morality" of the *K-Gruppen*. Later, the editors, in a further comic maneuver, placed their own faces into the masthead, symbolizing the turn to personal subjectivity and the DIY ethos of the undogmatic left. This sorting out of the images proceeded in parallel with the sorting out of the movement as, during the course of the 1970s, it splintered into its component parts. The visual practice of the high period of the movement in the late 1960s, by contrast, was characterized by the juxtaposition of images in ways that papered over rather than revealed basic contradictions, allowing the ambiguous allegiances at the heart of the antiauthoritarian revolt to exist, temporarily, in tandem.

A key feature of the collage style, with its ambiguous juxtapositions, was the recontextualization of images drawn from disparate sources. This recontextualization played a key role in the dialogue carried on by the underground press with the mainstream. Indeed, one of the key visual-discursive maneuvers of the underground press was the reappropriation of imagery from mainstream sources. Already with the earliest of the papers, a brash cut-and-paste layout was used to represent a postmodern analog to the sometimes dry and theory-laden pronouncements of the student left. Words and images were appropriated from diverse sources,

---

[54] *Schwarze Protokolle*, no. 6, 1973, HIS ZS 100 "Schwarze Protokolle."
[55] *Carlo Sponti*, no. 43, June 1978, HIS ZD 313.

Figure 5.4 Cover of *Rote Garde*. Hamburg Institute for Social Research.

Figure 5.5 Masthead image from *Schwarze Protokolle*. Hamburg Institute for Social Research.

Figure 5.6 Masthead image from *Carlo Sponti*. Hamburg Institute for Social Research.

then recontextualized in ways that exposed official hypocrisies and challenged dominant narratives. One of the techniques pioneered by *Linkeck* involved (re-)presenting media images in ways that subverted their original meaning. Issue no. 1, for example, used the logo of Springer's *Bild Zeitung*, putting the words "gas the commune" into mouth of Axel

Springer himself. The central image – gas bubbles coming from a human behind – was surrounded by terms such as"criminals," "pathological idiots," "left-fascists," "Vietcong whores," "Communist pigs," all lifted from the pejorative repertoire of the Springer milieu.[56] *Linkeck* no. 2 lifted the masthead from the Nazi Party newspaper *Völkischer Beobachter*, altering the phrase "Fighting Organ of the National Socialist Movement of Greater Germany" to appear without the word "National."[57] Yet another issue bore the logo of *Der Landser*, a small-format magazine of war stories catering to military buffs and ex-Wehrmacht soldiers. On the cover, the helmet of a German soldier attacking a tank with explosives bears the logo "APO," while a photo inset of a young Rainer Langhans (who had served briefly in the army before becoming a counterculture media star) is labeled "Sergeant Langhans."[58] A headline urged readers, in ironic reference to the Emergency Laws opposed by the APO, to "drive Bonn into a state of emergency."[59]

Such juxtapositions of the comical and the militant served a serious purpose, for they made political mobilization not boring, but sexy, fun, and cool. The use of recontextualized images, moreover, made it possible to level a withering critique at the media forces that sought to turn average citizens against the student movement. One of *Linkeck*'s special targets was Hans-Joachim Stenzel, a cartoonist for the *Bild Zeitung* and the *Berliner Morgenpost*. Stenzel's (quite entertaining) cartoons mercilessly lampooned the student movement, portraying students as dirty, threatening idiots. In *Linkeck* no. 4, some of Stenzel's cartoons, bracketed by the phrase "expropriate Springer," were accompanied by a mocking letter from editor Bernd Kramer. The letter suggested (among other things) that the female subject of the "love-in" depicted in one of the cartoons was none other than Frau Stenzel. (Stenzel subsequently sued for damages.) The cover of the issue bore a reproduction of one of Stenzel's most well-known images, a "biker-barbarian" student with a cigarette in one hand and a spiked club in the other. The figure was juxtaposed with a quotation from Marx's *Das Kapital*, "I welcome every judgment of scholarly criticism" ("Jedes Urteil wissenschaftlicher Kritik ist mir willkommen"), an act of cheeky erudition that, alongside Stenzel's crude caricature, made a sharp commentary about the depths to which a supposedly free and objective mainstream press was willing to stoop.[60]

[56] *Linkeck*, no. 1.
[57] *Linkeck*, no. 2. The issue seems to have appeared with at least two different cover designs, each featuring the *Völkischer Beobachter* masthead.
[58] *Linkeck*, no. 3a. [59] *Ibid.* [60] *Linkeck*, no. 4.

Figure 5.7 Cover of *Linkeck*, no. 4. Hamburg Institute for Social Research.

"GREET THE REVOLUTION – IN A BRILLIANT JACKET": THE COUNTERCULTURE BETWEEN REVOLT AND RECUPERATION

The struggle over the meaning of images at the heart of the underground press's semiotic guerrilla warfare against the mainstream press was emblematic of a larger struggle around the visual signifiers of countercultural membership. The visual nature of this membership, and in particular the fact that it was rooted in style and fashion, made it a central site of recuperation. Of all the aspects of a would-be revolutionary movement that consumer capitalism might attempt to turn to its own purposes, those aspects that were rooted in selective consumption from the outset were the easiest to coopt. At a fundamental level, the counter-culture was a visual phenomenon, inasmuch as the style codes that governed the surface level of membership in it were visual in nature. The rise of the underground, subculture(s), and counterculture was inextricably linked with visuality and the visual image. The style-based subcultures of the postwar period arose out of the nexus of social change (e.g. the birth of the teenager), youth consumption (of goods imbued with valued characteristics), and fashion. As we have seen, this development unfolded in a dialectic relationship with music and particular music genres, which helped create the space, physical and discursive, in which style-based sub-cultures could coalesce. Subcultures were thus both sonic and visual, but it was the latter that trumped, because visual markers were the ultimate expression of subcultural status. As scholars in media and cultural studies (and, to a lesser extent, history) have shown, subcultures based themselves on values of authenticity and "subcultural capital" that determined membership in them. Visual markers – hair length, clothing choices, various other aspects of comportment – were the defining features of membership in the community.

It is common, in discussing 1968, to speak in terms of *movements*, but in the realm of the visually defined style community even more than elsewhere, it is more proper to think in terms of *scenes*. The *scene* as a category of analysis has been the subject of a good deal of scholarly analysis in fields such as media and communication studies, but for our purposes the scene can be understood as a spatially and visually constructed set of relationships based on social, political, cultural, and aesthetic affinities; *spatial*, because typically constructed in terms of meeting places both semiprivate (music venues, pubs, and bars) and public (the street); *visual* because organized around readily accessible markers of group identity (in 1968, jeans, parkas, long hair, other and sundry aspects of "freak" appearance, for both men and women).[61] The spatial and the visual are here intimately related, for as much as the possession of "subcultural capital" depended on specialized spatial knowledge (e.g. of what bars to go to and knowledge of the spaces in which "scene" activities took place), membership in the scene (i.e. one's passport to acceptance within these spaces) was judged in heavily visual terms. It is not for nothing that the underground press was saturated with self-depictions of the "freak" look, whether famous (stars such as Langhans and Teufel) or generic (any one

---

[61] See, for example, Darcy Leach and Sebastian Haunns, "Scenes and Social Movements," in Hank Johnston, ed., *Culture, Social Movements, and Protest* (Aldershot: Ashgate, 2009), pp. 255–276.

of thousands of images culled from the globally available image field). The look of the antiauthoritarian/countercultural left, sometimes even more than its (highly variegated) ideas, acted as organizing principle number one.

Accounts by contemporaries strongly emphasize the impact of long hair on men. "It should be recalled that back in 1966," writes *International Times* correspondent Alex Gross, a male wearing long hair could still provoke controversy even in England and America, while in Germany it could elicit catcalls in the streets. "I was accustomed to hearing people shout after me 'Hey Gammler!' or 'Hey, Bayottle!' (this being the German pronunciation of 'Beatle') even though my hair was relatively short."[62] Hash Rebels Michael "Bommi" Baumann and Ralf Reinders write at some length about the social significance of long hair in the 1960s. For Baumann, long hair offered a means of achieving a "new identity" outside of a workaday normality constructed in overwhelmingly visual terms: "As long as you fit in, you don't get hassled."[63] Elsewhere he writes, "Everything started with the fact that we had long hair. They called us 'Gammler.' Someone who had long hair in West Berlin 1961/62 was automatically an outcast and was spit on and insulted in the street or arrested by the police."[64] The situation had hardly changed a few years later. "It is easily forgotten today," writes Ralf Reinders, that "[m]any people at that time lost their jobs, were chased out of apprenticeships because they had long hair ... You weren't served a beer, you were beaten up. Sometimes some bum [on the street] wanted to give someone a haircut. There were just continual problems."[65]

The situation was little different on the other side of the German–German divide, where, if anything, the subversive power of visual difference was even more pronounced, and deviation from the norm even more severely punished. The young generation of the 1960s in the DDR, as in other countries of the Eastern Bloc, readily adopted the outlook, mores, appearance, and behavior of Western "Beat culture." Music and fashion became a badge of identity, a totem of disengagement from the dull conformity of daily life. The importance of personal style as a political statement is captured strikingly in the term of self-identification employed in the reminiscences of members of the East Berlin

---

[62] Gross, *The Untold Sixties*, p. 190.
[63] Baumann, *How It All Began*, pp. 19–20.
[64] Michael Baumann with Christof Meueler, *Rausch und Terror: Ein politischer Erlebnisbericht* (Berlin: Rotbuch Verlag, 2008), p. 26.
[65] Reinders and Fritsch, *Die Bewegung 2 Juni*, p. 213.

underground scene collected in 2004 by Thomas P. Funk: "longhairs."[66] It is indicative that the threatened forced haircuts written about by Ralf Reinders in West Berlin were often actually administered in East Berlin, not by petit-bourgeois vigilantes but by the forces of the state. The subversive power of personal style on the two sides of the Iron Curtain was a matter of degree and not kind, its differential consequences determined only by the relative extent of the state's claims on the personal expression of the young.

In the West, the Kommune I acted as a dissemination point for the ideas and images of the nascent counterculture in which the visual occupied a central position. The communards differentiated themselves from the student movement not only in their disdain for the formal democratic procedures of the SDS, or in their willingness to use provocation unilaterally to win publicity for their cause, but in their physical appearance. Largely conventional at the time of the failed "pudding bomb" assault on Hubert Humphrey in April 1967, by the next year this had metamorphosed, especially in the case of the group's two stars – Rainer Langhans and Fritz Teufel – into the shaggy, beaded hippie look of the international counterculture. The appearance of Langhans and Teufel, especially at a time when *Gammler* were regularly demonized in the Springer Press, was a visual metaphor for the danger represented by the commune, the latter a term with a deep and chilling resonance for non-leftists in Germany.

In the sense that their appearance represented a social danger in the West Germany of the late 1960s, the communards were the successors to the *Halbstarken* of the 1950s and cousins to their contemporaries the *Gammler*; but if personal appearance was a visible sign of (dangerous) difference separating the countercultural tribe from mainstream society, it was simultaneously a mark of belonging and authenticity in the underground scene itself. Teufel's and Langhans's appearance, the former with his beard and spectacles, the latter with his easily recognizable Afro, helped popularize the idea of the commune for young people all around Germany better than a thousand manifestos. Indeed, those without access to the commune's printed proclamations could still see images of the communards in the mainstream press. The personification of the commune in the figures of Langhans and Teufel comes out strikingly in

---

66 See Thomas P. Funk, "Unterm Asphalt: Die Kunden vom Lichtenberger Tunnel," in Rauhut and Kochan, eds., *Bye Bye, Lübben City*, pp. 94–106.

Figure 5.8 Rainer Langhans and Uschi Obermaier as poster children of the counterculture in *Stern*. Photo: Klaus Mehner.

the commune's fan mail. One of the many postcards sent to the commune, addressed to "Mr. Teufel in Hell" ("Teufel" is the German word for "devil"), featured a drawing of Langhans's Afro, suggesting the extent to which, for one young correspondent at least, the two figures were synonymous, not only with the commune but with each other.

After the move of the commune to the Stephanstraße "Fabrik" in late summer 1968, and the arrival of Langhans's new girlfriend, the model Uschi Obermaier, the cult of personality intensified further. Langhans and Obermaier became media stars, regularly appearing in photo shoots that turned them into poster children for the new lifestyle revolution. Here, images of physical beauty and countercultural style became vehicles for transmission of a new attitude toward life with an implicitly political valence. In one feature in the photo-magazine *Stern*, Langhans and Obermaier demonstrated, step by step, how to roll a marijuana cigarette. Frequently appearing topless, the couple became symbols of the new sexual freedom and openness associated with the counterculture.

In gender terms, the "equality" symbolized by the joint nudity of Langhans and Obermaier concealed more ambiguous meanings. Either partner could function as a sex symbol, to be sure; but the juxtaposition of Langhans's bare-chested hippie look and Obermaier's bare breasts was an asymmetrical statement, to say the least. This was in keeping with the general trend according to which depictions of "revolutionary" women emphasized their sexuality, a point to which we shall return. Here, it may be noted that changes in women's fashions played a role similar to changes in men's in terms of telegraphing membership in the APO or the counterculture. In a few short years from the mid 1960s, men made the transition from suits and ties to jeans, casual jackets, and sometimes beards; women meanwhile sported shorter skirts and high boots, as well as jeans and second-hand American Army parkas, the latter a key antiauthoritarian fashion statement in both Germanys.[67]

The fame of Langhans and Obermaier was not universally approved on the left, less because of concerns about the exploitation of the female form than worry over the effect that "selling out" to the capitalist image machine could have on the legitimacy of the movement as a whole. Indeed, the Kommune I's role as an interface between underground and mainstream placed it in an ambiguous relationship with the political movement from which it arose. Langhans and Obermaier, for example,

---

[67] See Poiger, "Generations."

Figure 5.9 APO style. Outside the International Vietnam Congress, February 1968. Note the Vietcong flag. Landesarchiv Berlin.

faced charges that their main source of income, selling pictures of themselves to the capitalist press, was an unworthy method of earning one's daily bread. "Rainer and Uschi go out very seldom," the caption under a picture of the couple in the radical newspaper *883* sarcastically observed; "the curiosity of strangers is disagreeable to them."[68]

Such charges, part of a larger unhappiness about the ease with which the mainstream was able to gain access to and package the supposedly subversive surfaces of countercultural style, were not uncommon. Indeed, the counterculture that the Kommune I helped to launch became a site of struggle in which those who wished to preserve the purity and authenticity of the countercultural project fought against incursions that sought to sap that meaning. The visual nature of countercultural fashion meant that its elements could easily be repackaged. The surfaces of style were empty of meaning as such – meaning was, as it were, imparted to elements of

[68] "Der Sonderbare Drive der Kommune I," *883*, no. 40, November 13, 1969. The fact that Obermaier freely admitted having little interest in the "revolution" hardly helped to dampen such criticism.

style through a complicated process of association and articulation that I have explored elsewhere.[69]

The ultimate vehicle of recuperation was advertising. The young provided a ready-made body of consumers, and the importance of fashion to the construction of youth identity made the intervention at the forefront of youth style a profitable enterprise indeed. Advertising's *raison d'être*, after all, was to transform feelings, values, aspirations, and vague associations into commodity form. For the advertiser, the youth wave meant money; but for young people who associated elements of style with real values, that is, who saw them as marks of authenticity with an actual content, the incorporation of countercultural images and goods into the consumer sphere represented the death of the project. "The young are the most consumption-friendly group of consumers in the Federal Republic," noted a piece in *Pardon*,

[but] a great part of the youth are rebelling, profess the socialist idea, want to change society. Are the young thus already lost as consumers of the products of the capitalist economy? No! Because advertising exists as … the best way to make youth protest harmless and to make capital out of the revolutionary impulse of the young. This new trend in advertising … can, if consistently carried out, transform the attack on the capitalist system into a profitable capitalist search for wealth.[70]

The article was illustrated with recent examples of recuperative advertising strategies. "Greet the revolution – in a brilliant jacket," read one representative example. "Men, the moment of revolution is at hand," it continued.

The nights are getting longer, more colorful … And you want to show up at a demonstration looking like a grey mouse? You have to be seen. With your coat of DIOLEN cotton. DIOLEN cotton, that is the style for the breakout – for the revolution 68. Also in the stylish shock-colors Marcuse-red and Mao-yellow.[71]

The dapper white jacket in the advertisement was accessorized with cigarette, "Expropriate Springer" badge (badly superimposed on the image of the coat) and "Mao Bible."

The danger such developments represented for a movement that existed at the intersection of youth culture and radical politics was addressed in a number of fora. The Aktionszentrum Unabhängiger und Sozialistischer

[69] See Brown, "Subcultures."
[70] *Pardon: Die deutsche satirische Monatsschrift*, 7 Jahrgang, no. 8, August 1968, p. 22.
[71] *Pardon*, no. 8, August 1968, p. 22.

Figure 5.10 "Greet the Revolution – in a brilliant jacket." *Pardon*, no. 8, August 1968. Hamburg Institute for Social Research.

Schüler (AUSS; Action Center for Independent and Socialist School Pupils) took it up in a long contribution to *konkret* in August 1969:

> Olivetti is already advertising for young managers in the Italian daily newspapers using the "dynamic" image of Che Guevara; Christian Dior has learned to "subvert" [fashion shows]; *Twen* offers its readers group sex ... and [the youth magazine] *Underground* its readers the school revolt after school and via mail. All that's not so bad; it's a calculated risk of the cultural revolution that the established culture will lustily grab after all the attractive junk available. Much worse is that many of us are beginning to fit ourselves to the image that the old culture has cobbled together out of our revolutionary positions and symbols and with them rejuvenated itself.[72]

Here the AUSS touched upon an aspect of the development of radical movements that has often been overlooked: the question of generational turnover. The entry of younger new members into a subculture tends to amplify the importance of the surface marks of subcultural belonging at the expense of the ideas motivating the first generation of members.[73] As the AUSS put it: "Today in many classes and subcultural groups the very pupils are honored who have best imitated us, without however having really been touched by us, the very pupils who are able to put on the revolutionary façade most slickly."[74]

For the AUSS, this problem was intimately bound up with the broader problem of recuperation, since it was precisely from the stock of commercially produced images and markers of identity – e.g. clothes and music – that subcultural identity was constructed to begin with. The AUSS complained of a new type of local "matador" in some groups, who prized style over substance. This young person talked a radical game, "but only in German class, where it doesn't cost them anything."[75] The biggest problem with this type was his potential to serve – and notably, it is a *male* type spoken about here –

> as a false image of liberation for other pupils. Because he unifies in himself the attributes with which the shy, introverted, inhibited, and [oppressed] class comrades easily identify: He is narcissistic, verbally clever, clothes himself extravagantly (either extremely fine, or extremely confidently according to our own Gammel-aesthetic) and has a good-looking girlfriend. This type, that we ourselves have produced, already represents elements of the class enemy.[76]

---

[72] "Sexualität nach der Sexwelle," *konkret*, no. 17, August 11, 1969, p. 20.
[73] See Brown, "Subcultures."
[74] "Sexualität nach der Sexwelle," p. 20.
[75] *Ibid.*   [76] *Ibid.*

In the leading radical paper *883*, the possibilities of liberation through popular music and subculture were the subject of ongoing debate.[77] While recognizing that subcultural identity could play a role in freeing consciousness and strengthening resistance to capitalism's demands at the level of daily life, the paper also criticized the role played by hippies in the commercialization of the underground, and warned against supposedly "left-wing" pubs that, with a few radical posters on the wall, tried to capitalize on APO trade.[78] Terms such as "underground" and "subculture," despite efforts to popularize them by hip capitalists such as Rolf Ulrich Kaiser and theorist-participants such as Rolf Schwendter, came increasingly into disrepute with many of the people they were meant to represent. Schwendter himself criticized Kaiser in connection with the Essener Songtage and, though he refused to condemn him outright, wondered in print if Kaiser's involvement in the more political-theoretically oriented approaches to the question of counterculture could be divorced from his wider efforts to profit from it.[79]

Others recoiled from the increasingly commercial overtones of terms such as "counterculture" and "underground." "Underground has become such a perverted term that we feel distinctly uneasy when we are labeled with it," noted the editors of the underground newspaper *Dig. .it*;

[i]t is no longer possible to speak of the underground as the counterculture, the psychedelic youth movement, let alone as [part of] the new potential for social change. Rather, the ideas of the underground are absorbed and interwoven into a consumption-oriented lifestyle … with the aim of awakening the already near-dead culture business to an illusory existence.[80]

This attempt at recuperation had proven itself all too successful in

simulat[ing] freedom while in reality hindering its realization. In place of the original idea of reducing (pseudo-) necessities … the underground has, more or less unwillingly, supplied entire industrial sectors with new impulses through which millions of young people are brought to the point – with U-fashion, U-Musik, U-Literature, U-porno – of buying their lifestyle instead of creating it themselves.[81]

---

[77] See Weinhauer, "Der Westberliner 'Underground'," pp. 82–83.
[78] See "Sind Hippies Kulturrevolutionäre?," *Agit 883*, no. 35, October 9, 1969; Heidi Rühlmann, "Eine linke Kneipe in proletarischem Milieu: HIPETUK," *Agit 883*, no. 26, September 7, 1969.
[79] "Zur Gegenmedien Tagung am 11–14 Juni in Remscheid," *Roter Mohn*, no. 1, July 15, 1970, HIS ZR 563.
[80] *Dig. .it*, no. 1, in Wintjes and Gehret, eds., *Ulcus Molle Infodienst*, p. 92.
[81] *Dig. .it*, no. 1.

A similar critique was levied by the Hamburg anarchist journal *Befreiung*, in this case against the cooptation of the so-called "Jesus People." The turn of members of the hippie movement to an iconoclastic version of Christianity was a significant part of the more general turn to alternative, largely Eastern religions at the end of the 1960s. The hippies and *Gammler* of the 1960s, the journal observed in 1971, had wanted to escape from the old society. "They attempted to lead a free, unshackled life. They attempted not only to break out of the old society, but to … build a new one: the subculture or the counter-society."[82] These hippies and *Gammler* dressed differently and listened to different music, but then "cunning fashion-managers recognized that here a new industry could be cranked up. An entire jeans industry became rich, as well as large-capitalist concerns (fashion, makeup, records, and poster industry). The hippie-movement became commercialized and degraded to a [mere] fashion."[83] The danger that "an entire generation could break with capitalist values" required a stronger intervention, thus the Jesus People, who were hoodwinked by figures such as the evangelist Anton Schulte and by commercialized productions such as *Jesus Christ Superstar*.[84]

The cooptation of the counterculture became the target of direct action on more than one occasion. In West Berlin, members of the Blues scene attacked the West Berlin premier of the musical *Hair*. "We are well aware," read a flyer distributed in connection with the action, "that 'Hair' only appears in the guise of the subculture in order to gratify capitalist demands."[85] The flyer went on to link the protest against *Hair* with resistance to the pressure of the authorities on meeting places such as the Zodiak, thereby juxtaposing the make-believe counterculture of peace, love, and inclusiveness with the reality of police raids and arrests: "The performance of 'Hair,' this Pseudo-Subcultural troupe, attempts to demonstrate the outward impression: West Berlin, the 'free city', has a place for everyone! We demand the giving over of the Beautyfull [sic] balloons to the real subculture."[86]

---

[82] *Befreiung*, 25 Jahrgang, January 1972. Green Library, Stanford University, Germany. Extraparliamentary Opposition movement, 1967–1984 collection, box 23 (unnumbered folder), p. 8.

[83] *Befreiung*, 25 Jahrgang, January 1972.

[84] *Befreiung*, 25 Jahrgang, January 1972, p. 9. Anton Schulte was known as the German Billy Graham. See his book on the American Jesus Freaks: Anton Schulte, *Die Jesus-Bewegung in USA: Ein persönlicher Reisebericht* (Altenkirchen: Missionswerk Neues Leben, 1972).

[85] "Ist 'Hair' Subkultur?," in Kramer, ed., *Gefunde Fragmente, 1967–1980*, p. 24.

[86] *Ibid.*

Nikel Pallat, the manager of Ton Steine Scherben, made this sort of point in an even more spectacular manner during an appearance on the WDR television program *Ende offen* ... Pallat had been invited to take part in a roundtable discussion on "Pop und Co: Die andere Musik zwischen Protest und Markt" (Pop & Co.: The Other Music between Protest and the Market). Other panelists included the sociologist Heinz-Klaus Metzger, the journalist Wolfgang Hamm, and Rolf Ulrich Kaiser. After abusing Kaiser for several minutes – "you work for the oppressor and not against the oppressor" – Pallat attacked the studio table with an axe (for some thirteen seconds), afterward stuffing the studio's microphones into his pockets.[87] "So," muttered Pallat as he walked away from the shattered table, "now we can continue the discussion."[88]

CONCLUSION

The (tele)visual nature of Pallat's intervention reinforces, again, the extent to which the antiauthoritarian revolt relied on the subversive power of the image. But it also highlights, like Holger Meins's *The Making of a Molotov Cocktail* before it, how readily the visual, as still or moving image, could trump the reasoned discussion that it ostensibly sought to supplement. In Pallat's case, indeed, the intervention was directed precisely against that reasoned discussion. This dichotomy, between the visual as means of supplementing rational argument and the visual as means of short-circuiting it, was a characteristic feature of the antiauthoritarian revolt. In a broader sense, as the debates about recuperation discussed above indicate, the realm of the visual also represented a site of ideological contingency and ambiguity. Some of the very things that held the antiauthoritarian movement together, indeed, as we have seen in this chapter, the very visual signs that signified membership in it, were the same things that could tear it apart, the very things that could be used, from the perspective of activists themselves, to coopt and destroy it. From a scholarly perspective, the dovetailing of the antiauthoritarian movement with patterns of youth consumption is one of the reasons for its spread and staying power, or, perhaps more properly, for the staying power of a heavily mediated, consumption-based *version* of youth revolt that helped fuel the broader

---

[87] See Sichtermann et al., *Keine Macht für Niemand*, pp. 66–69. Also present at the roundtable discussion was Conny Weit, a member of the group Popol Vuh.

[88] A video of Pallat's appearance on *Ende offen* ... can be viewed at www.youtube.com/watch?v=H3AxGp5k-Qo (accessed December 31, 2008).

democratizing and liberalizing upsurge of the long sixties. It is important to remember, however, that from the perspective of the activists themselves, and here we refer not only to denizens of the subculture/counterculture, but also to student activists and left-wing intellectuals more generally, the signs and symbols of countercultural belonging, as well as the cultural-productive activities with which they were intimately bound up, served above all a *political* function. The visual was deployed in accordance with the antiauthoritarian and self-organizational imperatives that governed all actions in the movement; that is, it was conceived not as an invitation for mass acceptance but as a highly specific means of enacting a rebellion of the self, with potential (via the scene[s] of which the self was a part) to reshape society. That self-adopted signs of difference had the potential to win mass acceptance and thereby lose their meaning was a frustrating but inevitable consequence of a set of visual practices rooted in art/pop on the one hand, and in consumption and reconfiguration of consumer items on the other.

At the same time, as we saw in connection with the response to Holger Meins's Molotov Cocktail film, the prominence of the visual in the antiauthoritarian revolt could sometimes threaten to overwhelm the culture of reasoned debate that informed the activities of the SDS and its intellectual supporters. To be sure, images could be carefully deployed in the service of reasoned political critique, and, indeed, the multivalent associations and ironic juxtapositions characteristic of the use of images in the underground press often demonstrated, even when they were sometimes simultaneously crass and brutal, a precocious political and aesthetic sophistication. Yet these very images held the power to bypass reason, appealing directly to the emotions, and if the use of images in this way by political movements was by no means new – indeed, stretched back, in its modern form, to the French Revolution – in the media-driven moment of 1968 the dichotomy between words and images reached a particularly forceful expression.

Above all, the visual, alongside the performative impulse flowing out of its sources in the art world and the new political-provocational gambits of Provo and Situationism, were primary sites of the transnational in 1968. The doctrines feeding the developments of a performative politics of appearance and gesture were dominantly, if not exclusively, extra-German. Fluxus, as we have seen, originally a product of the New York art scene, represented the convergence of a group of artists, international in both provenance and orientation, with key West German art figures centered in Rheinland art institutes and departments. Literally transnational in inception – for example, through the travels of George Maciunas and the presence of artists such as Nam June Paik – Fluxus and related doctrines and movements were also globalizing in conception, representing the activity of networks of like-minded individuals across national borders. More generally, the image sphere out of which the antiauthoritarian revolt was constructed was, as we have seen, a global one. The proliferation of images, of everything from atrocities in Vietnam to the faces of revolutionary heroes to artifacts drawn from the whole range of popular culture, helped delimit the scope of the antiauthoritarian gaze. Simultaneously, antiauthoritarians expressed the global on their very persons. The "scurrilous rituals and symbols" written of by Michael Baumann, "like the army parkas with writing on them, signs saying 'Ban the Bomb,' slogans or names of rock groups, blues people, and so on," were visual markers of an identity drawn from multiple sources, in almost every case, extra-German.[89] Finally, the deployment of images drawn from this sphere in collages and other cultural productions not only demonstrated the range of the far left's commitments but became one of the primary ways in which the convergence of the global and the local, central to 1968, was expressed at the level of practice.

[89] Baumann, *How It All Began*, p. 21. See also Marion Grob, *Das Kleidungsverhalten jugendlicher Protestgruppen in Deutschland im 20 Jahrhundert: Am Beispiel des Wandervogels und der Studentenbewegung* (Münster: F. Coppenrath, 1985); and Kathrin Fahlenbrach, *Protest-Inszenierungen: Visuelle Kommunikation und kollektive Identitäten in Protestbewegungen* (Wiesbaden: Westdeutscher Verlag, 2002).

CHAPTER 6

Power

In February 1968, just a little over two weeks after the Springer Tribunal at which Holger Meins screened his *The Making of a Molotov Cocktail*, some 2,000 delegates gathered at the Technical University for the International Vietnam Congress. Drawn overwhelmingly from the Berlin SDS, the delegates included representatives of the international student revolution from locations throughout the world. Like the Springer Tribunal, the Vietnam Congress was aimed at taking the SDS's contest with authority to a new level. In this case, the goal was to bolster and make concrete the SDS's support for the Vietnamese people fighting against US imperialism. Just two weeks prior, the Vietcong had launched the surprise Tet offensive, which had shockingly demonstrated the vulnerability of the US superpower. Previous activism had succeeded in placing the Vietnam War at the forefront of the agenda; the goal now was to find a way to turn words into action. The slogan on the giant banner stretching around the hall, Che Guevara's "the duty of the revolutionary is to make the revolution," signaled this intention in striking terms. The following day, a massive demonstration involving 12,000–20,000 demonstrators turned the streets of West Berlin into a sea of red flags, accompanied by chants of "Ho Ho Ho Chi Minh!"

Marking the high-point of the identification with the national liberation struggles of the Third World as a solution for revolutionaries at home, the Vietnam Congress also demonstrated the limitations of the SDS's attempt to transform itself into an active revolutionary force within West German society. Within less than two months of the Congress, Rudi Dutschke would be convalescing from life-threatening wounds, and student activists would test the limitations of revolutionary rhetoric-turned-reality in raging street battles with police. The relative strength of the competing forces in West Berlin was cast into sharp relief by the anti-SDS counterdemonstration that took place the following weekend. On February 21, 1968, under the motto "Berlin stands for peace and

Figure 6.1 "Stop Dutschke Now!" *National Zeitung*. Hamburg Institute for Social Research.

freedom," some 80,000 citizens converged on the Rathaus Schöneberg, scene of many previous student protests.[1] The protest was explicitly conceived as a response to the student demonstration of the previous weekend. City and private workers were allowed off work early to attend. "Berlin demonstrates," proclaimed a flyer announcing the event, "against street terror and anarchy, for freedom and constitutional order. Against the intolerance of self-appointed elites, for respect for the opinion of the minority ... Against illusions and political suicide, for peace, freedom, and self-determination in the whole world."[2]

High-sounding rhetoric aside, the mood at the demonstration was ugly. Demonstrators carried signs bearing the name Dutschke over the legend "Public Enemy Nr. 1." Another sign bore a Germanized version of the classic American Cold War slogan "Better Red than Dead" ("Lieber tot als rot"). More than one shaggy-haired student was set upon by demonstrators. In one case, a young man bearing a passing resemblance to Rudi Dutschke, Lutz-Dieter Mende, was nearly torn apart before police intervened. "From the crowd I heard ever louder," he recalled, "it's Dutschke. It spread like a wild fire through the crowd ... I yelled: I'm a worker just like you. Then someone was brandishing a bottle. I felt blows all over my body. I fled into a tobacco shop ... I was deathly afraid. They screamed: Kill him, string him up."[3] In one case, amid threats and imprecations, students were packed onto S-Bahn cars and "sent to the east."[4] Afterward, the letters section of *konkret* was filled with reports of protesters roughed up by the crowd. A young worker, accompanied by his sister and fiancée sporting "Solidarity for Vietnam Campaign" buttons, was told they belonged "over the wall" in a "labor camp"; a young woman reported having a man tear off her badge and spit in her face.[5] In at least one incident, protestors fought with student counterdemonstrators.[6] A report in *Die Zeit* recounted the remark "When Adolf was around this wouldn't have happened."[7]

---

[1] "Massendemonstration in Berlin," *Frankfurter Rundschau*, February 22, 1968.
[2] Aktion demokratisches Berlin, "Berlin demonstriert," Hoover Institution, Notgemeinschaft für eine freie Universität, box 575, folder 33.
[3] "Verwaltungsangestellter," in "Schlägt sie tot: schneidet ihr die Haare ab!," *konkret*, no. 5, May 1968, p. 14. See the photos of Mende and other events of the day in Ruetz, *"Ihr müßt diesen Typen nur ins Gesicht sehen,"* pp. 110–118.
[4] Ruetz, *"Ihr müßt diesen Typen nur ins Gesicht sehen,"* p. 166.
[5] "Junger Arbeiter" and "Junges Mädchen" in "Schlägt sie tot: schneidet ihr die Haare ab!," p. 14.
[6] "Massendemonstration in Berlin."
[7] "Demonstration mit Nachhilfe: Antwort an die Studenten: Radikalismus der Bürger," *Die Zeit*, no. 9, March 1, 1968.

Figure 6.2 "Berlin stands for peace and freedom." Counterdemonstration in front of the Rathaus Schöneberg, John-F.-Kennedy-Platz, Berlin-Schöneberg, February 21, 1968. Landesarchiv Berlin.

Figure 6.3 Dutschke "Public Enemy Nr. 1." Counterdemonstration before the Rathaus Schöneberg, February 21, 1968. Landesarchiv Berlin.

The animus against the SDS was an artifact of the anti-Communist attitudes that characterized life in the Cold War garrison city of West Berlin. Portrayals of the student movement in the tabloid press as lazy hooligans at best and Communist (or Nazi) insurgents at worst helped shape these attitudes; but the tactics of provocation through which the antiauthoritarian faction established its dominance contributed to them as well. Spectacular actions – the "go-in" at the trial of Fritz Teufel in November 1967; the Christmas 1967 protest in the Gedächtniskirche (in which Dutschke was set upon by an enraged fifty-nine-year-old crutch-yielding engineer); the various street actions of the Kommune I – all depended for their effect on the outrage they produced, outrage intended to provoke conversation but which often only provoked anger. That the police violence that inevitably accompanied such demonstrations was always reconfigured in the popular imagination into *demonstrator* violence only intensified this effect.[8]

Still, the competing demonstrations of February 1968 illustrated the relative weakness of the SDS. Even though polls showed that students tended to support the SDS's positions, and even though the SDS could count on the support, in many of its demonstrations and initiatives, of other student groupings such as the Liberaler Studentenbund Deutschlands (LSD; Liberal Student Federation of Germany) and Die Falken, the SDS itself amounted to only some 2,000 activists in all of West Germany. A critical step in making the leap "from protest to resistance," as the matter was formulated by Ulrike Meinhof in a column in *konkret*, had thus to be to extend the struggle outside the universities.[9]

In the spring of 1968, however, the SDS was riding a wave of revolutionary expectation that seemed to span the globe. The representatives attending the Vietnam Congress made the international struggle concrete, and the revolutionary upheaval that struck France a mere two months later seemed to activists to make the revolution a real, living possibility. In the Federal Republic, the campaign against the Emergency Laws seemed to place the SDS near the head of a revolutionary wave of West Germany's own. The mass mobilization, which saw the participation of a range of student, trade-union, church and other civil groups, united the disparate elements of the extraparliamentary opposition in a way they had not happened before and would not happen again. The mass demonstrations of

[8] See Manfred Gailus, ed., *Pöbelexzesse und Volkstumulte in Berlin: Zur Sozialgeschichte der Straße (1830–1980)* (Berlin: Europäische Perspektiven, 1984).
[9] Formulated by Ulrike Meinhof, "Vom Protest zum Widerstand," *konkret*, no. 5, May 1968, p. 5.

May 1968 marked the apogee of the APO. On May Day, 40,000 marched in West Berlin alone.[10] The traditional antinuclear *Sternmarsch* (Star March) on Bonn on May 11 attracted 100,000 people. Over the next two weeks, actions around the second reading of the Emergency Laws involved 80,000 participants in fifty cities.[11] When, on May 30, 1968, the Emergency Laws were voted into effect, the limitations of the extraparliamentary coalition to effect real change were thrown into sharp relief. In the subsequent period, the difficulty of answering all the questions extant from the beginning of the antiauthoritarian revolt–Who was to make the revolution? How was it to be made? What *was* "the revolution," actually?– would come painfully to the fore.

GOING TO THE PEOPLE

Even before the failure of the campaign against the Emergency Laws, activists of the SDS were searching for alternatives to what they feared could become the dead end of student protest. In the period following the anti-Emergency Law campaign, the need to sustain the radical momentum and to extend it beyond the university resulted in the founding of so-called *Basisgruppen*. Coming into life in the course of the "Easter disturbances" that followed the assassination attempt against Rudi Dutschke, the first *Basisgruppen* began as *Stadtteilgruppen* (neighborhood groups). Eleven groups were in place in time for the May Day 1968 demonstrations, representing the Berlin districts of Moabit, Kreuzberg, Neukölln, Schöneberg, Wedding, Spandau, Wilmersdorf, Zehlendorf, Friedenau, Reinickendorf, and the Märkisches Viertel.[12]

At the beginning, the groups were largely composed of students, but they also included young workers, apprentices, and secondary-school pupils, many of whom had previously belonged to the working groups of the Critical University.[13] The most working-class group was the Socialist Club Neukölln, founded by disgruntled working-class SPD members the previous December and kicked out of the SPD at the beginning of 1968.[14]

---

[10] Henning and Raasch, *Neoanarchismus*, p. 99.

[11] Henning and Raasch, *Neoanarchismus*, p. 113.

[12] Johannes Brunner, Werner Hausmann, Michael Kaufmann, Karl Müller, and Walter Schneider, eds., *Aufbruch zum proletariat: Dokumente der Basisgruppen*. Eingeleitet und ausgewählt von Karl-Heinz Schubert (Berlin: Taifun-Verlag, 1988), p. 6.

[13] The *Basisgruppen* also attracted members of other groups including the SEW and Die Falken; Brunner et al., *Aufbruch zum proletariat*, p. 13.

[14] *Ibid.*

In cooperation with the growing movement among secondary-school pupils, the *Basisgruppen* quickly outgrew their status as junior partners to the SDS to become a key site of cross-class radicalism. Until the fall of 1968, when they began to focus more and more on establishing a presence in the factories, the *Basisgruppen* concerned themselves with neighborhood issues, especially the developing struggle around urban renewal in Kreuzberg. In keeping with the diverse makeup of the APO at the time of their formation, the *Basisgruppen* were markedly heterogeneous in ideological orientation and social makeup. In key questions such as authoritarianism versus antiauthoritarianism, the relationship to violence, or attitudes toward the Soviet Union, the *Basisgruppen*, like the APO as a whole, presented a complex and contradictory picture.

The newly formed *Basisgruppen* announced their presence in a "May 1st Campaign" for May Day 1968. A primary goal of the campaign was to support the campaign against the Emergency Laws. More fundamentally, the campaign sought to make concrete what had heretofore been but a vaguely defined goal: to extend the struggle within the universities to include the working class.[15] The goal, as the rank-and-file group Moabit put it, was to politicize the "objective interests" of the Berlin population, that is, to seize on those concrete areas in which Berliners experienced, in their own life situations, the contradictions of capitalism.[16] For Moabit, this effort involved attempts to connect with workers in the AEG-Turbine concern. The campaign was aimed at crystallizing and systematizing the theoretical work of the *Basisgruppen*, organizing the founding of new groups, and opening up new areas of initiative. The latter were to include a focus on worker's control, workers' communes, female workers and family conflicts, and sexual education.[17]

The problems inherent to such attempts at mobilization and self-organization from below come out poignantly in the self-assessments of the *Basisgruppen*. The case of the *Basisgruppe* Reinickendorf is particularly instructive. The group was founded in March 1968 as the "Political Working Circle in [the youth club] Prisma." The initial membership of the working circle consisted of three students (non-SDS members), one apprentice, one young worker, and ten school pupils who had previously

[15] "Bericht der Basisgruppe Wedding" (1968), p. 2, reprinted in Brunner et al., *Aufbruch zum proletariat*.

[16] "Bericht der Basisgruppe Moabit," *Basisgruppen-Info* no. 4/69 (1969), reprinted in Brunner et al., *Aufbruch zum proletariat*.

[17] "Strategie zum 1 Mai: Konzept der Basisgruppen," *Rote Presse Korrespondenz*, no. 5, March 21, 1969, p. 1, reprinted in Brunner et al., *Aufbruch zum proletariat*.

worked with a student newspaper. According to the group's account, the school pupils took the primary initiative. The youth center Prisma, as a space where "controlled self-activity of the youth" was possible, occupied a special place in the life of the group. Supplied by the district administration (another example of the liberalizing trends that underpinned the antiauthoritarian revolt), the center offered not only meeting rooms but also printing machines and material. Young people had joined the group, it was explained, because they had realized that youth centers were a liberal plot to contain and redirect the revolutionary energies of youth. The group's key areas of focus were, unsurprisingly given its makeup, schools and youth homes.[18]

The group's theoretical work included discussion of themes corresponding to the ongoing campaigns of the APO, including "the nature of democracy and parliamentarism, press concentration and so-called press freedom, Emergency Laws, Vietnam, socialist theory, etc."[19] Actions included the distribution of flyers about May Day, the anti-Springer campaign, and the anti-Emergency Law campaign at schools, outside of factories where young people worked, at youth homes, and in Prisma itself. Another initiative was the organization of a flyer-distribution network in schools in Reinickendorf and Wedding. This work, according to a report compiled in the fall of 1968, was beset with problems, including poor preparation, a false expectation of the results to be obtained, and a lack of knowledge about specific conditions (e.g. in the youth homes) that would have increased the impact of the propaganda.[20]

Work within the group had functioned well enough during the period of the APO's ascendency (late spring to early summer 1968), the report continued, but already at that time problems of organization and concept had begun to manifest themselves. A first main problem stemmed from one of the group's main strengths: "Everyone who declared themselves for the APO was admitted."[21] This meant that while the group was able to profit from the diverse radical impulses fueling the APO, it was difficult to stabilize. "Even before the 1st of May," the authors noted, "we could detect strong fluctuations, insufficient activities, untrustworthiness in connection with the distribution of flyers, and a disinterest in theoretical work."[22] The measures undertaken to stem these problems only made them worse. Discussions followed at which it was decided that all new members would

[18] "Bericht der Basisgruppe Reinickendorf" (1968), p. 1, reprinted in Brunner et al., *Aufbruch zum proletariat.*
[19] *Ibid.*   [20] *Ibid.*   [21] *Ibid.*   [22] *Ibid.*

have to be vetted by interview before admission, that all further group decision-making would be binding on individual members (majority rule), and that attendance at meetings of newly established theoretical working groups would be mandatory. In short, it was decided by the nominal leadership that the antiauthoritarian structure of the group was a liability and that the largely "emotional" orientation of the youth involved needed to be replaced by a more dedicated and theoretical approach.[23]

Time-consuming discussions and restrictions on individual autonomy hurt morale and prompted a number of members to leave the group. After the Christmas break, only a small group remained. It was decided to reconstitute the group on a "cadre basis." This reconstituted group quickly wore out its welcome at Club Prisma, where it faced disinterest and accusations that it was trying to manipulate young people for its own ends. Eventually the rump group was forced to relocate to a private apartment, where it decided, in the interest of rekindling youth enthusiasm, to launch a new campaign focusing on "sexual repression in capitalist society," with special attention to the "sexual difficulties of school pupils." Armed with this "attractive problematic," the group was able to gain entry once again into Club Prisma.[24]

The Kreuzberg rank-and-file group experienced similar problems, reporting the difficulty of transforming a radical "potential purely grounded in emotion" into a disciplined and effective political program.[25] Complaining of the "formulaic council-like model" that had governed the organization of the group, the report also noted the problems of mobilization and disinterest in theory that had dogged the *Basisgruppe* Reinickendorf.[26] In particular, the group noted a lack of interest in the May Day campaign and in the question of factory work. The report adduced an overall naivety with respect to the workers in particular. "People spoke about factory work," the report complained, "without realizing that there were already workers in the Basis-group [who] represented a concrete point of contact."[27] For their part, the workers had an ambiguous relationship with the students. The report noted of workers that

1. They could not stand lack of punctuality.
2. They often felt themselves discriminated against as "you workers." In general there was a noticeable tendency toward integration and

[23] *Ibid.*   [24] *Ibid.*   [25] *Ibid.*
[26] "Erfahrungsbericht der Basisgruppe Kreuzberg" (1968), p. 2, reprinted in Brunner et al., *Aufbruch zum proletariat.*
[27] "Erfahrungsbericht der Basisgruppe Kreuzberg" (1968), p. 3.

accommodation with the life of the students (change of cigarette brands, distancing from working-class life).

3. They expected sexual emancipation in the sense of an uncomplicated use of the women.

4. They wanted a clear political program (no long discussions, but action).

5. They had a mistrust of the genuineness of the students' engagement.[28]

Detectable in this reporting of workers' attitudes, and in the *Basisgruppen* reporting on the difficulties of mobilizing workers more generally, was an undifferentiated concept of the "proletariat" that would soon fuel the "Proletarian Cult" of the *K-Gruppen*.

Yet, the *Basisgruppen* faced a dilemma, for in their attempt to keep the dynamism of the antiauthoritarian movement alive, they came up against intractable problems of mobilization and organization that stretched back to the roots of the revolutionary left in the previous century. More than one group located the problems facing the *Basisgruppe* in the very nature of the APO itself, which had seemed a powerful movement during the period of convergence around the Emergency Laws, but which lacked any organizational or ideological mechanism for sustained struggle. "It must not be forgotten," observed the *Basisgruppe* Reinickendorf, "that the inability of the APO to build up an effective organization, to develop a halfway authoritative concept, and to provide an adequate analysis of social reality, has contributed decisively to the current situation."[29] Like the *Basisgruppen* more generally, the activists of the *Basisgruppe* Reinickendorf had seen at first hand the damage that a lack of organization could do. From their perspective, only a more disciplined and organized approach could have any chance of success.

In the end, the essential goal of the *Basisgruppen*, to achieve a synthesis of "antiauthoritarianism and organization," proved difficult to attain.[30] Far from providing a new model of organization that would aid the transition of the student movement to a socialist mass movement, the *Basisgruppen* revealed in striking terms the dichotomy at the heart of the APO. Their experiences demonstrated that papering over the differences between the different conceptions of the revolution was no longer a viable alternative. In this way, the *Basisgruppen* contained within themselves the seeds of

---

[28] *Ibid.*

[29] "Bericht der Basisgruppe Reinickendorf," p. 1.

[30] K.-H. Lehnardt and Ludger Vollmer, *Politik zwischen Kopf und Bauch: Zur Relevanz der Persönlichkeitsbildung in den politischen der Studentenbewegung in der BRD* (Bochum: Druckladen-Verlag, 1979), p. 240.

the subsequent split of the antiauthoritarian movement into *K-Gruppen* and Sponti scene. Indeed, as an assessment of the *Basisgruppen* published in *Neue Kritik* in 1969 argued, more or less from the perspective of the nascent *K-Gruppen*, the *Basisgruppen* were unable to play a decisive role in Berlin precisely because they were so differentiated in their conceptions. Rather than representing a cohesive movement, the groups were a collection point for the forces left homeless by the disintegration of the SDS.[31] At the same time, however, in providing a bridge from the student movement to the (young) working class, they provided a major vehicle of the generational turnover that would drive the next phase of radicalism.

"ALL ADULTS ARE PAPER TIGERS"

As noted above, a key source of radicalism feeding the *Basisgruppen* came from the secondary schools. Pupils from the *Oberschulen* (gymnasia and trade schools) constituted up to 50 percent of the membership of some *Basisgruppen*.[32] "Federal German pupils of all states and schools are uniting – by class outside the classroom – this year more and more than ever before," proclaimed *Der Spiegel* in November 1968; "Raucously they highlight their goal: a say in the decisions of the teacher."[33] As an untapped font of revolutionary potential, school pupils, as well as trade-school pupils and apprentices, proved an irresistible target for APO activists in search of the revolutionary subject.

The SDS played a leading role in helping to politicize school pupils. With its support, the AUSS was founded in Frankfurt in June 1967. Activists from seventeen different cities were in attendance.[34] The AUSS slogan, "There are school pupils who won't go along anymore," gave a good idea of the attitude underlying its aims. Demanding the "democratization of school and education," and "consciousness raising among the students,"[35] the AUSS poured its energy into criticism of curricula and the authoritarian relationships of instruction, collaboration with apprentice groups in the trade schools, and local "SEXPOL" campaigns.[36] Among

---

[31] Hannah Kröger, "Die organisatorische Situation in Berlin," *Neue Kritik*, no. 54, 1969.
[32] "Verfassungsschutz: Über 'Linksextreme Schüler'," reprinted in *Berliner EXTRA Dienst*, October 5, 1968, no. 80/II, pp. 5–7, available online at www.trend.infopartisan.net/1968/remember68_21. html (accessed May 5, 2011).
[33] "Wie im Kongo," *Der Spiegel*, no. 47, November 18, 1968.
[34] "Verfassungsschutz: Über 'Linksextreme Schüler'."
[35] *Ibid.*
[36] Jürgen Miermeister and Jochen Stadt, eds., *Provokationen: Die Studenten- und Jugendrevolte in ihren Flugblättern, 1965–1971* (Darmstadt, Neuwied: Luchterhand, 1980), p. 164.

Figure 6.4 "Who has betrayed us? School bureaucrats." Demonstration of school pupils in the Hohenstaufenstraße, Berlin-Schöneberg, March 1970. Landesarchiv Berlin.

the organization's goals were the creation of independent Schüler councils (soviets), sex education in the school curriculum, and the abolition of censorship of school newspapers.[37]

With the support of the local chapter of the SDS, an Unabhängige Schülergemeinschaft (USG; Independent School Pupils' Association) was founded in West Berlin the same month. The organization had a membership of 400, which included Peter Brandt, the nineteen-year-old son of the West German foreign minister Willy Brandt.[38] Aligned with the AUSS, the USG understood itself as an alternative to the existing system of *Schülermitverantwortung* (SMV) promulgated by the eleven state culture ministers a short time before.[39] A few months later, the Aktion

---

[37] "Verfassungsschutz: Über 'Linksextreme Schuler'."
[38] "Wie im Kongo," *Der Spiegel*, no. 47, November 18, 1968. On Brandt's activities, see "Schüler-Gewerkschaft: Im Kampf gegen die Lehrer ist Brandts Sohn Peter dabei," *Die Zeit*, no. 6, February 10, 1967.
[39] "Administration today means distribution of milk cartons and upkeep of the school grounds," complained an SMV representative from Hamburg; "We have been degraded to hand-brooms of the teachers. But being in charge?"; "Wie im Kongo," *Der Spiegel*, no. 47, November 18, 1968.

Schülerselbsthilfe (ASH; Action School Pupils' Self-Help) was founded in Berlin, with an initial membership of seventy students and teachers. Alongside these organizational initiatives, the SDS and the various Republican Clubs attempted to radicalize the younger students through events such as the September 1967 go-in at various Berlin gymnasia aimed at publicizing the judicial persecution of Fritz Teufel.[40] School-related questions figured heavily in the curriculum of the Critical University founded in November 1967. Initiatives included a weekend seminar on "The Democratization of School," and the founding of an Action Center for School Pupils.[41]

The SDS also agitated extensively among trade-school pupils (*Berufschüler*), with significant success, and, in practice, the radicalism of students in the two streams of West German education flowed together and overlapped. Apprentices became integrated into the revolt as well, motivated by unhappiness over the conditions of their training as well as their relationship to the trade-union bureaucracy. Their radicalism drew on a generalized anticapitalist attitude as well, which easily dovetailed with the antiauthoritarianism of a youth culture centered on rock music and countercultural style.[42] Entering into apprenticeships at a young age, sometimes as young as fourteen, apprentices found the strictures of the workplace, especially around such issues as long hair, clothing style, and smoking, an unhappy contrast to the relative laxness of school. As in the case of school pupils, the SDS actively sought the participation of apprentices, forming working groups aimed at politicizing them in the Republican and other political clubs.[43] Other suitors for the political affections of apprentices included the SDAJ (refounded by the illegal KPD in May 1968), the "Red Guards" of the fledgling KPD–ML, and the trade unions themselves, which in some cases leaned left in the direction of apprentice militancy. In practice, the radicalism of school pupils and apprentices tended to flow together. The two groups were treated as a common target group by the Red Guards and others, and a combined

[40] "Wie im Kongo."
[41] Arbeitsgemeinschaft 10: Sexualität und Herrschaft; Arbeitsgemeinschaft 17: Mitbestimmungsmöglichkeiten für Schüler, "Aufruf zur Gründung eines Aktionszentrums für Schüler," Berlin, January 23, 1968. APO-Archiv Berlin.
[42] Knud Andresen, "Die bundesdeutsche Lehrlingsbewegung von 1968 bis 1972: Konturen eines vernachlässigten Phänomens," in Peter Birke, Bernd Hüttner, and Gottfried Oy, eds., *Alte Linke, Neue Linke? Die sozialen Kämpfe der 1968er Jahre in der Diskussion* (Berlin: Dietz, 2009), pp. 87–102, at pp. 88–89.
[43] Andresen, "Die bundesdeutsche Lehrlingsbewegung von 1968 bis 1972," p. 91.

School Pupil and Apprentice Center was established in the Lehniner Platz in Berlin.[44]

In 1968 a *Verfassungsschutz* (Federal Office for the Protection of the Constitution) report noted that agitation among school pupils and apprentices had shown considerable success, with demonstrations attracting significant numbers of the two. These pupils, noted authorities, did "not shrink from altercations with the police" and, indeed, counted for some 20 percent of those arrested in demonstrations.[45] Although easily discernable in the analysis of the *Verfassungsschutz* is an implicit recourse to the categories of "(ring)leaders" and "led," which tended to underpin the thinking of officials concerned with the "subversion" of (presumably otherwise loyal) citizens by activists of the SDS, the government's own reports belied the picture of a passive secondary-student body being acted upon by outside agitators. The *Verfassungsschutz* noted the particular appeal of the left's focus on sexual questions, as well as that of the "countless happenings staged by the SDS and the APO," but it also acknowledged that a general sense of discontent with the allegedly authoritarian nature of school, especially among older pupils, easily dovetailed with the revolutionary aspirations of the SDS.[46]

Pupils regularly instigated and carried out actions in the schools, including mass meetings and strikes. In connection with the second reading of the Emergency Laws in May 1968, for example, 200 pupils of the Karl-Friedrich-von-Siemens-Schule skipped instruction en masse, assembling on a nearby sports field instead to discuss the Emergency Laws. In other cases, pupil "action committees" disrupted classes and sporting events, forcing their cancellation.[47] In West Berlin, the government noted extensive contacts between pupils' groups and the APO, calling special attention to the "Critical Pupil Group" at the Goethe-Gymnasium in Wilmersdorf, the "Anti-Emergency Law Committee" at the Freiherr-vom-Stein-Schule in Spandau, and the "Action Committee" at the Hermann-Hollerith-Schule in Steglitz.

Also of significance were the circles responsible for the publication of student newspapers (*Schülerzeitungen*) such as the *Roter Turm* at the Schadow-Schule in Zehlendorf and *Rote Sophie* at the Sophie-Charlotten-Schule in Charlottenburg.[48] These and other *Schülerzeitungen* proved to

[44] "Sozialistische Arbeiter- und Lehrlingszentrum Westberlin" (SALZ), available online at www.mao-projekt.de/BRD/BER/SMV/Berlin_Schuelerbewegung_1968–1969.shtml (accessed May 5, 2011).

[45] "Verfassungsschutz: Über 'Linksextreme Schuler'."

[46] *Ibid.*   [47] *Ibid.*   [48] *Ibid.*

be one of the most important vehicles of pupil radicalism, dovetailing notably, in both their concerns and their physical appearance, with the underground press. Although the institution of the *Schülerzeitung* long predated the radicalization of the 1960s, the first of the papers more or less explicitly related to the APO appear to have been in operation by mid 1965. A sociological study on the subject appearing that year surveyed over 1,000 *Schülerzeitungen* spread across the width and breadth of the Federal Republic, some eighty-one in West Berlin alone.[49] Over three-quarters of the editor-respondents claimed a political motivation for their activities, with close to 50 percent citing the desire to "fight undemocratic tendencies" as a chief concern.[50]

Unsurprisingly, articles on pop music and other artifacts of youth culture were strongly represented.[51] Although nominally directed by faculty sponsors, and thereby beholden to the administration of their schools, these papers were in practice fairly autonomous organs reflecting the concerns of the students. Students were typically given fairly wide latitude in their editorial policy, at least until such time as this policy began to encompass themes and topics disapproved of by the school administration. In many cases, students founded their papers under the guidance of left-wing teachers, in other instances in cooperation with fully fledged members of the APO, who were well represented among the students at the Pädagogische Hochschule in Berlin.[52]

Unsurprisingly, student newspapers presenting ideas associated with the APO very quickly ran afoul of school authorities. *Der Rote Turm*, published from early 1967 by students of the Schadow-Schule in Berlin-Zehlendorf, was closed down by the school after only two issues. The editors subsequently decided to continue production on an independent basis under the name *Neuer Roter Turm*. Willy Brandt's son Peter was one of the ten editors. A chief focus of the paper, like the majority of the *Schülerzeitungen*, was the attempt to uncover and bring to light instances of official malfeasance that revealed the harsh reality beneath the democratic-pedagogical façade of public education. Readers were invited to submit reports on instances of scandals or corruption in their schools, which were duly reported in subsequent issues. Such reports were not meant to narrow the lens onto the situation of the student;

[49] Jan-Peter Hintz and Detlef Lange, eds., *Schüler und ihre Presse* (Berlin: Verlag Junge Presse Berlin, 1967), p. 8.
[50] Hintz and Lange, *Schüler und ihre Presse*, p. 8.   [51] *Ibid.*
[52] "Verfassungsschutz: Über 'Linksextreme Schuler'."

rather, they were meant to reveal the school as a mirror of the authoritarian relations that governed society at large. "We are above all of the opinion," wrote the editors in the founding issue of the successor journal,

that the authoritarian structure of our schools is impossible to understand without coming to grips with the structure of our society. Therefore articles about the Grand Coalition, the DDR, Vietnam, Peru, and Greece. We see school issues and "grand politics" not as completely different thematic areas, but rather as two sides of the same coin.[53]

The genre of the *Schülerzeitung* very quickly burst the boundaries of the gymnasia. Papers were founded under the auspices of the several independent political organizations for school pupils, as well as by various publicistic entrepreneurs of the APO. Among the latter was *Underground*, a "*Schülerzeitung*" published by Erich Bärmeier and Hans Nikel beginning in November 1968. The layout and general appearance of *Underground* was very similar to Bärmeier and Nikels's satirical magazine *Pardon*. Slicker and more professional than the hectographed productions of the gymnasia, *Underground* was also more mainstream in its approach, hewing more closely to the (pop-)cultural youth-revolutionary end of the left-publicistic spectrum than the more radical and explicitly political *Schülerzeitungen* associated with the *Schüler-* and *Basisgruppen*. *Underground* was criticized for its pop-cultural style by the SDS, which argued that the visual material detracted from the political content of the articles and that the magazine failed to offer constructive solutions to the problem of "school misery." The magazine responded by pointing out that it did not intend to be political in the strict sense and sought to appeal to pupils beyond the small hard-core minority.[54]

The increasingly slick productions of the left-wing publishing houses made school pupils a major focus of their propagandistic efforts, sometimes focusing even on younger grade-school pupils. *Das kleine rote Schülerbuch* (*The Little Red Pupils' Book*), published by the Verlag Neue Kritik in Frankfurt, urged pupils to resistance in a sort of Maoism-for-children: "A tiger can cause someone fear," it read,

but when he is made out of paper, then he can't eat anyone. You believe too much in the power of the adults – and you believe in your own possibilities too

[53] *Neuer Roter Turm: Schülerzeitschrift*, no. 3, March 1967, Green Library, Stanford University, Germany. Extraparliamentary Opposition movement, 1967–1984 collection, box 87, folder 3.

[54] *APO aktuell, Heft 3: Die APO und die Oberschulen aus wehrpolitischer Sicht* (Sinzig: Boehlke, 1969), p. 71.

little. The adults possess great power. They are real tigers. But in the long run they can't exercise any power over you. They are paper tigers.[55]

Older pupils received more explicit instructions. The *Roter Kalendar 1972 für Lehrlinge und Schüler* (*Red Calendar 1972 for Apprentices and School Pupils*), published by the Wagenbach collective in West Berlin, helpfully suggested "flyer and poster actions, building seizures, actions against building owners and property speculators, against exploiters in luxury hotels, against bureaucrats in administrations, against the owners of rental properties. Further against the buildings or the property of exploiters or their abettors [Helfers-helfer]."[56] Elsewhere, readers were informed about topics relating to radical cultural production, including "how to create flyers" and "possibilities with video."[57] A list of *Lehrlingsgruppen* (apprentice groups) and Republican Clubs rounded out the volume, arming young people with the contact information necessary to follow the calendar's central injunction: "Organize yourselves."[58]

School pupils and apprentices were extraordinarily active. In Berlin-Spandau, the Aktionsgemeinschaft Spandauer Schüler (AGSS; Action Association of Spandau School Pupils) began publishing the *Schülerzeitung Radikalinski* beginning in fall 1968. In its physical layout and in its concerns, the paper was indistinguishable from the non-school-related underground press. The following year, *Radikalinski* released a joint issue with the West Berlin underground newspaper *Linkeck*. In Baden-Baden, where school-pupil activism centered on the Markgraf-Ludwig-Gymnasium, the *Schülerzeitung Ça Ira* began publication earlier the same year, in connection with the founding of a local chapter of the USG. The impetus was a 500-person teach-in on New Year's Eve 1967, which saw speeches by the Berlin USG's Peter Brandt and the doctoral student in sociology Günter Amendt. Urged to join the "rebellion of the students and workers," pupils founded a section of the USG three days later.[59] The twenty-six-year-old bookseller Bernhard Wette agreed to serve as editor

---

[55] Peter Jacobi and Lutz Maier, *Das kleine rote Schülerbuch* (Frankfurt: Verlag Neue Kritik, 1970), Green Library, Stanford University, Germany. Extraparliamentary Opposition movement, 1967–1984 collection, box 61, folder 2, p. 13.

[56] *Roter Kalender 1972 für Lehrlinge und Schüler* (Berlin: Verlag Klaus Wagenbach, 1971), Green Library, Stanford University, Germany. Extraparliamentary Opposition movement, 1967–1984 collection, box 55, folder 2, pp. 6–7.

[57] *Roter Kalender 1972 für Lehrlinge und Schüler*, pp. 69, 90.

[58] *Roter Kalender 1972 für Lehrlinge und Schüler*, p. 67.

[59] "Baden-Baden und die Revolution 1968," available online at www.bad-bad.de/gesch/baden-baden-1968.htm (accessed May 5, 2011).

without pay.[60] The first issue of the paper appeared on February 24, 1968, in an edition of 1,000. It immediately succeeded in provoking various scandals. Amendt's injunction in the first issue ("Get the horizontal bars and balance beam, cases and cabinets, in short, all the instruments of castration and deflowering, out of the gym, and leave nothing but blankets and matting, on which you lie by pairs, and make love (*à faire l'amour*)," caused particular consternation. The police quickly descended on the Markgraf-Ludwig-Gymnasium to search knapsacks for contraband issues of the paper, and criminal charges were mooted by various local dignitaries insulted in the paper's pages.[61]

The *Schülerzeitung Radikalinski* launched an attack on the director of the Luise von Gottorpschule, noting that he had joined the Nazi Party in 1934 of his own free will. At the Freiherr vom Stein Schule in Berlin-Spandau, pupils associated with the paper *Bumerang* became involved in a major feud involving a school official named Bethge. When a piece by Bethge equating democracy with "the mobilization of all forces for German industrial and economic capacity" was criticized in a follow-up piece by the newspaper's editor in chief Günther Hellmich, Bethge moved to have the paper closed down.[62] In the wake of Hellmich's resignation, a war of words developed between Bethge and the radical left in Berlin. Bethge's personal intervention against the underground press brought him into conflict with the editors of *Linkeck*, who weighed in with a series of vicious personal attacks against him.

The quickness of school pupils to take up the themes of the APO in their newspapers, to become indignant at attempts at censorship, to protest and even to fight with police, lent weight to the thesis that school pupils were a revolutionary subject in the making. "The school pupils represent a quantitatively enormous revolutionary potential," observed the authors of a study published by a Berlin *Basisgruppe* associated with the AUSS, "Will it be possible to transform this into a qualitatively meaningful factor?"[63] For many members of the *Basisgruppen*, as well as for the cadres of the main *Schüler* organizations and the activists of the nascent *K-Gruppen* (often in practice amounting to more or less the same people), the answer to this question often depended on being able to theorize the radical incidents

---

[60] "Affaären Schuler-Zeitung," *Der Spiegel*, no. 16, April 15, 1968.
[61] *Ibid.*
[62] *Neuer Roter Turm: Schülerzeitschrift*, no. 5, no date, Green Library, Stanford University, Germany. Extraparliamentary Opposition movement, 1967–1984 collection, box 87, folder 3.
[63] *Auss. Sozialistische Praxis im Schulkampf. Basisgruppen Arbeitsheft*, no. 1, p. 32.

unfolding in the schools. The above-mentioned *Basisgruppe* placed the Bethge incident at the Freiherr vom Stein Schule at the center of its study of "socialist praxis in the school struggle."[64] "That the book strikes one or another taste as too abstract," apologized the authors, "is not our fault, but lies rather in the nature of the thing. The core of dialectical materialism is, as Lenin said, the concrete analysis of a concrete situation."[65]

Yet, as the authors seemed to realize, jargon-filled prose rife with quotations from Lenin and Mao was out of step with the pop-fueled spirit of antiauthoritarian revolt percolating in the schools. Activists might pander to youth sensibilities all they wished (the *Infiltrator*, for example, included an "Infiltrator-Agit-Prop-Poster" bearing the legend "Together We Are Strong"), but attempts like this to capture the youthful imagination paled besides the efforts of the young people themselves.[66] The jargon of the nascent cadre groups presented a jarring contrast with the content of the *Schülerzeitungen*, anarchic collages of word and image in which calls to revolutionary struggle sat without apparent contradiction amid paeans to sex, drugs, and rock 'n' roll. The dividing line between anarcho-pop antiauthoritarianism and nascent K-Group dogmatism in the *Schülerzeitungen* was, as in the case of the *Basisgruppen*, by no means so clear cut in any case. Some *Schülergruppen* themselves became hotbeds of proto-cadre activism. *Radikalinski*, for example, came increasingly under the influence of the Red Guards, a Maoist youth organization that eventually became the youth wing of the KPD–ML. Scholars differ about the extent to which the Schülerbewegung embodied or helped to foster the dogmatic vanguardism of the *K-Gruppen*, but it seems accurate to say that, far from being monolithic, the Schülerbewegung reflected the range of positions characteristic of the antiauthoritarian revolt as a whole.[67]

"LIQUIDATE THE ANTIAUTHORITARIAN PHASE": THE RETREAT INTO ORGANIZATION

The *Basisgruppen* in which so many school pupils and apprentices received their first politicization had a relatively short-lived existence. After their

---

[64] *Ibid.*

[65] *Auss. Sozialistische Praxis im Schulkampf. Basisgruppen Arbeitsheft*, no. 1, p. 1.

[66] *Infiltrator: Sozialistische Schülerzeitung*, May 1971, Green Library, Stanford University, Germany. Extraparliamentary Opposition movement, 1967–1984 collection, box 61, folder 1.

[67] Jürgen Miermeister and Jochen Staadt argue that the Schülerbewegung was one of the sites where the "tendencies toward dogmatic oversimplification" that marked parts of the APO developed most quickly; Miermeister and Staadt, *Provokationen*.

initial period in the spring and summer of 1968, the *Basisgruppen* functioned as neighborhood groups focusing on whatever issues came to hand. Gradually, and for the bulk of their existence through the end of 1969, they focused on the factories as their primary site of engagement. Here, the *Basisgruppen* prefigured, and to a certain extent merged into, the emerging *K-Gruppen*. Unlike the *Basisgruppen*, however, the *K-Gruppen* quickly jettisoned ideological heterogeneity to embrace a dogmatic brand of Marxism–Leninism–Maoism that promised to make up for in ideological certainty what it lacked in ecumenism. Indeed, it was precisely the catchall quality of the *Basisgruppen*, combined with their lack of a clear unifying program, that the founders of the *K-Gruppen* rejected.

When, a short time later, activists began founding the *K-Gruppen*, the intention was to break decisively with the directionlessness of the so-called "antiauthoritarian phase," moving beyond the limitations of the student movement and its successors in the *Basisgruppen*. The new "socialist phase" would be inaugurated by a disciplined and theoretically grounded attempt to make contact with the working class that must form the basis of any revolution in West Germany. Here the *K-Gruppen* broke with much of what had animated the APO, rejecting specifically the unique mixture of radical politics, art, and popular culture that had fueled the antiauthoritarian revolt. Attempting to move forward using Maoism as a check against the bureaucratization that had infected the developments first launched by Lenin, they actually moved backward, retreating into the ideas, forms, attitudes, and emotional postures of the Old Left.

The first of the *K-Gruppen* was the KPD–ML, founded in late 1968 by Ernst Aust. By the spring of 1970 the group had split into two factions, each producing its own newspaper claiming to be the official organ of the KPD–ML. In December 1969, a contentious conference sponsored by the *Rote Presse Korrespondenz* demonstrated the lack of unity between the various factions of the extraparliamentary movement. In February 1970, Christian Semler and two others founded the KPD(AO) with the intention of laying the groundwork for the creation of a national Communist Party.[68] Other groups included the Kommunistische Bund founded in 1971 in Hamburg, and the Kommunistische Bund Westdeutschlands (KBW) founded in 1973. In 1971, the *Verfassungsschutz* estimated that in 1969–1970 there were active some twenty different Maoist groups, possessing some 800 members, each of which conceived of itself as a

---

[68] The "AO" was later dropped.

precursor group to a new, soon-to-be-founded revolutionary Communist Party.[69] In the mid 1970s, the membership of the *K-Gruppen* numbered 10,000–15,000.[70]

Despite their various differences, all of these groups had in common their rejection of the DKP founded in September 1968 as a successor to the illegal KPD banned in 1956. As a creature of the East German SED (and thereby a creature of Moscow) the "revisionist" DKP did not meet the standards of revolutionary respectability to which the *K-Gruppen* (aligned with Maoist China) aspired. The DKP did benefit from the dissolution of the SDS, receiving initial support from the Marxistische Studentenbund Spartakus (MSB Spartakus; Marxist Students Alliance Spartacus) founded in Essen at the beginning of 1969 from members of the traditionalist wing of the SDS.[71] Although it enjoyed a presence within or alongside SDS in a number of cities, especially in the Rheinland and in the south, the group counted only somewhere between 250 and 1,000 members nationwide. It was criticized for its connection with the DKP and denounced as "authoritarian, traditionalist, and Stalinist" both within and without the SDS.[72]

The *K-Gruppen*, too, were frequently condemned by others on the left. Their fanaticism and intolerance of dissent, their erasure of the individual in the service of the group, their demands for permanent around-the-clock service to the "revolution," gave them a cult-like aspect.[73] "Obedience replaced solidarity," wrote Peter Mosler, "[j]ust as the principles of the student revolt – freedom, equality, reciprocity – originated in the heroic period of the bourgeoisie, so the principles of the MLer [corresponded to] the feudal [forms] of ... primary accumulation of the S[oviet]

[69] Jahresbericht des BfV für 1969/70 (offene Fassung), November 24, 1971. BArch Koblenz, B106, Band 78917, p. 23.

[70] Geronimo, *Feuer und Flamme: Zur Geschichte der Autonomen* (Berlin: Id-Verlag, 2002), p. 68.

[71] StAM, Bayer. Staatsministerium des Innern, "An die Reigierung von Oberbayern z.H.des Herrn Regierungspräsidenten oViA München. Betreff: 'SPARTACUS,'" February 7, 1969. In some locations (notably Frankfurt, Göttingen, Mainz, and Cologne) SPARTACUS was identical with the remaining members of the "traditionalist" faction in SDS, who were otherwise too weak to form their own group; StAM, Bayer. Staatsministerium des Innern, "An die Reigierung von Oberbayern z.H.des Herrn Regierungspräsidenten oViA München. Betreff: 'SPARTACUS,'" April 9, 1969, Staatsarchiv München, p. 2.

[72] The 250-member figure comes from the Bavarian Ministry of the Interior. Authorities estimated that two-thirds of AMS members were simultaneously members of the DKP. StAM, Bayer. Staatsministerium des Innern, "An die Reigierung von Oberbayern z.H.des Herrn Regierungspräsidenten oViA München. Betreff: 'SPARTACUS,'" April 9, 1969, pp. 2–3. Approximately a year later, the membership had risen to around 1,000 members; Jahresbericht des BfV für 1969/70 (offene Fassung), November 24, 1971.

[73] On this theme, see the essays in *Wir warn die stärkste der Partein ... Erfahrungsberichte aus der Welt der K-Gruppen* (Berlin: Rotbuch Verlag, 1977), pp. 23–33.

U[nion]: un-freedom, un-equality, and one-sided exchange."[74] Drawing on the New Left (anti-)psychiatrist R. D. Laing, he continued, "The party took over the function of the family as defensive tribe, in order to create the 'one-dimensional man,' induce respect, conformity, and obedience."[75] Other commentators agreed that the *K-Gruppen* represented an atavistic retreat into the safety of old forms, ideas, postures, and emotions. For the anarchist chronicler Geronimo, writing some time later, the "regression to the party-concepts of the 1920s and the adherence to a completely anachronistic and backward-looking concept of the proletariat oriented on the male factory worker" made the activists of the *K-Gruppen*, as revolutionary strategists, "laughing stock[s]."[76] For Mosler, who saw the cadre parties as a turn to "barracks communism," the *K-Gruppen* were simply "new parties of an old type."[77]

These criticisms aside, the dividing line between the radicalized young workers of the *Schüler-* and *Basisgruppen* and the *K-Gruppen* was not initially as great as it would later become. Many of the longhaired countercultural types who populated the *Schüler-* and *Basisgruppen* naturally gravitated into the *K-Gruppen*, but many left just as quickly when it became apparent that the antiauthoritarianism that had fueled their overall orientation to politics had no place there. In particular, the austerity of the K-Group approach repelled those for whom nonconformist personal appearance represented a central component of resistance and rebellion. For the *K-Gruppen*, the need to win over the working class trumped the needs of individual self-expression; serious Marxism-Leninism demanded a corresponding seriousness of fashion and comportment. The question of the value of countercultural style was taken up by the KPD–ML, one of the sternest of the *K-Gruppen*. "Our position toward long hair, hippie-clothes, Beat- and Pop-fashion," read an article in *Roten Morgen*, the official party newspaper, "is decided according to the question of whether these aspects of fashion serve the capitalist class or the working class, the reaction or the revolution."[78] The generational revolt, the paper

---

74 Mosler, "Die Revolte frißt ihre Väter," p. 53.   75 *Ibid.*
76 Geronimo, *Feuer und Flamme*, p. 68.
77 Mosler, "Die Revolte frißt ihre Väter," p. 53. This, along with their uncritical worship of figures such as Chairman Mao, no doubt accounts for why it is overwhelmingly former members of the *K-Gruppen* who have been most vociferous in denouncing their former radicalism (e.g. Gerd Koenen, Götz Aly).
78 "Sind lange Haare fortschrittlich?" *Roten Morgen*, no. 2, January 5, 1974 and January 19, 1974; available online at www.mao-projekt.de/BRD/KUL/Lange_Haare.shtml (accessed May 10, 2011).

argued, was part of capitalism's attempt to divide the working class. "The bourgeoisie know very well," the article continued,

that youth are the most active and combative part of the people. For that reason, they wish to hinder youth from recognizing that their freedom is inseparable from the freedom of the working people, and that only under socialism, under the rule of the working class, are youth really free.[79]

The most important task was to prevent youth from being driven by capitalism into the "dead end of individual protest."[80]

By contrast, the reformed DKP, founded in 1968, displayed a much more open attitude toward countercultural deportment in an attempt to win youth. The party profited from the disintegration of the student movement, picking up many of the former traditionalists in the SDS. It sent condolences to the wife of Rudi Dutschke after the assassination attempt against him in April 1968, and senior party figures spoke approvingly of the hippie movement as a welcome turn away from the values of bourgeois capitalism.[81] The Maoist KPD–ML scorned this position, noting:

It is no accident that it is precisely the modern Revisionists [the DKP] who propagate long hair on their placards and try to trap youth with Beat music. The propagation of bourgeois youth culture by the DKP revisionists is an important factor in its desperate efforts to hold the working class back from the socialist revolution, to chain it to the capitalist system.[82]

The authors of the Hamburg periodical *SEXPOL-Info* complained in 1974 of the continued growth of the dogmatic groups, "each one more left than the next," who attracted members precisely because, in contrast to other groups, they looked not like "longhaired hippies" but like "proper revolutionaries."[83] Yet this insistence on "socialist morality" made the *K-Gruppen* anathema to the numerically much larger group of activists for whom personal appearance, and personal opinion, was not something to be sacrificed on the altar of the class struggle. The dogmatism of the *K-Gruppen* also repelled those who had been struggling to validate and politicize the concepts of sub- and counterculture. The theorist Rolf Schwendter, working in connection with the "Workshop Subkultur," highlighted this dichotomy in his notes for the planned "counter-media" day in Remscheid in June 1970: "A large part of the ... APO has ... hardened

79 *Ibid.*   80 *Ibid.*   81 See Brown, "Richard Scheringer."
82 "Sind lange Haare fortschrittlich?"   83 *SEXPOL-Info*, February 1974.

itself into dogmatic standpoints. In their claim to be the avant-garde of a Leninist Cadre party, these groups have taken themselves far from the content of their struggle, from the striving for emancipation,... democratization, solidarity."[84] It was nevertheless true, Schwendter admitted, that many radicals had "fetishized taking drugs and listening to music into an exclusive concern."[85]

The political content of drug-taking was a subject of fierce debate. For West Berlin's Hash Rebels (aka The Blues), drugs were a central component of the revolution. Operating in and around the Wieland commune in Charlottenburg, The Blues became militant defenders of the subculture's prerogatives, practices, and places. "The Hash Rebels," an inaugural flyer proclaimed, "are the militant core of the Berlin subculture. They fight against the slave-system of late-capitalism. They fight for their own right of decision about the body and lifestyle … Fuck this society [and its taboos]. Become wild and do beautiful things. Have a joint. Everything that you see that doesn't please you, destroy it."[86]

Self-consciously working-class, violence-prone, and unafraid of the police, the Hash Rebels represented the countercultural impulse at its most militant. The group's founding event was a "smoke-in" held in Berlin's Tiergarten in July 1969, where 400 "freaks" defiantly smoked dope in the open. Characteristically, even an event like a "smoke-in" was justified in international perspective and according to scientific-sociological precedent. A flyer announcing a subsequent Tiergarten smoke-in referenced an article published in the English underground newspaper *International Times* calling for the legalization of marijuana. The flyer went on to question why, since marijuana was proven to be nonaddictive and "from a medical standpoint" less harmful than alcohol or tobacco, it was nevertheless criminalized. Smoking together in the open, the flyer implied, not only asserted the right of the underground to determine its own course but also exposed the contradictions of a system in which substances were criminalized according to cultural prejudices rather than scientific evidence.[87]

---

[84] "Zur Gegenmedien Tagung am 11–14 Juni in Remscheid," *Roter Mohn*, no. 1, July 15, 1970, HIS ZR 563.

[85] *Ibid.*

[86] "Have a joint" appears in English in the flyer. "Scheisst auf diese Gesellschaft," flyer originally distributed in West Berlin the summer of 1969, reprinted in Kramer, ed., *Gefundene Fragmente*, vol. 1, p. 9.

[87] "Sonnabend 12 Juli, Smoke in Tiergarten," APO-Archiv Berlin, Ordner K I.

Even sympathizers were skeptical of the Hash Rebels' emphasis on the revolutionary imperative represented by drugs and the drug trade. Peter Paul Zahl, the editor of *Agit 883*, went on record to question the political value of the hash campaign. "Let's take a look around us," he wrote; "we see the cheery remnant of the KI [Kommune I] – pseudo-cheery dream dancers. We look in the pubs where hash is dealt in grand style – happy year's-end profit figures. And this does not prove that with hash one is better able to communicate."[88] In another piece in *883*, Werner Olles argued,

It is clear beyond a doubt that where pot is smoked, where flower power is practiced, that there Marx's *Kapital* and Guevara's *Guerilla – Theory and Method* are probably seldom read, and it has likewise been shown that the radicalism of the *Hascher* and the members of hippie-like subcultures never go beyond a non-committal pacifism containing thoroughly bourgeois elements.[89]

The problem with the Hash Rebels, the piece continued, was one of "general resignation. 'Nesting in the cracks of power' and 'living in the gaps' means nothing concrete other than integration into a [repressive] society."[90] Such complaints were met with contempt by the Hash Rebels, who accused Olles of trying to enforce a code by which "a socialist must look like a Spießer" (petit bourgeois). Olles, they argued,

totally overlooks [the fact] that the Central Committee does indeed smoke pot, but has never propagated flower power or any other "hippie ideology." We also do not "nest" in the "cracks of power" and we do not live in "gaps." We live in communes, wander about, and fight together against state power in the street.[91]

RELEASE: "WE ARE ON A PRODUCTION TRIP"

The Hash Rebels' extreme vision of individual autonomy represented the opposite pole from the *K-Gruppen*'s attempts to elaborate a form of radicalism that would elide distinctions between the generations in the interest of working-class unity. In the counterculture more generally, however, it was not the act of militant self-defense *as such*, but the act of creative self-organization that was key. We have already seen how initiatives in the realm of publishing and musical production grew out of and articulated with left-wing positions; by the beginning of the 1970s,

---

[88] Peter Paul Zahl, "Haschischkampagne oder Die Ideologie der 'Glücklichen Verbraucher'," *Agit 883*, no. 24, July 24, 1969, p. 4.

[89] Werner Olles, "Kiff und Revolution," *Agit 883*, no. 28, August 21, 1969, p. 5. Olles was a member of the Frankfurt branch of the SDS Frankfurt and later became near to the *K-Gruppe* KPD–ML.

[90] Olles, "Kiff und Revolution," p. 5.

[91] "Ein Sozialist muss aussehen wie ein Spiesser," *Gefunde Fragmente*, p. 17.

the self-organizational imperative produced something almost resembling an alternative society in urban environments around West Germany. In West Berlin, with its wastelands and liminal zones, a range of alternative institutions stood at the intersection of culture and politics. A full-size spread featuring "Berlin Collectives" in the underground newspaper *Hundert Blumen* gives an impression of just how far this process of self-organization in West Berlin had advanced by the beginning of the 1970s. The spread depicted the Georg von Rauch and Tommy Weissbecker houses; Ton Steine Scherben and the agit-prop collective "Rock Front"; Homosexual Action West Berlin; feminist groups including Brot und Rosen; the Wagenbach publishing collective; a number of underground newspapers, the *Sozialistisches Zentrum*, the *Rote Hilfe*; left-wing lawyers' collectives; street-theater, teachers' and children's groups; and various technical collectives (film and audiovisual, etc.).[92]

The range of initiatives depicted gives an idea of the extent to which, by the early 1970s, the left-wing underground had proceeded along the road to creating its own counterinstitutions. The advertisements and personals sections in *Agit 883* offer an unparalleled look into the state of the left-wing infrastructure in West Berlin at the end of the 1960s and the beginning of the 1970s. Left-wing commerce, as Thomas-Dietrich Lehmann points out, was seen as yet another means of politics, a way of achieving independence from shops and businesses run by the movement's political opponents.[93] Alongside record and clothes shops such as ZIP, flymusic, Shoppop, and Old-new-shop were to be found "the first socialist tailor" in the Uhlandstraße ("we sew only with socialist thread"), as well as numerous bookstores, pubs, and music venues.[94] On a more serious level, the "Socialist Lawyers Collective" run by Horst Mahler, Hans-Christian Ströbele, and Klaus Eschen in the Meierottostraße (its desk the large kitchen table formerly belonging to the Kommune I), provided legal defense for scene members run afoul of the law. Meanwhile, the "Socialist Center" at Stephanstraße 60, home to the final configuration of the Kommune I before its dissolution in November 1969, provided a meeting place for various left groupings.[95]

---

[92] *Hundert Blumen*, March 1973, APO-Archiv Berlin.

[93] Thomas-Dietrich Lehmann, "'Erscheint donnerstags mit Kleinanzeigen': Auf den Spuren einer linken Infrastruktur," in Rotaprint 25, eds., *Agit 883*, pp. 61–72, at p. 63.

[94] Lehmann, "'Erscheint donnerstags mit Kleinanzeigen'," p. 63.

[95] Lehmann, "'Erscheint donnerstags mit Kleinanzeigen'," p. 68. Personal ads became the site of a "secondhand culture" that bypassed the regular economy, providing a "scene" trade in clothes, apartments, and automobiles.

The Aktion Roter Punkt ("Aktion Red Dot") movement sought to strike back against the rising costs of public transportation. Founded in Hanover in 1969 and spreading to West Berlin and other cities, the movement sought to make it safe and effective to hitchhike, through cities and around the country. Drivers were advised to place a red dot on a 12 × 12 piece of white paper on their windshield. The sign would signal to hitchhikers the driver's willingness to accept passengers. In West Berlin, the movement aimed at blunting the increase in public transportation fares, which became a major area of left-wing mobilization in the spring and summer of 1969. The Roter Punkt movement was founded as a response to the raising of public transportation fares in June 1969. It was not seen as a single-issue mobilization, however. "We don't just talk, we act," wrote its organizers; "There are a lot of actions running, and we will do many more."[96] In Heidelberg and Hanover, the campaign led to flyer actions, teach-ins, boycotts, and even blockades of public transportation.[97]

Another key initiative of the radical scene was the drug self-help group Release. Founded in London in 1967 by Caroline Coon and Rufus Jones, Release aimed at helping drug users with legal and addiction troubles. The organization published a "Release Report on Drug Offenders and the Law" (which Scotland Yard tried and failed to suppress) and at one point handled up to a third of all drug busts in Great Britain.[98] Release groups were subsequently established in the Scandinavian countries and in the Netherlands, before coming to Germany. The Release group in Berlin was heavily influenced, as well, by the (controversial) American drug-treatment group Synanon. An explicit attempt to adapt foreign models to the needs of local activism, Release was another of the transnational exchanges that helped shape the West German 1968.

The founding of Release came at moment of transition in the role of drug use in the left scene. Through the end of the 1960s, drug use was either a casual adjunct to the APO lifestyle, or, as in the case of groups such as the Hash Rebels, the focus of attempts at politicization around the concept of drug consumption as a revolutionary act.[99] From the beginning of the 1970s, facile assumptions about the oppositional value of drugs began to give way to a younger and more or less depoliticized "drug

---

[96] "Aktion Roter Punkt," Hoover Institution, Notgemeinschaft für eine freie Universität, box 575, folder 40.

[97] See "Gescheiterte Rote Punkt-Aktion in Hannover," *Agit 883*, no. 54, March 26, 1970. See also "Rote-Punkt-Aktion in Heidelberg," *Rote Presse Korrepondenz*, no. 31, September 19, 1969.

[98] Barbara Ellen, "Still Fighting the Bad Guys," *The Observer*, Saturday, July 29, 2000.

[99] Weinhauer, "The End of Certainties," p. 384.

scene" in which criminality and personal decay became dominant over any previous political associations.[100] The situation became sufficiently bad to prompt the organization of an anti-drug conference sponsored by the journal *konkret* in Hamburg in March 1972.[101] The transition of the APO from the broadly defined antiauthoritarian movement to the Communist splinter groups assured that drug use lost much of its previous revolutionary cachet.[102]

Release was a response both to the concrete problem of drug addiction that was an all-too-visible adjunct to the "scene" in German cities at the beginning of the 1970s and to the interpretive problem stemming from the changing status of drugs within the scene. The first German Release center was founded by former heroin addicts in Hamburg in September 1970. According to the group's press release, 200 addicts had telephoned for help within the first week. Authorities subsequently allowed the group to set up a drug-addiction treatment center in the Vierlande Youth Prison in Hamburg-Bergedorf.[103] Funded through private contributions and by government subsidies, Release also supported itself through a range of business initiatives. In addition to the Release office at Karolinenstraße 7–9, the group ran a hostel, a macrobiotic restaurant (Ming), a multimedia lab, and a publishing house.[104] Other initiatives included a pair of boutiques in the area of the university and an initiative called "Rock-Lib" ("Rock Liberation Front" or "Association for the Promotion of Modern Rock Music"). Its goal was to "support new music groups and, at another level, to cream off the demand artificially created by the large profit-oriented pop-music manufacturers."[105] The latter suggested a broader mission, beyond just getting people off drugs, to create an alternative to capitalist society.

Release also helped organize five rural communities, established between 1971 and 1973, in Otterndorf, Velgen, Streuberg, Ellenberg, and Langwedel. "Release operates on the principle that the drug addict needs

---

[100] Christian von Wolffersdorff-Ehlert, "Drogen: Neugier, Krankheit, und Geschäft," in Wolfgang Gaiser et al., eds., *Immer diese Jugend! Ein zeitgeschichtliches Mosaik—1945 bis heute* (Munich: Kösel, 1985).

[101] *Arbeitspapiere zum Anti Drogen Kongress, 18–19 March, 1972* (Hamburg: Konkret Buchverlag and Co KG Eigendruck, 1972).

[102] Weinhauer, "The End of Certainties," p. 384.

[103] "Release Organization Hamburg, 'Help Yourselves' (Helft Euch Selbst)," HIS "Release Hamburg Texte, 1970–1976."

[104] The group's various initiatives are detailed in *Der Release Trip* (Hamburg: Release-Verlag, 1973); HIS, "Der Release Trip."

[105] "The organization co-operates with Riebe's musical journal and the groups Guru-Guru, Tomorrow's Gift, Clap Can, Störtebecker and Release-Music." *Der Release Trip*, p. 5.

a genuine alternative to the needle," read a press release. "This cannot be found in ordinary city life, precisely against which the addict has blindly and symptomatically taken up arms. Release prepares the way toward liberation from drug dependence and compulsive drug-taking through a return to healthy human relations."[106] The rural communities were similar to the urban initiatives in providing opportunities and facilities for independent cultural production. The Otterndorf Youth Hostel had a recording studio and put on theatrical productions. The Streuberg Youth Hostel also contained a recording studio, while the communities in Ellenberg and Langwedel focused on agriculture and "biologically-dynamic horticulture."[107]

A second Release group was founded in Heidelberg in October 1971. By the end of 1972 there were groups in West Berlin, Munich, and Frankfurt, as well as in Cologne, Freiburg, Bremen, Nuremberg, Oldenburg, Wiesbaden, Düsseldorf, Braunschweig, Bonn, and a number of other cities.[108] From the beginning, Release groups existed in a symbiotic relationship with state authorities. In and around Hamburg, as we have seen, Release relied on government subsidies and official support. In Frankfurt, the administration of the University of Frankfurt allowed activists to "seize" five empty university buildings in order to found a Release facility complete with tearoom and workshop. In Munich, the local Rotary Club helped fund the transformation of a building in the city center into a Release hostel.[109] In Heidelberg, a hotbed of drug addiction with some 200 known addicts at the beginning of the 1970s, Release enjoyed the enthusiastic support of Mayor Reinhold Zundel, and could rely on its own physician, Dr. Karl ("Chuck") Geck.[110]

Release groups sometimes faced the argument that ex-addicts, as non-professionals, were unqualified to administer a drug-treatment program. In other cases, it was noted that, given the persistence of "soft" drug use in the group's establishments, the group seemed less like a drug-treatment group and more like just a drug group. Sometimes protracted negotiations with state entities proved frustrating and helped contribute to the group's politicization.[111] Yet, in general, Release's success depended on the active

---

[106] *Der Release Trip*, p. 5.   [107] *Ibid.*

[108] Kai Krüger, "Release: die einzige Selbsthilfeorganisation, die von Ex-Fixern akzeptiert wird," *Die Zeit*, no. 49, December 8, 1972.

[109] Peter Brügge, "Wir wollen, daß man sich an uns gewöhnt," *Der Spiegel*, no. 33, August 1971.

[110] Martin Geier, "Heidelberg, Brunnengasse 20: Ein Versuch, Rauschgiftsüchtige zu heilen," *Stuttgarter Zeitung*, May 7, 1971, p. 3; Krüger, "Release: die einzige Selbsthilfeorganisation, die von Ex-Fixern akzeptiert wird."

[111] Weinhauer, "The End of Certainties," p. 385.

support of local and state administrations. In at least one case, success in winning support from local authorities (in this case the police in West Berlin), produced in-fighting and brought charges that Release's left-wing principles were being compromised by such cooperation.[112]

Support from the authorities notwithstanding, Release took a rather ambiguous stance on drugs, fighting hard to maintain a distinction between "hard" drugs (heroin and speed) and "soft" drugs (marijuana, hashish, and, nominally, LSD and other hallucinogens). Informed use of soft drugs, Release argued, could be separated from the use of known addictive substances such as heroin. This tightrope walk between combatting drug use and valorizing it was reflected in the group's notion of the "cool user," which became the title both of a book and of a self-produced television documentary. "The cool user recognizes dangerous drugs and does not become addicted," noted Release guidelines; "The cool user doesn't use or want any injections. Most drugs that need to be injected are addictive. The cool user wants to be *free*. No opiates, no speed ... The cool user informs himself about the provenance and effects of a drug. In cases of doubt he calls Release."[113] Another document, criticizing the inadequacy of drug-treatment facilities in Munich, was illustrated with a panel from the unequivocally pro-drug American underground comic *The Fabulous Furry Freak Brothers*.[114] A Release report on the purity of various street drugs analyzed eight different street brands of LSD with names such as "Black Widow" and "Heidelberger Filz." Out of eighty-five hits tested, fifty-four were "pure," nineteen "impure," and twelve "shit." "In *all* cases," readers were advised: "Mescaline and Psilocybin were crooked. The analyzed M & P trips were made out of milk-sugar, starch, paprika, etc. DON'T BUY ANY MESCALINE AND PSILOCYBIN IN MUNICH!" Local hashish was also found wanting. "Stay cool user," the document concluded, "don't let yourself be ripped off."[115]

Release's insistence on its right to parse the relative harm or worth of different drugs according to its own categories was part and parcel of its

---

[112] In this case, because activists split off from Release Heidelberg to found Release Berlin, on the basis of a different therapeutic conception, "To Release Berlin—Challenge," HIS, "Release Berlin. Texte 1971–1972 und Prop-Alternative."

[113] A reader captured by police was advised to "stay especially calm and cool with your mouth." "Release Info 2," reprinted in *Der Release Trip*.

[114] "Drobs macht zu—wir machen Release," (1972); HIS, "Release München vom 'Drob' bis zum Release. Texte, Protokolle, Konzepte, Infos."

[115] "Drogen in München," HIS, "Release München vom 'Drob' bis zum Release. Texte, Protokolle, Konzepte, Infos."

countercultural worldview as well as of its broader political program. On the one hand, the group adhered to the countercultural wisdom of the day, which held that drugs could be a valuable adjunct to the search for personal and spiritual fulfillment. Frequent reference to the use of drugs in primitive cultures, especially among Native Americans, sought to validate drug use as a font of more authentic sources of wisdom than those available in the modern West. On the other hand, in rejecting the logic of drug criminalization, Release claimed the right to intervene at the juncture of the state's right to control and the underground's claims to autonomy and self-management. Drug use, the group insisted, was not an individual problem but a social problem and therefore one that required help, both from above, via the government, and from below, via those most directly affected.

At the same time, Release refused to look at drug treatment as a compartmentalized adjunct to a return to bourgeois normalcy but rather as part of a broader self-empowerment. This self-empowerment was linked, above all, to creative acts, as Release Munich sought to make clear: "Release is liberation! Liberation from every type of addiction that we as a product of social relationships can only effectively attack at its roots."[116] This liberation was to stand as a direct antidote to the depoliticized resignation that could easily overcome members of the counterculture who had sunk into drug addiction; the goal was to "break through isolation, initiate collaboration, and stabilize the alternative society [*Gegengesellschaft*]. A long march, permanent learning-process, connections."[117] To this end, Release Munich sought to organize a contact bureau to coordinate "legal aid, bail, medical help, addresses, pregnancy, jobs, newspapers, events, plans, communal living arrangements, productions, advice, [and] kindergartens."[118] Around the same time, a circle called "Connections" (they used the English word) put out a call for an "information festival" to take place in winter 1972, which was to include "music groups, theater, macrobiotic, lightshow groups, underground newspapers, dealers, freaks, film people, painters, sculptors."[119] This overall approach, with its focus on creative self-management from below, was captured in a statement by the activists in Hamburg: "We're on a production trip."[120]

---

[116] "Fight for Release—Release sucht connections," HIS, "Release München vom 'Drob' bis zum Release. Texte, Protokolle, Konzepte, Infos."

[117] *Ibid.*   [118] *Ibid.*

[119] Themes of the festival were to be "drug use and misuse, alternatives to drug use, drugs in connection with music and groups"; see "Hallo Freunde!" in HIS, "Release München vom 'Drob' bis zum Release. Texte, Protokolle, Konzepte, Infos."

[120] "Hallo Freunde!"

SPACE: A SLIGHT RETURN

The self-organizational imperative that fueled the left-wing scene did not stop at cultural-productive activities or personal self-empowerment but involved attempts to organize previously unorganized groups seen to possess revolutionary potential. Not infrequently, these attempts unfolded in relationship to disputed spaces, either institutional (such as youth centers or group homes) or nominally independent (such as empty buildings seized for the express purposes of creating independent initiatives of one sort or another). Struggles around these groups and spaces represented one of the signature motifs of the radicalism of the early 1970s. This period was not, as it has often been portrayed, one that was less revolutionary because of the eclipse of the student movement but one that became more radical as new groups, actors, and concerns came to the fore. This shift was partly the result of generational turnover, reflecting in part the increasing prominence of youngsters entering the drug scene. In these and other cases, marginalized groups (institutionalized children, mental patients, criminals; in short, all the various groups assigned by Marx to the "lumpen-" or subproletariat), offered the promise of a new and untapped revolutionary potential. Here Marcuse's *Randgruppentheorie* (marginal-group theory) was a notable influence, although attitudes differed about the relative worth of marginalized groups in the revolutionary struggle.[121]

Youth homes represented a key site of intervention by antiauthoritarian activists. Here and elsewhere, official permissiveness on the terrain of sociological discourse and practice acted as a bridge for activists wishing to gain ingress into official institutions and a means of justifying their activism in terms designed to appeal to liberalizing authorities. The problem of runaways, so-called *Trebegänger*, thematized in the press and in the sociological literature, became a central feature of the efforts to resituate the antiauthoritarian revolt on the terrain of daily life at the end of the 1960s. Youth homes became, for activists, places where youth who did not or would not fit in were socialized into a capitalist system requiring subservience and docility.

Ulrike Meinhof famously made work with institutionalized girls a central focus of her activity before becoming involved in the RAF. Her television movie *Bambule: Fürsorge – Sorge für wen?*, about a riot in the Eichenhof girls' home in Berlin, was scheduled to be shown on West German television but was pulled from the schedule after Meinhof helped

---

[121] Sven Steinacker, "Die radikale Linke und soziale Randgruppen: Facetten eines ambivalenten Verhältnisses," in Rotaprint 25, eds., *Agit 883*, pp. 201–214, at pp. 204–205.

Andreas Baader escape from protective custody a few days before it was supposed to air.[122] Meinhof's comrades in the RAF, Andreas Baader and Gudrun Ensslin, induced kids to break out of youth homes, gathering a group of some fifty runaways around them, who became involved in communal living arrangements. The importance of socially marginal groups in the thinking of the nascent RAF was expressed in the group's founding declaration: "Find out where the homes are and the families with many children and the subproletariat and the proletarian women who only wait for the opportunity to smash the right face in. Those are the people who will take on the mantle of leadership."[123]

In Cologne, activists founded the Sozialpädagogische Sondermaßnahmen Köln (Social-Pedagogical Special Measures Cologne), subsequently renamed Sozialistische Selbsthilfe Köln (SSK). Fighting gentrification, securing the rights of tenants, and working with juveniles from youth homes and patients from psychiatric clinics, the organization received support from across the social spectrum.[124] The communes and *Wohngemeinschaften* (flat-sharing communities) of the SSK, many of them established in seized buildings, became the destination of first resort for youth fleeing conditions in the youth homes. This fact was officially recognized by the state, which in 1972 designated the SSK an official contact center for youth.[125] According to the agreement worked out between the state and the SSK, the latter was not required to send juveniles back to the homes from which they had fled. The relationship with the state soured, however, when the SSK refused to abide by any limitations on the number of juveniles it could house.[126] From 1974 on, operating independently of the local administration, the SSK played a leading role in exposing conditions in local psychiatric institutions, leading to the closure of the scandal-plagued Brauweiler psychiatric clinic.[127]

---

[122] The script was published in 1971; see Ulrike Marie Meinhof, "Bambule: Fürsorge—Sorge für wen?" *Rotbuch*, no. 24, 1971.

[123] Cited in Franz-Werner Kersting, "Juvenile Left-Wing Radicalism, Fringe Groups, and Antipsychiatry in West Germany," in Schildt and Siegfried, eds., *Between Marx and Coca-Cola*, pp. 353–375, at p. 363.

[124] Sozialistische Selbsthilfe Köln, *Sanierung macht Angst, Angst macht krank, Sanierung macht krank, Eine Dokumentation* (Cologne: SSK, 1981).

[125] Lothar Gothe and Rainer Kippe, *Aufbruch, 5 Jahre Kampf des SSK: von der Projektgruppe für geflohene Fürsorgezöglinge über die Jugendhilfe zur Selbsthilfe verelendeter junger Arbeiter* (Cologne: Kiepenheuer & Witsch, 1975).

[126] Geschichts-LK des Geschwister-Scholl-Gymnasiums Jahrgangsstufe 12, "'Menschen wie Vieh gehalten.' Der Skandal um die Schließung der Fachklinik für Psychiatrie und Neurologie des Landeskrankenhauses Brauweiler 1978," http://armeirre.blogsport.de/images/Brauweiler_MenschenwieViehgehalten_Geschichtswettbewerb2011.pdf, accessed May 3, 2011.

[127] The group eventually expanded to six communes encompassing 100 people; see Stadtbuch Köln, '84–'85; *Kölner Volksblatt* (Cologne, December 1983), pp. 395–396, in Saral Sarkar,

In Munich, the so-called "Aktion Südfront" (Action Southern Front) attempted to mobilize apprentices and juveniles from the youth homes into a revolutionary force. Founded by sixty activists in May/June 1969, this campaign of *Randgruppenagitation* (marginal-group agitation) focused on helping young people run away from state-administered youth homes.[128] The campaign focused especially on the Piusheim in Glonn, southeast of Munich (characterized by activists as "a ghetto for youth with difficulty in adapting themselves to late-capitalist society"), and the nearby Girls Home Zinnenberg.[129] At least 100 young people ran away from these two youth homes in the summer of 1969, with some forty moving into communes and *Wohngemeinschaften* in Munich.[130]

One of the founders of Südfront, Dr. Winfried "Schwammerl" Hauck, was arrested in April 1969 on suspicion of, among other things, hiding runaways from youth homes in his Schwabing apartment. Five hundred of Hauck's students at the Thomas Mann Gymnasium demanded his release and reinstatement. Hauck had been dismissed after a father complained about an essay he assigned on the theme "What is forbidden for the young?"[131] On September 24, 1969, prompted by Südfront's attempt to disrupt a CSU meeting on September 5, as well as its role in a demonstration against Franz-Josef Strauß, a massive police force raided fourteen different left-wing apartments, the Student Council of Munich University, and the left-wing Trikont publishing house.[132]

In response, Trikont, which had been targeted in the police action because of its contact with institutionalized young people in the context of a book project on youth homes, released a detailed analysis of the Südfront campaign and the raids. The police had hoped to find evidence of "'immoral conduct' (hash, orgies, seduction of minors, inducement to theft)," they wrote, but from their perspective, the real problems lay in

Green-Alternative Politics in West Germany, vol. 1: *The New Social Movements* (New York, Paris, and Tokyo: United Nations University Press, 1993), pp. 246–247.

128 "Über die Aktion Südfront ist folgendes bekannt geworden," Bayer. Staatsministerium des Innern 8 München 22, den 14. November 1974; available online at http://protest-muenchen.sub-bavaria.de/artikel/1809 (accessed May 15, 2011).

129 "Polizeiaktion. Im Morgengrauen: 16 Wohnungen und AStA-Räume durchsucht," *MSZ. Münchner unabhängige Studentenzeitung*. Sondernummer Oktober 1969, 1; available online at http://protest-muenchen.sub-bavaria.de/artikel/1795 (accessed May 15, 2011).

130 "Flusslandschaft 1969. Jugend," available online at http://protest-muenchen.sub-bavaria.de/artikel/394 (accessed May 15, 2011).

131 "Flusslandschaft 1970. Alternative Szene," available online at http://protest-muenchen.sub-bavaria.de/artikel/410 (accessed May 15, 2011).

132 "Flusslandschaft 1969. CSU," available online at http://protest-muenchen.sub-bavaria.de/artikel/388 (accessed May 15, 2011).

Südfront's "ambivalent" political position. Instead of fighting to develop their own self-organization within the existing homes, youth had simply fled to the city, where they encountered, unprepared and untutored, the "subcultural code of ethics (total self-liberation)." There, unable to grapple with the pressures of their new environment, with its sexual freedom and rejection of social norms (e.g. regular work), the youth had easily fallen into the criminal activity for which they had been pre-programmed by their prior, oppressive capitalist (mis)education. Only when the youth began to engage in political activity, as they had done beginning in August, did the authorities, fearing the coming together of young workers and students, decide to crack down.[133]

From a broader perspective, the attempt to work with working-class youth, wayward or otherwise, was fueled by essentialist ideas about the "fighting qualities" of the proletariat. In his memoir, Michael Baumann made much of this thesis, noting that his working-class acclimation to violence prevented him from having "hang-ups" about it.[134] This thesis was echoed in the press materials from Trikont Verlag publicizing Baumann's memoir. "Bommi's story," the press observed, "is important above all because it shows the development of a person who didn't come out of the typical milieu of the APO comrades, that is, not out of bourgeois security ... [but] from the proletariat."[135] Baumann represented, in this context, a sort of "organic intellectual" who heralded a coming together of workers and students that had begun to unfold with the advent of the *Basis-* and *Schülergruppen*. Elsewhere, socially marginalized groups were praised for their skill in street combat.[136] The Hash Rebels made much of their roots as working-class rockers, mythologizing their battle against police at the Rolling Stones concert in Berlin's Waldbühne in 1965 as a key moment when working-class truculence added much-needed backbone to the antiauthoritarian revolt.[137] Similarly, Hamburg anarchists seeking to mobilize working-class youth argued that "Rockers and apprentices must demonstrate together" because both sought "to live their life and not [the life] that capitalist society prescribes for them."[138]

---

[133] "Flusslandschaft 1969. CSU."

[134] Baumann, *How It All Began*, pp. 27–28.

[135] "KOMMT NACH BERLIN. NACHWORT zu Bommi Baumann: 'Bommi' Baumann. Wie alles Anfing: Trikont," International Institute for Social History, Amsterdam.

[136] Steinacker, "Die radikale Linke und soziale Randgruppen," p. 204.

[137] Reinders and Fritsch, *Die Bewegung 2 Juni*, pp. 16–20.

[138] Anarcho-Kollektiv, Section "Freiheit für den Rocker," Kampfgemeinschaft "Rettet die Rocker," and Vereinigung "Erkennt die Rocker an," "Rocker! Lehrlinge!" in Schulenburg, ed., *Das Leben ändern, die Welt verändern!*, pp. 350–351.

The rocker was key in this alliance, above all, because "the Rocker is not afraid of the police."[139]

Rockers and other marginalized and (or simply unpolitical) subcultural groupings proved highly problematic revolutionary subjects, however. A "Central Committee of Youth Communes" founded in Berlin at the beginning of 1969 recognized and sought to organize the influx of runaways and other wayward youth seeking support and succor within the student and left-wing milieus. Appealing to the Berlin Senator for Youth and Sports for aid to fund apartments and "teaching and research groups" to administer them, the group argued for the need for official support for left-wing institutions that were beginning to assume informal responsibility for youth upbringing no longer taking place within the parental home or state-institutional facilities.[140] The commune subsequently founded in the Kluckstraße suffered grave difficulties. The rocker club "One" moved in and essentially took over the premises. Both the rockers and runaways from the youth homes proved largely impervious to the ministrations of the left-wing activists who sought to mobilize them. For their part, the activists were disappointed at the gulf between the truculent young people they were attempting to work with and the "the historical, militant, class conscious proletarian" of their dreams. The hoped-for "synthesis of the theoretical socialism of the students and the goal-less uprising of the proletarian youth," in the laconic judgment of the authors of a retrospective analysis, "was not possible."[141]

A more successful self-organizational project involving runaways and other marginal youth was the Georg von Rauch Haus in Berlin-Kreuzberg, although here too problems arose. The seizure of the Georg von Rauch house "was such a great achievement that was talked about [by radicals] all around Germany," recalls Gert Möbius;

but in the house itself there were always big problems, for [at least the first] three years. Because there were factions who wanted to go to work and didn't care about becoming professional revolutionaries; many did want to become

---

[139] Anarcho-Kollektiv, Section "Freiheit für den Rocker."
[140] Steinacker, "Die radikale Linke und soziale Randgruppen," p. 206.
[141] Autorenkollektiv cited in Steinacker, "Die radikale Linke und soziale Randgruppen," p. 207. The radical left were not the only ones interested in penetrating and instrumentalizing the Randgruppe milieu. One of the initiators of the "Project Group Youth Communes" announced in the pages of *Agit 883* in February 1969, the Schöneberg teacher Irmgard Kohlhepp, was actually an NPD activist pursuing the classical *Querfronttaktik* of the German radical right. In another instance, two young girls claiming to be runaways from the Berlin girls' home Eichenhof sought refuge in a Berlin *Wohngemeinschaft*, only later to turn over stolen information on the commune and the left scene to the NPD; Steinacker, "Die radikale Linke und soziale Randgruppen," pp. 205–206.

professional revolutionaries; children were supposed to go to school, but didn't want to, a revolutionary can't go to school; but where was the money to come from?[142]

One of the groups seeking to work with the squatters was the "Basisgruppe Heim- und Lehrlingsarbeit" (Rank-and-File Group Home- and Apprenticework) for whom the activity in the Rauch Haus represented "a model of emancipatory youth work." Setting up shop on two floors of the house along with young workers and apprentices, the *Basisgruppe* justified the seizure of the building not only in terms of general need (they cited the lack of open space, parks, kindergartens, and youth facilities in Kreuzberg) but also in terms of the imperative of giving "the underprivileged and ... socially damaged [*sozial Geschädigten*] ... the opportunity to emancipate themselves from their socially oppressed position and to oppose capitalist interests."[143] The *Basisgruppe* took this argument to the authorities, negotiating with sympathetic local officials to preserve the seizure of the house, even in the face of a full-scale campaign in the Springer Press to demonize the house and its occupants. Against this realistic approach, activists of another group, the "Gruppe SH-Trebe-Arbeit" (associated with the anarchist Schwarze Hilfe) declared themselves to be "professional revolutionaries" and argued against any accommodation with the authorities. In the event, the Schwarze Hilfe activists were shown the door by their more practical-minded colleagues.[144]

These early exchanges marked the beginning of a bitter struggle over urban space that was to rage throughout the rest of the decade and beyond. In all cases, a discourse of anticapitalist "self-organization" coexisted with the language of social pedagogy via which activists claimed the right to intervene on the terrain of daily life where capitalism failed to deliver the goods. These battles over urban space also intersected with debates about the nature and status of cultural production and leisure activity. This came to particular expression in the campaign to create self-organized youth centers, which, along with building seizures dedicated to gaining and holding living space against the predations of speculators and government projects for urban renewal, became one of the key sites of conflict of the 1970s. Involving activists and young people who demanded autonomy within government-funded centers, or, where necessary, seized buildings to initiate the creation of self-administered centers on their own, the campaign not only issued a stark challenge to the rights of private property

---

[142] Möbius, "Hoffmanns Comic Teater."   [143] *Ibid.*
[144] Steinacker, "Die radikale Linke und soziale Randgruppen," p. 212.

and government control but also connected long-running debates about authenticity and recuperation to conflicts over the disposition of urban space.[145] Beginning in 1971, the campaign rapidly gathered steam. Some 500 "initiative groups" were in existence by 1972, with the number growing to 2,200 by 1975.[146] An *Aktionskreis Jugendzentrum* (Action Circle Youth Center) was founded near Stuttgart in April 1971, quickly attracting members from around the country. In addition to organizing mutual support among initiative groups, the *Aktionskreis* sought to put activists in touch with social workers, lawyers, psychologists, and architects – anyone, in short, who could help buffer the interaction between activists and state authorities.[147]

In Hanover, activists of the group "Music Initiative Hanover," in cooperation with activists involved with underground newspaper *Agit 883*, launched a campaign for an independent youth center. The two groups drew an explicit link between the status of leisure time and the status of work. "The bosses have institutionalized our leisure time, and program it in *their* sense," read an article in *Agit 883*; "Leisure time has been torn away from us, we don't have any influence over it, we must accept authoritarian house-rules, home-leaders, and so-called 'youth workers.'" Like everything else in capitalist society, leisure time had been "commercialized and institutionalized" for the benefit of the ruling class. It was therefore no mere side issue but reproduced the conflicts at the heart of capitalist society.[148] As a flyer produced by Music Initiative Hanover and *Agit 883* put it: "The bosses are afraid. They know if we shaped our own leisure time, we might come up with other dumb ideas: Self-organization in the factories. Self-organization in the schools. Self-organization everywhere. We demand an independent youth center now!!!"[149]

A vacant factory building in the Arndtstraße was chosen for the new center, which was to be modeled on the independent youth center established at Mariannenstraße 13 in Berlin-Kreuzberg following the Ton Steine Scherben concert at the Technical University in July. There, after

---

[145] See Sebastian Haumann, "'Stadtindianer' and 'Indiani Metropolitani': Recontextualizing an Italian Protest Movement in West-Germany," in Klimke, Pekelder, and Scharloth, eds., *Between Prague Spring and French May*, pp. 141–153.

[146] Egon Schewe, *Selbstverwaltete Jugendzentren Entwicklung, Konzept und Bedeutung der Jugendzentrumsbewegung* (Bielefeld: Pfeffer, 1980), p. 27.

[147] Schewe, *Selbstverwaltete Jugendzentren Entwicklung*, p. 28.

[148] "883 Hannover für ein unabhängiges Jugendzentrum," *Agit 883*, no. 85, November 15, 1971.

[149] "flugblatt no 2, work is killing us, programmed leisure time too!!!!!," reprinted in *Agit 883*, no. 85, November 15, 1971.

an initial police action resulting in more than seventy arrests, the city reached a modus vivendi with the squatters, the administration promising 5,000 deutsche mark in funding and local police donating furniture(!).[150] Providing living quarters, space for trade-school pupils', school pupils', sex information, and legal advice groups, as well as rehearsal space for the Rote Steine theater group, the seized building became, depending on the viewpoint of the observer, a model of anarchist self-organization or a nest of subversives being assisted by the local administration to destroy society from within.[151]

In Hanover, activists hoping to draw on the mobilizing power of popular music planned their action to coincide with the Ton Steine Scherben concert set for Saturday night, December 11, 1971, an event at which they knew a large number of youth would be concentrated.[152] Over 300 young people took part in the seizure of the building. The police declined to act immediately but instead waited to ask the city administration for advice. Over the weekend, activists proved their seriousness about the principle of self-organization, undertaking repairs and setting up a canteen. A general assembly agreed to distribute thirty-seven rooms, some to families with children and some to youth escaping bad homes. Others were set aside for working groups, which included "Kindergarten, Music Group, Film AG, Political Working Group, and Release-Center."[153] In contrast to the situation in Berlin, and in the absence of a sympathetic left-wing SPD official like Erwin Beck, who at that very moment in Berlin was helping the activists of the Georg von Rauch Haus maintain their precarious hold on the building, seized only three days before, the decision was quickly made to evict the Arndtstraße squatters. On Monday night, police rampaged through the rooms of the building attacking young people with truncheons and arresting 108 of them.[154]

The battle of the youth center in the Arndtstraße in Hanover was only one of countless other struggles around the use of vacant buildings in the Federal Republic at the beginning of the 1970s. Squatting became a new locus of the search for fields of radical engagement and a means of locating

---

[150] "If they would only be allowed to help with the renovation!," the article observed; "Die Kreuzberger Genossen haben gehandelt," *Agit 883*, no. 85, November 15, 1971.
[151] "Die Kreuzberger Genossen haben gehandelt."
[152] *Befreiung*, 25 Jahrgang, January 1972, p. 3.
[153] *Ibid.*
[154] The building was occupied for fifty-six hours; during that time 1,000 youths visited or moved in; *Befreiung*, 25 Jahrgang, January 1972, pp. 4–5.

the struggle concretely on the terrain of daily life. The first building seizures took place in West Berlin, Frankfurt, Munich, Cologne, Göttingen,
and Hamburg. In Frankfurt, the so-called "building war" (*Häuserkampf*)
became a signature radical campaign of the 1970s. From the beginning,
activists sought to unite work with out-groups, in this case, foreign guest
workers and impoverished families, with the struggle over urban space.
With substantial support in both the population and in the press, and
with a left-SPD administration reluctant to crack down too forcefully on
squatters, the campaign quickly developed into something resembling a
broad-based social movement.

The building war was driven by a diverse set of groups drawn overwhelmingly from the antidogmatic left. These Sponti groups became the
primary vehicle of antiauthoritarian radicalism in West Germany from
the beginning of the 1970s. Already by the end of the 1960s, these groups
began to pursue an alternative course of revolution in which the working
class appeared not as a monolithic entity waiting for a vanguard, as in
the conception of the *K-Gruppen*, but as a revolutionary subject ready,
with assistance, to unfold its own potential in relationship to its own,
local concerns, according to the principle of self-organization. This conception was fundamentally anarchist in orientation, drawing as it did,
always implicitly and sometimes explicitly, on the concept of the "affinity group," which was to help the masses without assuming a position of
leadership over them.

The Sponti scene was fundamentally transnational in orientation and
makeup. One major influence was the French May, which had demonstrated the potential for students and workers to join in a common struggle. What began as student unrest at two Paris campuses had spread, with
the assistance of police brutality, to become a general strike involving
10 million workers and threatening, for a time at least, to overthrow the
French government. The French May was seen as a model for what could
happen in the Federal Republic under the right conditions. As Hans
Magnus Enzensberger put it in a speech against the Emergency Laws, the
goal must be to "create French conditions in Germany."[155] The French May
was more than simply an inspiration, however, for one of its main figures,
the French-German activist Daniel Cohn-Bendit, provided a direct link

---

[155] Hans Magnus Enzensberger, in Bernhard Pollmann, ed., *Lesebuch zur deutschen Geschichte*, vol.
III, *Vom deutschen Reich bis zur Gegenwart* [From the German Reich to the Present] (Dortmund:
Chronik Verlag, 1984), pp. 253–254.

to West Germany through his connections to the Sponti stronghold of Frankfurt.

Another key source for the development of the Sponti scene in the Federal Republic in general, and in Frankfurt in particular, was the antiauthoritarian movement in Italy. The theory of "Operaismus" associated with the Italian group Lotta Continua ("Continuous Struggle") offered a way out of a theoretical and practical impasse facing activists who wished to make an approach to the concrete struggles of workers without assuming the vanguard party position of the *K-Gruppen*. So-called *Betriebsprojektgruppen* (Factory Project Groups) were formed in a number of cities, including "Revolutionärer Kampf" (Revolutionary Struggle) in Frankfurt, "Proletarische Front" (Proletarian Front) in Hamburg and Bremen, "Arbeiterkampf" (Workers' Struggle) in Cologne, and "Arbeitersache" (Workers' Cause) in Munich. The groups published a joint newspaper, *Wir wollen Alles* (*We Want Everything*) beginning in February 1973. In contrast to the *K-Gruppen*, and in keeping with the model of "Operaismus," these groups treated the approach to industrial workers as a sort of experiment out of which new tactics and concepts could be developed. Rather than imposing theory *on* workers, they sought to derive theory *from* workers' concrete struggles.[156]

In particular, the Factory Project Groups sought to organize foreign guest workers, many of them Italian, who were traditionally left out of the industrial trade-union equation. Lotta Continua was an influential model. Founded in the fall of 1969, it focused on spreading radicalism to the working class, with emphasis on marginalized (e.g. young and immigrant) workers in large factories such as Fiat in Turin. Revolutionärer Kampf in Frankfurt was particularly influenced by Lotta Continua, especially its emphasis on spontaneity and decentralized direct action. The attempt to organize and support immigrant workers met with some notable local successes, such as the October 1971 action at Opel in Rüsselheim and the August 1973 Ford strike in Cologne. Ultimately, however, activists were forced to acknowledge that the gulf they were trying to bridge between immigrant and German, between young activist and older worker, was simply too wide and that the very different character of Italian industrial labor relations made the importation of Italian models of activism problematic.[157]

---

[156] Geronimo, *Feuer und Flamme*, p. 19.
[157] Geronimo, *Feuer und Flamme*, pp. 19–21.

The housing struggle into which Sponti activists began to pour their energy met with more success. Indeed, the refocusing of activist energy on the housing struggle made it possible to overcome the difficulties of mobilization that had dogged the Factory Project Groups. Agitation around living conditions, rent strikes, and building seizures proved the perfect way of concretizing the struggle against capitalism, of making capitalism and the means of fighting it visible on the surface of everyday life. The meaning of the housing struggle was expressed in striking terms by the group Proletarische Front writing in *Wir wollen Alles*:

Seizing buildings means destroying the capitalist plan in the city districts. Means not paying rent, means abolishing the capitalist shoe-carton structures. Means building communes and centers, means reorganizing the social life of the city districts, means conquering helplessness. In the seizure of buildings and in rent strikes lies the pivot point for the fight against capital outside the factories.[158]

The housing struggle took its most prominent form in Frankfurt and Hamburg, two cities with reform-oriented Social Democratic administrations. Again, as in the case of the Bethanien, radical measures unfolded in part through tacit cooperation with liberal-minded city authorities, cooperative radicalism in action once again. Yet provisional accommodation was never far removed from the potential for police raids, as subsequent events would demonstrate. In Frankfurt, as already mentioned, the housing movement achieved substantial early success. The focus was the Westend district targeted by developers as the center of a new commercial district. Already at the end of the 1960s, speculators had been moving in to buy up buildings, leading to the departure of previous residents, increased rent, and limited availability of apartments for students and others. In 1972–1973, members of the Sponti scene, above all militants of Revolutionärer Kampf, in many cases working with Italian immigrants who had been members of Revolutionärer Kampf's Italian model Lotta Continua, launched a parallel campaign of rent strikes and building seizures that forced a temporary halt to developers' plans for the district. The SPD, which had originally declared its intention to clear all seized buildings, had to back off as it became clear that, in the course of countless demonstrations, street battles, rent strikes, and building seizures, Sponti militants had won considerable popular support.[159]

[158] Proletarische Front, in *Wir wollen Alles*, no. 4, May 1973, quoted in Geronimo, *Feuer und Flamme*, p. 21.
[159] Geronimo, *Feuer und Flamme*, p. 22.

The rent-strike movement involving Italian and Turkish immigrants, hampered to an extent by communication problems with the Sponti activists, lost steam by early 1973. Afterward, the emphasis shifted to the defense of seized buildings and attendant street battles with the police assigned to clear the buildings. The police assault on the Kettenhofweg Haus in early 1973, in particular, lead to robust defensive countermeasures, including the formation of mobile self-defense teams called *Putzgruppe*.[160] "Strong points for waging civil war are being created in the big cities," worried the *Frankfurter neue Presse*; "It is not out of the question that, following on the Frankfurt example, a sort of parallel government is being created in the middle of the big cities ... Yesterday University-Soviets, today housing Soviets, tomorrow possibly 'Soviets of the occupied factories'."[161] This fevered vision of anarchist revolution significantly overshot the reality of the situation, but it did illustrate the extent to which the occupation movement had succeeded in something resembling a temporary urban autonomous zone in Frankfurt.[162]

Ultimately, however, militants proved unable to resist police assaults on their strongpoints. The February 1974 surprise attack of 2,500 police on the "Block," as the squat at Bockenheimerstraße/Schumannstraße was called, broke the back of the movement in Frankfurt, despite the 10,000-person-strong demonstration that followed it.[163] Nevertheless, as in Berlin-Kreuzberg, the squatter movement prevented the destruction of many old, beautiful buildings slated to be replaced by 1970s-style modernist office buildings, to the ultimate enrichment of the cityscape.

In April 1973, activists in Hamburg, inspired by the defense of the Kettenhofweg squat in Frankfurt, decided to seize the large building at Ekhofstrasse 39. The situation in the Hohenfelde district in Hamburg where the building was located was similar to the one in Frankfurt. It was marked by speculation, the forcing out of old residents, a lack of apartments while buildings stood vacant, and increased rents. Also as in Frankfurt, the local population showed considerable solidarity with the squatters. Police harassment, accompanied by demonization of the squatters as "terrorists" and "gangsters" in the press, led to a situation of almost

---

[160] Geronimo, *Feuer und Flamme*, p. 23. The term *Putzgruppe* appears to stem from the phrase "Pig ist Pig und Pig musst put"—"A pig is a pig and a pig must be destroyed" (i.e. be rendered "kaputt").

[161] *Frankfurter neue Presse*, April 1973.

[162] Proletarische Front, in *Wir wollen Alles*, no. 4, May 1973, quoted in Geronimo, *Feuer und Flamme*, p. 22.

[163] Geronimo, *Feuer und Flamme*, p. 23.

open warfare that quickly consumed the squatters' political energies. In late May, after a little over a month of existence, the squat was cleared in an assault by 600 police including commandos armed with machine guns. Seventy persons were arrested and thirty-three charged under Section 129 concerning "membership in or support of a criminal organization."[164] The assault on Ekhofstrasse 39 clearly demonstrated that any accommodation with squatters on the part of Social Democratic administrations was purely tactical in nature. It also demonstrated that, short of the military capability and political will to defend seized buildings, the housing struggle could never be more than a holding action against the combined force of capital and state power.

"WHEN WE ARE HAPPY, THAT'S ALREADY REVOLUTIONARY"

The struggle over urban space in student metropoles such as Frankfurt, Hamburg, Munich, and Berlin produced a mixed result. Where activists were able to reach accommodation (of whatever type) with authorities, alternative projects based in seized buildings were allowed to stand, becoming staples of the subsequent period of the "alternative movement" in the 1980s and 1990s. A similar process unfolded after the fall of the wall in 1989, with empty buildings in the liminal zone between former East and West Berlin becoming home to various initiatives, many of which survive, with official sanction, to the present day. From the perspective of activists seeking to maintain the momentum of the student movement and to search out new directions of revolutionary action, however, the "building war," like the attempts of the *K-Gruppen* to mobilize the working classes or the efforts of the Hash Rebels to turn smoking marijuana into a revolutionary act, was ultimately a dead end.

As a consequence, many activists began leaving these sorts of struggles behind altogether, searching out new terrain where the personal costs of activism were not so high. Going "back to the land," founding rural communes across West Germany, they attempted to give fresh meaning to the idea of the "revolution of everyday life" that had haunted the antiauthoritarian revolt since its inception. This goal had, of course, been central to the urban communes founded from the end of the 1960s. Communes such as the Kommune I and Kommune 2 (Berlin), the Horla Commune

---

[164] Proletarische Front, in *Wir wollen Alles*, no. 4, May 1973, quoted in Geronimo, *Feuer und Flamme*, p. 25.

(Cologne), the Anarsch, Linkeck, Pots, Bülow, and Wieland communes (Berlin), the Haifisch Kommune (Munich), and the Ablassgesellschaft (Hamburg), all to a greater or lesser extent focused on combining both personal and political transformation. Many of these communes were also associated with creative initiatives, whether underground newspapers, rock bands, theater groups, or other cultural-productive projects. The Linkeck Commune in West Berlin and the Päng Commune outside Nuremberg published eponymous newspapers; the Pots Commune in West Berlin produced the paper *Charlie Kaputt*, while members of the Ablassgesellschaft in Hamburg published *Die neue Scheisse*. The rock band Amon Düül lived in a rural commune as did, from 1975, Ton Steine Scherben.[165] That so many communes served a cultural-productive function is hardly surprising; rather, it expressed the communicative imperative that governed the communes' posture both internally and externally.

The initial wave of commune foundings launched a widespread movement, the term "commune" increasingly being replaced by the less heavily freighted *Wohngemeinschaft*. The movement expanded rapidly. Some 2,000 *Wohngemeinschaften* existed in 1971. By the end of the decade, that number had expanded to some 40,000.[166] Though they generally jettisoned some of the broad claims of political transformation associated with the first communes, many *Wohngemeinschaften* persisted in attempting to revolutionize personal and sexual relations. This made them, as the sociologist Heide Berndt pointed out in *Kursbuch* in 1969, hotbeds of interpersonal conflict beset by problems of jealousy, insecurity, and isolation.[167] "The 'destruction of privacy' or 'smash the bourgeois family,' were slogans with which, it was imagined, one might counteract authoritarian character formation and late-capitalist isolation," writes Sven Reichardt; group discussions of "private disputes between lovers" were seen as correctives to parental programming around "bourgeois correct behavior and obsessive cleanliness."[168] The attempt to make the *Wohngemeinschaft* a "counter-model to the coercive community of the nuclear family" could make it a difficult place to live; yet, as Reichardt has pointed out, these

---

[165] See Steve B. Peinemann, "Aus der Grossßtadtszene aufs Land geflohen: Ton Steine Scherben," in Steve Bernhard Peinemann, ed., *Die Wut, die du im Bauch hast. Politische Rockmusic: Interviews, Erfahrungen* (Hamburg: Rowohlt, 1980).

[166] Sven Reichardt, "Is 'Warmth' a Mode of Social Behaviour? Considerations on a Cultural History of the Left-Alternative Milieu from the Late 1960s to the Mid 1980s," *Behemoth*, 3 (2) (2010): 84–99, at p. 88.

[167] Heide Berndt, "Kommune und Familie," *Kursbuch*, no. 17, June 1969.

[168] Reichardt, "Is 'Warmth' a Mode of Social Behaviour?" p. 88.

institutions also offered forms of sociability that, in valorizing feelings of openness, authenticity, and "warmth," expressed and fostered key values of the left-wing habitus.[169]

The urban commune experiments, either in their revolutionary-trans-formative or practical-realistic variants, paved the way for excursions both into new vistas of personal subjectivity and out of the city, into the coun-tryside. Here, activists sought to escape the hothouse environment of the cities with their constant conflict and either/or political postures. "When at the beginning of the 1970s the idea matured that we should together move to the country," wrote Bernd Leineweber and Karl-Ludwig Schibel, two leading figures in the commune movement,

> our decision was formulated like this: We stop working in the institutions – in our case, in schools and universities – and practicing leftist politics, we move out of the city. Not because we consider work in the institutions to be ... wrong ..., nor because we consider the urban centers to be unimportant ..., but because we want to do something different. We want to organize our everyday life together in a small, manageable group, to keep ourselves free from the market nexus as far as possible and to produce as much of our own food as possible; we want to work – on the basis of joint living and working – on those conceptions of liber-ation and emancipation which in the previous years had produced chaos among the leftists in their efforts to become new human beings.[170]

Hoping to retain the transformative goals of the antiauthoritarian movement, Leineweber and Schibel wished to jettison the seemingly fruitless struggle over political alternatives that characterized the last days of the APO. The goal was no longer to be, as in the fashion of the student intellectuals and activists of the *K-Gruppen*, to "think for others, for the 'people' or for the 'proletariat'"; rather, it was to change the concrete situ-ation of the group to which one belonged. "We are accomplishing – in a 'utopian' manner – what left-wing intellectuals always want ... but just for us. Not for others."[171]

The impulse to escape from the hopeless impasse of left-wing polit-ics in an increasingly polarized society was already becoming widespread at the beginning of the 1970s, and even more so near their end, when

---

[169] *Ibid.*

[170] Bernd Leineweber and Karl-Ludwig Schibel, "'Die Alternativbewegung': Ein Beitrag zu ihrer gesellschaftlichen Bedeutung und politischen Tragweite, ihren Möglichkeiten und Grenzen," in Wolfgang Kraushaar, ed., *Autonomie oder Getto? Kontroversen über die Alternativbewegung* (Frankfurt: Verlag Neue Kritik, 1978), pp. 95–128.

[171] *Ibid.*, pp. 119–120.

terrorism and counterterrorism, as well as more prosaic problems such as unemployment, were making life increasingly untenable for many in the left-wing scene. "Dreams of alternative villages haunted the freak-districts of Kreuzberg, München-Haidhausen, and Frankfurt-Bockenheim," noted the author of a profile of Leineweber and Schibel, fueling the desire to "'finally just get out of this cold country of the German Autumn.'"[172]

This step away from any sort of vanguardism, even of the antiauthoritarian variety, was easily misinterpreted as a step away from all political engagement, as a 1971 *Spiegel* cover story on communes demonstrated. Reckoning the number of rural communes at about sixty, the piece profiled the Päng Commune outside Nuremberg. Founded by Raymond Martin and others in 1970, Päng was one of the earliest and most successful of the rural communes. The piece cast the "back to the land" movement as a decisive turn away from politics, an interpretation to which Martin's comments, at least on the surface, lent weight. "Revolution? Nonsense and over with!," the article paraphrased Martin as saying; "'All the revolution now! screamers, APO-aggressors, terrorists and fashion-Maoists' should learn from him and his American underground-masters, for the present, how one makes a revolution with oneself: 'stoned,' free from force and violence, eating in accordance with nature ('you are what you eat') and full, full of love." Portrayed as both confused and unoriginal ("Anglicisms of an international Pop-, Underground-, and drug-jargon, old APO-words ... concepts from Yoga, macrobiotic and psychedelic technology flow gently across the lips of these flipped-out apprentices"), the communards were presented as a decisive step away from the politics of the antiauthoritarian revolt. "The clenched fist," observed the author with characteristic condescension, "has opened."[173]

This facile interpretation misjudged the content of the back to the land moment. First, at least as far as the Päng Commune was concerned, moving from the city to the countryside did not shatter old political allegiances. The commune could be seen as an unpolitical act only inasmuch as the definition of politics was seen to be synonymous with the overheated rhetoric of the student movement and the *K-Gruppen*. What counted as a rejection of politics – and this counts for Martin's comments to *Der Spiegel* as well – was often only a rejection of the thankless task of trying to create a certain type of prepackaged revolutionary movement

---

[172] Matthias Horx, "Das verlorene Paradies," *Zeit-Magazin*, 1988.
[173] Peter Brügge, "Wir wollen, daß man sich an uns gewöhnt," *Der Spiegel*, no. 33, August 1971.

where none in fact existed, with all the dogmatism, exhaustion, anger, and self-deception that that entailed. According to Leineweber and Schibel, defending themselves against the "embittered resistance" and "massive condemnation" directed against their decision to move to the countryside, the problem was that professional revolutionaries could only think in terms of rigid antinomies: "here Communist orthodoxy, there the political subculture, here out-of-touch dogmatism and proletariat-fetishism, there the cult of innerness and social romanticism ... What the left needs," they wrote, "is complementary thinking in practical questions, not the insistence on a [party] line."[174]

The move back to the land was accompanied by a turn to new concerns and a new set of tropes. Already implicit in the countercultural turn of the late 1960s, these ideas began to take serious root at the beginning of the 1970s. One of the most important figures in the rural-Communist imaginary was the Native American. In Germany, fascination with the Native American had deep cultural roots, popularized above all by the best-selling German author Karl May (1842–1912). May's adventure stories of the American frontier featuring the Apache Indian chief Winnetou and his white trapper companion Old Shatterhand were enormously influential, helping to foster a cult of the American frontier and the noble savage whose influence continues until the present day.[175] For young radicals of the 1960s, the Native American took on an additional significance as a symbol of resistance against the system. The figure of Chief Geronimo, crouched with rifle at the ready, was already a stock image in the underground press on both sides of the Atlantic, environmentally conscious authenticity and anticolonial militancy rolled into one.[176] "It is probably just [my] personal view," wrote a "Waltraud W." in *Päng* in a piece entitled "Indians Today," "when I maintain: the Indians see their contest not as class struggle, as is so often heard from left-wing groups. They are in a deeper sense revolutionaries from birth – they don't need to create any subcultures, they [already] have them."[177]

---

[174] Leineweber and Schibel, "'Die Alternativbewegung', at p. 122.
[175] Yolanda Broyles González, "Cheyennes in the Black Forest: A Social Drama," in Roger B. Rollin, ed., *The Americanization of the Global Village: Essays in Comparative Popular Culture* (Bowling Green, Ohio: Bowling Green State University Popular Press, 1989), pp. 70–86.
[176] See Timothy Scott Brown, "The Sixties in the City: Avant-gardes and Urban Rebels in New York, London, and West Berlin," *Journal of Social History*, 46 (4) (2013): 817–842.
[177] Elsewhere in the same issue, *Päng* presented detailed instructions for building a teepee. The cover of issue no. 6 bore a photo of armed Native Americans, accompanied by the legend: "Violence is neither good nor evil. It is only so good or bad as those who employ it."

Such valuations were part of a broader process of cultural adoption through which the group borrowed from abroad the tropes, imagery, and cultural products necessary to construct and make sense of the radicalism they were already putting into practice. As we have already seen, both the idea-world and the visual iconography of the West German countercultura were drawn almost entirely from the American hippie movement. Whereas early influences on the German underground had, with exceptions such as the literature of the American Beats and American musical artists such as Jimi Hendrix and Frank Zappa, come predominantly from the UK, influences at the beginning of the 1970s came primarily from a very robust American hippie culture, which had pioneered many of the countercultural ideas and visual tropes at an early stage. Particularly influential were American underground comics such as Gilbert Shelton's *Fabulous Furry Freak Brothers* and the various works of R. Crumb. Like Rolf Dieter Brinkmann, Martin took pains to ensure that the best of the international counterculture was available in West Germany. Martin founded the underground comics magazine *U-Comix* in 1969, which reprinted much of the American underground comics scene. Martin also imported American underground comics and translated and reprinted the works of psychedelic guru Timothy Leary.

Above all, however, the rural communes were about finding peace, away from the divisive and exhausting struggles of the urban movement. "We live in a small Bavarian village, far away from the city," wrote Martin in *Päng*;

Through our tribe the population of Kucha (that's what the village is called) has increased from 200 to 220. We have a [large] acreage and a large garden in which we have planted or are planting oats, potatoes, various vegetables, and marijuana. The inhabitants of the village like us a lot, which is expressed in presents and positive communication. Although Kucha is made up of CSU and NPD voters, the inhabitants accept us, because, unlike many rural groups, we don't act out the same shit as in the city and therefore fail to join in the harmony of the countryside. Who can enjoy going barefoot over meadows, fresh milk from healthy cows, self-gathered nourishment, wildlife, handiwork, etc., will find here in the country a paradise. We are happy to be here.[178]

To the extent that they were still revolutionary, the communards' gesture was a revolution of the self. "We have often been accused of retreating, building our own little world of illusions," they write; but "we've had it, having to pay rent for our lives, and we want to do what we want,

---

[178] "Das Land is Frei," *Päng*, no. 4.

to the extent that that is possible here in the BRD ... WE are our new morning!"[179] In the final analysis, this led to the ultimate turn to personal subjectivity. As Martin put it in *Päng*: "When we are happy, that's already revolutionary."[180]

In the event, country living did not always prove as paradisaical as hoped. The same conflicts with authority that governed relations in the city cropped up there as well. Martin described in a special report in the underground journal *Ulcus Molle Infodienst* how, after moving to a new location in nearby Jobstgreuth, the commune, now operating a press named UPN-Volksverlag, was subjected to a massive police raid.[181] Ostensibly searching for hashish (which they found), the authorities also discovered an American Army deserter named "Mike" (subsequently arrested by American military police) and a postcard from RAF terrorist Astrid Proll. "This pack of cops no doubt wanted to put a scare into us drug-addicted rabble, us Communist pigs," wrote Martin, "and hinder our underground press work. Typical case of metamorphic jealousy. Caterpillars envy butterflies."[182]

CONCLUSION

The concerns expressed by Martin and others in the rural commune movement prefigured the alternative movement that gathered force in the later 1970s and flowered in the 1980s. Indeed, rural communes and urban *Wohngemeinschaften* represented key phenomena bridging the antiauthoritarian movement of the 1960s and 1970s and a later era marked by a less explicitly revolutionary but nevertheless radical-democratic attempt to reshape the face of daily life. In terms of the arc of the radical moment of 1968, however, it represented the culmination of tendencies inherent in the antiauthoritarian movement itself. The attempt to realize the revolution on the terrain of personal experience – not through the overheated psychological one-upmanship of the first commune experiments but through practical attempts to create new ways of living and relating to others – represented *one* answer, ultimately one of the more satisfying ones, to the question of what the term "revolution" actually meant. If it

[179] *Ibid.*   [180] *Päang*, no. 4.
[181] UPN stood for Undefinierbare Produkte aus Nürnberg: "Indefinable Products from Nuremberg."
[182] Raymond Martin, "Kommune Päng Landfreaks schmützige Hände Gendarme," *Infodienst*, February 1, 1973.

represented a step away from the dreams of student theoreticians of the revolution, it simultaneously reflected a long-standing schism within the left, not only between dogmatic and nondogmatic forms of socialism but between internal and external visions of revolutionary change.

More generally, the history of the alternative projects of the late 1960s and early 1970s, from *Wohngemeinschaften*, to independent youth centers in squatted buildings, to various sorts of cultural-productive installations, illustrates a basic fact about 1968: that radical gains often happened in concert with, rather than in diametric opposition to, liberalizing tendencies in government and society. Yet the democratizing imperative that drove grassroots radicalism had a strongly cumulative effect. The more areas of life found wanting when viewed through the radical-democratic lens – whether the university, the secondary school, the youth home, etc.–the more demands were made for self-management and autonomy; and the more these demands met with success, the more emboldened activists became. In the end, activism always continued until it came up against the point where authority could budge little further without fatally undermining the basic power arrangements underpinning liberal democracy, up to, and including, challenging the state's monopoly on the use of violence.

At the same time, unanimity on the left was impossible to achieve, because there was and could be no agreement about basic issues, from the identity of the revolutionary subject, to the ideal balance between organization and spontaneity, to what, in the final analysis, a revolution actually represented. These questions were not products of the 1960s but were deeply rooted in the left-revolutionary tradition(s). Activists thus sought their answers in the revolutionary past; but they also sought them beyond Germany's borders. From the influence of English and American countercultural drug-treatment models on the formation of Release to the inspiration of revolutionary events such as the Paris May and models such as the Italian group Lotta Continua – each heavily stamped by the presence of activists from abroad – the antiauthoritarian revolt in West Germany was a product of transnational exchanges and global vision.

In cobbling together components of current events and past traditions, activists produced a unique mixture neither fully old nor wholly new. For a brief moment of revolutionary convergence, leading up to the spring of 1968 and the campaigns against the Springer Press and the Emergency Laws, activists in and around the SDS found themselves riding the wave of a radical-democratic citizens' movement. When this movement failed to produce the desired changes, the outstanding questions of revolutionary tactics and organization were revealed in glaring fashion. While some activists enacted a retreat into organization, falling back into Old Left forms and postures, others attempted to carry the radical-democratic remaking of everyday life at the heart of the antiauthoritarian revolt to its logical conclusion. It was precisely at this moment, at the apogee of the APO, that the nature of the revolution was challenged from an entirely different and – for those not paying attention – unexpected direction.

CHAPTER 7

Sex

On September 13, 1968, the Twenty-Third Delegate Conference of the SDS took place in Frankfurt. The conference occurred at a time of transition for the organization, as it struggled to define its goals and mission while coping with an ever-more demanding contest of wills with the authorities. In the midst of the usual discussions, the floor was granted to Helke Sander, a student at the DFFB. Sander proceeded to deliver a fiery speech accusing the male leaders of the SDS of ignoring, patronizing, or otherwise oppressing the women in the organization. The responsibilities of motherhood and housework, she argued, effectively excluded women from meaningful participation in politics. "The helplessness and arrogance with which we are forced to present ourselves," said Sander, "is not particularly fun. We are helpless because we actually expect progressive men to realize the shattering effect of our conflict. We are arrogant because we see what blinders you have before your eyes." Sander concluded by warning the male leadership of the SDS that it must take the attitude of the women seriously. "Comrades," she said, "if you are not ready for this discussion ... then we will have to conclude that the SDS is nothing more than an overinflated counter-revolutionary yeast dough. The female comrades will know then what consequences to draw."[1]

Amid a mix of laughter and boos (some of the latter from women in the audience) Sander took her seat. The dialogue she hoped to initiate failed to materialize. The panelists politely thanked her without further comment, and the speaker, Hans Jürgen Krahl, moved on to other business. At this, a woman named Sigrid Rüger stood up shouted "Comrade Krahl! You are objectively a counterrevolutionary and an agent of the class enemy as well." Taking a ripe tomato out of her bag, the heavily pregnant Rüger

[1] Helke Sander, "Rede des 'Aktionsrates zur Befreiung der Frauen," in Ann Anders, ed., *Autonome Frauen: Schüsseltexte der neuen Frauenbewegung seit 1968* (Frankfurt: Athenäum, 1988), pp. 39–47.

Figure 7.1 "Penistagon: We can get no Satisfaction" [sic]. Anti-Vietnam War demonstration, West Berlin, October 20, 1967. Landesarchiv Berlin. Photo: Wolfgang Schubert.

hurled it at the SDS's star theoretician, hitting him squarely in the head.[2] What Peter Mosler called "the revolt within the revolt" had begun.[3]

"THE PRIVATE IS POLITICAL"

Rüger's theatrical piece of direct action, commonly cited as the beginning of the women's movement in West Germany, expressed frustrations that had been brewing for some time. Ironically, Rüger was not a supporter of any female-separatist position per se; a well-known SDS activist since the mid 1960s, she had arranged for Sander to be able to speak at the meeting. What enraged her was the contemptuous dismissal of Sander's speech.[4] Women were more heavily represented in the SDS than

---

[2] Rüger is alleged to have comforted Krahl as he later cried over the incident; see Katharina Rutschky, *Emma und ihre Schwestern: Ausflüge in den real existierenden Feminismus* (Munich: Carl Hanser, 1999).

[3] Peter Mosler, *Was wir wollten, was wir wurden: Studentenrevolte – zehn Jahre danach. Mit einer Chronologie von Wolfgang Kraushaar* (Reinbek b. Hamburg: Rowohlt – Verlag, 1977), p. 159.

[4] Kätzel, *Die 68erinnen*, p. 169.

any other student organization, in no small part because the organization allowed them more opportunities to get involved than elsewhere. Helke Sander joined the SDS in 1959, attracted by the fact that women in the organization, even though few in number, held a different intellectual status than elsewhere. "[A] sexist climate did not dominate," she remembers, "but rather a neutral comradely climate. It wasn't the case that women felt like exhibition items, or that people talked badly about them or considered them a minority, but that they were simply like the others, men as well."[5] Against this theoretical equality, however, was the fact that men did most of the talking; and the expectations that women placed on the SDS as a site for their agency and activism only increased the potential for their dissatisfaction, especially as women in the SDS began to realize the political implications of the fact that they were not men.

Helke Sander spoke in Frankfurt as a representative of a Berlin group called the Aktionsrat zur Befreiung der Frauen (Action Council for the Liberation of Women). Established by Sander and six others in early 1968, the Aktionsrat was an outgrowth of meetings held in January to discuss issues of child care. These meetings took place in an atmosphere of tension in which women intent on politicizing the private sphere felt ignored and silenced, and men concerned with making "the revolution" felt irritated by the sudden intrusion of "women's crap." This open contempt fanned flames that were already burning. In the run-up to the Twenty-Third Delegate Conference, the Aktionsrat was already developing a line of analysis that would underlie Helke Sander's speech and help fuel the group's subsequent activities. "The class division of the family with the man as bourgeois and the woman as proletarian – master and slave – implies the basic function of men as the class enemy" read a resolution prepared for the meeting. Women and mothers, with their pressing and personal stake in the matter, were to serve as guarantors of a determined assault on the "authoritarian rationality principle" that governed patriarchal society in general and the SDS in particular.[6]

The revolt launched at the Twenty-Third Delegate Congress revolved around a demand for the right to speak, the right to express ideas and positions other than those defined by the male theoretician media stars who dominated the movement. Against this backdrop, the revolt was an attempt to assert egalitarianism against elitism, which was simultaneously

[5] Kätzel, *Die 68erinnen*, p. 183.
[6] "RESOLUTION für die 23. o. DK des SDS. Vorgelegt von Aktionsrat zur Befreiung der Frauen Berlin," Bundesarchiv Koblenz, Zsg 153–12, p. 2.

a denial of the primacy of the male voice. The left-wing scene had long been dominated by aggressive male personalities known for theoretical and rhetorical self-confidence. The activist Antje Vollmer, later a Green member of parliament, remembers: "I would never have trusted myself to try and mix in the debates. The pressure around rhetorical brilliance, aggressive gesture, word-play and demagogy was enormous."[7] It was little different in the Kommune I, its reputation for fun and free love notwithstanding. Founder Dieter Kunzelmann presided over a competitive rhetorical regime in which intellectual cut and thrust was the order of the day. The group-psychology sessions that earned the Kommune I the name "horror commune," in which members tried to "deprogram" themselves with the aid of aggressive probing by their fellow communards, intimidated men and women alike.[8] Status in the commune, as in the SDS, had very much to do with the ability to prove oneself in verbal combat. Dominance rested on skill in deploying the ideological concepts and jargon that served as cultural capital in the movement.

Inga Buhmann experienced the oppression of male rhetorical dominance both as a member of the circle around Subversive Aktion in Munich in the early 1960s and later in the decade as a student in Frankfurt. "I was very quickly disappointed with the Frankfurt School and the milieu around it," she wrote;

The seminars I attended were more like rituals than occasions where actual debate took place. Adorno's seminar was ruled by a restrained style, almost solemn; in Habermas' [seminar] gathered the sociological elite, against whom there would have been nothing to say, had they not dragged around their freshly-learned jargon to every appropriate and inappropriate occasion, to parties, to bars, to sex, to SDS, and had they not overwhelmingly used them to browbeat others.[9]

This offensive deployment of jargon, Buhmann argued, was one of the key weapons used to silence women. "My biggest criticism," she wrote, "is that they used their knowledge as an arrogant instrument of power, above all against women. It often occurred that when I asked a question, I received in response a sermon consisting of an uninterrupted series of quotations put together from the five books that everybody had to read to be 'in.'"[10]

---

[7] Quoted in Renner, *1968*, p. 70.
[8] See the comments by Gunther Langer: "Meine Schüler finden es irre, dass ich Hippie war."
[9] Buhmann, "Frankfurt," p. 310.   [10] *Ibid.*

Buhmann saw the state of affairs as broadly indicative of relations between men and women in the movement more generally. "A woman in the SDS was supposed to be as beautiful as an advertising image," she writes, "even in Frankfurt, when possible, with stylish clothes, chic, conventionally attractive; she was supposed to function in bed the same way as in the office, sexy and simultaneously a fast typist ... and intellectual enough that she could 'join in conversation'; loyal or alternating companion to her boyfriend-comrade, who she should make as comfortable as possible so that he could withstand the stress of hard political times."[11] Of the cognitive dissonance involved in this situation Buhmann writes: "It was a great disappointment for me that politically aware men did not behave any differently toward women than other men, yes sometimes even more brutal and exploitative, and that embellished with the pretense of liberation."[12]

The idea of sexual liberation according to which women were to be perpetually available for sexual activity – implicit in the oft-cited slogan "Wer zweimal mit derselben pennt, gehört schon zum Establishment" ("Who sleeps more than once with the same person already belongs to the establishment") – placed women in a situation of double jeopardy. Reingard Jäkl, a member of the Red Women's Front in Munich (later a Green politician), recalls: "The first doubts came to me in the course of the so-called 'Sex Revolt' when I refused the demand of a comrade that I go to bed with him and received the answer: 'But you're frustrated!' That sounded a lot like 'You're frigid!' I was pissed."[13] Frigga Haug of the Socialist Women's League West Berlin recalls: "I hated the term 'sexual revolution' at the time, because ... we knew that it was only a revolution for men and that women were supposed to be available without hesitation, as often as possible, and if possible, on a rotating basis."[14] As Jäkl put it:

The Sexual Revolution was (and is) for the world of men a feast they've come upon, on which they greedily pounce, because they get big advantages out of it. For many women it was a bitter awakening, after the liberating breath of fresh air, to find themselves in a new dilemma: not to be able to say "no" without being placed under suspicion as a counterrevolutionary.[15]

Such experiences fueled the impetus for women to create a separate space for themselves. "Lots of women experienced the same thing," recalls

---

[11] Buhmann, "Frankfurt," p. 313.   [12] *Ibid.*
[13] Reingard Jäkl, "Eine kleine radikale Minderheit," in Becker, ed., *Unbekannte Wesen*, pp. 145–148, at p. 147.
[14] Kätzel, *Die 68erinnen*, p. 197.
[15] Jäkl, "Eine kleine radikale Minderheit," p. 147.

Jäkl, "and we often stood around in the pubs together and began to talk about it. That alone provoked a lot of the men. The comrades reacted unbelievably aggressively to these first autonomous impulses."[16] Another member of the Munich Women's Commune, Katrin Seybold, stresses repeatedly in her unpublished memoirs the oppressive effect of the dominance of men in the movement. During a stay in the Kommune I Fabrik in 1969, Seybold had the opportunity to observe Uschi Obermaier and Ina Siepmann while their respective boyfriends, Rainer Langhans and Dieter Kunzelmann were imprisoned on a bomb charge.[17] In their absence, the attractive and confident Siepmann was a center of attention, writing an essay and constantly surrounded by leather-jacketed Hash Rebels. Uschi, meanwhile, mostly lounged on a mattress, "happy when someone visited who didn't just talk to Ina." When Langhans and Kunzelmann returned from prison, in Seybold's telling, "the women changed. Ina became completely quiet, and waited until Dieter had something to say. Uschi started to bounce around on the mattress, or to sit up very straight, because she knew that Rainer liked that. She often repeated what Rainer said in a loud voice."[18]

Sickened by the women's subordination to their male "pashas," Seybold, a keen observer of the commune scene, concludes: "Yes, everything was very human there. But for women there was no possibility of existing … The men emancipated themselves only among themselves, it was the most woman-hostile commune that I had ever seen."[19] Members of a commune in Mannheim complained in *Agit 883* of the "group boss, or several, the so-called Obergenossen," who "don't look at the sub-comrades or especially the female comrades when they speak to them," and who "almost always secure their stupid dogmatism and spread an atmosphere in which no one is allowed to contradict them."[20] This treatment landed especially on the females, the authors complained, girls "regularly being degraded to disempowered little hangers-on."[21]

The journalist Alice Schwarzer, moving in very different circles, recalls similar experiences during her time as a journalist for the *Düsseldorfer*

---

[16] *Ibid.*

[17] A police search of the commune on March 5 uncovered a bomb planted by the police agent Peter Urbach, leading to the arrest of Kunzelmann and Langhans.

[18] Katrin Seybold, "Frauenkommune Türkenstraße 68a," unpublished manuscript, Archiv Heinz Korderer, Munich.

[19] Seybold, "Frauenkommune Türkenstraße 68a."

[20] Cited in Massimo Perinelli, "Lust, Gewalt, Befreiung. Sexualitätsdiskurse," in Rotaprint 25, eds., *Agit 883*, pp. 85–99, at p. 94.

[21] Cited in Perinelli, "Lust, Gewalt, Befreiung," p. 94.

Nachrichten and later for the Frankfurt-based left-wing magazine *Pardon*. In May 1968, shortly after her return from a visit to Paris, where she had joined French students in protests against the shooting of Rudi Dutschke, Schwarzer took part in an anti-Emergency Law demonstration in Düsseldorf. Taking the microphone to call for solidarity with the student protests then breaking out in the Latin Quarter, Schwarzer was surprised to hear the shout "Hey Bonnie" accompanied by wolf whistles. "It was the time of *Bonnie and Clyde*," she recalls (the Arthur Penn film starring Warren Beatty and Faye Dunaway had appeared the year before) "and I was wearing ... the full Bonnie look, beret included. I never went to a demo looking conspicuously stylish again."[22] Later, at *Pardon*, Schwarzer was shocked again when a colleague drunkenly remarked (in reference, Schwarzer believes, to the fact that she had not slept with any of her co-workers during her six months with the magazine), "You're actually quite nice. It's too bad you're frigid."[23]

Sexist attitudes were not always expressed with such egregious candor, but the overall atmosphere reinforced a feeling of alienation for women. Schwarzer recalls feeling strange in *Pardon*'s editorial offices, not just because she was the only female journalist on staff but because of the magazine's notoriously salacious cover illustrations. "When once a month we had to choose a cover image," she recalls,

the photos for which the editors were contracted out were projected on the wall. Most were photos from a rural commune in which beautiful girls thrust out their boobs for the camera while waving a red flag for the revolution. "No not that one, the previous one was better, you could see all of the nipples," commented the completely charming publisher and chief editor Hans Nickel. I was silent. What could I have said to that? We women didn't yet have words for our discontent.[24]

Disgust with this state of affairs lent much of the force to Helke Sander's comments to the delegate conference in September 1968.[25] "Comrades," said Sander, "your events are unbearable. You are full of inhibitions that you unleash in the form of aggression if someone says something dumb or something that you already know."[26] Rüger's tomato was aimed precisely at breaking through this wall of heretofore-unassailable speech, a

---

[22] Alice Schwarzer, "Mein 68," *Emma*, May/June 2008.
[23] *Ibid.* [24] *Ibid.*
[25] Monika Steffen, "Was die Studenten in Frankfurt gelernt haben," January 25, 1969; *SDS-Info*, January 26, 1969, no. 4, pp. 19–24.
[26] Helke Sander, "Die Anfänge der Frauenbewegung," in Eckhard Siepmann, *CheShahShit: Die Sechziger Jahre zwischen Cocktail und Molotow* (Berlin: Elefanten Press, 1984), pp. 170–172.

suggestion that, behind the emphasis on the correct line and the correct terminology lay a failure to recognize conditions of oppression that lay so close as to be invisible for those who had hitherto found no important reasons to look.

For Sander, resistance against the theoretician-patriarchy had an additional dimension, one closely linked to the broader goals of the nascent women's movement. In her comments, she called for a turn toward practicality, a concern with the concrete bases of a future revolutionary praxis. "Why don't you finally just admit that you're exhausted from the year just passed," she asked, "that you don't know how you can bear the stress any longer of burning yourselves out bodily and spiritually in political actions, without any increase in satisfaction? Before you plan new actions, why don't you discuss how people are actually going to carry them out?"[27]

Sander's comments were a poignant reflection of the impasse in which the SDS found itself near the end of 1968, in the wake of the assassination attempt against Rudi Dutschke, and the failure of subsequent actions to fundamentally alter the balance of power in the contest with the authorities. But they also represented a call to realize and to concretize the focus on the transformation of daily life, along principles of direct democracy and self-management, that had underpinned the antiauthoritarian movement from its inception. If this shift in focus represented a turn away from the grand rhetoric of confrontation and revolution, it was equally a rejection of the impulse to drop out of society to focus on personal fulfillment free from constraints, or ambiguous concepts such as "sexual revolution." Rather, the focus was now to be on issues such as child-rearing, gender relations, education – issues that were seen to be central not only to the real, existing conditions of daily life but to future hopes for a transformation of society.

This emphasis on the concrete bases of a future revolutionary praxis underpinned the initiatives undertaken in the wake of the Twenty-Third Delegate Congress. Immediately after the tomato-throwing incident, female activists gathered in the kitchen of the Kolb student hostel in Frankfurt to found so-called *Weiberräte* ("Old Wives Soviets"). These groups were to serve as the basis of continued (women-only) discussions of issues relevant to women. "Immediately after returning to their home towns, [women] founded *Weiberräte*," writes Alice Schwarzer, "women's

---

[27] Sander, "Die Anfänge der Frauenbewegung."

groups, to which men were not admitted. Here only women spoke, at long last, without being run down by eloquent male comrades."[28]

Eight *Weiberräte* established themselves between the delegate conference in September and the next conference two months later in Hanover. In October, the Frankfurt Weiberrat disrupted the government's celebration of the fiftieth anniversary of the female franchise in Frankfurt's Paulskirche, storming the stage with placards bearing slogans such as "Equality stops where wages begin" and "Where is the emancipation for men?" The women were prevented from speaking and roughly expelled by police, an incident immortalized in a cartoon strip by New Left cartoonist Alfred von Meysenbug.[29] At the meeting in Hanover, another, more threatening provocation was launched at the men in the SDS. Activists prepared a flyer in which a witchy-looking female huntress with axe in hand reclined on a divan, before a wall of mounted penis-trophies, each labeled with the name of a male "star" of the SDS. The text read:

We're not opening our mouths. When we open it anyway nothing comes out. When we leave it open it's stuffed for us: with petit bourgeois cocks, socialist screw-pressure, socialist children, love-making … bombast, socialist potent horniness, socialist intellectual pathos, socialist care-giving, revolutionary futzing around, sexual-revolutionary arguments, total societal orgasm, socialist-emancipatory-drivel, claptrap! when we manage to get up, then: socialist back-slapping, fatherly fussiness; then we are taken seriously; then we are wondrous, astonishing, we are praised, then we are allowed at the Stammtisch, then we are identical; then we type, pass out leaflets, paint slogans, lick stamps, we are theoretically turned on! If we can't take it, we are penis-envying, frustrated, hysterical, uptight, asexual, lesbian, frigid, short-sighted, irrational, penis-envying, pleasure-adverse, hard, virile, prickly, bitchy, we are compensating, we are over-compensating, we are penis-envying, penis-envying, penis-envying, penis-envying, penis-envying. Women are different!

The flyer concluded with a rallying cry, modeled on a well-known SDS slogan, with a threatening twist: FREE THE SOCIALIST EMINENCES FROM THEIR BOURGEOIS COCKS![30]

The flyer, as one scholar puts it, evoked "real fear."[31] Not all the women involved easily embraced the implicit violence of the presentation, but all

---

[28] Alice Schwarzer, *10 Jahre Frauebewegung: So fing es an* (Cologne: Emma-Frauenverlag, 1981), p. 13.

[29] Kraushaar, *Frankfurter Schule und Studentenbewegung*, p. 365.

[30] Sibylle Flügge, "Der Weiberrat im SDS," in Siepmann, ed., *CheShahShit*, pp. 173–174.

[31] Mona Steffen, "SDS, Weiberräte, Feminismus?" in Kraushaar, ed., *Frankfurter Schule und Studentenbewegung*, vol. III, pp. 126–140, at p. 133.

understood the message. In a report to the Weiberrat, one of the women involved in the distribution of the flyer noted:

In Hannover, we wanted to pass out the flyer with the agreement of the other female comrades. These reacted coolly at first to the aggressiveness of the flyer. We called everyone together and cited examples of the types of oppression listed in the flyer. In the course of this concrete exemplification everyone confessed that it was the same in their groups as well. Thereupon all the members of the eight SDS women's groups present agreed to stand behind the leaflet.

The men, she continued, acted as expected: "enraged, chaotic, aggressive-authoritarian."[32] The women kept silent, as agreed upon beforehand. But the impact of the action helped inaugurate a new era of self-confidence for women in the SDS. "Back at home, we worked some more," remembered the activist quoted above:

[f]or the first time female comrades at an SDS meeting sat all together in a corner, and one could observe that the male comrades understood this as a demonstration of power. When a female comrade made a presentation, she was listened to. Furthermore, she felt far more sure of herself, because she knew she had the other women behind her, and she knew that, if necessary, one of them would help her.[33]

Alongside Berlin and Frankfurt, Munich emerged as a hotbed of the nascent women's movement. A host of initiatives founded in 1968 and 1969 included the "Working Circle Emancipation," a small commune around former Kommune I member Dagmar Przytula and her husband Horst (not to be confused with the contemporaneous "Working Circle Emancipation" in the Munich Republican Club); the "Women's Commune" (Germany's first) in the Türkenstraße 68a in Schwabing; a free kindergarten at the Akademie der Bildenden Künste; and the Red Women's Front. These were accompanied from 1971 by women's groups among the *Basisgruppen* at the firms Siemens and Agfa, the latter around the feminist Hannelore Mabry.[34]

The Women's Commune, a major APO address in Munich, originally consisted of six young women in their twenties and two children. Men were not excluded from the commune, and some later joined as "associate members."[35] The commune stood in regular contact with the Kommune I

---

[32] Frauenjahrbuch '75, reprinted in Sander, "Die Anfänge der Frauenbewegung."
[33] *Ibid.*
[34] Heinz Korderer, "Anfänge der neuen Frauenbewegung in München" (unpublished manuscript), Archiv Heinz Korderer, Munich.
[35] Elisabeth Zellmer, *Töchter der Revolte? Frauenbewegung und Feminismus in den 1970er Jahren in München* (Munich: Oldenbourg, 2011), p. 83.

and 2 in Berlin, and Uschi Obermaier and Rainer Langhans spent time there during the filming of the movie *Rote Sonne*. The women of the commune were very active, "liberating" some of the local male-dominated scene pubs and taking part in the first rank at demonstrations.[36] They were active in the APO legal campaign, traveling to Frankfurt to protest harsh judicial measures against imprisoned activist Reinhard Wetter. There they took the opportunity, with colored hair, dressed in purple corduroy trousers, black boots, and tight sweaters, to disrupt a sociology seminar led by Hans-Jürgen Krahl, who had them ejected for their "unscholarly appearance."[37]

Such provocations were underpinned by a new self-confidence, based on the fact that, in contrast to the SDS as a whole (where it was proving increasingly difficult to match social-revolutionary aspirations with effective actions), women could fall back not only on their need to come out from under the shadow of their male comrades but also on an obvious series of concrete and very personal issues crying out for attention. The first of these, as mentioned above, had to do with child care. Helke Sander had experienced the need for women to organize when she attempted to participate in the work of the SDS anti-Springer campaign. Concerned that the activists involved were not paying any attention to the portrayal of, or the appeals to, women in the Springer newspapers, she recalls being told, "'go in the kitchen, Marianne [presumably Herzog, girlfriend of Jan-Carl Raspe] is in there working on something like that.' In that moment I was speechless, but I actually did go in the kitchen, and got to know Marianne, and out of that developed the first meeting of what would become the Aktionsrat."[38]

A week or two later, the group distributed a flyer (to women only) at the Free University, inviting women to a meeting on the theme of motherhood and child care. "Approximately 100 people came to this first meeting," Sander recalls; "There were a few men there, who we didn't send away ... What was notable about this meeting is that we were able to agree right away. We found it simply unbelievable, what we were forced to come up against."[39] The Aktionsrat met on Wednesday evenings in the Republican Club; within a short space of time it had some 700 members. Frigga Haug, a founder of the Frankfurt New Left journal *Das Argument*, was awed when she first attended a meeting of the Aktionsrat: "The meeting took place in the Republican Club, and I can only put the alarming feeling I had like this: 'The room was full of hair.' That was really my main impression, just hair! ... and I realized that before this I had only been to men's meetings."[40]

The first meeting of the Aktionsrat saw the founding of the first so-called *Kinderläden*.[41] These were daycare facilities set up in empty store-fronts where children were taken care of collaboratively on a volunteer basis, thus freeing time for young mothers to pursue other activities. The *Kinderläden* idea had been developed the previous year by the Frankfurt-based sociologist Monika Seifert, who was informed by the writings of Wilhelm Reich. They met with major demand. "We have such an enormous influx [of interested parties]," Sander reported at the Twenty-Third Delegate Congress, "that we can barely handle it organizationally."[42] Yet, for all their success, the *Kinderläden* did not fulfill their function of freeing up time for women to engage in politics; rather, they themselves became the political project, one that actually took more time rather than less.[43] Characteristically, men, who had initially lacked interest in the project, stepped in to assert control over it. To this end, they founded a Zentralrat der Kinderläden (Central Council of Storefront Daycare Centers), arguing that because they were theoretically more advanced, they had a responsibility to oversee these projects.[44]

If motherhood held a powerful mobilizing potential, it did not provide an unproblematic theoretical basis for female activism. Key to the self-understanding of these early women's groups was that they were a part of a socialist movement that had begun in the SDS. From the beginning, the goal of liberating women – alleviating the oppression of the female self – sat uneasily alongside the goal of overthrowing capitalism. The dichotomy at the heart of the pre-feminist project between personal, subjective experience on the one hand, and objective, scientific-socialist theorizing on the other, cut right through the middle of the women's groups formed out of the SDS. Was the women's movement being advanced by socialists who were above all *women* or by women who were first and foremost *socialists*?

Very quickly, both the Berlin-based Aktionsrat zur Befreiung der Frau and the Frankfurt Weiberrat reproduced within themselves versions of

[40] Kätzel, *Die 68erinnen*, p. 189.
[41] Alice Schwarzer, "Männer, wir kommen! Deutsche Frauen im Aufbruch," *Pardon*, no. 6, June 1972.
[42] "Rede von Helke Sander (Aktionsrat zur Befreiung der Frauen) auf der 23 Delegiertenkonferenz," cited in Sander, "Die Anfänge der Frauenbewegung."
[43] Kätzel, *Die 68erinnen*, pp. 167–168.   [44] Kätzel, *Die 68erinnen*, p. 167.

some of the same splits cutting through the antiauthoritarian movement as a whole. The Aktionsrat split into what can roughly be designated "feminist" and "socialist" factions. A faction around Helke Sander calling itself "Against the Old and for the New" argued for the centrality of motherhood and family. Insisting, in the spirit of the first *Kinderläden* initiatives, that children were the responsibility not of the family (which reproduced bourgeois patterns of repression) but of society as a whole, the group demanded concrete financial support for collective child-care initiatives.[45]

The majority group in the Aktionsrat criticized this position as a "bourgeois reduction of the political struggle of left-wing women to the sector of children and family," insisting that the focus must remain on the deep-economic bases of female repression. To this end, it launched a monthly discussion group on Marx's *Das Kapital*. A similar initiative was undertaken in the Frankfurt Weiberrat, by this time referring to itself as the Socialist Women of Frankfurt.[46] Within a year of this exchange, these diverging tendencies led to splits within the two Räte. In November 1970, the theory-oriented group in Frankfurt split off and joined the DKP en masse. In Berlin, the majority Aktionsrat changed its name to Sozialistischer Frauenbund West Berlin (SFB; Socialist Women's League West Berlin), leading the "feminists" around Helke Sander to split off and form the group Brot und Rosen, named after the American socialist women's organization Bread and Roses.[47]

The influence of American feminism, as this choice of name suggests, was key. Indeed, the development of Second Wave Feminism not only in West Germany but in Europe as a whole, is inseparable from the transnational exchanges out of which it arose. "Women's Liberation," as an autonomous response to sexism in general and sexism among left-wing students and radicals in particular, was first and foremost a product of the USA. Key feminist texts such as Betty Friedan's *The Feminist Mystique* (1963), Germaine Greer's *The Female Eunuch* (1970), and Shulamith Firestone's *The Dialectic of Sex* (1970) were widely circulated in Europe. Helke Sander's original speech on behalf of the Aktionsrat bore the clear stamp of writings by American feminist figures such as McAfee, Wood,

---

[45] Gruppe: Gegen dass Alter und für das Neue, "Bekanntmachung des Aktionsrats zur Befreiung der Frauen," *Rote Pressekorrespondenz*, no. 33, October 3, 1969.

[46] "Zur Frauenemanzipation: Für eine Politisierung des Aktionsrates zure Befreiung der Frau," *Rote Pressekorrespondenz*, no. 35, October 17, 1969.

[47] The group took its name from the foundational essay by American Second Wave feminists Kathy McAfee and Myrna Wood, "Bread and Roses," *Leviathan* (June 1969).

Marge Pierce, and Marlene Dixon.[48] Sander's own thought, above all her speech from the Twenty-Third Delegate Conference of the SDS, attracted an international readership. Her writings on West German kindergartens was published in the journal *Radical America* as early as 1970.[49]

First-person exchanges were also key. Both American and West German women were active in the first women's groups in London in the period 1968–1970.[50] German feminists meanwhile adopted American texts, protest methods, language, and concepts. Yet, as in all cases of transnational exchange, local needs shaped reception of the global source material. It seems clear, for example, that West German feminists placed a greater emphasis on child care and motherhood than did their American counterparts. The history of the German version of Bread and Roses very much reflected the dilemma facing the West German left at the moment of its founding. Tellingly, the group expressed its intention to work with the SEW, the DKP's West Berlin affiliate, a move that must be understood against the background of the workerist turn taken by the remnants of the SDS *circa* 1969–1970. The attempt of the women's groups to cast their advocacy for women in a "proletarian-revolutionary" framework was a natural outcome of a moment in which activists, searching for a way forward, placed their hopes in a proletariat that, with the strike wave of September 1969, and with the increased involvement of young workers and apprentices in the *Schüler-* and *Basisgruppen*, seemed to be flexing its muscles.[51]

At a deeper level, the drive to theorize on the basis of the Marxist classics was an expression of a search for legitimacy, both against the male theoreticians who had dominated the SDS and against society at large. Recourse to Marxist categories of analysis provided a basis of authenticity that many members of the nascent women's movement felt was essential to being taken seriously. Soon, however, the transition to the women's movement proper involved the emergence of a new, more fundamental site of authenticity. This turn occurred in connection with the issue that would become the centerpiece of the West German women's movement properly defined: the campaign to legalize abortion. In this campaign,

[48] Edith Hoshino Altbach, Jeanette Clausen, Dagmar Schultz, and Naomi Stephan, eds., *German Feminism: Readings in Politics and Literature* (Albany, NY: State University of New York Press, 1984).

[49] Helke Sander, "Project: Company Kindergartens," *Radical America*, 4 (2) (1970): 68–79. Sander's essay originally appeared as "Projekt Betriebskindergarten," *Rote Presse Korrespondenz*, no. 27–8 (August 29, 1969).

[50] Geoff Eley, *Forging Democracy: The History of the Left in Europe, 1850–2000* (Oxford University Press, 2002), pp. 376–377.

[51] Sarkar, *Green-Alternative Politics*, p. 186.

the new organizing power of politicized women came to forceful expression, spreading beyond the boundaries of the SDS milieu to become the basis of a social movement in its own right.

As is characteristic of the West German 1968 as a whole, the campaign to overturn Paragraph 218, the anti-abortion law still on the books from the Wilhemine period, was fundamentally transnational in both makeup and genesis. French and German women activists had mingled before, demonstrating together outside the International Vietnam Congress in February 1968 and in other contexts.[52] Yet these early contacts mostly predated the development of an independent women's movement. The driving force in the West German campaign against abortion was Alice Schwarzer, who by 1970 was living and working as a freelance journalist in Paris. Impressed by news of the American "Women's Lib" movement and the Dutch "Dolle Minas," and inspired by the increasing availability of feminist texts, Schwarzer recalls remarking to some French friends in the spring of 1970: "We've got to have something like that here – a women's movement. A few months later, we did."[53]

The catalyst was provided by a group of women arrested for trying to lay a wreath for "the Unknown Woman of the Unknown Soldier" under the Arc de Triumph on the anniversary of the defeat of Nazi Germany. Inspired by this incident, Schwarzer and others founded the first French feminist group, the Mouvement de Libération des Femmes (MLF; Movement for the Liberation of Women). Heavily international in makeup, the group had expanded to several hundred members by the end of the year. A number of activists were veterans of the French student movement, "frustrated by the machismo of their own comrades," writes Schwarzer. Others came from outside the ranks of the movement, attracted by the chance to voice long-simmering concerns.[54] "In any case," writes Schwarzer, "we were anti-hierarchical, anti-capitalist, anti-guy. And I was living sort of a double life: as left-wing journalist for Germany, and active feminist in France."[55]

This double life was instrumental in the genesis of the campaign against Paragraph 218 in the Federal Republic. In France, on April 5, 1971, at the instigation of the actress Jeanne Moreau, the women of the MLF published the "Manifesto of the 343" in the *Nouvel Observateur*. Penned by Simone de Beauvoir, the declaration contained the signatures of 343 women, including Beauvoir and a number of other high-profile figures,

---

[52] See, for example, the photo in Ruetz, *"Ihr müßt diesen Typen nur ins Gesicht sehen,"* p. 103.
[53] Schwarzer, "Mein 68."　　[54] *Ibid.*　　[55] *Ibid.*

who admitted to having had illegal abortions. The effect of this act of civic bravery was immense. Reported on internationally, it helped prepare ground for the subsequent legalization of abortion in France. Back in West Germany a month later, Schwarzer convinced Wilfried Maaß at *Stern*, the Federal Republic's largest circulation news magazine, to publish a similar declaration. On June 6, 1971, the "Manifesto of the 374" appeared in *Stern*.[56] A signature campaign called Aktion 218 had been begun by student women's groups in Munich, Cologne, Frankfurt, and West Berlin, with help from organizations such as the Humanistic Union and the Young Socialists. As in France, the declaration had a explosive effect. In its aftermath, pro-abortion groups were founded around the country. A number of prominent men, including Ernst Bloch and Günter Wallraff, expressed solidarity by admitting their "complicity." Eventually, a group of 329 progressive physicians published a declaration in support of the overturn of Paragraph 218. A scheduled episode of the television program *Panorama* in which fourteen doctors were to perform an abortion was cancelled at the last minute.[57]

The campaign against Paragraph 218 marked the beginning of a mass women's movement in West Germany. "Aktion 218" groups were founded around the country, drawing in women who had never previously participated in politics. The Federal Women's Conference in Frankfurt of March 1972 displayed the mobilizing power of the abortion issue, with some two-thirds of the thirty-six groups involved having been formed expressly for the abortion-rights campaign.[58] Yet, as Alice Schwarzer observed in a piece on the conference in *Pardon*, the abortion campaign revealed fundamental tensions in the nascent women's movement.[59] Three hundred of the women in attendance at the conference belonged to the women's groups hatched out of the student movement: the Frankfurter Weiberrat, the Münchener Rote Frauenfront (Munich Red Women's Front), and the Sozialistische Frauenbund West Berlin (West Berlin Socialist Women's League). These were groups, Schwarzer argued, who had "barricaded themselves in a theoretical ghetto," holding fast to a theory-centric cadre-political model more in step with the dogmatism of the *K-Gruppen* than to the ecumenism of the emerging women's movement. "Hardly could

---

[56] "Wir haben abgetrieben," *Stern*, no. 24, June 6, 1971, pp. 16–23.
[57] George Katsiaficas, *The Subversion of Politics: European Autonomous Social Movements and the Decolonization of Everyday Life* (Oakland, Calif.: AK Press, 2006), p. 106.
[58] Schwarzer, "Männer, wir kommen! Deutsche Frauen im Aufbruch."
[59] *Ibid.*

they stand," she archly observed, "before they were trying to march in lock-step."[60]

The socialist women's groups initially greeted the campaign with suspicion. The Sozialistische Frauenbund West Berlin joined immediately, but the Münchener Rote Frauenfront split on the issue. The Frankfurter Weiberrat, adhering to their long-standing opposition to reformism of any type, rejected it out of hand.[61] As they put it in an early statement:

We ... are a *political group* ... We engage with the problems of women in our society, but we are *no bourgeois emancipation movement*. We see the problems of women not as something pertaining to the individual, do not restrict ourselves to legal demands, or the call for help from the state – in short any form of reformism, that doesn't call decisively into question the social basis of our capitalist competition-society.[62]

This stance, de rigueur on the radical left at the beginning of the 1970s, was exemplified in the introduction to a 1971 edition of the writings of the German socialist Clara Zetkin, published by the Roter Stern Verlag. Paraphrasing Max Horkheimer, the authors observed:

The initiatives of West German illustrated magazines and their actresses-clientele for the repeal of paragraph 218 is not any different from the narrow-minded representation of corporate interests practiced by the bourgeois women's movement at the turn of the century. One who speaks of the emancipation of women and does not even mention its connection with anti-capitalist struggle, had better keep quiet.[63]

Ironically, for the socialist women's groups, this insistence on the primacy of deep structural issues came dangerously close to relegating women to the status of a "secondary contradiction," the very thing for which the Aktionsrat had criticized the men in the SDS to begin with. Moreover, it begged the question of how the intimate relationship between women's issues and social issues was to be tackled at the level of praxis. For many women, the turn toward theory and the study of the Marxist classics, especially after the initial breakout centered on women's right to speak about the issues affecting them, seemed a poor substitute for action. "We ourselves could not say why we met regularly," observed a member of the Red Women; "There was a certain uneasiness ... Yes, and

---

[60] *Ibid.*   [61] Sarkar, *Green-Alternative Politics*, pp. 188–189.
[62] "Selbstverstandnis des Aktionsrats zur Befreiung der Frauen," October 16, 1968, in *Sozialistische Kinderladen Info* no. 3, February 6, 1969, pp. 13–14, Green Library, Stanford University, Germany. Extraparliamentary Opposition movement, 1967–1984 collection, box 61, folder 3.
[63] Quoted in Sarkar, *Green-Alternative Politics*, p. 194.

then the political schooling started. Karl Marx, Volume I. We hated that like the devil. But nobody dared say anything."[64] Against this backdrop of simmering unease, the campaign against Paragraph 218 proved irresistible, drawing in even the Frankfurter Weiberrat, which continued to warn against the dangers of reformism even as it helped to collect signatures for Action 218.[65]

The idea of a *women's* movement as an autonomous political force provoked distinct unease on the dogmatic end of the left spectrum, where the idea of an emancipatory movement that sought to free itself of Marxist categories was highly suspicious. "Like before the big Paragraph 218 demonstration in Bonn in September 1975," recalls Gerd Koenen, at that time a member of the Maoist KBW,

as the autonomous women with their white-painted faces, wild Indian howling, and obscene chants (THE POWER OF DICKS HAS ITS LIMITS ...) boarded the special train that we – or rather, our female comrades and their "218 Committees" – had tirelessly organized in Frankfurt ... What a bunch of reactionary nonsense, we thought, that these crazed petit-bourgeois women wanted to handle the question of abortion as a purely female affair ("My Belly Belongs to Me"); that they actually wanted to do everything alone and themselves; or that they in all seriousness really believed that in a class society "the women," *all* women, could have common interests.[66]

The KBW's party newspaper attacked the demonstration, charging: "Feminism as a version of bourgeois individuality wants to talk at proletarian women instead of taking part in the class struggle, to split them apart, for starters getting them to fight against their own men as 'chauvinists,' before capitalism is fought." Regarding the demonstration in Bonn, the article explained that the party had felt it necessary to distance itself from the "pop music-playing, costumed, color-blotted feminist parade spreading an evil ideological stench through the quarter."[67]

Activists of the nascent women's movement struggled at first to defend themselves against this withering contempt. In a retrospective account published the same year as the Bonn demonstration, members of the Frankfurter Weiberrat described the painful transition of their group into a fully "feminist" organization. We had "asserted officially that we wanted to struggle for the legalization of abortion for proletarian women,"

---

[64] *Ibid.*
[65] Peter Mosler, "Die Macht der Schwänze hat ihre Grenze," in Scibold, ed., *Die 68er*, at p. 328.
[66] Koenen, *Das rote Jahrzehnt*, p. 239.
[67] Mosler, "Die Macht der Schwänze," p. 327.

recalled one activist; "Particularly at the beginning we tried to justify ourselves by emphasizing that we wanted to bring socialist goals into the 'liberal mass movement' and that we considered the campaign only as a training ground for the 'real' praxis to follow it."[68] Another recalled:

> Only when we came out for the first time with a campaign of our own did we land properly in the cross-fire of leftist critics, who at once rejected the struggle against the prohibition of abortion as "reformist," i.e. wrong. However, they did not take the trouble to explain why the demand for the repeal of paragraph 218 was more reformist than the demand for higher wages.[69]

In the campaign against 218 and its aftermath, women activists increasingly ceased feeling the need for such explanations. Now marching firmly under the banner of feminism as a distinct political force, they were no longer interested in shoving the round peg of their activist concerns into the square hole of dogmatic Marxism.

SEXUAL REVOLUTIONS

These campaigns around the concrete issues affecting women's social roles and women's bodies, campaigns that reproduced fundamental disagreements at the heart of the antiauthoritarian revolt, unfolded against the background of the so-called "sexual revolution." The changes signaled first and foremost by the arrival of the pill, introduced to the Federal Republic in June 1961, accompanied and helped drive changes in sexual mores that characterized the decade of the 1960s. These changes were the object of both sociological and journalistic investigation at the time they were taking place, the increased sexuality of young people in general and young women in particular receiving extended and repeated coverage. These changes were, it goes almost without saying, far broader than the activist wave in and around the SDS and the women's groups that arose out of it. But these groups helped to shape aspects of the sexual revolution in West Germany, and, more importantly, were shaped by it.

By 1966, the accelerating sexualization of West German society had come under the heading of the "sex wave," a term that, with its implication of a deluging force sweeping away all obstacles, captures well how many West Germans experienced it. This sex wave consisted of what Dagmar Herzog has described as "a thorough saturation of the visual

---

[68] Sarkar, *Green-Alternative Politics*, p. 195.   [69] *Ibid.*

landscape with nude and semi-nude images of women's bodies and the unabashed marketing of a multitude of objects via these images," combined with "a liberalization of sexual mores and of the terms surrounding sexuality so profound that it acquired the name 'sexual revolution.'"[70] The latter, driven both from above (via the interpretive work of sexual experts) and from below (by young libidos newly liberated by the advent of the birth-control pill), dovetailed with attempts by New Left groups and the nascent women's movement to challenge conservative sexual mores. A complex phenomenon with both commercial, social, and sexological components, the sex wave encompassed, and was constructed by, a range of actors with differing motivations.

There was hardly any other area in which the radical activism of the 68ers intersected more with the sphere of liberalizing expertise more than in questions of sexuality. There was considerable overlap between the sexological positions expressed by the 68ers and those taken up by mainstream experts.[71] Sexuality, alongside pedagogy – or, often, in connection with it – was one of the sites where the scholarly scientific imperative was hardest at work. The sexological interventions of the 68ers and their allies in the scholarly disciplines dovetailed with the work of sexual popularizers such as Oswalt Kolle and Beate Uhse, who became highly visible faces of the sex wave. Kolle's popular "Unknown Entity" (*"unbekannte Wesen"*) series in the major illustrated journals – e.g. "Your Wife, the Unknown Entity" – helped popularize the notion of sexuality as a site of enlightened self-help. His films synthesized the latest findings of sociology, psychology, and sexology for a mass audience. The films, featuring "naked couples talking through their sexual problems, framed by expert voice-overs assuring people that marriages could be mended through open communication," blurred the boundaries between sex education and soft-core pornography.[72] His 1967 film *The Wonder of Love: Sexuality in Marriage*, was seen by over 5 million West German viewers within four months of its release.[73] Beate Uhse's sex-shop empire, similarly, helped lend respectability to the sexual urges

---

[70] Dagmar Herzog, "Between Coitus and Commodification: Young West German Women and the Impact of the Pill," in Schildt and Siegfried, eds., *Between Marx and Coca-Cola*, pp. 261–286, at p. 261.

[71] Dagmar Herzog, *Sex after Fascism: Memory and Morality in Twentieth-Century Germany* (Princeton University Press, 2007), p. 152.

[72] Herzog, "Between Coitus and Commodification," p. 273.

[73] Kerstin Brückweh, *Mordlust: Serienmorde, Gewalt und Emotionen im 20. Jahrhundert* (Frankfurt: Campus Verlag, 2006), p. 171.

of the bourgeoisie, making sexual materials available in normal shops in normal urban shopping complexes.[74]

Adolescent sexuality was a major theme in both the mainstream and left press, countless articles on the changing sexual mores and practices of the young appearing both in left-wing journals such as *konkret* and *Pardon* and mainstream magazines such as *Der Spiegel* and *Stern*. The example of neighboring East Germany, which strove to present a liberal image regarding issues such as equality for women and youth sexuality, figured prominently in some of these depictions. *konkret*'s features on the DDR highlighted the vibrancy of East German youth and young women in particular.[75] As early as December 1966, the magazine was reporting approvingly on the "Sex Wave in the DDR."[76] The sexual revolution in other countries was also featured, as were, later in the decade, sensational feminist protests in countries such as Denmark, the Netherlands, and the USA.[77]

Early on, sexuality came to feature prominently among the themes under consideration by the West German student movement. In 1965/1966, the Allgemeiner Studentenausschuß at the Free University was sponsoring colloquia on sexuality dealing with themes stretching from premarital sex to abortion to homosexuality.[78] By the end of the decade, working groups on the theme "Sexualität und Herrschaft" (Sexuality and Governance) were being formed throughout the SDS.[79] Meanwhile, themes of free love and the assault on the bourgeois family increased in prominence as a result of the sexual-publicistic antics of the Kommune I, the theoretical work of the Kommune 2, and the practical application of liberated sexuality in the subsequent commune movement. Around the same time, a "porno wave," made possible by the liberalization of pornography laws in the summer of 1969, made sexually explicit images more

---

[74] Elizabeth Heinemann, "Jörg Schröder, linkes Verlagswesen und Pornographie," in Sven Reichardt and Detlef Siegfried, eds., *Das Alternative Milieu: Antibürgerliche Lebensstil und linke Politik in der Bundesrepublik Deutschland und Europa, 1968–1983* (Göttingen: Wallstein, 2010), pp. 290–312, at pp. 298, 292.

[75] See, for example, Hans Apel, "Das ganze neue DDR-Gefühl," *konkret*, no. 8, August 1967.

[76] Charles Trefflinger, "Im Sexschritt marsch! Sexwelle in der DDR," *konkret*, December 1966.

[77] Wolfgang Röhl, "In Kopenhagen gehen die Frauen auf die Barrikaden: Rot-strümfe an die Front," *konkret*, no. 12, June 1970; "Playboy-Protest: US-Studentinnen demonstrieren gegen das Herrenmagazin," *konkret*, no. 8, April 8, 1969.

[78] FU Berlin, Flugblätter, 1965/66 HIS.

[79] Sven Reichardt, "Von 'Beziehungskisten' und 'offener Sexualität'," in Reichardt and Siegfried, eds., *Das Alternative Milieu*, pp. 267–289, at p. 282.

available than ever before. Spurred by the legalization of pornography in Denmark (texts in 1967, images in 1969) and Sweden (both texts and images in 1971), West Germans became the most important consumers of Scandinavian pornography.[80]

The "sexual revolutionaries" of the student movement enjoyed an uneasy relationship with this sex wave, even as they helped contribute to it. Their basic approach to questions of sexuality, much like that of the socialist women's groups, was to insist upon the fundamental interconnectedness of sexual and social questions. The notion that sexuality could not be separated from the social structures in which it was imbricated was codified by Reimut Reiche in *Sexuality and Class Struggle* (1968), which argued that "[n]o sexual revolution is possible without social revolution."[81] Yet, if sexuality was a site of progress in the fight against capitalism, it was also a site where the danger of capitalist recuperation loomed large. Even as they fought against the remnants of a restrictive sexual morality – under attack from all sides but far from vanquished – activists had to face the uncomfortable fact that the banner of sexual liberation had been seized by persons for whom liberation stopped at the bedroom door (that is, for whom there was no social, let alone socialist component to sexual liberation). They also faced the knowledge that sex was increasingly becoming just another commodity, a product of the "consumption terror" rather than an antidote against it.[82]

Purveyors of the mainstream sex wave such as Beate Uhse and Oswalt Kolle came in for special criticism. Günter Amendt's *SexFront* criticized them for their advice on "spicing up" the fundamentally oppressive institution of marriage.[83] A SEXPOL group charged that Kolle offered nothing more than a

purely mechanical illusory freedom that degrades the sexual act to a gymnastics exercise. We seek to start exactly where Kolle stops, because we believe that sexual education and the anti-baby-pill are merely minimum technical requirements for a free sexuality. We formulate our critique of the inhuman sexual morality of this society in connection with our critique of the existing social order – and that is what Kolle definitely does not do![84]

---

[80] Heinemann, "Jörg Schröder," p. 298.
[81] Serialized in Reimut Reiche, "Sex und Revolution," *konkret*, no. 4, April 1968.
[82] Herzog, "Between Coitus and Commodification," p. 270.
[83] Herzog, *Sex after Fascism*, p. 155. See also Günter Amendt, "Sexfront Revisited," *Zeitschrift für Sexualforschung*, 19 (2) (2006): 159–172, at p. 164.
[84] *SEXPOL-Info* 3, p. 169.

The profusion of sexual images posed a similar dilemma, as the AUSS pointed out in a piece on its SEXPOL campaign in *konkret*: "In the last two years it has become evident," wrote the AUSS, "that the advertising industry, the culture- and consumption monopoly, and the school bureaucracy are giving our sexual demands a reactionary content, even before we are able to give them a revolutionary content."[85] This situation carried a very real danger for activism. "If we declare ourselves content with the industrially exploitable symbols of the 'sexual revolution,' we become, whether we wish to or not, the avant-garde of a new capitalist ideal of culture and consumption instead of the avant-garde of the social revolution."[86]

Wilhelm Reich figured so prominently in the idea-world of the anti-authoritarian revolt precisely because his insistence on the interrelatedness of sexual and social revolution seemed to offer a way to integrate sexuality into the revolutionary struggle. Reich's basic thesis was that the suppression of true sexual nature – tantamount for Reich to the suppression of the universal life energy itself – was the root cause of psychosis. The suppression of sexual needs could not be reduced to the individual, however, but must be understood in the context of the society that produced that individual. Neither Freudian psychoanalysis nor Marxian class analysis alone was sufficient to understand and rectify the problem of man in society. A fusion of the two offered the promise of uncovering root causes of both personal and social misery. Reich's interwar attempts to put these revolutionary ideas into practice saw him expelled from two left-wing parties (the Austrian SPD and the German KPD), as well as from the International Society for Psychoanalysis. A prophet of sexual revolution and himself a victim of every major strand of authoritarianism – he was purged from the Stalinized KPD, chased out of Germany by the Nazis, and hounded to his death by the authorities in American exile – Reich embodied both the powerful thrill of the forbidden and the sparkle of an intellectual "find" whose day had finally come.

Indeed, the outpouring of Reich bootlegs – some seventy-five bootleg editions of Reich's works appeared between 1965 and 1970 – was the sign of a popularity that transcended mere intellectual concerns.[87] In analytic terms, Reichian texts such as *The Function of the Orgasm* (1927), *The Mass Psychology of Fascism* (1933), and *The Sexual Revolution* (1936), seemed to

---

[85] "Sexualität nach der Sexwelle," p. 20.
[86] "Sexualität nach der Sexwelle," p. 19.
[87] Reichardt, "Von 'Beziehungskisten'," p. 283.

offer a blueprint not only for the attempt to situate sexuality alongside Marxism to the benefit of both but to come to grips with the deep roots of the authoritarian personality at the heart of fascism. In this connection, Reich seemed to offer an antidote to "lessons about proper behavior" offered by the older generation, lessons that, from the perspective of young left-wing activists, had proven all too consonant with Nazi criminality.[88]

The recourse to Reich represented yet another face of the scholarly scientific imperative, not merely because of the extent to which Reichian theory informed the revolutionary sexology of the student movement (thereby creating lines of communication with other sites of sexological expertise), but because of the role it played in supplying a scientific language for what amounted to, as it were, a praxis-based phenomenon. For, unlike the proletarian revolution that the *K-Gruppen* hoped to facilitate, the actors of the sexual revolution, in the beginning stages at least, needed little encouragement to "make the revolution." From this perspective, the infamous banner at Frankfurt University – "Read Reich and Act Accordingly" – was more than just a clever joke; it suggested the extent to which theory functioned as an *ex post facto* justification for libidinal impulses already at work.

These ideas were infused into the antiauthoritarian movement through the SEXPOL campaign, which sought to bolster the organizational basis for the melding of the private and the political while providing a theoretical-political basis for the free play of raging adolescent hormones. Taking its name, SEXPOL, from the organization established by Reich in 1932 (Deutscher Reichsverband für Proletarische Sexualpolitik; German Association for Proletarian Sexual Politics), the movement represented yet another attempt to mine the past for material useful in the revolutionary present. Straddling the discursive line between sex education and sexual revolution, the movement found that sex proved the revolutionary focus par excellence for adolescent rebels. Whether it was the antiauthoritarian politics that added frisson to the idea of adolescent sexuality unchained, or whether it was the other way around, the mixture proved potent. With its dual message of enlightenment and revolution, SEXPOL was a consistently popular attraction for young revolutionaries in the secondary schools.

The SEXPOL campaign unfolded especially in connection with the Schülerbewegung, not only encompassing students in the gymnasia but

[88] Herzog, *Sex after Fascism*, p. 159.

also playing a key role in the increasing presence of working-class pupils in the antiauthoritarian movement via the *Basisgruppen* and youth centers. The leadership of the AUSS presided over a series of local campaigns beginning in 1967, making no secret of their instrumental nature. Because "a large number of pupils suffer subjectively from sexual oppression, dependency, and ignorance," the AUSS observed, "even those who are not consciously able to perceive political oppression and domination … [t]he … existing sexual oppression and exploitation is relatively easily and concretely depicted as an expression of economic exploitation and political oppression."[89] Teacher – pupil and other authoritarian relationships had necessarily to express themselves in the sexual realm, meaning that sexuality became an ideal site at which to expose oppression. The authors went on to claim that 50 percent of AUSS groups had their origins in local SEXPOL groups.[90]

Pupils appear occasionally to have been put off by the didactic tone of the sexual revolutionaries. A "Project Group Sexuality and Politics" active in Rheinland-Palatinate acknowledged that its target audience sometimes failed to see the "inner relationship" between sexuality and politics. More probably they objected to jargon-filled lectures about the relationship. But, in general, the chance to link sexuality with an antiauthoritarian stance directed at parents, teachers, and society at large met with great enthusiasm.[91] This is hardly surprising given the extent to which ideas of sexual and political revolution were bound up in the minds of the young. Observers ranging from the cultural critic Klaus Theweleit to the journalist Sabine Weissler were struck by the centrality of sex to the antiauthoritarian revolt. The former adduced a "special sort of sexual tension" underpinning the revolt, while the latter wrote of a veritable "flood of articles, lectures, discussion events, and reading circles on the question of sexual enlightenment as a part of political emancipation." In this context, the SEXPOL campaign was merely codifying something that was already going on.[92]

Leading figures in the SDS such as Reimut Reiche and Peter Gäng lent their weight to the campaign, as did the sexologist Günter Amendt, whose left-wing sex education manual *Sexfront* (1970) represented a major publishing success for Jörg Schröder's März Verlag. A SEXPOL working

[89] "Sexualität nach der Sexwelle," p. 18.   [90] *Ibid.*
[91] Quoted in Miermeister and Staadt, *Provokationen*, p. 164.
[92] Quoted in Herzog, "Between Coitus and Commodification," p. 275.

group was founded in the West Berlin and other Republican Clubs, featuring frequent discussions on sexual themes, including discussion of Reiche's *Sexuality and Class Struggle*. Local SEXPOL groups founded by the *Basisgruppen* and/or in connection with school papers and groups pursued a steady program of scandalizing school and government authorities. On more than one occasion, editors of school papers were brought up on charges around sexually explicit discussion and imagery, teachers who supported them suspended or fired.[93]

One of the most visible of the local SEXPOL groups was the Gruppe SEXPOL-Nord, founded in fall 1968 by Hubert Bacia and Jürgen Werth as a working group in the youth club Prisma in Berlin-Reinickendorf. As we have already seen, the Gruppe SEXPOL-Nord was one of the more successful initiatives of the *Basisgruppe* Reinickendorf, helping to solidify its presence in the Club Prisma where other avenues of approach to working-class youth failed. The group entered the discussion about sexuality in a major way, publishing its discussions under the title *SEXPOL-Protokolle* (1969). The protocols, which featured frank discussion by young people about their sexual relations, were serialized in *konkret* and discussed with Ulrike Meinhof and Peter Homann.[94]

The Gruppe SEXPOL-Nord made its most spectacular intervention through its advocacy of free access to the birth-control pill, distributing it to young women for free. The authorities – cooperative radicalism now breaking down at the threshold of free contraceptives passed out without a doctor's note – closed the club. In response, in January 1969, the SEXPOL group, in conjunction with the Trotskyist Spartakus, the Maoist Red Guards Berlin, and the West Berlin section of the East German FDJ made a show of publicly distributing free pills in front of the closed doors of the youth center.[95] Not everyone approved of such efforts. In an analysis of the work of the *Basisgruppen*, one activist wrote:

Through an ahistorical adoption of the positions of Reich & Co., a way of looking at things is promoted in which protest against existing sexual norms is taken to be already a revolutionary act. From today's vantage point it has to be said that the SEXPOL movement has as its main object the living out of male fantasies of promiscuity.[96]

---

[93] Miermeister and Staadt, *Provokationen*, p. 164.
[94] *konkret*, no. 12, June 2, 1969.
[95] See "Gruppe Sexpol-Nord Westberlin," www.infopartisan.net/archive/1967/266756.html.
[96] Karl-Heinz Schubert, "Zur Geschichte der westberliner Basisgruppen," in Brunner et al., eds., *Aufbruch zum proletariat*.

Figure 7.2 Cover of *konkret*, no. 3, March 1968. Hamburg Institute for Social Research.

Such a critique is clearly an artifact of the more general conflict between the hedonism and asceticism in the antiauthoritarian revolt; but even more clear – as the enthusiastic participation of women in campaigns around the pill indicated – is that the SEXPOL campaign hit upon a popular and effective site of antiauthoritarian engagement.

Sex radical and/or Reichian ideas could fuel a whole range of activities and initiatives. In the Eichenhof group home featured in Ulrike Meinhof's teleplay *Bambule*, young women demanded the free distribution of the pill and other contraceptives as part of their assault on the "fascist" character of the home leadership.[97] In Berlin's *Kommune 99*, fueled by intensive discussions of Reich's *The Function of the Orgasm*, communards policed each other's sexuality, in one case badgering a roommate with no outwardly apparent sex life about the consequences of his failure to have sex. "One needed to have an orgasm," a female member recalls of the underlying thinking, "or something backs up, and you become as a personality no longer usable, politically no longer usable."[98] Accounts in the Gruppe SEXPOL-Nord's *SEXPOL-Protokolle* made other charges, complaining that girlfriends were expected to be politically active and in-the-know but discouraged from any meaningful participation.[99]

That the SEXPOL campaign represented a key site of the scholarly scientific imperative in action only added to its impact: the claim to relevance based on the latest empirical knowledge, legitimized by the way it intersected with the positions of liberalizing experts, dovetailing with the urgent desires of young people for whom the ability to theorize and legitimize what they already wanted to do anyway was a godsend. "What does the sexual life of youth look like?" asked SEXPOL activist Hubert Bacia in a contribution to the Schülerzeitung *Neuer Roter Turm*; "W. Reich established thirty years ago that complete abstinence, that is, no sexual activity at all after entering into puberty, only appears in severely inhibited and neurotic boys. Today Kinsey offers the concrete figures to back that up."[100] The theoretical sexual discourse drawn from Reich and Marcuse, popularized through the SEXPOL campaigns and other means, even filtered down into the left-wing personals ads. As one characteristic ad put

---

[97] Cited in Perinelli, "Lust, Gewalt, Befreiung," pp. 86–87.

[98] Sabine Porn, "Kollektiv-Beischlaf und Steinwurf-Terror: Die Frauen der ersten Kommunen," in Becker, ed., *Unbekannte Wesen*, pp. 169–174, at p. 172.

[99] Cited in Perinelli, "Lust, Gewalt, Befreiung," p. 94.

[100] Hubert Bacia, "Uber die Schädlichkeit der Enthaltsamkeit," *Neuer Roter Turm: Schülerzeitschrift*, no. 3, March 1967, Green Library, Stanford University, Germany. Extraparliamentary Opposition movement, 1967–1984 collection, box 87, folder 3.

it: "Who knows a psychoanalyst who holds to the theories of Wilhelm Reich? What patient, conscious girl (17–20 y.) is ready to help me out of my sexual need and in the process help me overcome the bourgeois-repressive fetters of my environment[?]. The attempt won't be simple."[101]

Reich also underpinned attempts to develop antiauthoritarian models of child-rearing in the context of the *Kinderläden* movement. For all their status as an attempt to offer concrete solutions to a concrete and pressing problem, the *Kinderläden* became, for many activists, opportunities to transform Reichian and Marcusian theory into reality. The original project of providing child care for left-wing women became very quickly bound up with notions of antiauthoritarian child-rearing and the fostering of childhood sexuality as an antidote to social repression. The turn to antiauthoritarian child-rearing was in turn bound up with the historical recovery project fueling the antiauthoritarian movement more generally. Seeking to find useful material to support the practical and theoretical needs of the present, activists looked back to the sex radicals of the 1920s, above all Reich.[102]

Alongside attempts to infuse political activism with Reichian sex theory came efforts to instrumentalize a more banal facet of sexual engagement: pornography. From fairly early on, pornography was imbued by a portion of the antiauthoritarian movement with a political legitimacy that warranted its inclusion in the panoply of left-wing action forms. It is not hard to see why. Pornography held the unique power to simultaneously offer cultural rebellion, tweak mainstream sensibilities, and bring into play the repressive power of the state. Even more, pornography was understood as part of a complex of subversive activities. This formula was codified in the name of the Cologne underground newspaper edited by Henryk M. Broder, Reinhard Hippen, Rolf Ulrich Kaiser, and Fred Viebahn: *PoPoPo* ("Zeitung für Pop & Politik & Pornografie," "Newspaper for Pop & Politics & Pornography").

A key figure in the intersection of pornography and politics was the left-wing publisher Jörg Schröder. Schröder began his publishing career in 1967 as an editor at the Melzer Verlag where, alongside revolutionary texts by Che Guevara and Fidel Castro and cutting-edge works of transatlantic letters (Brinkmann, Chotjewitz, Kerouac, and LeRoi Jones), he published a highly successful German-language edition of Dominique Aury's *The Story of O*.[103] After going on to found the März Verlag in 1969,

---

[101] Quoted in Perinelli, "Lust, Gewalt, Befreiung," pp. 85–99.
[102] Steffen, "SDS, Weiberräte, Feminismus?" p. 134.
[103] Heinemann, "Jörg Schröder," p. 298.

Schröder took over the German branch of the French erotic publishing house Olympia Press, where he presided over the creation of the first porno films to be openly produced and sold in West Germany. At the same time that he was publishing key New Left texts such as Günter Amendt's *SexFront*, Schröder was releasing porno films that openly sought to blur the boundaries between sex and politics. The six films produced by Olympia between 1971 and 1972 depicted scenarios set up as commentaries on themes of sexual and social exploitation, consumption, and class conflict. At least one film drew explicitly on the theories of Reimut Reiche and Herbert Marcuse, others depicted lesbianism, and one – *Die Amazonen* (*The Amazons*) – was dedicated to Warhol assailant Valerie Solanas and her SCUM (Society for Cutting Up Men).[104]

The mixture of porno and politics in Schröder's films, though unique for the genre, was characteristic of the cultural productions of the countercultural or "hedonistic" end of the radical left spectrum. The stock in trade of the underground press was the juxtaposition of female nudity against the symbols of revolutionary activism, especially violence. The image from *Pardon* showing a young woman holding two round fizzing bombs in front of her breasts (see Fig. 7.3) was only a particularly striking example of a more general phenomenon. Everywhere, from magazines such as *konkret* and *Pardon* to the underground press proper, female nudity and revolution existed in a metonymic relationship. In practical terms, pornography helped finance the publication of left-wing literature. This was true for Jörg Schröder as well as for Klaus Rainer Röhl, publisher of *konkret*. Röhl saw the use of nude or semi-nude women on his covers as a way of paying the bills, further justifying it as a way of winning readers to left-wing ideas. Yet, notions of sexual revolution and political revolution synergized with each other, the tandem deployment of female nudity and symbols of "the revolution" lending a greater subversive charge to both.[105]

In this context, the female image did a sort of triple duty: it titillated, lending a prurient interest to the complex of ideas and images in which it was imbedded; it telegraphed a powerful idea of sexual revolution that could articulate with other sorts of revolution; and it sometimes presented an image of the "revolutionary heroine" who combined within herself the virtues of female beauty and political militancy. The latter is notable in the work of Alfred von Meysenbug, left-wing cartoonist and illustrator

104 Heinemann, "Jörg Schröder," pp. 303–305.
105 Heinemann, "Jörg Schröder," p. 290.

Figure 7.3 "Time for a little more revolution!" *Pardon*, no. 1, 1968.
Hamburg Institute for Social Research.

of Amendt's *SexFront*. In his Frankfurt School-inspired consumerism critique *Super-Mädchen* (*Super Girl*), with its eponymous bare-breasted heroine, woman functions simultaneously as sex object and revolutionary protagonist. Meysenbug's renderings of the (fully clothed) women involved in the October 1968 protest in Frankfurt's Paulskirche have, aside from the nudity, a similar quality.[106]

This heroization of the female radical had its flipside in the mainstream response to the significant presence of women in terror groups such as the RAF and Movement 2 June. In the early days, women were taken seriously neither by their comrades nor by the authorities. Dagmar Przytula remembers how, during the arrest of the Kommune I members before the attempted pudding bombing of Hubert Humphrey, the women were immediately released: "we were supposedly just appendages of the men, and therefore not responsible. How wrong this assessment was later shown by the case of Gudrun Ensslin."[107] Later, when the radicalism of women was an undeniable fact, women received a disproportionate amount of attention from journalists and commentators, who wrote as if women terrorists outnumbered the men. Alan Rosenfeld and others have traced this distortion to anxieties about changing gender relationships in West Germany broadly and to worries over the dynamizing effects of women's liberation in particular. "Excessive" liberation for women, the thinking went, helped to explain the prominence of women in these groups. In contrast to the reality of such groups, in which the sexist attitudes typical of the antiauthoritarian revolt seem to have been in play, women were often assigned a leading role, if not held responsible as driving forces.[108]

More commonly, women functioned, both in underground comics (particularly in the popular R. Crumb comics imported from America) and in the underground and "mainstream underground" press (e.g. *Pardon* and *konkret*) as pure sex objects. The deployment of the naked female form as a symbol of an undifferentiated sexual revolution, a sort of "vulgar sex-radicalism," concealed that it was often just being used in a way little different than in the boulevard newspapers of the Springer Press. The use of naked (and, increasingly, bound) women on the cover of *konkret* became an object of dispute both from outside and from within the editorial staff. In a forum in the April 22, 1969 issue, Hubert Bacia

---

[106] Kraushaar, ed., *Frankfurter Schule und Studentenbewegung*, p. 364.
[107] Kätzel, *Die 68erinnen*, p. 207.
[108] Alan Rosenfeld, "'Anarchist Amazons': The Gendering of Radicalism in 1970s West Germany," *Contemporary European History*, 19 (4) (2010): 351–374.

and Jürgen Werth took the magazine to task for its increasing tendency to feature women in bondage on the cover:

The chained woman signals nothing less than the unacknowledged fear of the konkret decision-makers that they share with countless gender comrades: Bind the woman securely in her role as an object of the male gaze (Schaulust), bind her drastically with the traditional chains of kitchen and childbearing. This picture expresses in purest form the sado-masochistic triumph of the man in this society.[109]

Elsewhere, images of bondage and sado-masochism were used in ways that seemed simultaneously to critique and exploit such representations, criticizing "bourgeois uptightness" about sexuality while exploiting prurient interests. In Rolf Ulrich Kaiser's book *Protokolle einer Kommune und 23 Trips*, a passage criticizing attempts to smear the counterculture by equating murderous outliers such as Charles Manson with the "mainstream" of the underground was illustrated with a drawing of a naked and bound Sharon Tate menaced by a knife-yielding hippie. Laying the responsibility for itself, as it were, at the feet of the bourgeoisie, the image condemned mainstream hypocrisy even as it sought to titillate with its lurid depiction of sex crime.[110]

In addition to its general function as a means of attacking bourgeois authoritarian taboos, sexual or pornographic images were also deployed as a political weapon. In the pages of *Agit 883*, as Massimo Perinelli writes, pornography was a site in which were "intermingled every possible discourse: from anti-repressive politics vis-à-vis antiprostitution laws and paragraphs against same-sex sexual practices, sexual denunciation of political enemies and their rape by über-potent comrades, to crude sexual statements about women."[111] Above all, sexual imagery provided a ready series of metaphors for the contest with authority. In the pages of *Agit 883*, and in other underground newspapers as well, "the relationship between the rebels and the state was depicted as a sexualized relationship of violence" in which "the state as a woman was 'fucked' by potent comrades, while the gentleman politicians were lampooned as sexually impotent."[112]

Alongside sexual-denunciatory attacks on specific enemies was to be found a more generalized symbolic depiction of enemies in terms designed to reveal their true inner nature as sexually repressed beings.

---

[109] *konkret*, no. 9, April 22, 1969, p. 14.
[110] Rolf Ulrich Kaiser, *Protokolle einer Kommune und 23 Trips* (Düsseldorf: Droste, 1970).
[111] Perinelli, "Lust, Gewalt, Befreiung," p. 89.
[112] Perinelli, "Lust, Gewalt, Befreiung," p. 97.

This sort of "unmasking" has a long history on both the left and the right, but in the context of the flowing together of sexual and political revolution in the antiauthoritarian revolt it was particularly notable for the way that a popularized/vulgar rendering of Reichian and Marcusian ideas was deployed to attack the legitimacy of state authority. Policemen and judges were routinely depicted in perverted sexual activity, their sexual inadequacy a sign of the illegitimacy of their authority, or their sexual maladjustment a symbol of the corrupt system that they represented. Sexual denunciation was practiced not just against the forces of the state, but within the movement as well. The charges of impotence and/or sexual perversion leveled against policemen and judges – figures only depicted as *potent* when engaged in the brutalization of political opponents – were deployed within the movement as well, by one faction against another, or by women against men. This practice was only one, if a striking example, of the popular deployment of theory. Sex radicalism in the Reichian or Marcusian mold was a means not just of healing the self but of breaching the inner defenses of otherwise heavily armored enemies.

The nude or semi-nude female continued to persist in the underground press as a visual trope representing the new sexual freedom well into the 1970s. Increasingly, however, this facile deployment of the female form came to be out of step with developing feminist currents, women directly intervening to dispute the way they were being depicted. In one case, women of the Gegendruck publishing collective launched an attack on Joseph Wintjes of *Ulcus Molle Infodienst*. Gegendruck had begun printing *Ulcus Molle Infodienst* in 1976. The women at Gegendruck had from the beginning suppressed their unease at the journal's illustrations depicting women in various states of undress or involved in sexually compromising situations.[113] The dispute began when the Gegendruck women refused to print the proposed cover of *Ulcus Molle Infodienst*, August 7, 1977, which contained an illustration by Walter Hartmann depicting a nude woman squatting over an upturned book in a sexually provocative pose. Wintjes was forced to change the cover, but the incident unleashed a firestorm of charges and countercharges.

Many left-wing critics accused the Gegendruck women of practicing a censorship no less odious than the one the government was practicing against the left as a whole. The Verlag Association in Hamburg asked, "How can we wholeheartedly defend ourselves against censorship ... when

---

[113] There was one man among the staff as well, but his role in the dispute is unclear.

our own camp stinks of puritanism, hypocrisy, and base blackmail?"[114] Raymond Martin, publisher of underground newspaper *Päang*, sarcastically recommended that the women of Gegendruck pay a visit to the AAO commune, notorious on the left for its cult-like program of mind control.[115] The outraged artist Walter Hartmann (using the English for greater subcultural credibility), accused the Gegendruck women of "female pig chauvinism."[116] The Gegendruck women responded by calling on women's groups and publishers to reject any further cooperation with Wintjes. "Can you imagine how it is," they asked in a leaflet,

in the evening in the women's group to consider how to fight for our rights. To do actions, to do demonstrations, to collect signatures, and then to go into the press the next day and there lies the artwork for *Ulcus Molle Info*, which contains exactly the stuff we are fighting against?"[117]

Such incidents demonstrated with great clarity that facile notions of sexual revolution, as encoded in the visual iconography of the antiauthoritarian movement but elsewhere as well, were no longer tenable.

"OUT OF THE PUBLIC TOILETS, INTO THE STREETS!"

The women's movement was not the only site of the antiauthoritarian revolt where politics and the politics of everyday life intersected over the terrain of sexuality. Like the women's movement, the homosexual rights movement also grew directly out of the antiauthoritarian revolt, even as it diverged from it at key junctures. Like the women's movement, the homosexual rights movement in West Germany was both a response to international currents and an attempt to take care of unfinished business from the past. In 1968, homosexuality in West Germany remained criminalized in terms little different from those that obtained in the imperial period. The Weimar Republic had seen forceful efforts to normalize and decriminalize homosexuality, Magnus Hirschfeld's Sexological Institute

---

[114] Verlag Association Hamburg, "Stellungnahme zum Vorgehen von Gegendruck zum Thema Titelgrafik," September 9, 1977, Green Library, Stanford University, Germany. Extraparliamentary Opposition movement, 1967–1984 collection, box 55, folder 1.

[115] Raymond Martin, "Auschnitte aus Leserbriefen," in "Stellungnahme des 'linken' Verlags," Verlag Association, Green Library, Stanford University, Germany. Extraparliamentary Opposition movement, 1967–1984 collection, box 55, folder 1.

[116] Hartmann to Gegendruck collective, reprinted in Verlag Association Hamburg, "Stellungnahme zum Vorgehen von Gegendruck zum Thema Titelgrafik."

[117] "Stellungnahme von Gegendruck order wie drückt man sprachlose Wut schriftlich aus," in Verlag Association Hamburg, "Stellungnahme zum Vorgehen von Gegendruck zum Thema Titelgrafik."

being in the forefront. The rise of the Nazis foreclosed all such attempts at experimentation and liberalization. The persecution of homosexuality under Nazism is well known. The Nazis retained and extended Paragraph 175 of the penal code making male homosexuality a crime, supplementing the existing penal regime with the use of the concentration-camp system. Some 100,000 men were arrested for homosexuality during the Nazi period, 50,000 sentenced, and up to 15,000 sent to concentration camps on top of whatever prison sentences had already been served. Lesbians were not openly persecuted, although lesbian associational life was dramatically curtailed.

Under the Christian-Democratic administrations of the post-1945 period, there was no return to the liberalizing trends of the Weimar period. Rather, Paragraph 175 was maintained virtually intact. Male homosexuals were denied victim status after the war, the extent to which they had been persecuted by the Nazis downplayed. Worse, in the early postwar period, some liberated homosexual concentration-camp inmates were remitted to prison to serve out the remainder of their sentences under Paragraph 175. It is characteristic of the moral regime in post-1945 West Germany that as many homosexuals were persecuted in the Federal Republic (44,000 men) as under the Nazis.[118] Paragraph 175 was upheld by the federal government as late as 1962, but already liberalizing trends were beginning to come to the fore. The annual congress of German lawyers in 1968 came out in support of the liberalization of criminal penalties for sexual acts. As Robert Moeller has pointed out, the persistence of homophobia was evident in the debates on decriminalization, even on the part of supporters. Homosexual men were not called in to testify in debates about decriminalization, in part because their open appearance as homosexuals would have placed them in legal jeopardy under Paragraph 175. More fundamentally, their appearance would have torn away the veil of silence that continued to lay over homosexual life generally and the persecution of homosexuals under Paragraph 175 in particular.[119]

In East Germany, homosexuality had been decriminalized in 1968 by a regime newly confident in the success of economic reforms and a new constitution. Prior to this, despite sexological initiatives in the direction of greater liberalization, undertaken with an eye toward ongoing debates in West Germany, and, in some cases, inspired by the work of Magnus

[118] Robert Moeller, "Private Acts, Public Anxieties, and the Fight to Decriminalize Male Homosexuality in West Germany," *Feminist Studies*, 36 (3) (2010).
[119] Moeller, "Private Acts."

Hirschfeld, the regime had continued to use Paragraph 175, still in force in East Germany as well, to police and protect "socialist morality." In the event, the dismantling of Paragraph 175 was accompanied by additional scrutiny on the sex lives of teenagers, so that the net effect was arguably one of greater repression.[120]

In the West, the accession of Gustav Heinemann to the post of justice minister with the entry of the SPD into power as part of the Grand Coalition in 1966 raised hopes for a reform of Paragraph 175.[121] By mid decade, the weight of expert opinion was firmly in support of liberalization. As the director of the Institute for Sexual Research at the University of Hamburg put it in the foreword to a 1967 book on the question of Paragraph 175, the topic had been "talked to pieces."[122] All that remained was for politicians to act accordingly. The election of the Social Democrat Willi Brandt to the Chancellorship in 1969 created the space for liberalization. In 1969, homosexual sex for men over twenty-one years old was decriminalized. The age of consent was further reduced in 1973 to eighteen. Part of a wave of partial decriminalizations across Europe in 1969–1973, these measures represented the recognition that blatant legal discrimination was no longer viable. They did not signal an end to homophobia nor defuse the subversive power of same-sex relations.[123] They did, however, open the space for the emergence of a gay (alternative) public sphere that both intersected with the emerging alternative scene and helped to create a broader acceptance of homosexuality in mainstream society.

Characteristically, the formation of the gay-rights movement in West Germany was inspired by a piece of independent media. The 1971 film *Nicht der Homosexuelle ist pervers, sondern die Situation in der er lebt (It's Not the Homosexual Who Is Perverse, but Rather the Situation in Which*

---

[120] Jennifer V. Evans, "Decriminalization, Seduction, and 'Unnatural Desire' in East Germany," *Feminist Studies*, 36 (3) (2010), at p. 560.

[121] Gerald Kienast, "Schwul! Paragraph 175 in Deutschland," *konkret*, January 1967. Such hopes were not shared by everyone; as one reader of *konkret* put it, "Anyone who expects the elimination of Paragraph 175 by SPD Justice Minister Heinemann will lose their hair over it, or at least go gray." An SPD willing to compromise thoroughly enough so as to be able to enter a coalition government with the CDU, the reader maintained, could not be expected to live up to any of its other promises either. "Leserbriefe, Betr. 'Schwul' Paragraph 175, konkret 1+3/67," *konkret*, no. 6, June 1967.

[122] Hans Giese, *Homosexualität oder Politik mit dem §175* (Reinbek bei Hamburg: Rowohlt, 1967).

[123] As Geoff Eley points out, "cold war sexualities had been dangerous ground, the Left's uncharted territory, and same-sex relations provided the frontier that was most assiduously policed"; Eley, *Forging Democracy*, p. 473.

He Lives), co-directed by Rosa von Praunheim (Holger Mischwitzky) and Martin Dannecker, played a key role in jump-starting the gay pride movement in West Germany. Its concluding slogan "Out of the public toilets, into the streets!" signaled the arrival of a new and more militant mindset. The movie was screened around the country, accompanied by public discussions, and in 1973 it was also shown on West German television. The film helped foment discussion around gay issues, leading to the formation of gay-rights groups around the country, and indeed, even outside the country. East Germans who caught the airing of the Praunheim and Dannecker film on West German television founded the group Homosexual Initiative Berlin (HIB), which represented the first gay liberation group of the Eastern Bloc.[124]

The first and most important gay liberation group in the Federal Republic was Homosexual Action West Berlin (HAW). Founded on August 15, 1971, in the wake of the screening of the Praunheim and Dannecker film at the *Berlinale*, the group quickly became a trendsetter in West Berlin and throughout West Germany.[125] The founding of HAW was part of an international wave of homosexual rebellion. The Stonewall riots in New York City had broken out just two years before, news of them quickly spreading to Europe. The formation of the Gay Liberation Front in America, a group launched in the aftermath of Stonewall and notable for its radical linking of gay rights with issues of antiracism and Third World liberation, inspired the founding of parallel groups in Europe. A Gay Liberation Front was founded at the London School of Economics in October 1970, with similar groups founded in France and Italy the following year.[126] HAW was part of this wave of "liberation front" foundings, the German answer to the perceived need to take the struggle for gay rights to a new level of militancy and direct action.

Like the Gay Liberation Front in America, and its British and Continental European spin-offs, HAW was based on the notion that gay liberation was inseparable from broader struggles over equality, both cultural and economic. Characteristically, the struggles of gays at home were linked with the struggles of gays and others abroad. Drawing connections

---

[124] George E. Haggerty and Bonnie Zimmerman, eds., *Gay Histories and Cultures: An Encyclopedia* (New York: Garland, 2000), p. 116.
[125] Initial discussions about the formation of the group were undertaken in a series of meetings at the Arsenal cinema in Berlin-Schöneberg, the group subsequently relocating to the "Hand-Drugstore" in the Motzstraße. Beginning the following year, the group organized a yearly Pfingsttreff, and marched en bloc in the annual May Day parade. A women's section was added the same year.
[126] Eley, *Forging Democracy*, p. 475.

Figure 7.4 Demonstration of Homosexual Action West Berlin against the Pinochet dictatorship in Chile, November 3, 1973. Landesarchiv Berlin.

between gay rights at home and the persecution of gays by the military dictatorships of Latin American (see Fig. 7.4), HAW activists insisted on the fundamental connection between different types of repression. Gerhard Hoffmann and Reinhard von der Marwitz, two key figures in the early West German gay-rights movement, argued in 1976:

At the moment it is above all the women and men in the Latin American states who need our solidarity and that of the entire socialist movement. Since the military putsch in Chile in September 1973 homosexuals have been imprisoned in concentration camps along with other political and racially persecuted. In Argentina the organ of the welfare ministry calls for a general pogrom against gays and lesbians. The Argentinian right sees foreign Marxism as the original font of "sexual deviancy."[127]

The connection between the concentration camps in which the Nazis had imprisoned homosexual victims and the concentration camps in which Latin American juntas now did the same was too obvious to miss.

---

[127] Gerhard Hoffmann and Reinhard von der Marwitz, *Schwanz und Ordnung* (Vienna: Neues Forum, 1976), p. 57.

In contrast to many foreign gay-rights movements, HAW was explicitly Marxist in orientation. Many of the initial group of some forty members of HAW were members of New Left groups such as the SEW and KPD(AO), and, indeed, the group required that each member also belong to another political group so as to avoid constituting a "gay ghetto."[128] Characteristically, HAW's founding document declared that homosexual emancipation could only take place in conjunction with the emancipation of the working classes. The slogans deployed in the group's public outings clearly reflected this orientation. In the 1973 May Day parade, 150 gays and lesbians marched through West Berlin with a banner reading "Homosexual or not, solidarity in the class struggle" ("Homosexuell – ob ja ob nein – im Klassenkampf heißt's solidarisch sein"). For the Pfingsten Meeting, a more complex affair with Info-stands, "kiss-ins," and a demonstration on the Kurfürstendamm, the slogan was: "The oppression of homosexuality is only a special case in the general sexual oppression."[129]

These seemingly simple formulae, much as in the case of the women's groups such as the Aktionsrat zur Befreiung der Frauen, concealed latent lines of conflict.[130] First, like their feminist counterparts, activists confronted the fact that the oppression of homosexuals, like the oppression of women, was understood through the Marxist lens as a "secondary contradiction." The very framework according to which the struggle against sexual oppression had to be grouped as a subset of more overarching structures of oppression (general sexual oppression, capitalism itself) was empowering inasmuch as it connected their personal situation to the situations of others and to larger social structures that needed changing; but it carried with it the risk that specific pleas for redress could be shoved off in favor of "the revolution" that must happen before anything else could happen. It hardly helped matters that, in accordance with the group's dual membership policy, significant numbers of the group's activists belonged to Marxist cadre organizations, these being the least likely to eschew dogmatic adherence to Marxist analytic categories.[131]

---

[128] Haggerty and Zimmerman, eds., *Gay Histories and Cultures*, p. 116.

[129] Egmont Fassbinder, "Mein schönes 'schwules' Schöneberg," in *Berlin-Schöneberg: Blicke ins Quartier, 1949–2000* (Berlin: Jaron-Verlag, 2001), pp. 153–160.

[130] See http://blog.aidshilfe.de/2011/08/15/homosexuelle-aktion-westberlin (accessed February 1, 2012).

[131] Elmar Kraushaar, "'Nebenwidersprüche': Die neue Linke und die Schwulenfrage in der Bundesrepublik der siebziger und achtziger Jahre," in Detlef Grumbach, ed., *Die Linke und das Laster: Schwule Emanzipation und linke Vorurteile* (Hamburg: MännerschwarmSkript Verlag, 1995), p. 148.

Indeed, with their restrictive morality and insistence on the primacy of the revolution above all other factors, the *K-Gruppen* could sometimes provide hostile environments for homosexuals who wished to combine the struggle for gay rights with the struggle against capitalism. In response to an open letter from Homosexual Action Bremen urging the importance of winning support for gay-rights issues among the masses, the Communist League West Germany replied: "We are … opposed to social interest groups of homosexuals as homosexual, since that can result in nothing more than life reform, and we in no way endorse the work of Communists in such bourgeois arrangements."[132] The KPD–ML similarly dismissed gay activism as a legitimate field of endeavor, quoting Lenin on the dangers of justifying a "hypertrophic [gay] sexual life" on the basis of bourgeois morality or of seeking reform within the existing system.[133] Members who emphasized their sexuality, the party charged, were placing "the founding principles of the dictatorship of the proletariat on their head."[134]

Reluctance to grapple with the status of homosexuality in and of itself was not confined to the *K-Gruppen*. When gay activists disrupted a "Portugal Teach-In" at the Technical University in May 1975 at which Portuguese leftists had been invited to speak, they once again came up against comrades who saw gay rights as a distraction from the urgent matter of revolution. Protesting the fact that Portuguese journalists had recently been dismissed by the revolutionary government for being, variously, "fascists," "racist bourgeois," and "homosexuals," the activists were prevented by their German comrades from reading a statement criticizing the Portuguese.[135] Frustrated gay activists marched out chanting "Freedom for gays! Freedom for women! See you again in the KZ" (concentration camp). Later, they published a declaration in *InfoBUG* serving notice to comrades across the left spectrum:

So long as you, from the Spontis to the *K-Gruppen*, attempt to push aside our problem with: not here and now! "Gays out!," and "you are agents of social democracy!," you don't understand that this discrimination against gays means

[132] KBW, "Brief des ständigen Ausschuß des Zentralen Komitees des KBW an die HAB vom 14. Dezember," in Los Angeles Research Group, *Zur materialistischen Analyse der Schwulenunterdrückung* (Berlin: Verlag Rosa Winkel, 1977), pp. 73–75, at p. 75, quoted in Kraushaar, "'Nebenwidersprüche'," p. 153.

[133] KPD–ML Ortsleitung Bremen, "Stellungnahme zur Diskussion über Homosexualität," in Los Angeles Research Group, *Zur materialistischen Analyse der Schwulenunterdrückung*, pp. 77–78, quoted in Kraushaar, "'Nebenwidersprüche'," p. 153.

[134] KPD–ML Ortsleitung Bremen, "Stellungnahme zur Diskussion über Homosexualität."

[135] Kraushaar, "'Nebenwidersprüche'," pp. 142–143.

nothing else other than: you have to function in your crappy roles as men and women![136]

The incomprehension of left-wing comrades aside, the attempt to mix politics and sexual identity held a number of potential problems. These reared their head as early as the conversation following the first showing of the Praunheim and Dannecker film, which some gay discussants accused of worsening the situation of gays through its unapologetic depiction of the gay subculture.[137] This dispute about the proper way to be gay, which was also a dispute about how gays should present themselves within society and within the left-wing movement, came to a head in connection with the Pfingsten Meeting of 1973. Founded the previous year as a means of bringing to West Berlin members of the Homosexual Action groups from the rest of West Germany, the meeting also attracted visitors from the rest of Europe. In the 1973 meeting, in yet another striking example of the power of transnational exchanges to synergize events in the Federal Republic, the intervention of French and Italian drag queens sent the nascent movement in a new and unexpected direction. Egmont Fassbinder, one of the founders of HAW, recalls: "A few gays from romance countries found our 'traditional' method of demonstrating ridiculous and pulled up along side us marching in Prussian Goosestep, caricaturing us and chanting 'We want a pink Volkswagen!'" This seemingly innocuous episode became the occasion, later that evening back in the group's Dennewitzstraße headquarters, for an extended and heated discussion about, in Fassbinder's words, "our 'un-gay' behavior, our ingratiating ourselves with the left-wing men of the student movement."[138]

Thus began the so-called *Tuntenstreit* (drag queens' dispute), in which the proper content of gay identity was put to the test in a way that challenged the political conceptions at the heart of the movement.[139] The issue split the group into two factions, roughly correlating to the "dogmatic" and "undogmatic" members of the group: one "feminist" (i.e. blatantly queer), the other arguing that ostentatious displays of queer identity such as drag detracted both from the attempt to gain acceptance from the mainstream and from the struggle against capitalism. The feminist faction argued that drag was indeed political, both in its ability to

[136] *InfoBUG*, no. 59, 1975, quoted in Kraushaar, "'Nebenwidersprüche'," p. 143.
[137] See http://blog.aidshilfe.de/2011/08/15/homosexuelle-aktion-westberlin (accessed February 12, 2012).
[138] Fassbinder, "Mein schönes 'schwules' Schöneberg," pp. 153–160.
[139] *Tuntenstreit: Theoriediskussion der Homosexuellen Aktion Westberlin* (Berlin: Verlag Rosa Winkel, 1975).

upset notions about correct gender roles and as a point of contact with the lesbian and feminist movements. A number of lesbians did belong to HAW but eventually split off to found the Lesbian Action Center.[140] Meanwhile, in the wake of the *Tuntenstreit*, members of the integrationist faction of HAW's male membership, committed to a Marxist, trade-union-oriented approach, split off to found the Allgemeine Homosexuelle Arbeitsgemeinschaft (AHA; General Homosexual Working Group).[141]

This splintering, characteristic of the historical moment in which the gay-rights movement came into being, did not blunt the emergence of the broader movement. The overturning of Paragraph 175 created an opening that was quickly filled by a nascent gay-pride culture. The first nationwide gay-rights demonstration took place in the Catholic stronghold of Münster in 1972, challenging religious authorities who were among the most vocal opponents of gay rights. The creation of a homosexual public sphere saw the appearance of a host of new men's publications with titles such as *Him* ("for men, who men want") and *Sunny* ("Color magazine for friends"). The key importance of the overturning of Paragraph 175 to homosexual life in West Germany was captured in the subtitle of one of the new magazines, *du & ich*: "The after-September magazine."[142]

CONCLUSION

Both the abortion and gay-rights movements represent an expansion of the fundamental maneuver at the heart of 1968: the establishment of the right to speak – in this case, the right to speak about the most intimate concerns, whether of the disposition of the female reproductive capacity or of the right to openly pursue true sexual identity. Both were, characteristically, also constructed in transnational terms, drawing inspiration from their membership in imagined emancipatory communities and foreign action models that they imported into the Federal Republic. From the influence of American feminism or the French abortion-rights campaign

---

[140] Monika Kühn, 'The Lesbian Action Centre, West Berlin: The Formation of Group Solidarity,' in Altbach et al., *German Feminism*, pp. 311–314.

[141] Such problems were not unique to HAW but paralleled developments elsewhere. The British Gay Liberation Front, for example, was "torn apart" in the course of the early 1970s "by tensions between women and men, drag queens and machos, socialists and counterculturalists"; Barry D. Adam, *The Rise of the Gay and Lesbian Movement* (New York: Twayne, 1995), quoted in Eley, *Forging Democracy*, p. 474.

[142] Peter P. Dahl, "Dr.homo.phil.: Über drei Zeitschriften für das Leben zu zweit," *konkret*, no. 14, July 2, 1970, p. 12.

on the West German women's movement, to the example posed by East Germany's comparatively liberal gender politics, to the influence of the international gay-rights movement on the development of a similar movement in the Federal Republic, emancipatory West German initiatives around gender and sexual orientation were heavily stamped by influences beyond the borders of West Germany. Although both had their roots in the activism of the antiauthoritarian movement and were products of the sexual-revolutionary space opened up by the intersection of that activism with liberalizing trends from outside the movement, both were a long way from the undifferentiated notions of sexual revolution that drove the antiauthoritarian movement at its height. At the same time, however, both were a product of that moment of revolutionary conflation in which there seemed to be no fundamental separation between the myriad of issues at play, and retained something of that character even during the long separating-out process of the 1970s.

Almost from its very beginning, the women's movement demonstrated a separatist potential that would come more fully into its own by the mid 1970s. The first independent women's centers were established in 1972. A dozen independent women's centers were in existence by the spring of 1974, seventeen by the end of the year.[143] A host of autonomous institutions – women's bars, publishers, bookstores, film festivals, rock bands – followed. By the end of the decade, mass-circulation women's magazines such as *Emma* and *Courage* helped solidify the arrival of women and women's issues on the national stage. The separatist tendency was a source of tension, as we have seen, but the potential for it was implicit in the antiauthoritarian project from the beginning. All that was needed for it to become manifest was for the dream of a revolutionary mass movement to be exposed, as it was in the latter half of 1968, as a fiction. This realization, occurring simultaneously with the realization that women were relegated to a secondary status within the emancipatory movement to which they belonged, lent strength to the idea, nascent all along, that practical activity in the service of daily life issues might represent the revolution after all.

[143] Katsiaficas, *The Subversion of Politics*, p. 106; Kristine von Soden, ed., *Der grosse Unterschied: Die neue Frauenbewegung und die siebziger Jahre* (Berlin: Elefanten Press, 1988), p. 89.

CHAPTER 8

Death

On April 25, 1977, the student newspaper of the University of Göttingen published an "obituary" for a government official recently assassinated by the RAF. The official, Attorney General Siegfried Buback, had been a leading figure in the government's war against left-wing terrorists. Killed three weeks earlier, along with his driver and another passenger, by a motorcycle-borne assassin, as he sat at a red light en route from his home to the federal court in Karlsruhe, Buback represented the first victim of a renewed wave of terror that would climax in the paroxysm of violence known as the German Autumn. The author of the obituary, an anonymous student writing under the pseudonym "a Mescalero from Göttingen," observed that although the murder of Buback, a former Nazi Party member, had left him with a feeling of "clandestine joy," it was nevertheless now necessary to question the wisdom of revolutionary violence as a means of struggle against the state. "Our way to socialism," he concluded, "cannot be paved with corpses."[1]

Subsequently published in newspapers and periodicals across the student left spectrum and in the mainstream press, the second thoughts about violence frequently excised but the "clandestine joy" always left glaringly intact, "Buback – Ein Nachruf" caused an uproar. "This 'clandestine joy'," observed the author of a retrospective press account,

exploded like a bomb in a state shaken by terrorist hysteria, that had initiated a massive manhunt-machinery, messed around with the constitution (Basic Law), and started a witch-hunt against [terrorist] "sympathizers." The Mescalero was made into a representative object of hate ... against everything that was left and suspicious.[2]

The so-called "Mescalero Affair" also caused soul-searching about how West Germany had come to the point where an anonymous student could

---

[1] "Buback – Ein Nachruf," *Göttinger Nachrichten*, April 25, 1977, pp. 10–12.
[2] "MESCALERO: Klammheimlich ade," *Der Spiegel*, January 7, 1980.

Figure 8.1 Crime scene: Rudi Dutschke's shoes, Kurfürstendamm,
April 11, 1968. Landesarchiv Berlin.

experience "joy" at the murder of a government official. In an article in *Der Spiegel*, the SPD politician Peter Glotz condemned the "inhuman language" of the Mescalero letter, while insisting on the need to come to grips with the communicative gulf that had opened up in the Federal Republic. Glotz argued that this gulf had opened so wide that it was now possible to speak of "two cultures" in West Germany – one encompassing mainstream society, the other the counterculture in the universities and elsewhere. Tellingly, Glotz distinguished the two cultures by the sources of information that shaped their worldviews: on the one hand, readers of the "stinknormal" ("stinkingly normal") mainstream press; on the other, the members of the "info-culture" who gained their knowledge of the world through left-wing flyers, newspapers, and periodicals (e.g. *InfoBUG*). "He who lives for three years in the Info-Kultur," Glotz observed, "speaks an entirely different language than the people of the other culture, and ... the ability of each to understand the other is being destroyed."[3] Glotz's position would prove to be influential, especially on

[3] *Der Spiegel*, no. 41, October 10, 1977.

the left, where, as we will see, his call for rapprochement met with an unexpected resonance.

The murder of Siegfried Buback came against the dramatic backdrop of the trial of leading members of the so-called "first generation" of the RAF. Prior to their capture in June 1972, the group had been responsible for a series of attacks – the so-called "May Offensive" – that included bombings of US Army bases in Frankfurt and Heidelberg, the offices of the Springer Press in Hamburg, and the car of a judge in Karlsruhe (the judge's wife was injured in the explosion instead). After a period of incarceration in separate prisons, the group was moved to the fortress-like Stammheim prison, purpose-built for their imprisonment and trial. Holger Meins succumbed to a hunger strike in Wittlich, where he was imprisoned separately, in November 1974; Ulrike Meinhof was found hanged in her cell at Stammheim a year and a half later. The "murders" (as the terrorists saw it) of Meins and Meinhof, as well as that of Siegfried Hausner, blown up by his own bomb during the siege of the West German embassy in Stockholm, were cited as justification for the murder of Buback. The surviving defendants, despite solitary confinement, maintained contact with each other and with the outside world through their attorneys. Outside, alongside a broadly based campaign against the conditions of the group's imprisonment, the "second generation" of the RAF prepared and carried out new actions aimed at gaining their release. Buback's murder was one of these.

Against this backdrop, the publication of the Mescalero letter unleashed a firestorm. Unable to identify the author, the authorities instead punished those responsible for publishing his work. Over 140 persons, beginning with members of the Göttingen Student Council, faced charges. A group of forty-eight educators who reprinted the text with a foreword criticizing the government's attempt to stifle debate on the letter, were disciplined and/or brought up on charges.[4] One of the most vocal signatories of the pamphlet, the social psychologist Peter Brückner, had already once been suspended from his teaching position at Hanover Technical University for his alleged support of the RAF. Brückner was accused, among other things, of having sheltered Ulrike Meinhof when she was on the run. In the wake of the Mescalero Affair, on the basis of his refusal to sign a loyalty oath, he was suspended once again and had his salary cut.[5] That Brückner, a fierce critic of the RAF's violence, was demonized in this

---

[4] "Andere Gewalt als Al Capone," *Der Spiegel*, no. 34, August 15, 1977, p. 28.
[5] See Peter Brückner, *Die Mescalero-Affäre: ein Lehrstück für Aufklärung und politische Kultur* (Hanover: Internationalismus Buchladen und Verlagsgesellschaft, 1977).

way is evidence of the extent to which the prolonged terrorist crisis of the 1970s had seen emotion trump reason.[6]

The state response to the Mescalero Affair was no isolated incident, moreover, but merely one in a series of steps over the course of the 1970s in the government's effort to close down the left-publicistic sphere that had begun to open up over a decade earlier. The state's response was rooted in an analysis focusing on alleged support for terrorism in the left scene generally, an analysis that was not without a basis in fact. The Mescalero Affair seemed to provide further proof, if any were needed, that the left in general, and the left-wing publicistic sphere in particular, was a bastion of support for terrorism. To be sure, the RAF was very far from enjoying universal support on the left and was fiercely criticized for carrying out what was increasingly a private war against the government. As the decade progressed, the justification for revolutionary violence was a subject of fierce debate. But, as we will see, the very existence of this debate came too close to support for the government's comfort.

"STOP DUTSCHKE NOW!"

The turn of a portion of the antiauthoritarian movement to violence unfolded in small steps but over a relatively brief period. The signal moments of this radicalization were the murder of Benno Ohnesorg on June 2, 1967, and the assassination attempt against Rudi Dutschke on Thursday, April 11, 1968. Dutschke was shot in the head by the deranged Joseph Bachmann as he stood outside a pharmacy on the Kurfürstendamm, where he had gone to buy medicine for his son Hosea Che. An avid reader of both the Springer Press and the far-right *National Zeitung*, Bachmann expressed hatred for the "Communist Dutschke." It is now known that Bachmann was not only attracted by the anti-Communist rhetoric of the Springer Press or the *National Zeitung* but had active ties to the NPD and other far-right groups, including a neo-Nazi group later involved in bomb attacks.[7] In the wake of the attack, activists were quick to point to the link between Bachmann and the Springer Press. After initially denying that he read Springer papers, Bachmann admitted

---

[6] See the discussion of Brückner's position in Jeremy Varon, *Bringing the War Home: The Weather Underground, the Red Army faction, and Revolutionary Violence in the Sixties and Seventies* (Berkeley, Calif.: University of California Press, 2004), pp. 239–240.

[7] See "Enthüllung durch Stasi-Akte: Dutschke-Attentäter hatte Kontakt zu Neonazis," *Der Spiegel*, December 5, 2009, available at www.spiegel.de/politik/deutschland/enthuellung-durch-stasi-akte-dutschke-attentaeter-hatte-kontakt-zu-neonazis-a-665334.html (accessed March 15, 2012).

that he was a *Bild* reader and claimed to be acting on behalf of all those whose opinions found their expression there.[8] As the Student Council of Göttingen University put it, "in the person of Josef Erwin Bachmann, Springer's demands have found their executioner."[9]

The day following the shooting, when it was widely believed that Dutschke had died in the assault, activists marched on the Springer building in the Kochstraße, trying to storm the building and setting fire to Springer delivery trucks amid cries of "Springer murderers" and "Springer burn."[10] Demonstrators were encouraged in their violence by the police agent provocateur Peter Urbach, who distributed Molotov cocktails. A massive battle between police and demonstrators raged on the Kurfürstendamm. Mass meetings at the Technical University on Saturday saw repeated calls for violence as a response to the attack on Dutschke.[11] Post-assassination riots raged for days afterward around the country. Anti-Springer actions took place in at least twenty other cities, including Frankfurt, Cologne, Essen, Hamburg, and Munich.[12] In massive protests over Easter weekend, the demonstrator Rüdiger Schreck and the Associated Press photographer Klaus Frings were killed in Munich. Despite strong evidence that Schreck's death came at the hands of the police, the press characteristically placed all the blame for the events on the demonstrators.[13]

These events intensified ongoing discussions about the role of violence. The following month, the independent West Berlin "Editorial Collective," formed to contribute to the journal *konkret*, published a major piece dealing with the question of violence. The collective, composed of Rudi Dutschke, Bahman Nirumand, Hans Magnus Enzensberger, Michael Schneider, Peter Schneider, Jürgen Horlemann, Eckhard Siepmann, and Gaston Salvatore, parsed the types of violence that might legitimately be employed, positing the legitimacy of "counterviolence" as a potential response to state- (or press-inspired) violence of the sort that had claimed Ohnesorg, Dutschke, and the others. "Who shot on June 2?" they asked;

---

[8] Thomas, *Protest Movements*, pp. 69–70.

[9] Thomas, *Protest Movements*, p. 170.

[10] Thomas, *Protest Movements*, p. 171.

[11] Thomas, *Protest Movements*, p. 173.	[12] *Ibid.*

[13] Thomas, *Protest Movements*, p. 174. Frings appears to have been killed by a stone coming from the direction of the demonstrators. Neither case has ever been clarified. See "Die 68er: 40 Jahre danach – Zwei vergessene 68er-Opfer," available online at http://web.archive.org/web/20090606003717/www.br-online.de/kultur/gesellschaft/die-68er-40-jahre-danach-DID1202381431011/68er-osterunruhen-klaus-frings-ruediger-schreck-ID1205848656242.xml (accessed March 14, 2012).

We didn't shoot the Shah, but Benno Ohnesorg was shot by the police. Who cast the students as rioters, disturbers of the peace, red fascists, [stormtroopers], as *Polit-Gammler* to millions of readers, and encouraged them not to leave the dirty work to the police alone? It wasn't us who called for violence against persons, but Springer.[14]

Crucially, the collective also grounded the legitimacy of counterviolence in Western capitalist society in the context of the struggles in the Third World, and in the American ghetto, sites where the "permanent violence" of capitalism and especially colonialism was most forcefully felt.[15]

The collective's assertion of the defensive nature of any potential violence practiced by the left was no mere rhetorical strategy. The Springer Press may have blamed violence on demonstrators, but there is ample documentary evidence that, for a surprisingly long time, it was students who were overwhelmingly on the receiving end of violence. Eyewitness accounts collected in connection with June 2, 1967, and with subsequent protests from around the country document this unequivocally. Notwithstanding the facile attempts of a handful of scholars to decontextualize debates about violence – lifting them out of the reality of massive police violence against students in order to insert them into a narrative in which the violence debate seems at best perverse and at worst marks a direct line of continuity with the terrorism of the RAF and other groups – it is clear that the left's attempts to come to grips with the prospect of violence (short of some sort of Gandhian alternative) was one it was forced into by the nature of the state's response to protest.[16]

It is little surprise, in this context, that the "counterviolence" theorized by the Berlin Editorial Collective began to materialize. The extent to which praxis was already outstripping theory was indicated a few months

---

[14] Berliner Redaktionskollektiv, "Gewalt," *konkret*, no. 6, June 1968, pp. 24–28, at p. 26.

[15] Berliner Redaktionskollektiv, "Gewalt," p. 27.

[16] See for example, Wolfgang Kraushaar, "Rudi Dutschke und der bewaffnete Kampf," in Wolfgang Kraushaar and Jan Philipp Reemtsma, *Rudi Dutschke Andreas Baader und die RAF* (Hamburg: Hamburger Edition, 2005). For a trenchant critique of this book and its facile (and highly politicized) assumptions about the links between the 68er movement and the RAF, see Ingrid Gilcher-Holtey, "Transformation by Subversion? The New Left and the Question of Violence," in Davis et al., eds., *Changing the World, Changing the Self*, pp. 155–169. Martin Klimke is correct when he writes, contra Kraushaar: "Although drafted in highly military jargon [in his handwritten notes published verbatim in Lönnendonker et al., *Die antiautoritäre Revolte*] Dutschke's primary aim was not to build up an urban guerilla force, but to implement [Che's foco theory] in his mobilization strategies"; Klimke, *The "Other Alliance,"* p. 67; "[T]he question of violence," writes Ingrid Gilcher-Holtey, cannot be separated from the movement's alternative scheme of order, or from its method to alter society by subversion ("Transformation by Subversion?" p. 157).

later in the so-called "Battle of Tegeler Weg." This street battle, launched on November 4, 1968, in connection with the disciplinary proceedings against Horst Mahler for having taken part in the attack on the Springer building after the assassination attempt against Rudi Dutschke, represented the first time that activists prepared ahead of time to wage battle with the police. Up to 1,000 students, their ranks supplemented for the first time by rockers, outfitted with motorcycle helmets, drove back the police with a fierce attack.[17] This first foray into offensive operations was an unqualified success from the tactical perspective, with 130 police injured compared to only twenty-two activists.[18] The authorities reacted by giving the police new equipment, hard helmets with face shields replacing the old Weimar-era Tschako helmet.[19]

The response to the Battle of Tegeler Weg indicates the variety of opinion in the antiauthoritarian revolt on the question of violence. The Republican Club weighed in on the violence on Tegeler Weg, releasing a statement about it and organizing an open discussion, a transcript of which was subsequently published in *Berliner Extra-Dienst*. The issue addressed the question of whether or not the riots should be seen as a part of the class struggle and tried to come to grips with the meaning of the involvement of new actors who belonged to groups previously unassociated with the APO.[20] That members of the club had taken part in the fighting caused a major disagreement within the Republican Clubs nationwide, leading to debate about whether, in the words of club member Helmut Gollwitzer, the club was supposed to be "an assemblage of the radical democratic left" or a "Trotskyist or whatever other kind of sect."[21]

At the same time, these developments were the product of a larger process via which the rhetoric of violent confrontation transformed itself slowly from symbolic play to reality. Although the antiauthoritarian revolt had largely rejected violence against persons (splitting, however, on the question of violence against property), it was rife from the beginning with symbolic violence, notable especially in the actions of the Kommune I. Actions involving fire – either actual (the burning of the Christmas tree on the Kudamm in December 1966) or symbolic (the "burn" flyers) – or bombs

[17] Baumann, *How It All Began*, p. 48.
[18] Stefan Aust, *Baader-Meinhof: The Inside Story of the RAF* (Oxford University Press, 2009), p. 43.
[19] Aust, *Baader-Meinhof*, p. 43.
[20] *Berliner Extra-Dienst*, December 11, 1968.
[21] Gollwitzer, quoted in "Auf dem Wartebänkchen der Revolution," *Der Spiegel*, no. 52, December 23, 1968.

(the Pudding Attentat of April 1967) were standard items in the repertoire of provocation. More generally, the tactics of direct action (go-ins, etc.) imported from America, particularly where they involved the penetration of privileged spaces (as in Dutschke et al.'s protest in the Kaiser Wilhelm Memorial Church at Christmas 1967), were effective precisely because they provoked conflict, conflict that could by definition easily turn violent. The same was true of those other actions – impersonating police officers, for example – for which violence was, if not an inevitable, certainly a predictable result.

The valorization of the Third World guerrilla struggles, moreover, was rich with violent content. The moral certainty that came with supporting what were seen as freedom-fighting underdogs suffering under the industrial killing might of the USA and other postcolonial powers turned bloodthirstiness into a virtue. Images of violence, from the (increasingly bloody) popular cinema, from reportage on the postcolonial struggles of the Third World or battles between students and police in the capitals of the First, along with the terroristic revolutionary vocabulary adopted from Maoism and elsewhere, combined to create a violent background noise. As the editors of the *Schülerzeitung Der Brocken* put it: "If we speak brutally, it's not down to us, but to the circumstances, which are brutal."[22]

Violent rhetoric, more generally, had a life of its own. It was difficult to rail against oppressors and praise those who struggled against them without being drawn inexorably toward acts of physical resistance. Although nominally a proponent of the traditional distinction in the student movement between violence against persons and violence against property, Dutschke's advocacy of support for the Third World guerrilla struggles in the metropole necessarily entailed an ambiguous attitude toward revolutionary violence. In a joint statement issued in connection with the 1967 annual SDS conference in Frankfurt, Dutschke and Hans-Jürgen Krahl declared that "the propaganda of gunfire in the Third World must be completed by the propaganda of action in the metropole, which historically makes the urbanization of rural guerrilla tactics possible. The urban guerrilla is the quintessential organizer of irregularity for the destruction of the system of repressive institutions."[23]

It is against this background that we must read the aborted attempt by Rudi Dutschke to bomb the antenna mast of the American Armed Forces Radio network in Frankfurt, recently highlighted as evidence of

---

[22] Quoted in "Schülerzeitung Gestern und Heute," *Die Pest*, no. 2, September 1968.
[23] Quoted in Thomas, *Protest Movements*, p. 149.

the violent proclivities of the 68ers.[24] The historian hardly needs to cite this incident, or Dutschke's transporting of unused explosives in his baby's pram, or his alleged plan to travel to Latin America to join the guerrilla struggle, in the prosecutorial yet ultimately speculative detail in which they have recently been treated to conclude that the antiauthoritarian movement was pregnant with the potential for violence from its onset. The willingness to consider violence was woven into the very fabric of the antiauthoritarian revolt, inasmuch as this revolt, as the assault on peaceful demonstrators on June 2, 1967, demonstrated, and as subsequent events reinforced, faced a violent response. Short of a Gandhian commitment to nonviolence, a commitment that, in this case, would have involved turning the other cheek to police batons, and, at its logical extreme, advocating that the Vietnamese and other national liberation movements lay down their arms and submit to imperial demands, counterviolence had inevitably to be on the table. From this perspective, attempts to turn Rudi Dutschke and Andreas Baader into "colleagues" attack a straw man: the either–or question of whether the "terrorists" were also "68ers" (or vice versa) holds less significance for our understanding of the antiauthoritarian revolt in West Germany than it does as an entry in the ongoing war over the politics of memory in Germany.

"IT IS TIME TO DESTROY"

It is true, however, that once the ground for counterviolence was prepared by the realization of the lengths to which the state was willing to go to combat challenges to the status quo, violence could become a project in its own right. In the period after the Battle of Tegeler Weg, as the new radicalized subculture of the Blues took shape in West Berlin, both the rhetorical and actual resort to violence gathered force. Members of this militant subculture had long been in the forefront of the push to break through the psychological barriers against open conflict with the authorities, beginning as early as the Stones riot of 1965. The famous Tiergarten smoke-in of July 1969 was explicitly conceived as a means of preparing for personal and group self-defense, while attempts to defend subcultural hangouts in West Berlin in the summer of 1969 led to serious combat with police involving stones and Molotov cocktails.[25]

---

[24] See the discussion in Kundnani, *Utopia or Auschwitz*.
[25] Reinders and Fritsch, *Die Bewegung 2 Juni*, p. 24.

In the commune in the Wielandstraße, activists supported themselves through bootleg publishing and shoplifting while poring over texts on guerrilla struggle and political violence. Coining slogans such as "It is time to destroy" and "Be high, be free, terror's gotta be," they placed the rhetoric of violence at the heart of countercultural identity. The growth of this violent identity was heavily shaped by drugs. Ingesting massive quantities of hash, marijuana, LSD, STP, mescaline, magic mushrooms, and other drugs, activists created a sort of militant fantasy world. "We blanked out reality," wrote Michael Baumann many years later, "not dissimilar from soldiers before a battle. Drugs and warriordom were always intimately bound together for us ... Back then we wanted to create the New Man. We wanted with drugs to expand our consciousness and penetrate into new spheres."[26] With its combination of drugs, humor, and pop-cultural references, the militancy of the Blues often seemed more like countercultural play run amok than the product of a well-thought-out commitment to political violence. In the event, however, it was to have deadly consequences.

A key jumping-off point in the development of the terror scene was the so-called *Knastcamp* ("clink-camp"), organized for July 1969 in the village of Ebrach near Bamberg. The occasion for the meeting was the imprisonment in Ebrach of the student Reinhard Wetter. Wetter had been involved in a number of colorful actions. In October 1967, he boarded a Munich street car without a ticket to pass out flyers against the rise in transportation fares. In January 1968, he was one of the students who entered classrooms in police uniform to "protect" ex-Nazi professors. The same month he threw a stone at the Greek embassy in protest against the military dictatorship, and a month later he took part in disrupting a ceremony at the Munich Amerikahaus. The initiative for the *Knastcamp* was taken by Wetter's friend Fritz Teufel, who had been living in Munich in the commune "Wacker Einstein," which he had co-founded with Irmgard Möller and others in the waning days of the Kommune I. The event was co-organized by the Rote Hilfe and the SMASH shop in Erlangen. Teufel had already visited Ebrach in May, accompanied by eighty students, but

---

[26] "Ex-Haschrebell Bommi Baumann: 'Meine Kumpels könnten einen Friedhof füllen,'" *Spiegel* online, April 5, 2009, available at www.spiegel.de/kultur/gesellschaft/ex-haschrebell-bommi-baumann-meine-kumpels-koennten-einen-friedhof-fuellen-a-617431.html (accessed March 20, 2012).

had been unable to carry out the plan of smashing in the wooden jail door with a battering ram.[27]

The *Knastcamp*, set to begin on July 15, was to be a more involved affair. Even at this late date, on the cusp of the transition to the terror movement that would consume the lives of a number of the *Knastcamp* participants, the line between hard-political militancy and countercultural fun was blurry in the extreme. The tenor of the affair was captured in the slogan on a flyer advertising the event: "mit dem joint in der hand, revolution auf dem land!" ("with a joint in the hand, revolution in the countryside!").[28] The organizers rented a meadow and arranged food and drink, envisioning a week-long festival ("Red Knast Week") that would make up, as Teufel envisioned it, a sort of "political Woodstock." Events were to include performances by the bands Tangerine Dream and Amon Düül, as well as an assault on the lockup in which Wetter was being held. Forbidden by local authorities from camping in their chosen location, the participants resettled at a nearby lake. In the event, the storming of the jail did not take place, but a group of forty activists led by Dieter Kunzelmann did assault the district office in Bamberg in protest against the camping ban.

Among the 150–200 participants in the *Knastcamp* were a who's who of the radical scene in West Germany, including militants from the Kommune I and the Hash Rebel scene in West Berlin. Clearly visible in the 16mm film of the event by Gerd Conradt and Katrin Seybold are activists such as Dieter Kunzelmann, Fritz Teufel, Tommy Weisbecker, Georg von Rauch, Irmgard Möller, Ina Siepmann, Rolf Heißler, Rolf Pohle, Astrid Proll, Bernward Vesper, Gudrun Ensslin, Andreas Baader, Brigitte Mohnhaupt, and others, many of whom were shortly to go on to play leading roles in groups such as the Tupamaros West-Berlin, the RAF, and Movement 2 June.[29] The mentality behind the camp comes out clearly in the iconography of the announcements, each of which figured a bomb with a burning fuse.[30]

A list of "anarchist terrorists" compiled by the *Verfassungsschutz* in the wake of the *Knastcamp* contained eighteen names, almost all of which

[27] See the account at www.haschrebellen.de/werdet-wild. See also Werner Kohn, *In Bamberg war der Teufel los: K(l)eine 68er Apologie* (Bamberg: Collibri, 1993).
[28] "Kommt zur roten Knast Woche nach Ebrach," in *Der Blues: Gesammelte Texte der Bewegung 2 Juni* (Dortmund: Antiquariat "Schwarzer Stern," 2001), p. 53.
[29] "Wilde Tiere," Rote Knastwoche (1969/1970) (dir. Gerd Conradt and Katrin Seybold).
[30] On Ebrach, see Marco Carini, *Fritz Teufel: Wenn's der Wahrheitsfindung dient* (Hamburg: Konkret Literatur Verlag, 2003), p. 137.

were shortly to be associated with the founding of the Tupamaros West-Berlin, Movement 2 June, or the RAF.[31] The militants were sought under Paragraph 129 (belonging to a criminal organization) and for a bomb attack on the Munich house of the senior prosecutor Wilhelm Lossos, who afterward received a postcard asking if he had "enjoyed the lightning."[32] The attack was carried out by members of the group on their way out of the country on a trip to meet up with terrorist groups in Italy. When this plan misfired, Dieter Kunzelmann, Georg von Rauch, Albert Fichter, Roswitha Conradt, and Ina Siepmann continued on to Jordan, there to receive terrorist training from representatives of the Palestinian Liberation Organization. Siepmann stayed on in Jordan, while Kunzelmann and Teufel returned via Istanbul, Munich, and Frankfurt to Berlin.

Back in Berlin, Teufel and Kunzelmann helped organize the Tupamaros West-Berlin, named after the Uruguayan guerrilla group. The Tupamaros were organized into cells with names such as "Schwarze Ratten" (Black Rats), "Schwarze Front" (Black Front), "Onkel Tupa" (Uncle Tupa), and "Amnestie International" [sic].[33] The group first announced its presence through the attack on the Jewish community center in Berlin on November 10, 1969, coinciding with the anniversary of the Nazi pogrom on the Night of Broken Glass in 1938. This attack, intended as a blow against "Israeli imperialism" in the territories occupied in the 1967 Six Day War, was followed by a whole series of assaults on judges, lawyers, and American and Israeli installations. A parallel group founded by Fritz Teufel, the Tupamaros München, launched a series of Molotov cocktail attacks on state officials, businesses, and a US Army post exchange.[34]

This turn to revolutionary violence – as the "Tupamaros" name suggests and the refocusing of energies from the Vietnam War to the conflict in the Middle East further indicates – was constructed in fundamentally global, transnational terms: global because it based itself on an analysis of imperialism and anticolonial struggle encompassing continents; transnational because it depended on exchanges of radical ideas, texts, and

---

[31] The militants named were Fritz Teufel, Dieter Kunzelmann, Horst Mahler, Irmgard Möller, Brigitte Mohnhaupt, Ina Siepmann, Georg von Rauch, Michael Baumann, Karl Heiz Pawla, and Ulrich Enzensberger; Kriminalpolizei, München, September 18, 1970, "Betreff: Anarchistische Terrorgruppen in München und Berlin," Staatsarchiv München, Pol. Dir. 9846, p. 5. The letter was sent on behalf of the "Provisional Committee for the burning of state's attorneys," *konkret*, no. 17, August 11, 1969, p. 2.

[32] Kriminalpolizei, München, September 18, 1970, "Betreff: Anarchistische Terrorgruppen," p. 5.

[33] Kriminalpolizei, München, September 18, 1970, "Betreff: Anarchistische Terrorgruppen," p. 7.

[34] Kriminalpolizei, München, September 18, 1970, "Betreff: Anarchistische Terrorgruppen," p. 9.

personnel across national borders. The transnational element derived in part from the dovetailing of the aims of West German terrorists with those of Palestinian guerrillas, who found common cause in their antipathy to the state of Israel and/or that state's actions.[35] It had a German–German component as well. The East German Stasi was well informed about the makeup and activities of the left-wing terror scene in the Federal Republic, in no small part because militants leaving from or returning to West Berlin were subject to seizure and interrogation, on more than one occasion giving detailed information to Stasi investigators.[36]

The East German regime provided terrorist groups with varying levels of support, mostly passive but in some cases active.[37] To be sure, East German leaders disapproved of the anarchistic cultural provocation and general nonconformism of groups such as Movement 2 June; but shared goals – opposition to West Germany, the USA, Israel, and so on – generally outweighed such considerations.[38] For their part, West German terrorists regarded the East German state with the same mixed feelings as did the APO as a whole. But with the DDR willing to aid, or at least turn a blind eye to, activities directed against the Federal Republic, the operative principle seems to have been "the enemy of my enemy is my friend."

The attack on the Jewish community center in the Fasanenstraße in November 1969 casts into sharp relief the role of the transnational in the development of West German terrorism. Since Israel's victory and territorial expansion in the 1967 Six-Day War, the traditional philo-Semitism of the West German left was placed into conflict with the anti-imperialist commitments dictating automatic support for guerrilla groups fighting

[35] The Israeli use of napalm came in for special criticism by the West German left; see "Accused: Israels Napalm Krieg," *konkret*, no. 8, August 1967. Simultaneously, the claims of Palestinian guerrillas received more or less unbiased attention; see "Al Fatah – Terroristen oder Partisanen," *konkret*, no. 8, April 8, 1969.

[36] The most famous such case involved Michael "Bommi" Baumann. Arrested by East German border police and interrogated by the Stasi in November 1973, Baumann provided his captors with a wealth of information about the left-wing scene in West Berlin. See Wunschik, "Die Bewegung 2 Juni," p. 1019. A copy of Baumann's Stasi file exists at the Hamburger Institut für Sozialforschung and at the APO-Archiv Berlin.

[37] See, for example, Michael Müller and Andreas Kanonenberg, *Die RAF-Stasi Connection* (Berlin, 1992); Tobias Wunschik, "'Abwehr' und Unterstützung des internationalen Terrorismus: Die Hauptabteilung XXII," in Hubertus Knabe, ed., *West-Arbeit des MfS: Das Zusammenspiel von "Aufklärung" und "Abwehr"* (Berlin: Ch. Links, 1999), pp. 531–561; Martin Jander, "Differenzen im antiimperialistischen Kampf: Zu den Verbindungen des Ministeriums für Staatssicherheit mit der RAF und dem bundesdeutschen Linksterrorismus," in Kraushaar, ed., *Die RAF und der linke Terrorismus*, vol. II pp. 696–713.

[38] See Martin Jander, "Vereint gegen Israel? Die DDR und der westdeutsche Linksterrorismus," *Deutschland Archiv*, no. 3 (2008), pp. 416–422. See also Wunschik, "Die Bewegung 2 Juni," p. 1017.

occupations around the world. The bombing of the Jewish community center was by no means typical of the approach of the left as a whole to the Israel–Palestine conflict. It did, however, represent one logical extrapolation from the left's more general anti-imperialism. The bomb supplied by a government agent and laid by Tilman Fichter's younger brother Albert, plied with LSD and hectored into the deed by Dieter Kunzelmann, happily failed to detonate. But the timing of the attack, taken in context with Kunzelmann's apparent tendency to conflate the state of Israel with "the Jews," suggests that, for Kunzelmann at least, the line between anti-Zionism and anti-Semitism could be rather thin. The journalist Alex Gross, who spent significant time with Kunzelmann in the days of the Kommune I, recalls that Kunzelmann "went further than being merely party-line correct in his anti-Zionism – he was even rather outspokenly anti-Semitic, which was unusual among German students during the Sixties."[39]

For Kunzelmann, by this stage, as Gross and other writers have pointed out, the Nazi extermination of the Jews was simply no longer relevant; or, more accurately, it was relevant primarily as a psychological "hang-up" that could prevent a new generation of Germans from dealing with the facts of "imperialism" in the Middle East.[40] But the bombing of the Jewish community center was not the only indication of where anti-imperialist logic could ultimately lead. As early as 1972, Ulrike Meinhof penned a celebration of the murder of Israeli athletes at the Munich Olympics from her prison cell, accusing Israel, in a tortured Holocaust metaphor, of having sent its own athletes to the ovens as "fuel for [its] imperialist politics of extermination."[41] When, in the 1976 hijacking of an Air France jet, members of the Revolutionary Cells, in a grim replay of the death-camp selection process, separated Israeli from non-Israeli passengers, the dark path down which anti-Zionism could potentially lead became all too apparent.[42] Far from demonstrating the power of the National Socialist past to trump all other considerations, however, as in some oversimplified accounts, these incidents represented the power of

[39] Gross, *The Untold Sixties*, p. 266.

[40] Dieter Kunzelmann, "Brief aus Amman," *Agit 883*, no. 4, November 7, 1969, p. 5.

[41] Ulrike Meinhof, "Zur Strategie des antiimperialistischen Kampfes," November 1972, in Martin Hoffmann, ed., *Rote Armee Fraktion: Texte und Materialen zur Geschichte der RAF* (Berlin: ID-Verlag, 1997), p. 151.

[42] For an approach to the question of "left-wing anti-Semitism" with a helpful review of the literature, see Knud Andresen, "Linker Antisemitismus: Wandlungen in der Alternativbewegung," in Reichardt and Siegfried, eds., *Das Alternative Milieu*, pp. 146–168.

global-contemporary commitments to trump local-historical ones.[43] As a justification of the attack on the Jewish community center published in *Agit 883* put it, the bombing was not to be mistaken for the work of right-wing radicals, but seen as a decisive link [in the forging of] international socialist solidarity."[44]

The transition to outright terrorism pushed the debate on violence into a new register. Previously revolving around the necessity of self-defense against the police or the (somewhat tendentious) distinction between violence against property and violence against persons, the debate now came to center on the necessity for revolutionary violence that was already taking place. This debate was centered in the radical-left milieus out of which the terror groups had been hatched. In West Berlin, the RAF and Movement 2 June defined two poles of the urban guerrilla movement, the former adhering closely to an authoritarian Marxist-Maoist model, the latter representing an antiauthoritarian, anarchist-inspired alternative. In both groups, members went underground and fought until killed or captured. In Frankfurt, the Revolutionary Cells operated according to an alternative model via which anonymous members tried to avoid going underground, maintaining contact through a loose network of cells and staying in their normal lives as long as possible. A spin-off of the Revolutionary Cells, Rote Zora, added a feminist twist to the armed struggle movement from 1974. In all cases, the resort of a minority to "armed struggle" forced the radical-left majority onto the defensive, forcing them to choose between (often critical) analysis of the terrorists' actions and the demands of solidarity with terrorism against a state for which they had no love, no matter how much they might disagree, either on moral or tactical grounds.

The pressures of solidarity, indeed, played a role in the very founding of the RAF. After going on the lam in the wake of the arson trial of October 1968, Andreas Baader and Gudrun Ensslin fled to Paris, where they holed up for a time in the apartment of the leftist writer Regis Debray before moving on to Italy. In late February 1970, the two showed up at the door of Ulrike Meinhof in Berlin. Moving into a separate apartment, they rejected an offer by Dieter Kunzelmann to join his Tupamaros West-Berlin, deciding instead to join an urban guerrilla group being founded by

---

[43] Examples of the popularizing overemphasis on the National Socialist past are Kundnani, *Utopia or Auschwitz* and Jillian Becker's execrable *Hitler's Children: Story of the Baader-Meinhof Terrorist Gang* (London: Michael Joseph, 1977).

[44] "Schalom + Napalm," *Agit 883*, no. 40, November 13, 1969, p. 9.

attorney Horst Mahler. This nascent RAF (the use of the name was still a little ways off), included Baader, Ensslin, and Mahler, as well as Mahler's secretary Monika Berberich, a nineteen-year-old hairdresser named Petra Schelm, her boyfriend the Bundeswehr deserter Manfred Grashof, and Astrid Proll, the sister of Thorwald Proll. (The latter had been ditched by Baader and Ensslin in Strasbourg before their trip to visit Meinhof in Berlin.) Subsequent members of the "first generation" were to include Holger Meins, Jan-Carl Raspe, Ingrid Schubert, Christa Eckes, Angela Luther, and Thomas Weissbecker. On April 4, Baader was arrested at a police roadblock and jailed. Spurred by Ensslin, who helped concoct an escape plan involving a fake "book deal" that would allow the journalist Meinhof to meet with the prisoner Baader, Meinhof agreed to cross the Rubicon, converting words into deeds. Arriving to meet with Baader at the reading room of the German Central Institute for Social Questions in the Miquelstraße 83 (the scholarly scientific imperative as well as the state's measured judgment glaringly at work in both the nature of the ruse and the government's accommodating posture toward it), Meinhof and her accomplices sprang him instead, shooting and seriously wounding security guard Georg Linke in the process.

In the wake of the action, the group published the first communiqué referring to itself as the Rote Armee Fraktion, although the mainstream press preferred the more sensational "Baader–Meinhof Gang." In June, members of the group snuck into East Berlin and traveled from there on to Jordan, where they trained with Palestinian commandos. The culture clash between the young German libertines and their culturally conservative Palestinian hosts – the latter nonplussed, among other things, by the sight of sunbathing bare-breasted German revolutionary women – produced enough tension that the group decided to return to West Berlin. Here, it began to prepare its first series of actions, beginning with two simultaneous bank robberies in Kassel on January 15. In April, the group published its theoretical platform, "Das Konzept Stadtguerilla" ("The Urban Guerilla Concept"), which was heavily indebted to the Brazilian revolutionary Carlos Marighella's *Minimanual of the Urban Guerilla*, published in Germany for the first time the previous May.

Around the same time, the RAF shifted its primary base of operations from West Berlin to Frankfurt. Its campaign resonated more strongly in the former city than in the latter, however. The freeing of Baader prompted an initial surge of solidarity in the West Berlin scene, centered in particular on the journal *Agit 883*. In June 1970, the editorship was taken over by a group calling itself the "Communist Rebels," which included soon-to-be

RAF member Holger Meins.[45] The new editorial collective published the founding communiqué of the RAF–"Build a Red Army"–on June 2 and continued to offer support in the face of intensified police pressure. Meins, who had already helped to kindle the fires of revolutionary violence with his *The Making of a Molotov Cocktail* film of February 1968, had continued to fan the flames with his graphic work for *883*. This famously included a widely seen poster, "Freedom for All Prisoners," in which the names of the world's armed rebel groups (the Vietcong, the Japanese Zengakuren, the American Black Panthers and Weathermen, the Palestinian El Fatah, the Brazilian MR8 [Movimento Revolucionário 8 de Outubro], Chilean MIR [Movimiento de Izquierda Revolucionaria], and the Algerian Front de Libération Nationale) formed the petals of a flower whose central disk held a hand grenade. A striking example of the global conception at the heart of the "armed struggle" movement, the image was carried by militants in the May Day 1970 demonstration in West Berlin and was left at the scene of a bombing in Berlin-Lichterfelde that destroyed part of the facility of American company IBM.[46]

In Frankfurt, where the "Building War" was in full swing and where groups such as Revolutionary Struggle were sucking up much of the militant oxygen, the urban guerrilla strategy of the RAF was initially less attractive. From 1972, however, RAF sympathizers in Frankfurt began to found the Revolutionary Cells, while in West Berlin the Movement 2 June was created out of the Tupamaros/Blues milieu. The latter group, founded in the wake of the shooting death of Hash Rebel Georg von Rauch, announced its presence in May 1972 with the bombing of the British Yacht Club in West Berlin. The bombing, which accidently killed a sixty-six-year-old German boatbuilder (the bomb failed to explode in the middle of the night as allegedly intended) was carried out in support of the Irish Republican Army, then locked in an increasingly bloody struggle with the British. The RAF spent most of 1971 robbing banks, in some cases with fatal consequences, and avoiding police roadblocks, sometimes with attendant shoot-outs. The following year, the group upped the ante, embarking on its so-called May Offensive. Launched in protest against US actions in Vietnam, it included the bombing of the US Army 5th

---

[45] Knud Andresen, Markus Mohr, and Hartmut Rübner, "Unruhe in der Öffentlichkeit: Agit 883 zwischen Politik, Subkultur und Staat," in Rotaprint 25, eds., *Agit 883*, pp. 17–44, at pp. 33–34.

[46] Zahl recalls that when the detective discovered the poster in the *883* premises, he grinned and, in a wry statement of the gulf separating the worldviews of left-wing radicals and their adversaries, said: "That must also apply to the prisoners in Russia"; Peter Paul Zahl, "This Is the End My Friend," in Conradt, ed., *Starbuck*, pp. 114–117, at p. 114.

Corps Headquarters in Frankfurt, police headquarters in Augsburg and Munich, the Springer building in Hamburg, and the headquarters of the US Army in Europe in Heidelberg, among other targets. This series of attacks was followed very closely by the arrest and incarceration of the group's key members and the launching of a second generation of the RAF to take their place.

From here, the RAF's campaigns began to revolve less around the original issues that had motivated the group than around attempts to free the imprisoned first generation. Punctuated by hunger strikes, the private war between the terrorists and the government was marked by a grim tit-for-tat in which revenge actions became the order of the day. In November 1974, in response to the death by starvation of Holger Meins, Movement 2 June murdered Günter von Drenkmann in a botched kidnapping attempt. The following February, Peter Lorenz, the CDU candidate for mayor of Berlin, was kidnapped by Movement 2 June and freed in exchange for the release of prisoners. In the spring and summer of 1975, the actions planned by the German terrorists became steadily more international in focus. In April 1975, militants seized the West German embassy in Stockholm, executing two hostages before accidently blowing themselves up with their own bomb. In December, Red Cells member Hans-Joachim Klein took part in the raid on the OPEC (Organization of the Petroleum Exporting Countries) conference in Vienna, Austria, led by the infamous Carlos the Jackal.

The swell of violence reached its apogee in the events of 1977. The assassination of Siegfried Buback in April – justified as a response to the deaths of Holger Meins, Siegfried Hausner and Ulrike Meinhof – took place during the closing phases of the trial of Baader, Ensslin, and Raspe, who were convicted on April 28, 1977. The murder of the banker Jürgen Ponto on July 30, 1977, marked the beginning of the German Autumn, a paroxysm of violence that saw the kidnapping and murder of Hanns-Martin Schleyer, the President of the Confederation of German Employers' Associations, the hijacking of the Lufthansa jet "Landshut" by a Palestinian terror squad, and the mass suicide of the RAF inmates in Stammheim prison after hearing news of the successful commando assault on the hijackers in Mogadishu, Somalia.

"THE BÖLLS ARE WORSE THAN BAADER–MEINHOF"

The first major wave of terror attacks, the RAF's May Offensive of 1972, met with near universal condemnation on the left. Prior to this, the RAF had received the benefit of the doubt from many in the radical scene, who shared important aspects of the RAF's critique of the West German establishment. A poll published by the Allensbach Institute in July 1971 revealed that one in five West Germans under the age of thirty felt "a certain sympathy" for the RAF. Five percent of the respondents admitted that they would harbor a member of the RAF, with another nine percent responding that they would consider doing so. Even then, the RAF's actual supporters numbered a few thousand at most.[47] The shift from avoiding capture to acts of spectacular and deadly violence, however, effected a decisive shift in attitudes. Not only did the attacks provoke fear and anger in the general public, they also caused the left to "sharpen ... its objections to a program of violence that now included planned political murder and, if unintentionally, injuries to civilians."[48]

In two major conferences in May and June 1972, West German leftists expressed, in Jeremy Varon's words, a "near unanimous" condemnation of the RAF.[49] This condemnation remained somewhat tempered, however, by a reluctance to violate the principle of solidarity, which seemed to dictate that, even when the RAF's actions were wrong for either tactical or moral reasons, to condemn them too outwardly risked placing one on the side of the forces with whom the left had long been in conflict.[50] It was very easy, in this context, for the state and the establishment to posit the figure of the "sympathizer," who, while not directly involved with the RAF, nevertheless lent it at least moral support. The discourse of sympathizers came to occupy a central position in the discursive battle over terrorism in the Federal Republic.

The term and concept was sufficiently vague, however, as to admit to any definition the authorities wished to give it. As Hanno Balz observes, a "sympathizer" was not simply someone willing to provide material aid to the RAF or other groups but someone who failed to distance themselves strongly enough from terrorism or who made arguments (e.g. against state

---

[47] In polls taken in 1971, a quarter of West Germans under the age of thirty expressed sympathy with the RAF, while fourteen percent of the population overall declared a willingness to aid the RAF with shelter or other support; Hauser, "Terrorism," p. 272.

[48] Varon, *Bringing the War Home*, pp. 212–213.

[49] Varon, *Bringing the War Home*, p. 213.

[50] As Dorothea Hauser writes, the RAF "played on the ambivalent sentiments of a broad radical leftist milieu that did not necessarily embrace terrorist acts as a means to further the revolutionary cause, but in its fundmental opposition to a democratic system despised as 'fascist' still felt obliged to a certain solidarity which ranged from – often critical – sympathy to practical support." Hauser, "Terrorism," pp. 270–271.

repression) similar to those made by terrorists.[51] The empirical useless-
ness of the term was captured by *Der Spiegel* at the height of the German
Autumn:

> Everybody is a sympathizer who is called one. The term ... cannot distinguish
> between supporters of violence and those who call themselves "critics of the sys-
> tem" or think of themselves as "revolutionary" but oppose violence. And it does
> not distinguish between those who sympathize with terrorism and those who
> doubt the legality of how the state reacts to terrorism.[52]

Jeremy Varon perceptively captures the significance of the sympathizer
when he writes that, in the imagination of his or her critics, the sympathizer had "neither fully assimilated democratic values nor been properly
integrated into the norms of the postwar state. The sympathizer was thus
an internal other, a shadowy expression of the failure of the West German
state to command the basic allegiance of its citizens and complete the
desired evolution toward democracy."[53]

The imprecision of the term, or perhaps more properly its flexibility as
a tool for stamping out opinions inconvenient to the government, stands
out clearly in the establishment response to any attempt on the left to
encourage a nuanced approach toward the terrorism problem. As early as
January 1972, even before the first major wave of RAF bombings, the novelist Heinrich Böll unleashed a firestorm when he suggested in an article
in *Der Spiegel* that the Springer Press exaggerated the danger of the RAF
and in fact helped to perpetuate it. Criticizing what he called the RAF's
"war against society," Böll nevertheless argued that Meinhof should be
offered an amnesty.[54] The predictable backlash saw Böll branded as a sympathizer and sympathizers in general conflated with the terrorists they
supposedly aided. As the right-wing tabloid *Quick* put it: "The Bölls are
worse than Baader–Meinhof."[55] These other "Bölls" – intellectuals such
as Peter Brückner, Günter Grass, Kurt Scharf, Helmut Gollwitzer, or
Heinrich Albertz – faced charges of sympathizing with the RAF, even
though they held impeccable democratic credentials, uncategorically

[51] Hanno Balz, "Der 'Sympathisanten'-Diskurs im 'Deutschen Herbst'," in Klaus Weinhauer, ed.,
Terrorismus in der Bundesrepublik (Frankfurt: Campus, 2006), p. 320.
[52] "Mord beginnt beim bösen Wort I," *Der Spiegel*, no. 41, October 3, 1977, p. 28.
[53] Varon, *Bringing the War Home*, pp. 257–258.
[54] Heinrich Böll, "Will Ulrike Gnade oder freies Geleit?" *Der Spiegel*, no. 3, January 10, 1972,
p. 54.
[55] Quoted in *Der Spiegel*, no. 4, January 17, 1972, p. 118.

rejected violence, and backed even further away from the RAF than they already were after the first major wave of terrorist attacks in May 1972.[56]

The conservative and establishment response to this episode represents an early entry in the argument that terrorists and the left-wing milieu from which they sprang were one and the same, a position that continues to the present day. Friedrich Vogel of the CDU made an emblematic statement of this case, claiming that "terrorists move[d] like fish in the water of the left-affiliated parties."[57] In the aftermath of Movement 2 June's murder of court president Günter von Drenkmann in November 1974, Franz-Josef Strauß accused even the parliamentary delegations of the SPD and FDP of harboring terrorist sympathizers.[58] In the wake of the Buback obituary, the sympathizer discourse entered a hysterical new key. The forty-eight professors and teachers who weighed in in favor of a more nuanced reading of the text were widely criticized and smeared as sympathizers in the right-wing press.[59] The murder of Hanns-Martin Schleyer and the Lufthansa hijacking in the fall of 1977 intensified this discourse. For Bernhard Vogel, the CDU minister president of Nordrhein-Westfalen, simply referring to the RAF as the "Baader–Meinhof Group" instead of the "Baader–Meinhof Gang" was enough to reveal one as a terrorist.[60] Professors, students, student organizations, and the universities themselves were criticized as breeding grounds of terrorism, with the Buback obituary representing exhibit A that proved that higher education was a hotbed of sedition.[61]

One of the key weapons in the government's legislative war against the left was the Decree on Radicals in Public Service, the so-called *Berufsverbot* (Ban on Careers) as it was known on the left. Passed in January 1972, the decree was a joint project of the SPD and CDU/CSU. Not a new law per se but an attempt to codify and systematize existing laws, the decree required that all public servants – a category that included teachers, lawyers, and many other professions – uphold the West German Basic Law both publicly and privately. Actions deemed suspicious by the government were grounds for denying employment or for dismissal from current employment. As Axel Schildt has pointed out, the timing of the

---

[56] "Mord beginnt beim bösen Wort V," *Der Spiegel*, no. 46, November 7, 1977, p. 36.
[57] "Zucker vor der Hoftür," *Der Spiegel*, no. 25, June 12, 1972, p. 31.
[58] "Den Rechtsstaat retten: blödes Zeug," *Der Spiegel*, no. 11, March 10, 1975, p. 19.
[59] Clemens Kaupa, "The Multi-Causal and Asynchronous Development of Terrorism Laws in Germany from the 1970s to the Present," Diplomarbeit, University of Vienna, 2009, p. 13.
[60] "Mord beginnt beim bösen Wort I," *Der Spiegel*, no. 41, October 3, 1977, p. 28.
[61] On the terrorism and sympathizer debates and their effects, see Karrin Hanshew, *Terror and Democracy in West Germany* (Cambridge University Press, 2012).

decree had much to do with Willy Brandt's desire to mollify conservatives angered by his policy of rapprochement with East Germany.[62] But the law was equally an attempt to "drain the swamp" of the sympathizer scene while limiting the influence of the new left-wing parties, especially the *K-Gruppen* and the DKP.

Despite its stated intentions, the decree very quickly turned into a blunt instrument deployed not only against Communists but also potentially against any sort of political nonconformist, including persons who had previously engaged in activities such as protesting the Emergency Laws.[63] In the year following the decree,

> screenings of applicants and of public servants became an all-embracing operation. In October 1973 alone, 64,800 applicants were screened in Baden-Württemberg, and 55 of them were rejected with the agreement of the *Radikalenerlass*. All in all, 3.5 million persons (applicants and public servants) were screened, 2,250 were barred from application, and 2,000 to 2,100 public servants were subject to disciplinary proceedings, of which 256 were dismissed … From the very beginning, critics complained that in practice leftists were almost exclusively affected. In total, Braunthal reports that at least 92% of the barred applicants were leftists.[64]

The Action Committee against the *Berufsverbot* at the Free University Berlin published a collection of documents laying out the effects of the ban on individuals in education, medicine, social services, and the judiciary. One applicant was denied employment in the civil service for having taken part in a demonstration against the Pinochet dictatorship in Chile organized by a group with ties to the SEW. Another woman was denied employment as a teacher on the basis of, among other things, having previously been a member of the Communist-affiliated League against Imperialism. Yet another teacher was laid off on the basis of the claim that she had belonged to the SEW, a charge she forcefully denied. These and other cases detailed in the pamphlet highlighted the fundamentally arbitrary nature of the *Berufsverbot*, revealing its character as a thinly veiled attack on political nonconformism.[65]

---

[62] Axel Schildt, "'Die Kräfte der Gegenreformation sind in breiter Form angetreten': Zur konservativen Tendenzwende in den Siebzigerjahren," *Archiv für Sozialgeschichte*, 44 (2004), p. 467; see also Frank Fischer, "Von der 'Regierung der inneren Reformen' zum 'Krisenmanagement'," *Archiv für Sozialgeschichte*, 44 (2004): 398.

[63] "Charakter offenbart," *Der Spiegel*, no. 28, July 7, 1975, p. 21.

[64] Kaupa, "The Multi-Causal and Asynchronous Development of Terrorism Laws," p. 73.

[65] Aktionskomitte gegen Berufsverbote and Komitee zur Verteidigung Demokratischer Grundrechte, *Überprüfung der Politischen Treuepflicht. Berufsverbot Dokumente IV* (Berlin: Freien Universität Berlin, 1976).

Subsequent measures tightened the noose further. These include changes in 1976 to the criminal code making it a crime to form, support, or promote a "terrorist" organization (§129a); to produce or disseminate texts glorifying violence (§130a); or to advocate or approve of criminal offenses against the constitution (§88a). As more than one scholar has observed, a measure such as §129a went far beyond normal legal practice to allow the police to arrest persons whether they were actually involved in criminal actions or not.[66] Similarly, §88a, in proscribing every phase of publicistic activity from creation to distribution, and everything in between, stretched the definition of the criminal far beyond its normal boundaries. Like the *Berufsverbot*, these measures became tools for the state's attempt to police conscience and to quash the left-wing public sphere that had accompanied the rise of the antiauthoritarian revolt from its beginning. It is little surprise, for example, that the very first application of §88a involved raids on left-wing bookstores accused of selling terrorist texts or that subsequent applications of this and other judicial measures targeted left-wing publishers and printers.[67]

Two celebrated cases demonstrate the lengths to which the authorities were willing to go to control the left-wing public sphere. The first involved the publication of former terrorist Michael Baumann's *Wie alles anfing* (*How It All Began*) by Munich's Trikont Verlag. Baumann, an original Hash Rebel and founding member of the Movement 2 June, came to sour on the urban guerrilla project. His memoir, published in 1975, represented a leave-taking from the movement but was far from an unambiguous piece of turncoat literature. Describing in feverish and imaginative detail the path that had led him from the workplace to the commune to the violent underground, Baumann gave an unprecedented look into the mindset of the radical scene. Baumann decisively criticized the continued violence of the urban guerrilla groups, even pleading in *Der Spiegel* for comrades to "throw away the gun."[68] In a raid of Trikont's offices in November 1975, authorities confiscated some 1,600 books, the printing plates for *How It All Began*, and the press's business records.[69] Trikont responded by reprinting the book and waging a fierce public-relations campaign justifying its importance. An international group of some 300 left-wing writers and publishers weighed in to protest this obvious case of

---

[66] See Varon, *Bringing the War Home*, p. 256.

[67] Varon, *Bringing the War Home*, p. 262.

[68] "Freunde, schmeißt die Knarre weg," *Der Spiegel*, no. 7, February 2, 1974.

[69] "Polizeiaktion gegen den Trikont Verlag," in *Dokumentation über die Beschlagnahme von Literatur!* (Trikont-Verlag, undated), pp. 2–4. Papiertiger Archiv, Berlin.

censorship, seeing to the publication of a new edition of the book. Writer Heinrich Böll's claim was characteristic: that rather than being confiscated the book should be made widely available and should be widely discussed.[70]

An even more striking case of censorship was the case of a group of printers from the Agitdruck collective in Berlin-Steglitz. The "Agitdrucker," as they became known – Jutta Werth, Gerdi Foß, Martin Beikirch, and Henning Weyer – became a cause célèbre on the left, living examples of the extent to which the government had used the excuse of terrorism to silence voices it did not wish to hear. The Agitdruck Verlag was a leading press of the undogmatic left in Berlin. It had been founded, like so many other presses, in response to the large number of left-wing groups looking for an outlet for their political writings. From 1974, Agitdruck printed the *Info Berliner Undogmatischer Gruppen* (*InfoBUG*). A weekly with a wide circulation outside West Berlin, *InfoBUG* (sometimes also known as *BUG-Info*), was a key organ of the undogmatic left. Supplying information on events and protests, it was a critical forum for discussion of issues affecting the left-wing scene.

State action against Agitdruck began in the spring of 1975 with the confiscation of issues of *InfoBUG*. Further confiscations followed in 1976. Legal action began in February of 1977, ending with the arrest of Werth, Foß, Weyer, and Beikirch in October of that year on charges of supporting terrorism. The raid on *InfoBUG* and Agitdruck took place amid police raids on left-wing bookstores throughout Berlin. Fifty warrants were issued against the largely unknown publishers and contributors of *InfoBUG*. The four arrested, two of whom no longer even worked with the press, were targets of opportunity – they were the only ones who the authorities could lay their hands upon. The raids took place on the basis of §§88a and 129a. For having published communiqués from the Revolutionary Cells, Movement 2 June, and the RAF over a period of months in 1977, the defendants were accused of being part of the West Berlin sympathizer scene and thereby helping to create a psychological climate conducive to terrorism.[71]

The trial, which began in June 1978, lasted over seven months. The Action Committee against the *Berufsverbot* at the Free University deemed

---

[70] Heinrich Böll, "Stimme aus dem Untergrund," *konkret*, no. 2, 1976, p. 206.
[71] "Agit-druck kollektive, 22: Mai Aktionstag für die Agit-Drucker," Hoover Institution, Notgemeinschaft für eine freie Universität, box 575, folder 22. The printing of such materials coincided with the arrival of the three defendants in the collective.

it a "far-reaching danger to opinion and press freedom" in the Federal Republic. Pointing out that *InfoBUG* had only printed things that mainstream papers such as the *FAZ*, the *Tagesspiegel*, and *Die Welt* had also published, they argued that it was really opinion that was being punished.[72] One of the defendant's attorneys got into trouble for saying much the same thing.[73] Leftists and liberals criticized the conditions of imprisonment, including solitary confinement, which had left defendant Jutta Werth in a state of "psychic exhaustion." Werth was deemed only partly fit to stand trial, and even a court official spoke out in her support.[74]

The Tübingen professor Walter Jens appeared on behalf of the defendants, arguing that it was misleading to seize on individual articles in *InfoBUG* in a way that made the publishers look like terrorist sympathizers. *InfoBUG*, he argued, was characterized by "open discussion, pronounced contradictions, a wide spectrum of left-[opinion], and self-irony."[75] Although many opinions expressed in the paper were "cynical and inhuman," many more criticized terrorist violence. Given its lack of central editorship, he argued, *InfoBUG* should be seen more as a "collection of letters to the editor" than a periodical with a uniform message.[76] Two representatives of the Verband Deutscher Schriftsteller attending the trial were forced to write their criticism of it as individuals and not as representatives of the organization, after the latter came into conflict over the question with the Gewerkschaft Druck und Papier (Printing and Paper Union) to which it belonged.[77] In Frankfurt, a similar case developed around the Fantasia printing collective. Printers Doris Braune and Dorit Brücher were arrested in May 1978, accused of supporting criminal organizations for having printed hunger-strike declarations of imprisoned terrorists.

"COME WITH US, SAID THE DONKEY, WE'LL FIND SOMETHING BETTER THAN DEATH EVERYWHERE"

The overheated environment of the Federal Republic in the high period of left-wing terrorism increasingly resulted in a tendency toward dropping out as a means of escape from an increasingly intolerable situation. The

---

[72] Aktionskomitte gegen Berufsverbote an den freie Universität, "Erklärung zum Prozess gegen die Agit-Drucker," Hoover Institution, Notgemeinschaft für eine freie Universität, box 575, folder 22.

[73] "Verfahren gegen Drucker-Anwalt," *Der Tagesspiegel*, February 27, 1979.

[74] "Angeklagte im Agit-Drucker Prozeß nur beschränkt Verhandlungsfähig," *Der Tagesspiegel*, June 20, 1978.

[75] "Walter Jens im Drucker-Prozeß," *Der Tagesspiegel*, November 17, 1978.

[76] *Ibid.*

[77] "Agit-Drucker aus Haft entlassen," *Der Tagesspiegel*, July 14, 1978.

back to the land movement was one expression of this impulse, although even here the pressures of "sympathy" worked their influence. The first issue of the eponymous newspaper of the Päang Commune outside Nuremberg, for example, bore the logo of the nascent RAF, a subsequent cover demanding the release of the imprisoned Gudrun Ensslin.

In keeping with the general view that the eclipse of the APO in late 1968 had signaled the death knell of the utopian hopes of the 1960s, the turn of the decade saw attempts to find ways forward not just by staking out new terrains of personal and collective fulfillment in rural communes or urban *Wohngemeinschaften* but in the turn to New Age spirituality, Eastern mysticism, and other esoteric traditions. By the time of the German Autumn, this trend was in full swing. Characteristic of the turn was the decision of the Trikont publishing house, fresh from its battle with the authorities over the publication of Michael Baumann's *How It All Began*, to shift its publishing program from a political one to one focusing almost exclusively on Taoism, Buddhism, and other Eastern esoterica.

The move away from open political struggle per se did not, however, signal a complete breach with the concerns of the antiauthoritarian revolt. On the contrary, key currents in the turning away from the violent struggle between the armed groups and the state had less to do with a rejection of politics than with a re-envisioning of the nature of politics and the terms in which it was carried out. This re-envisioning entailed an emphasis on the cultural-productive aspects of the antiauthoritarian revolt, an emphasis that, as we have seen, ran through the revolt from its inception. It also heralded a tipping of the scales in the direction of individual over collective liberation, in the sense not that the collective was abandoned but that it was reimagined in a fresh way. The attempt to escape the either – or straitjacket imposed by the war between the state and its terrorist opponents was, in this sense, not an abandoning of the political but an attempt to reclaim an agency that allowed for a better fit between the political and the personal.

This trend was codified in the name of the TUNIX ("Do Nothing") Congress held in West Berlin in February 1978. The Congress was organized by members of the Sponti scene as a response to the German Autumn and the splintering of the left that was both its cause and its result. Modeled on the conference against repression that took place in Bologna, Italy, in September of the previous year, the Congress attracted an estimated 20,000 attendees from around the world. Its goal was to reconstitute the left out of the dual shadow cast by the terrorism of the RAF and the state repression directed against it. "We no longer want to do the same job, see the same faces over and over again," read the congress announcement; "They have bossed us around enough, have censored our thoughts and ideas, checked our apartments and passports, and bashed us in the face. We will no longer let ourselves be bottled up, made small, and made the same."[78]

The TUNIX Congress aimed at codifying and making explicit a desired transition from protest to creativity:

For years we have believed that things could be changed by actions under the motto "away with" and "down with," if only one tried at it hard enough. Our fantasy was mangled, euthanized, or shattered. Instead of, like always, engaging at this traditional level of resistance, this time we want not only to talk about new forms of resistance, but practice them in the course of our gathering. We want to develop new ideas for a new struggle, that we ourselves decide upon, and not let ourselves be forced by the technicians of "Modell Deutschland."[79]

Uniting Spontis, hippies, counterculturalists of every stripe, ecological and antinuclear activists – in short, all the multiple shades of the undogmatic left – TUNIX posited both an ending and a new beginning.

The TUNIX Congress was cast in terms of a journey – a trip out of a West Germany dominated by a no-longer-tolerable environment: "We decorate our dream-ship with the most colorful flags and sail with them to the South – to TUNIX."[80] Yet the Congress was by no means simply an effort at escape. Much more, it was an attempt to regain agency, to upset stifling categories of thought and action imposed both from outside the scene (by the government and media) and from within (by those for whom all-or-nothing revolutionary logics – of the proletarian revolution, of armed struggle – had come to dominate all other considerations). "The mood in the scene in those days," remembers organizer Diethard Küster, "was at a low. The RAF assassinations had led to more repression and pressure to conform. The *K-Gruppen* in the universities were in a crisis of meaning and purpose. And the Spontis, they hung around depressed in the bars or played football."[81] The idea for the festival was launched in December 1977 in the Abrosius pub, near the Tiergarten where Küster and his friends played football [soccer] every Saturday afternoon. "It was meant to be a farewell," he says, "a noisy festival of the utopians … The name TUNIX expressed the life-feeling of many students, for whom

---

[78] "Aufruf zur Reise Nach Tunix," Green Library, Stanford University, Germany. Extraparliamentary Opposition movement, 1967–1984 collection, MO613, box 35.
[79] *Ibid.*   [80] *Ibid.*
[81] Diethard Küster, interviewed in "Tunix-Kongress: Am Strand von Utopia," *Der Tagesspeigel*, January 27, 2008.

work was a synonym for the deprivation of freedom."[82] But the festival was not just a farewell; rather, it was seen as a vehicle for new, positive initiatives. The theme of rebirth was captured in the slogan of the movement, drawn from the Bremer Stadtmusikanten (Town Musicians of Bremen): "Come with us, said the donkey, we'll find something better than death everywhere."[83]

The organizers were shocked by the response, with thousands registering for the congress over the holiday break. Figures such as the French philosopher Michel Foucault, the German writer and undercover journalist Günter Wallraff, and the radical lawyer and future Green politician Christian Ströbele signed on for the event. Up to 20,000 people attended the congress, which took place from January 27 to January 29, 1978. Events included a podium discussion on "The Theory of Two Cultures" ("Mescalero-mentality: Culture versus Subculture") with Peter Brückner, Daniel Cohn-Bendit, President of the Free University Lämmert, SPD official Glotz, and "three representatives of the subcultural scene"; a discussion of Jean-François Lyotard's influential book *The Patchwork of Minorities*; a panel on self-administered youth centers with representatives of the Georg von Rauch Haus; panels on city district work; "psychiatry and anti-psychiatry"; the alternative press and left-wing bookselling; "homosexual autonomy theory"; and various ecological themes. Urgent contemporary issues in the left-wing scene – the "murders" in Stammheim; the *Berufsverbot*; the imprisonment of the Agitdrucker – were well represented. Cultural events – music nights, puppet shows, street performances – took place between the panel discussions. A two-day TUNIX film festival screened films by underground and more established directors, including Volker Schlöndorff's *The Lost Honor of Katarina Blum*, which thematized the campaign of repression currently dominating the left scene in the BRD.[84]

The imaginary landscape of TUNIX became a field for all sorts of projections in the minds of the festival attendees. "What does TUNIX mean?" a young man was asked by a roving interviewer at the festival: "No streets, no cops, no weapons," he replied.

I mean that it's not right that the big shots sit up on the fifth floor while I work in the cellar, and I think that one has to do away with this situation, and if one

---

[82] Küster, interviewed in "Tunix-Kongress."

[83] "Treffen in TUNIX, Westberlin 27–29.1.78," Green Library, Stanford University, Germany. Extraparliamentary Opposition movement, 1967–1984 collection, MO613, box 35.

[84] *Ibid.*

Figure 8.2 TUNIX demonstration. Note the banner of the Spanish anarcho-syndicalist organizations FAI–CNT. Photo: Klaus Mehner.

thinks a little logically, then one won't build atom power installations any more, and then one will hack up the cars, and then make a nice pickaxe, and then one can do agriculture, that's my opinion, and that is also TUNIX.[85]

Another interviewee responded that, after finishing his studies, he planned to go to the country and join a rural commune.[86]

Imaginary landscapes and rural destinations aside, the impulses fueling TUNIX were transnational in orientation and genesis. Above all, the birth of the autonomous movement in Italy made a profound impression in West Germany and elsewhere. The movement spread first to Amsterdam and Zurich before taking root in German cities such as Berlin and Hamburg. We have already seen how influential Italian groups such as Lotta Continua were on the formation of the Sponti scene in the Federal Republic. Around the time of TUNIX, the "Urban Indian" movement became extremely influential as well, with Italian activists traveling to West Germany to

---

[85] Radio show by Ernst Editz and Peter Sandmeyer, "Impulses from the Subculture" (SFB/WDR), published as "Tunix O-Ton," in Dieter Hoffmann-Axthelm, Otto Kallscheuer, Eberhard Knödler-Bunte, and Brigitte Wartmann, eds., *Zwei Kulturen? TUNIX, Mescalero und die Folgen* (Berlin: Verlag Ästhetik und Kommunikation, 1985), p. 94.

[86] Editz and Sandmeyer, "Impulses from the Subculture," p. 98. On Urban Indians, see Jens Huhn, "Die Stadtindianer auf dem Kriegpfad," in Kraushaar, ed., *Autonomie oder Getto?*

spread the word, and groups being founded around the country. The success of these proselytizing efforts caused the theorist Johannes Agnoli to worry that overidentification with Italian "Urban Indians" and autonomists was contributing to, rather than lessening, a lack of confidence on the part of West German activists in fighting to change the system.[87]

The Urban Indian phenomenon was, of course, yet another iteration of the traditional German fascination with the figure of the Native American. More importantly, it was attractive in West Germany precisely because it seemed to offer a path out of the impasse created by the terrorism – counterterrorism dynamic. In this respect, it represented merely the latest in a string of transnational adaptations by German activists to fill perceived needs in the Federal Republic. At TUNIX, the Urban Indian phenomenon was strongly in evidence. One young man with a painted face was asked: "It's always said, people that go around painted like that are Urban Indians, what do you think of that expression?" He replied: "A few are Urban Indians, maybe we're all Urban Indians, because we live in a ghetto; because we, I believe, push ourselves there, because we don't want to be like the others, don't want to go along."[88] A flyer from the "Council of the Tribes of the Berlin Mescaleros" proclaimed in florid prose:

Many tribes have come together in the land of TUNIX, and we will be as countless as the stars in heaven. You will recognize us by our open, brightly-painted, cheerful faces, resolved for any struggle. We will wake your stony grey wigwams to life with our bright colors … Our dance and our electric guitars will destroy your ears, but give us eternal energy and strength. Jimi Hendricks [sic] comes back from the eternal hunting grounds. We will tear down these grey walls that you name prisons. We will blow the smoke from our pipes to the four winds, so that you will know the cheerfulness of our lives.[89]

The attitude of many was summed up in a banner spotted at the festival: "Long live the short-lived, pessimistic, rebel youth."[90]

Aside from a panel on "feminism and ecology," the women's movement was notably absent from the proceedings. Women's groups reacted with scorn to this state of affairs:

1968: In the beginning was the tomato-hurling … 1978: A new specter haunts the scene: Neo-chauvinism! Today the undogmatic left meets in Berlin. Whether Sponti or Chauvi – they have a dogma in common: in the entire program the

[87] Katsiaficas, *The Subversion of Politics*, p. 102.
[88] Editz and Sandmeyer, "Impulses from the Subculture," p. 98.
[89] Editz and Sandmeyer, "Impulses from the Subculture," pp. 99–100.
[90] Editz and Sandmeyer, "Impulses from the Subculture," p. 94.

women's movement is excluded. **No** single event for the women's movement! Our own fault? Coincidence?[91]

No doubt the omission reflected not only the continued marginalization of women's issues within the left scene but also lingering tension outside the women's movement over the extent to which that movement had built its own free-standing counter-institutions. In the event, women's call for a protest during the festival at the women's prison in Moabit was integrated into the official program of the Congress.

The TUNIX Congress was also criticized by the *K-Gruppen* and by portions of the armed left. In a long open letter, Dieter Kunzelmann, now in his "Communist phase" as a member of the KPD(AO), took Diethard Küster to task for his alleged failure to take sides in the struggle between the left and the authorities. He wrote:

> That thousands are not simply trying to escape, going to the country, and letting themselves lie back onto their drug mattresses, but instead coming here together to the TUNIX-Congress to see how many of them there are and to counsel themselves about what to do in the face of the daily intensifying political repression, is to be praised [... but the] individual way out, even when there are a lot of individuals going this way, is no way out, but a dead end.

Kunzelmann rejected in particular the model of two cultures that seemed to offer the possibility of working, if not within the system, then at least with it. Talk of "self-liberation" and the creation of "liberated space," Kunzelmann argued, obscured the need to take sides. "Isn't the Schmidt-Genscher government just now encouraging the 'alternative projects,' of which Herr TUNIX is constantly talking, precisely in order to deflect the only alternative that remains ... to organize the intransigent struggle against the fascist danger in our country."[92]

Another critic wrote, "It is not the Stadtmusikanten who are journeying to TUNIX. It is the four ostriches! According to the motto 'Head in the (underground) sand.'"[93] The inhabitants of the "TUNIX ghetto"– "the rural communes from the Westerwald, the football players from the Tiergarten, the pub-collectives from Kreuzberg to Charlottenburg"– were accused of ignoring the critical issues such as freedom of the press

---

[91] "Ohne Frauen–Tu-Nix Läuft Nix!," Green Library, Stanford University, Germany. Extraparliamentary Opposition movement, 1967–1984 collection, MO613, box 35.

[92] "An die Genossen TUNIX und an den HERRN TUNIX!," Green Library, Stanford University, Germany. Extraparliamentary Opposition movement, 1967–1984 collection, MO613, box 35.

[93] "Es sind nicht die Stadtmusikannten, die nach TUNIX reisen. Es sind vier Vogelstrausse!" Green Library, Stanford University, Germany. Extraparliamentary Opposition movement, 1967–1984 collection, MO613, box 35.

(personified by the imprisoned Agitdrucker) and the overall deteriorating human-rights situation in the Bundesrepublik. Worse, the organizers of the Congress had failed to reach out to a broader public in any meaningful way. Special scorn was heaped on Lyotard's "patchwork" concept: "The walls of communications-angst ... [between us and] those outside of our ghetto will not be torn down through such a cynical-elitist Patchwork out of the brains of philosophers."[94]

Members of Movement 2 June imprisoned in Moabit similarly took the occasion of the TUNIX Congress to issue a critique of the left scene in general and the armed struggle in particular. "We find it good," they wrote,

that here comrades have taken the initiative, to initiate a long-needed discussion. We would find it even better if through TUNIX it would finally be possible to succeed in overcoming the total fragmentation of the left. It isn't necessary for everyone to have to paint the same star on the wall with the same colors. It would be enough, to break through together to TUWAS ["do something"].[95]

The biggest problem, they argued, "was the fragmentation of the left into dozens of groups [that] made it [too] damned easy for the ruling class to isolate them, to paralyze the dangerousness and appeal of the concentrated revolt in the streets."[96] The TUNIX Congress did little to alleviate this isolation. "What was thought of as an alternative to society," they argued, "ended up as an alternative to struggle."[97]

Important practical initiatives of long-term significance were nevertheless launched at the TUNIX Congress. A panel on the initiative to produce a left-wing daily newspaper for West Germany led directly to the founding of the *Tageszeitung*, Germany's longest-running left-wing daily. Panels on antinuclear and ecological topics tapped into and provided support for the growing antinuclear movement. And the initiative to found a new ecologically oriented political party gave birth to the Green Party. More fundamentally, the TUNIX Congress represented a culmination of the various attempts at creating an alternative public sphere that had marked the development of the New Left in West Germany. In this sense it was a successor not only to events such as the Frankfurt "Anti-Book

---

[94] "Es sind nicht die Stadtmusikannten."

[95] "Zum Treffen in Tunix," in *Der Blues: Gesammelte Texte der Bewegung 2 Juni*, vol. II, pp. 639–650, at p. 639.

[96] "Zum Treffen in Tunix," pp. 639–640.

[97] "Zum Treffen in Tunix," p. 640. See Klaus Hartung, "Versuch, die Krise der antiautoritären Bewegung wieder zur Sprache zu bringen," *Kursbuch*, no. 48, 1977, pp. 14–43; see also Klaus Hartung, "Über die langandauernde Jugend im linken Getto: Lebensalter und Politik – Aus der Sicht eines 38jährigen," *Kursbuch*, no. 54, 1978, pp. 174–188.

Fair" and "Literary Book Fair" of 1968 but also to the whole range of creative and publicistic activities of the antiauthoritarian revolt. A response to the hardening of the lines created by the cycle of state and terrorist violence and counterviolence, and to the dogmatization represented by the *K-Gruppen* founded in the wake of the SDS's demise, the congress aimed at retrieving the discursive and organizational fluidity that had originally characterized the antiauthoritarian revolt, now married to an infinitely broader set of activities and perspectives than had existed when that revolt began.

CONCLUSION

The TUNIX Congress, in this sense, marks a fitting end point to the antiauthoritarian revolt in West Germany. Not only did it serve as a launching point for the manifold initiatives of the alternative movement – initiatives that bridged the historical period of the antiauthoritarian revolt and the period that followed it in the 1980s and beyond – but it also marked the moment at which, for the historian, the shape of the West German episode in the larger event known as 1968 or the global sixties comes into sharp relief. This moment, formally beginning in the early 1960s but with roots in the 1950s (and indeed, in some cases earlier) extended to the period of the late 1970s, marked here by the TUNIX Congress. This period of roughly a decade and a half may be understood as a period of convergence followed by a period of divergence. First, against a backdrop of a rising youth culture, dovetailing with bohemian currents of disaffection from bourgeois society represented by the Beats and expressed in particular by the devotion of young people to rock music and its attendant mores, a heavily politicized cultural revolution rooted in the arts and bohemian intellectual circles took place. This revolution made explicit what had only heretofore been implicit: a rebellion against capitalist consumer society that rooted itself not in the mass militancy, Marxist parties, and labor struggles of the interwar period but in the conditions, problems, and perspectives of daily life. This rebellion encompassed not only members of the proletariat but students, bohemians, and young people generally.

As we have seen, the primary bearers of this avant-garde impulse were Situationist-influenced bohemian intellectuals and artists associated first with Munich's Gruppe Spur, and subsequently with the group Subversive Aktion. Through the latter group, this bohemian intellectual avant-gardism became infused with a highly theoretical neo-Marxist approach borne by East German refugee intellectuals, above all figures such as Rudi Dutschke and Bernd Rabehl. This mixture of artistic avant-garde and political forms of radicalism gave a distinctive shape to the nascent antiauthoritarian revolt in West Germany, above all through its influence on the student organization the SDS.

The impact achieved by the student revolt spearheaded by the SDS was only possible because of the wide-ranging coalition that evolved around key issues of concern, namely the war in Vietnam, opposition to the SPD's entry into coalition with the CDU, the Emergency Law legislation, and the Springer Press monopoly. The civic engagement represented by the coalition of which the SDS was a part, a coalition made up of trade unions, clergy and confessional groups, journalists, older intellectuals, and other student groups such as the LSD, was rooted in the citizen activism of the previous decade, above all the movements against West German rearmament as part of NATO and the Bundeswehr's adoption of nuclear weapons. It was as part of this coalition that the SDS rose to prominence, and the degree of its impact on West German society would have been unthinkable outside of its collaboration with the broader extra-parliamentary opposition of which it was a part.

This great convergence, which saw pop-cultural youth revolt, the subversive efforts of self-appointed avant-gardes in the artistic-political underground, and liberal-democratic citizens' engagement all sucked into a general stream of rebellion (in appearance, at least, even if their goals were often at odds), swelled into the middle of the year 1968. By the spring and summer of that year, key campaigns against the Emergency Laws and the Springer Press monopoly had failed to produce the desired results, and the increasing radicalization of portions of the student movement made continued cooperation with bourgeois-liberal critics of the system increasingly difficult.

At every stage, as we have seen, these domestic developments were spurred and shaped by West Germany's relations with the world. This was true in several senses. First, and most obviously, the antiauthoritarian revolt was shaped by West Germany's position on the front lines of the Cold War, a position that embraced both its relationship with its East German twin and its imbrication in a system of alliances that reproduced global tensions on the soil of the Federal Republic in concentrated form. Second, they were shaped by a globalizing imagination that linked activists to the broader world, both in terms of a commitment to human-rights issues in countries under (neo-)imperial domination, whether of the capitalist or Communist variety, and in terms of those various communities

of affinity (Third World liberation movements, the international counterculture) through which activists and young people constructed their
identities. Third, they were synergized at every step by transnational
exchanges, whether *receptive* (e.g. those involving the presence of Third
World or other foreign student radicals, the reception of foreign texts,
music, or other cultural products) or *active*, that is, exchanges in which
West Germans acted themselves as agents of the transnational, either
through travel abroad and the attendant relations thus formed or through
their role in importing political strategies and ideas, texts, and other cultural goods with a political valence into West Germany.

The impact of these imaginings and exchanges did not cease with the
transition of the antiauthoritarian revolt from convergence to divergence;
on the contrary, as everything from the terror scene, to the Sponti scene,
to the development of the women's and gay-rights movements illustrates,
the impact of foreign developments and transnational exchanges continued to be key. Just as in the early period of the student movement, ideas
from abroad, as well as the concrete presence of foreign radicals (from
as nearby as the Netherlands and as far away as Iran, Africa, and South
America) played a critical role in synergizing the antiauthoritarian revolt,
in the period of divergence after 1968, foreign examples and transnational
exchanges and networks of affinity connecting activists with citizens'
movements in other countries, whether the American women's movement
or the Italian Urban Indians, continued to function as key inspirations
and sources of knowledge.

From this perspective, both the German Autumn and the TUNIX
Congress that followed it mark an ambiguous caesura; it is perhaps a cli-
ché to observe that 1977/1978 represented both a death and a new beginning, since so much of what shaped German political culture in the
decades to follow arose out of that moment. To be sure, it is possible to
argue that the transition moment from convergence to divergence – the
crisis year of 1968–in itself marked a death of the ecumenical spirit and
sense of limitless horizons that marked "1968." But it would not make
sense to exclude the divergent phase of the movement from the overall
moment of 1968, for it was during this phase that the contradictions of
the antiauthoritarian revolt became exposed, its divergent strands separating out to run along courses of their own.

Equally important, it was in this phase that important developments
and tendencies, only really nascent until 1968, began to unfold, theories
and practices – e.g. radical democratic self-management – coming more
fully into their own. At the same time, it was the phase in which the dead

hand of the past tightened its grip on the shoulder of the living, with radicals cast adrift by the loss of the seeming unity of the high period of the APO turning back to older models of organization and analysis. Thus, it is only in the yin and yang of convergence and divergence that the shape of the complicated phenomena of 1968 in West Germany becomes clear.

Conclusion

This book has demonstrated the decisive importance of transnational exchanges and global imaginings in the genesis of the West German 1968. From the travels of radicals to the transplantation of books, movies, music, and other cultural goods; from solidarity with Third World liberation struggles to attempts to import the goods and ideas of the international counterculture, key West German events were constructed out of non-German materials and in relationship to extra- and trans-German patterns of emotional and ideological affiliation. Yet, as important as the role of the global – or, more properly, the global – local interactions fueled by transnational exchanges and global imaginings – in the West German 1968, the West German case has the capacity to make us think twice about the putative globality of 1968. As we have seen, the evidence is absolutely clear that West Germans constructed their 1968 in a hundred ways out of the material of the global, but West Germans arguably needed to do this in a way that the French and the Americans did not. To be sure, all around the world young nonconformists borrowed the ideas and practices of the (Anglo-)American counterculture and drew inspiration (and sometimes tactics) from movements such as the English Campaign for Nuclear Disarmament or the American free-speech and civil-rights movements. Yet their borrowing was not as extensive, nor did it carry the same level of urgency as elsewhere; for in West Germany, the "national deficit" produced by the multiple erasures of National Socialism and West Germany's Cold War status made borrowing a necessity, in both political and cultural terms.

This is a reason for the urgency of both the active transnationalism and the historiographical activism that stamped the antiauthoritarian revolt. Reaching abroad but also back into the past, activists sought to construct new traditions out of both the material of the local past and the global present. This syncretism is one reason for the complex and sometimes bewildering appearance of the antiauthoritarian revolt; but it is not the only one. Speaking in the broadest terms, the revolt was characterized by four basic antinomies. In spatial terms, as we saw in the first chapter, the revolt was a product of global/local intersections; yet these spatial relationships enfolded a series of contradictions: between the "good" America, embraced for its contributions to alternative lifestyle and radical praxis, and the "bad" America responsible for napalming Vietnamese peasants; between East Germany as a repository of Stalinism (which must therefore be rejected) and East Germany as a bugaboo of hysterical West German anti-Communists whose claims must necessarily be treated with skepticism; between the logic of internationalism, which dictated that the theories and practices of Third World liberation attempted must necessarily function in the Federal Republic, and the needs of local activism. Straddling the front lines of the Cold War, which were simultaneously the front lines of the postwar struggles over decolonization and those of the war over the fate of divided Germany itself, activists struggled to enact a revolt about German issues that took place in a global context.

As they struggled to create a West German answer to a series of global revolutions breaking out seemingly all around them (the international youth revolution, the anticolonial revolution, the revolution against bureaucracy behind the Iron Curtain, and so on), activists faced not only a spatial conundrum but also, as we saw in Chapter 2, a temporal one. Protagonists of a New Left representing new concerns, in many ways representatives of an historically unprecedented moment of newness and confluence, they had to grapple back into history in a dual recovery project aimed simultaneously at coming to terms with the fascist past and unearthing the lost radical ideas and practices of the revolutionary past. The splintering of the revolt in the period of divergence after 1968 embodied this temporal dichotomy as a significant minority of activists sought to reestablish the forms and practices of the old left as a necessary continuation of the new while others followed out the logic of self-management and independent cultural practice to extend the gains that had been made, even if these failed to resemble the notion of "revolution" as previously conceived. To be sure, no political movement is ever a purely fresh creation of the present moment, but, for all its newness and rushing hard toward the future, the antiauthoritarian revolt in West Germany, with all the ideological-archeological work before it, was a more than usually hybrid phenomenon.

A third major antinomy, one connected to the very nature of the politics pursued in the antiauthoritarian revolt, was a natural outgrowth of the first two. The attempt to come up with the right kind of politics for the West German situation necessarily yielded more than one answer, the solutions depending to a large extent on the (current or historical) source material selected. Was the revolution to be the work of artists and avant-garde cultural troublemakers? A revolution of serious-minded students allied with trade unions and older generation of intellectuals? A revolution of pop-cultural youth consumers? A revolution of workers led by revitalized Marxist-Leninist vanguard parties? A revolution allied with, or opposed to, Eastern Communist orthodoxies? A revolution of the people or a revolution of the self, or of both simultaneously? To the question "What *kind* of politics?" there could, in the final analysis, be no agreed-upon answer.

Moreover, the operative imperatives that underpinned the movement – the antiauthoritarian, self-organizational, communicative, scholarly scientific, and transnational – provided no unified concept and approach. On the contrary, they were by their very nature inconsistent and sometimes contradictory. In particular, as we have seen with respect to the organizational debate that followed the eclipse of the APO in mid to late 1968, antiauthoritarianism itself became a bone of contention. A significant minority of activists embraced the proposition that to be effective politically it was necessary to jettison what they saw as the excessive reliance on being against authority as such, by which they meant to suggest that discipline was an integral component of the success of political movements that could not be overlooked with impunity. The idea of self-organization, similarly, elided questions about the nature of political practice that, as we saw especially in Chapter 6 but in other chapters as well, often revealed themselves painfully in concrete situations.

The realm of cultural production, too, was shot through with contradictions, not least by dint of its uneasy relationship with the explicitly political facets of the revolt. If the interpenetration of culture and politics was a key feature of 1968, the terms of the relationship between them was open to interpretation. The questions of *if* culture should (or could) be political, or of *how* it should be political, were central to the antiauthoritarian revolt. This was true not only because of the importance of the revolution of daily life (e.g. of personal style or habitus), or because of the key role of the arts and artists, but also because of the absolute centrality of cultural production to the revolt. As we saw in the three central chapters of this book – Word, Sound, and Vision – cultural production, whether of the literary-publicistic, musical, or visual-cultural variety, was key to the antiauthoritarian revolt. The founding of journals, publishing houses, and bookshops; bands and record labels; film and authors' and other artistic collectives; the organization of underground festivals, and so on, were all expressions of the central act of the antiauthoritarian revolt: the assertion of the right to speak and, in particular, the right to express previously forbidden truths. At the same time, they were sites where the most important organizing principle of the revolt – direct democratic self-organization from below – came most fully into its own.

These areas of initiative became battlefields over the central questions of the revolt: about the value of popular culture (particularly popular culture imported from America); the worth of "hedonism" as a revolutionary principle; or the meaning of revolution more generally. In particular, they embodied tensions about the connection between art and politics, especially the question of whether or in what way writing, music, filmmaking, and so on, could be political. Debates about the value and meaning of concepts such as "counterculture," "subculture," and "underground" were in turn connected to questions of the extent to which it was correct to penetrate and change society as a whole as opposed to seceding from it into an autonomous world of one's own. They were also connected to worry about capitalist recuperation – that is, about the question of whether it was possible to seek revolutionary ends through nonrevolutionary means. Was radical literature, for example, really "radical" if it was produced and distributed by a mainstream publishing house? Such conflicts became increasingly bitter when the battle over capitalist recuperation took place not between the underground and the mainstream but within the underground itself, as in the criticism leveled at hip capitalists such as Rolf Ulrich Kaiser or left-wing media stars such as Rainer Langhans and Uschi Obermaier. The perceived problem of recuperation became especially acute in the realm of the visual, where symbols of countercultural identity – in many cases themselves simply consumer items, such as blue jeans, that had been adopted and assigned left-wing meanings by militants – were easily packaged and sold back to young people as symbols of rebellion meant to replace the real thing.

The visual was a key site of contradiction in another way, as we have seen. Visuality was central to the revolt, not just because of the importance of visual signifiers (e.g. the countercultural look) and performative politics rooted in artistic models of nonverbal provocation (e.g. impersonations of policemen, Shah masks, the processions and public rituals of the Kommune I). The very ubiquity of images drawn from the ever-expanding global image sphere, the ease with which activists with access to new reprographic technologies could collage them together to create new meanings, gave the visual a power out of all proportion to other means of communication. This trump power of the visual, linked to the new importance of provocative self-representation derived from artistic-political movements such as Fluxus and Situationism, as well as the possibilities of recuperation in a media-saturated landscape, made the visual a key site of contention in the antiauthoritarian revolt. It drove conflicts like the ones between the Kommune I and the traditionalists in the SDS or between Rolf Dieter Brinkmann and left-literary critics of the "hedonistic" turn.

The latter conflicts expressed one of the biggest unresolved tensions of the antiauthoritarian revolt – that between individualism and collectivism; that is, a conflict between the claims of personal and group identity and rebellion. This tension came out clearly in the battle between the undogmatic and Marxist cadre left after 1968 (of which the struggle between the Kommune I and the traditionalists in 1967 represented an opening salvo), but it underpinned the entire antiauthoritarian revolt. In the period of convergence before 1968, these two impulses were mutually supporting, or, at least, often seemed to be so. In the euphoric optimism of this phase, it was increasingly taken as a given that personal liberation fed into the project of social transformation. There was disagreement about this issue, as we have seen; but, in general, few could argue that, on some level, the two projects did not go hand in hand. In the period of divergence that followed, the inherent contradictions in this position came to the fore, the two tendencies reproducing themselves in increasingly exaggerated iterations (e.g. the Hash Rebels, the *K-Gruppen*).

With the transition to the 1970s, the tension between the need to achieve a concrete bettering of one's own life situation and the need to act collectively to change society came to even more forceful expression with the rise of the women's and gay-rights movements. The difficulty of reconciling the needs associated with motherhood and child-rearing (for heterosexual women) and sexual preference (for homosexual men and women) with the increasingly stringent demands of Marxist ideology all but forced straight women and homosexual men and women to seek new vistas of meaning and action outside of the narrow structures left over from the APO, vistas in which the maxim "the personal is political" could come more fully into its own. Tellingly, however, as activists' concerns turned away from world revolution toward the revolution of the self and the possibilities of daily life, transnational connections and global vision remained as important as ever.

Subsequent developments have done little to diminish the relevance of 1968. If 1960s activists in West Germany recognized themselves as actors on a continuum stretching back to the French Revolution of 1789 and the pan-European revolutions of 1848, the historian can point to more recent events and phenomena such as the fall of Communism in 1989, the antiglobalization movement, or the mass protests of the Arab Spring as evidence that fundamental questions about the organization of societies – particularly those having to do with democratic participation – remain open. Once again, a populist transnational Zeitgeist is unsettling established orthodoxies and power structures; once again, new communication technologies are allowing ideas and images to spread like wildfire; and once again, activists with emancipatory aims look across borders for solutions to problems at home, imagining themselves into a global community. For this reason, to investigate the history of the 1960s is to investigate the problems and trends of today.

For scholars, the political and theoretical debates bound up in 1968 constitute another reason for its continuing relevance. The questions posed by the protagonists of 1968 – What constitutes a "revolution"? Who must be its actors? – are precisely those that must be answered by the historian or social scientist, albeit from a different perspective. In particular, the unresolved issues related to the problems and prospects of self-organization in the realm of cultural production – questions about the possibilities of a political art, about the limits of representation, about issues of authenticity and recuperation – cut across the theoretical concerns of a number of disciplines, marking out 1968 as a site of genuine interdisciplinarity. The attempts of the 1960s to develop new forms of political praxis under the sign of participatory democracy, moreover, subsequently informed both the New Social Movements of the 1970s and 1980s and the global anti-corporate movement of the 1990s to the present. With both the themes (radical egalitarianism, the democratization of the mass media, the relationship of the Third World to the First) and the forms (self-organization from below, decentralized direct action, creation of alternative media) of the 68er movement appearing increasingly precocious at the beginning of the twenty-first century, 1968 remains unfinished business in more ways than one.

Select bibliography

ARCHIVES AND ARCHIVAL COLLECTIONS

APO-Archiv München (Archiv Heinz Corderer), Munich
Archiv "APO und soziale Bewegungen," Free University Berlin
Archiv Peter Hein, Berlin
Archiv Rainer Langhans, Munich
Archiv Uwe Husslein, Cologne
Bayerisches Hauptstaatsarchiv
Bundesarchiv Berlin
Bundesarchiv Koblenz
Green Library, Stanford University
Hamburg Institute for Social Research
Hoover Institution, Stanford University
International Institute for Social History, Amsterdam
Kreuzberg Museum, Berlin
Landesarchiv Berlin
Papiertiger Archiv, Berlin
Rio-Reiser-Archiv, Berlin
Staatsarchiv München, Munich

SECONDARY WORKS

Ahlberg, René, *Ursachen der Revolte: Analyse des studentischen Protestes*, Stuttgart: Kohlhammer, 1972.

Albrecht, Willy, *Der Sozialistische Deutsche Studentenbund (SDS): Vom parteikonformen Studentenverband zum Repräsentanten der neuen Linken*, Bonn: Dietz, 1994.

Allerbeck, Klaus R., *Soziologie radikaler Studentenbewegungen: Eine vergleichende Untersuchung in der Bundesrepublik Deutschland und den Vereinigten Staaten*, Munich: Oldenbourg, 1973.

Allinson, Mark, *Politics and Popular Opinion in East Germany, 1945–1968*, Manchester University Press, 2000.

Anders, Ann, ed., *Autonome Frauen: Schüsseltexte der neuen Frauenbewegung seit 1968*, Frankfurt: Athenäum, 1988.

Angster, Julia, *Konsenskapitalismus und Sozialdemokratie: Die Westernisierung von SPD und DGB*, Munich: Oldenbourg, 2003.

"'Safe by Democracy': American Hegemony and the 'Westernization' of West German Labor," *Amerikastudien/American Studies*, 46 (4) (2001): 557–572.

Aurdich, Rolf and Ulrich Kriest, *Der Ärger mit den Bildern: die Filme von Harun Farocki*, Konstanz: UVK Medien, 1998.

Aust, Stefan, *Der Baader Meinhof Komplex*, Hamburg: Hoffmann & Campe, 1985.

Baas, Jacquelynn, ed., *Fluxus and the Essential Questions of Life*, University of Chicago Press, 2011.

Baberowski, Jörg, *Der Sinn der Geschichte: Geschichtstheorien von Hegel bis Foucault*, Munich: C. H. Beck Verlag, 2005.

Bacia, Jurgen, "Von der subversiven Aktion zur Sponti Bewegung (1964–1973): Eine empirische Studie," Doctoral thesis, Free University of Berlin, 1984.

Bandy, Joe and Jackie Smith, eds., *Coalitions across Borders: Transnational Protest and the Neoliberal Order*, Lanham, Md.: Rowman & Littlefield, 2005.

Barnard, Malcolm, *Approaches to Understanding Visual Culture*, New York: Palgrave, 2001.

Barron, Stephanie, ed., *Art of Two Germanys: Cold War Cultures*, New York: Abrams, 2009.

Bauerkämper, Arnd, Konrad H. Jarausch, and Marcus M. Payk, eds., *Demokratiewunder: Transatlantische Mittler und die kulturelle Öffnung Westdeutschlands 1945–1970*, Göttingen: Vandenhoeck & Ruprecht, 2005.

Baumann, Michael with Christof Meueler, *How It All Began*, Vancouver: Arsenal Pulp Press, 1977.

Rausch und Terror: Ein politischer Erlebnisbericht, Berlin: Rotbuch Verlag, 2008.

Baumgartel, Tilman, *Vom Guerillakino zum Essayfilm: Harun Farocki – Werkmonographie eines Autorenfilmers*, Berlin: Bbooks, 2002.

Bauß, Gerhard, *Die Studentenbewegung der sechziger Jahre in der Bundesrepublik und Westberlin: Handbuch*, Cologne: Pahl-Rugenstein, 1977.

Beckett, James, *Barbarism in Greece: A Young American Lawyer's Inquiry into the Use of Torture in Contemporary Greece, with Case Histories and Documents*, New York: Walker, 1970.

Benedict, Hans-Jürgen, "Vom Protest zum Widerstand: Die Vietnamkriegs-Opposition in den USA und in der BRD," *Friedensanalysen*, 4 (1977): 79–106.

Benedikt-Jansen, Stephanie, *Joseph Beuys: Geordnetes Chaos oder Chaotische Ordnung*, Gelnhausen: Triga, 2001.

Benjamin, Walter, "The Author as Producer," in Victor Burgin, ed., *Thinking Photography*, Basingstoke: Macmillan, 1992, pp. 15–31.

Bergfelder, Tim, *International Adventures: German Popular Cinema and European Co-productions in the 1960s*, New York and Oxford: Berghahn Books, 2005.

Bergmann, Uwe, Rudi Dutschke, Wolfgang Lefèvre, and Bernd Rabehl, *Rebellion der Studenten oder die neue Opposition*, Reinbeck: Rororo Aktuell, 1968.

Beuckers, Klaus Gereon, *Zero-Studien: Aufsätze zur Düsseldorfer Gruppe Zero und ihrem Umkreis*, Münster: Lit, 1997.

Beuys, Joseph, *Kunst und Politik*, Wangen: Freie Volkschochschule Argental, 1989.

Bieling, Rainer, *Die Tränen der Revolution: Die 68er zwanzig Jahre danach*, Berlin: Siedler, 1988.

Bingel, Horst, ed., *Literarische Messe 1968: Handpressen, Flugblätter, Zeitschriften der Avantgarde*, Frankfurt: Metopen-Verlag, 1968.

Zeitschriften, Pressen und progressive Literatur, Frankfurt: Affenpresse, 1963.

Bock, Hans Manfred, *Geschichte des "linken Radikalismus" in Deutschland: Ein Versuch*, Frankfurt: Suhrkamp, 1976.

Böckelmann, Frank and Herbert Nagel, eds., *Subversive Aktion: Der Sinn der Organisation ist ihr Scheitern*, Frankfurt: Verlag Neue Kritik, 1976.

Bokina, John, ed., *Marcuse: From the New Left to the Next Left*, Lawrence, Kans.: University Press of Kansas, 1994.

Borer, Alain, *The Essential Joseph Beuys*, Cambridge, Mass.: MIT Press, 1997.

Bourdieu, Pierre, *Die feinen Unterschiede: Kritik der gesellschaftlichen Urteilskraft*, Frankfurt: Suhrkamp, 1994.

Die männliche Herrschaft, Frankfurt: Suhrkamp, 2005.

Bracher, Karl Dietrich, *The German Dictatorship: The Origins, Structure, and Effects of National Socialism*, New York: Praeger, 1970.

Braunthal, Gerard, *Political Loyalty and Public Service in West Germany: The 1972 Decree against Radicals and Its Consequences*, Amherst, Mass.: University of Massachusetts Press, 1990.

Breines, Paul, ed., *Critical Interruptions: New Left Perspectives on Herbert Marcuse*, New York: Herder, 1970.

Breiteneicher, Hille Jan, *Kinderläden: Revolution der Erziehung oder Erziehung zur Revolution?* Reinbek: Rowohlt, 1971.

Brennan, Teresa and Martin Jay, eds., *Vision in Context: Historical and Contemporary Perspectives on Sight*, London and New York: Routledge, 1996.

Briem, Jürgen, *Der SDS: Die Geschichte des bedeutendsten Studentenverbandes der BRD seit 1945*, Frankfurt: Paedex-Verlag, 1976.

Brill, Dorothee, *Shock and the Senseless in Dada and Fluxus*, Hanover, NH: Dartmouth University Press, 2010.

Brinkmann, Reinhold and Christoph Wolff, *Driven into Paradise: The Musical Migration from Nazi Germany to the United States*, Berkeley, Calif.: University of California Press, 1999.

Brinkmann, Rolf Dieter and Ralf-Rainer Rygulla, eds., *ACID: Neue amerikanische Szene*, Darmstadt: März Verlag, 1969.

Brown, Timothy S., "East Germany," in Martin Klimke and Joachim Scharloth, eds., *1968 in Europe: A History of Protest and Activism, 1956–1977*, London: Palgrave Macmillan, 2008, pp. 189–197.

Brown, Timothy S. and Lorena Anton, eds., *Between the Avant-garde and the Everyday: Subversive Politics in Europe, 1957 to the Present*, New York and Oxford: Berghahn Books, 2011.

Brückner, Peter, *Selbstbefreiung: Provokation und soziale Bewegung*, ed. Axel-R. Oestmann, Berlin: Wagenbach, 1984.

Budde, Gunilla, Sebastian Conrad, and Oliver Janz, eds., *Transnationale Geschichte: Themen, Tendenzen und Theorien*, Göttingen: Vandenhoeck & Ruprecht, 2006.

Bude, Heinz, *Das Altern einer Generation: Die Jahrgänge, 1938–1948*, Frankfurt: Suhrkamp, 1995.

Bude, Heinz and Martin Kohli, eds., *Radikalisierte Aufklärung: Studentenbewegung und Soziologie in Berlin 1965 bis 1970*, Weinheim: Juventa, 1989.

Burke, Peter, *Eyewitnessing: The Use of Images as Historical Evidence*, London: Reaktion Books, 2001.

Butterwegge, Christoph, et al., eds., *30 Jahre Ostermarsch: Ein Beitrag zur politischen Kultur der Bundesrepublik Deutschland und ein Stück Bremer Stadtgeschichte*, Bremen: Steintor, 1990.

Calzavara, Maria, et al. (Autorenkollektiv), *Demokratische Studentenbewegung in den USA, der BRD, Frankreich und Großbritannien: Stand und Probleme*, East Berlin: Institut für Hochschulbildung, 1978.

Caute, David, *The Year of the Barricades: A Journey through 1968*, New York: Harper & Row, 1988.

Chapman, Tia Ann, "Helke Sander and the Roots of Change: Gaining a Foothold for Women Filmmakers in Post-war Germany," AB thesis, Harvard University, 1994.

Chaussy, Ulrich, *Die drei Leben des Rudi Dutschke*, Berlin: Fischer, 1993.

Chollet, Laurent, *L'insurrection situationniste*, Paris: Éditions Dagorno, 2000.

Claessens, Dieter and Karinde Ahna, "Das Milieu der Westberliner 'scene' und die 'Bewegung 2 Juni'," in Wanda von Baeyer-Katte, Dieter Claessens, Hubert Feger, and Friedhelm Neidhardt, *Analysen zum Terrorismus, hrsg. vom Bundesministerium des Innern*, Opladen: Gruppenprozesse, 1982, vol. III, pp. 19–181.

Claussen, Detlev, ed., *Spuren der Befreiung: Herbert Marcuse – Ein Materialbuch zur Einführung in sein politisches Denken*, Darmstadt: Luchterhand, 1981.

Cohen, Robert, "The Political Aesthetics of Holocaust Literature: Peter Weiss's *The Investigation* and Its Critics," *History and Memory*, 10 (2) (1998): 43–67.

Cohn-Bendit, Daniel, *Wir haben sie so geliebt, die Revolution*, Frankfurt: Athenäum Verlag, 1987.

Cohn-Bendit, Daniel and Reinhard Mohr, *1968: Die letzte Revolution, die noch nichts vom Ozonloch wußte*, Berlin: Wagenbach, 1988.

Colvin, Sarah, *Ulrike Meinhof and West German Terrorism: Language, Violence and Identity*, Rochester, NY: Camden House, 2009.

Conrad, Christoph and Martina Kessel, eds., *Geschichte schreiben in der Postmoderne: Beiträge zu einer aktuellen Diskussion*, Stuttgart: Reclam, 1994.

Conradt, Gerd, *Starbuck: Holger Meins – Ein Porträt als Zeitbild*, Berlin: Espresso, 2001.

Davis, Belinda, Wilfred Mausbach, Martin Klimke, and Carla MacDougall, eds., *Changing the World, Changing Oneself: Political Protest and Collective Identities in West Germany and the U.S. in the 1960s and 1970s*, New York and Oxford: Berghahn Books, 2010.

Della Porta, Donatella, Hanspeter Kriesi, and Dieter Rucht, eds., *Social Movements in a Globalizing World*, New York: Palgrave Macmillan, 1999.

Della Porta, Donatella and Herbert Reiter, *Policing Protest: The Control of Mass Demonstrations in Western Democracies*, Minneapolis, Minn.: University of Minnesota Press, 1998.

Deppe, Frank, ed., *2 Juni 1967 und die Studentenbewegung heute*, Dortmund: Weltkreis-Verlag, 1977.

Deutschmann, Christian, "Lehrfilme der Westberliner Studentenbewegung," in Friedrich Knilli, ed., *Semiotik des Films: Mit Analysen kommerzieller Pornos und revolutionärer Agitationsfilme*, Munich: Hanser, 1971, pp. 199–206.

Dirke, Sabine Von, *"All Power to the Imagination!": The West German Counterculture from the Student Movement to the Greens*, University of Nebraska Press, 1997.

Divers, Gregory, *The Image and Influence of America in German Poetry since 1945*, Rochester, NY: Camden House, 2002.

Doering-Manteuffel, Anselm, *Wie westlich sind die Deutschen? Amerikanisierung und Westernisierung im 20 Jahrhundert*, Göttingen: Vandenhoeck & Ruprecht, 1999.

Dreyfus-Armand, Geneviève, Robert Frank, Marie-Françoise Lévy, and Michelle Zancarini-Fournel, *Les Années 68: Le temps de la contestation*, Brussels: Éditions Complexe, 2001.

Eckhard, Fred, et al., *Massen, Kultur, Politik*, Berlin: Argument-Verlag, 1978.

Eisenhardt, Hermann, *Klassenbegriff und Praxisverfall in der Neuen Linken: Zur Geschichte der Studentenbewegung in der Bundesrepublik*, Munich: Raith, 1975.

El Kurdi, Hartmut, *Schwarzrote Pop-Perlen: Keine Macht für Niemand–Ton Steine Scherben. The Essence of Rock*, vol. II, Hannover: Wehrhanverlag, 2001.

Elber, Rolf and Svend Hansen, eds., *Beiträge zur Geschichte des Sozialistischen Deutschen Studentenbundes*, Berlin: AStA der FU Berlin (Hochschulreferat), 1987.

Ellwein, Thomas, *Krisen und Reformen: Die Bundesrepublik seit den sechziger Jahren*, Munich: dtv, 1989.

Enderwitz, Ulrich, *Die Republik frißt ihre Kinder: Hochschulreform und Studentenbewegung in der Bundesrepublik Deutschland*, Berlin: DiA, 1986.

Enzensberger, Hans Magnus, "Klare Entscheidungen und trübe Aussichten," in Joachim Schickel, ed., *Über Hans Magnus Enzensberger*, Frankfurt: Suhrkamp, 1970, pp. 225–232.

Enzensberger, Ulrich, *Die Jahre der Kommune I: Berlin 1967–1969*, Cologne: Kiepenheuer & Witsch, 2004.

Ermen, Reinhard, *Joseph Beuys*, Hamburg: Rowohlt Taschenbuch, 2007.

Evans, Jessica and Stuart Hall, eds., *Visual Culture: The Reader*, London: Sage Publications, 1999.

Eyerman, Ron and Jamison, Andrew, *Music and Social Movements*, Cambridge University Press, 1998.

Fahlenbrach, Kathrin, *Protest-Inszenierungen: Visuelle Kommunikation und kollektive Identitäten in Protestbewegungen*, Wiesbaden: Westdeutscher Verlag, 2002.

Famulla, Rolf, *Joseph Beuys: Künstler, Krieger und Schamane – die Bedeutung von Trauma und Mythos in seinem Werk*, Giessen: Psychosozial-Verlag, 2008.

Faulstich, Werner, *Die Kultur de Sechziger Jahre*, Munich: W. Fink, 2003.

Zwischen Glitter und Punk: Tübinger Vorlesungen zur Rockgeschichte Teil III, 1972–1982, Rothernburg-Oberdorf: Wissenschaftler Verlag, 1986.

Fels, Gerhard, *Der Aufruhr der 68er: zu den geistigen Grundlagen der Studentenbewegung und der RAF*, Bonn: Bouvier, 1998.

Felshin, Nina, ed., *But Is It Art? The Spirit of Art as Activism*, Seattle, Wash.: Bay Press, 1995.

Fenemore, Mark, *Sex, Thugs and Rock 'n' Roll: Teenage Rebels in Cold-War East Germany*, New York and Oxford: Berghahn Books, 2007.

Fichter, Tilman, *SDS und SPD: Parteilichkeit jenseits der Partei*, Opladen: Westdeutscher Verlag, 1988.

"Vom linken Offiziersbund zur Revolte: Vier SDS-Generationen," in Jürgen Seifert, Heinz Thörmer, and Klaus Wettig, eds., *Soziale oder sozialistische Demokratie? Beiträge zur Geschichte der Linken in der Bundesrepublik. Freundesgabe für Peter von Oertzen zum 65. Geburtstag*, Marburg: SP-Verlag, 1989, pp. 11–20.

Fichter, Tilman and Siegward Lönnendonker, *Kleine Geschichte des SDS: Der Sozialistische Deutsche Studentenbund von 1946 bis zur Selbstauflösung*, Berlin: Rotbuch, 1977.

Fink, Carole, Philipp Gassert, and Detlef Junker, eds., *1968: The World Transformed*, Cambridge University Press, 1998.

Finney, Gail, *Visual Culture in Twentieth Century Germany*, Bloomington, Ind.: Indiana University Press, 2006.

Floh de Cologne, *Profitgeier und andere Vögel: Agitationstexte, Lieder, Berichte*, Berlin: Wagenbach, 1971.

François, Etienne, ed., *1968: Ein europäisches Jahr?* Leipzig: Leipziger Universitätsverlag, 1997.

Fraser, Ronald, et al., *1968: A Student Generation in Revolt*, New York: Pantheon, 1988.

Frei, Norbert, *1968: Jugendrevolte und globaler Protest*, Munich: Deutscher Taschenbuch Verlag, 2008.

Adenauer's Germany and the Nazi Past: The Politics of Amnesty and Integration, New York: Columbia University Press, 2002.

Friebel, Harry, *Initiativ- und Aktionsgruppen: zur Theorie und Praxis von Selbsterfahrung und politischen Aktion: am Beispiel Kinderläden*, Cologne: Kiepenheuer und Witsch, 1977.

Fried, Johannes, *Der Schleier der Erinnerung: Grundzüge einer historischen Memorik*, Munich: C. H. Beck Verlag, 2004.

Friedman, Ken, *The Fluxus Reader*, New York: Academy Editions, 1998.

Füssel, Stephan, ed., *Die Politisierung des Buchmarkts: 1968 als Branchenereignis*, Wiesbaden: Harrassowitz, 2007.

Gehret, Jens, *Gegenkultur: von Woodstock bis Tunix 1969–1981*, Asslar: MarGis, 1985.

Geulen, Benedikt and Peter Graf, *Mach mal bitte platz, wir müssen hier stürmen: Als der Beat nach Deutschland kam. Fotografien von Jens Hagen*, Cologne: M7 Verlag, 2007.

Gibbs, David N., *The Political Economy of Third World Intervention: Mines, Money and US Policy in the Congo Crisis*, Chicago University Press, 1991.

Gilcher-Holtey, Ingrid, ed., *1968: Vom Ereignis zum Gegenstand der Geschichtswissenschaft*, Göttingen: Vandenhoeck & Ruprecht, 1998.

"Die Phantasie an die Macht": Mai 68 in Frankreich, Frankfurt: Suhrkamp Verlag, 1995.

"Der Transfer zwischen den Studentenbewegungen von 1968 und die Entstehung einer transnationalen Gegenöffentlichkeit," *Berliner Journal für Soziologie*, 10 (4) (2000): 485–500.

Glomb, Ronald, "Auf nach Tunix," in J. Gehret, ed., *Gegenkultur heute. Die Alternativbewegung von Woodstock bis Tunix*, Amsterdam: Azid Presse, 1979.

Goffman, Irving, *Wir alle spielen Theater: die Selbstdarstellung im Alltag, München 1988: Ludolf Herbst – Komplexität und Chaos. Grundzüge einer Theorie der Geschichte*, Munich: C. H. Beck, 2004.

Goltz, Anna von der, ed., *"Talkin' 'bout My Generation": Conflicts of Generation Building and Europe's 1968*, Göttingen: Wallstein, 2011.

Grob, Marion, *Das Kleidungsverhalten jugendlicher Protestgruppen in Deutschland im 20 Jahrhundert: Am Beispiel des Wandervogels und der Studentenbewegung*, Münster: Coppenrath, 1985.

Gross, Alex, *The Untold Sixties: When Hope Was Born – An Insider's Sixties on an International Scale*, New York: Cross-Cultural Research Projects, 2009.

Grossarth-Maticek, Ronald, *Radikalismus: Untersuchungen zur Persönlichkeitsentwicklung westdeutscher Studenten*, Basel: Karger, 1979.

Revolution der Gestörten? Motivationsstrukturen, Ideologien und Konflikte bei politisch engagierten Studenten, Heidelberg: Quelle & Meyer, 1975.

Grunenberg, Christoph and Jonathan Harris, ed., *The Summer of Love: Psychedelic Art, Social Crisis and Counter-culture in the 1960s*, Liverpool University Press, 2005.

Grünewald, Guido, "Zur Geschichte des Ostermarsches der Atomwaffengegner," *Blätter für deutsche und internationale Politik*, 27 (1982): 303–322.

Guggenberger, Bernd, *Die Neubestimmung des subjektiven Faktors im Neomarxismus: Eine Analyse des voluntaristischen Geschichtsverständnisses der Neuen Linken*, Freiburg: Alber, 1973.

Wem nützt der Staat? Kritik der neomarxistischen Staatstheorie, Stuttgart: Kohlhammer, 1974.

Wohin treibt die Protestbewegung? Junge Rebellen zwischen Subkultur und Parteikommunismus, Freiburg: Herder, 1975.

Habermas, Jürgen, ed., *Observations on "The Spiritual Situation of the Age":* *Contemporary German Perspectives*, Cambridge, Mass.: MIT Press, 1984.

Haggerty, George E. and Bonnie Zimmerman, eds., *Gay Histories and Cultures: An Encyclopedia*, New York: Garland, 2000.

Halbach, Robert, ed., *Linkeck: Erste antiautoritäre Zeitung – Jedes Urteil wis-senschaftlicher Kritik ist mir willkommen*, Berlin-Neukölln: Kramer-Verlag, 1987.

Han, Woo-Chang, "Entwicklung und Bestimmungsfaktoren des politischen Protestes in der Bundesrepublik," Ph.D. dissertation, University of Mainz, 1991.

Hansen, Klaus, "APO und Terrorismus: Eine Skizze der Zusammenhänge," *Frankfurter Hefte*, 34 (1979): 11–22.

Hanshew, Karrin, *Terror and Democracy in West Germany*, Cambridge University Press, 2012.

Harlan, Volker, *Was ist Kunst? Werkstattgespräch mit Beuys*, Stuttgart: Urachhaus, 1986.

Hartig, Hilmar, "Die Entwicklung des Kommunismus in der Bundesrepublik," in Wolfgang Schneider and Jürgen Domes, eds., *Kommunismus inter-national, 1950–1965: Probleme einer gespaltenen Welt*, Cologne: Verlag Wissenschaft und Politik, 1965.

Hartong, Konrad, *Schülerbewegung und Schulerfolg in den weiterführenden allgemeinbildenden Schulen: dargestellt am Beispiel des Regierungsbezirks Osnabrück*, Lingen, Ems: R. van Ecken, 1961.

Harvey, Sylvia, *May '68 and Film Culture*, London: BFI Publishing, 1978.

Hebard, Andrew, "Disruptive Histories: Toward a Radical Politics of Remembrance in Alain Resnais's *Night and Fog*," *New German Critique*, 71 (spring–summer, 1997): 87–113.

Hecht, Jessica-Gienow, "American Cultural Policy in the Federal Republic of Germany, 1949–1968," in Detlef Junker, ed., *The United States and Germany in the Era of the Cold War, 1945–1968: A Handbook*, 2 vols., Cambridge University Press, 2004.

Hecken, Thomas, *Avantgarde und Terrorismus: Rhetorik der Intensität und Programme der Revolte von den Futuristen bis zur RAF*, Bielefeld: Transcript Verlag, 2006.

Gegenkultur und Avantgarde 1950–1970: Situationisten, Beatniks, 68er, Tübingen: Francke, 2006.

Heinemann, Karl-Heinz and Thomas Jaitner, *Ein langer Marsch: 1968 und die Folgen*, Cologne: PapyRossa-Verlag, 1993.

Herding, Klaus, *1968: Kunst, Kunstgeschichte, Politik*, Frankfurt: Anabas-Verlag, 2008.

Herf, Jeffrey, "The 'Holocaust' Reception in West Germany: Right, Center and Left," *New German Critique*, 19 (special issue 1) (1980): 30–52.

Herlemann, Beatrix, "Communist Resistance between Comintern Directives and Nazi Terror," in David E. Barclay and Eric D. Weitz, eds., *Between*

Reform and Revolution: German Socialism and Communism from 1840 to 1990, New York and Oxford: Berghahn, 1998, pp. 357–371.

Hermann, Kai, *Die Revolte der Studenten*, Hamburg: Wegner, 1968.

Hertle, Hans-Hermann and Wolfgang Günther, eds., *Zwischen Kooperation und Konfrontation: Beiträge zur Geschichte von außerparlamentarischer Bewegung und Gewerkschaften*, Marburg: SP-Verlag, 1988.

Hertz, Richard, *Twentieth Century Art Theory: Urbanism, Politics, and Mass Culture*, Englewood Cliffs, NJ: Prentice Hall, 1990.

Herzog, Dagmar, "Pleasure, Sex and Politics Belong Together: Post-Holocaust Memory and the Sexual Revolution in West Germany," *Critical Inquiry*, 24 (winter 1998): 393–444.

Sex after Fascism: Memory and Morality in Twentieth-Century Germany, Princeton University Press, 2007.

Higgins, Hannah, *Fluxus Experience*, Berkeley, Calif.: University of California Press, 2002.

Hildebrand, Klaus, *Von Erhard zur Großen Koalition, 1963–1969*, Stuttgart: Deutsche Verlags-Anstalt, 1984.

Hildebrandt, Dietrich, *"… und die Studenten freuen sich!" Studentenbewegung in Heidelberg 1967–1973*, Heidelberg: Esprint-Verlag, 1991.

Hobsbawm, Eric, *The Jazz Scene*, New York: Pantheon, 1993.

"The Year the Prophets Failed," in Eugene Atget and Laure Beaumont-Maillet, eds., *1968 Magnum throughout the World*, Paris: Distributed Art Publishers, 1998, pp. 8–10.

Hochkeppel, Willy, *Die Rolle der Neuen Linken in der Kulturindustrie*, Munich: R. Piper, 1972.

Hochstetter, Dorothee, *Motorisierung und "Volksgemeinschaft": Das National-sozialistische Kraftfahrkorps (NSKK), 1931–1945*, Munich: R. Oldenbourg Verlag, 2005.

Hodenberg, Christina Von, *Konsens und Krise: eine Geschichte der westdeutschen Medienöffentlichkeit, 1945–1973*, Göttingen: Wallstein, 2006.

Hodenberg, Christina Von and Detlef Siegfried, "Mass Media and the Generation of Conflict: West Germany's Long Sixties and the Formation of a Critical Public Sphere," *Contemporary European History*, 15 (2006): 367–395.

eds., *Wo 1968 liegt: Reform und Revolte in der Geschichte der Bundesrepublik*, Göttingen: Vandenhoeck & Ruprecht, 2006.

Hoffmann, Reiner and Ulrich Mückenberger, *Die Wahrheit der Träume: 1968 und heute, ein Kaleidoskop*, Münster: Westfälisches Dampfboot, 1994.

Hoffmann-Axthelm, Dieter, Otto Kallscheuer, Eberhard Knodler-Bunte, and Brigitte Wartmann, eds., *Zwei Kulturen? TUNIX, Mescalero und die Folgen*, Berlin: Verlag Asthetik und Kommunikation, 1985.

Holl, Kurt and Claudia Glunz, *1968 am Rhein: Satisfaction und Ruhender Verkehr*, Cologne: Verlag Schmidt von Schwind, 1998.

Hollstein, Walter, *Der Untergrund: Zur Soziologie jugendlicher Protestbewegungen*, Neuwied and Berlin: Luchterhand, 1969.

Holz, Hans Heinz, *Die abenteuerliche Rebellion: Bürgerliche Protestbewegung in der Philosophie – Stirner, Nietzsche, Sartre, Marcuse, Neue Linke*, Darmstadt: Luchterhand, 1976.

Holzhey, Magdalena, *Im Labor des Zeichners: Joseph Beuys und die Naturwissenschaft*, Berlin: Reimer, 2009.

Horn, Gerd-Rainer, *The Spirit of '68: Rebellion in Western Europe and North America, 1956–1976*, Oxford University Press, 2006.

Horn, Gerd-Rainer and Padraic Kenney, *Transnational Moments of Change: Europe 1945, 1968, 1989*, Lanham, Md.: Rowman & Littlefield, 2004.

Horx, Matthias, *Aufstand im Schlaraffenland: Selbsterkenntnisse einer rebellischen Generation*, Munich: Hanser, 1989.

Hospelt, Charlotte, *Jugendprotest im Spiegel der Presse: Eine Inhaltsanalyse von Zeitungsartikeln in der Bundesrepublik Deutschland*, Aachen: Shaker, 1997.

Howells, Richard, *Visual Culture*, Cambridge: Polity, 2003.

Huffell, Angelika, *Schülerbewegung, 1967–77: Erfahrungen, Porträts, Dokumente*, Giessen: Focus-Verlag, 1978.

Husslein, Uwe, "'Heidi Loves You!' in Knallgelb – oder: Pyschedelia in Germania," in *Summer of Love: Art of the Psychedelic Era*, Stuttgart, 2006.

Husson, Édouard, "1968: événement transnational ou international? Le cas de la France et de la République Fédérale d'Allemagne," *Revue d'Allemagne et des pays de langue allemande*, 35 (2) (2003): 179–188.

Iriye, Akira, "On the Transnational Turn," *Diplomatic History*, 31 (3) (2007): 373–376.

Jarausch, Konrad H., *Deutsche Studenten: 1800–1970*. Frankfurt: Suhrkamp, 1984.

  ed., *After Unity: Reconfiguring German Identities, 1990–1995*, Oxford University Press, 1997.

  ed., *Dictatorship as Experience: Towards a Socio-Cultural History of the GDR*, New York and Oxford: Berghahn Books, 1999.

Jarausch, Konrad H. and Martin Sabrow, eds., *Weg in den Untergang: Der innere Zerfall der DDR*, Göttingen: Vandenhoeck & Ruprecht, 1999.

Jarausch, Konrad H. and Hannes Siegrist, eds., *Amerikanisierung und Sowjetisierung in Deutschland, 1945–1970*, Frankfurt: Campus, 1997.

Jaspers, Karl, *Wohin treibt die Bundesrepublik? Tatsachen, Gefahren, Chancen*, Munich: Piper, 1966.

Jobs, Rick, *Riding the New Wave: Youth and Rejuvenation of France after the Second World War*, Stanford, Calif.: Stanford University Press, 2007.

Juchler, Ingo, *Rebellische Subjektivität und Internationalismus: Der Einfluß Herbert Marcuses und der nationalen Befreiungsbewegungen in der sog – Dritten Welt auf die Studentenbewegung in der BRD*, Marburg: Verlag Arbeiterbewegung und Gesellschaftswissenschaft, 1989.

  Die Studentenbewegungen in den Vereinigten Staaten und der Bundesrepublik Deutschland der sechziger Jahre: Eine Untersuchung hinsichtlich ihrer Beeinflußung durch Befreiungsbewegungen und–theorien aus der Dritten Welt, Berlin: Duncker & Humblot, 1996.

Judt, Tony, *Postwar: A History of Europe since 1945*, New York: Penguin Press, 2005.

Kahn, Robert Andrew, *Holocaust Denial and the Law: A Comparative Study*, New York: Palgrave Macmillan, 2004.

Kappelt, Olaf, *Braunbuch DDR: Nazis in der DDR*, Berlin: E. Reichmann, 1981.

Karl, Michaela and Rudi Dutschke, *Revolutionär ohne Revolution*, Frankfurt: Verlag Neue Kritik, 2003.

Kater, Michael H., *Different Drummers: Jazz in the Culture of Nazi Germany*, Oxford University Press, 2003.

Katsiaficas, George, *The Imagination of the New Left: A Global Analysis of 1968*, Boston, Mass.: South End Press, 1987.

Kätzel, Ute, *Die 68erinnen: Portrait einer rebellischen Frauengeneration*, Berlin: Rowohlt, 2002.

Kellein, Thomas, *The Dream of Fluxus: George Maciunas – An Artist's Biography*, London: Thames & Hudson, 2007.

Kersting, Franz-Werner, "Entzauberung des Mythos? Ausgangsbedingungen und Tendenzen einer gesellschaftsgeschichtlichen Standortbestimmung der westdeutschen '68er'-Bewegung," in Karl Teppe, ed., *Westfälische Forschungen–Zeitschrift des Westfälischen Instituts für Regionalgeschichte des Landschaftsverbandes Westfalen-Lippe, 48/1998*, Münster: Aschendorff, 1998, pp. 1–19.

Kießling, Simon, *Die antiautoritäre Revolte der 68er*, Cologne: Bohlau, 2006.

Klein, Thomas, *SEW: Die Westberliner Einheitssozialisten – Eine "ostdeutsche" Partei als Stachel im Fleische der "Frontstadt"?* Berlin: Ch. Links Verlag, 2009.

Kleßmann, Christoph, *Zwei Staaten, eine Nation: Deutsche Geschichte 1955–1970*, Göttingen: Vandenhoeck & Ruprecht, 1988.

Klimke, Martin, *The "Other Alliance": Global Protest and Student Unrest in West Germany and the US, 1962–72*, Princeton University Press, 2010.

Klimke, Martin, Jacco Pekelder, and Joachim Scharloth, eds., *Between Prague Spring and French May: Opposition and Revolt in Europe, 1960–1980*, New York and Oxford: Berghahn Books, 2010.

Klimke, Martin and Joachim Scharloth, eds., *1968: Handbuch zur Kultur- und Mediengeschichte der Studentenbewegung*, Stuttgart: J. B. Metzler, 2007.

Knabe, Hubertus, *Der diskrete Charme der DDR: Stasi und Westmedien*, Berlin: Propyläen, 2001.

ed., *West-Arbeit des MfS: Das Zusammenspiel von "Aufklärung" und "Abwehr,"* Berlin: Ch. Links Verlag, 1999.

Knoch, Habbo, "The Return of the Images: Photographs of Nazi Crimes and the West German Public in the 'Long 1960s'," in Philipp Gassert and Alan E. Steinweis, eds., *Coping with the Nazi Past: West German Debates on Nazism and the Generational Conflict, 1955–1975*, New York and Oxford: Berghahn Books, 2006, pp. 31–49.

Knorr, Heribert, "Die Große Koalition in der parlamentarischen Diskussion der Bundesrepublik 1949–1965," *Aus Politik und Zeitgeschichte*, B33 (74) (1974): 24–47.

Koch, Albert, *Angriff auf's Schlaraffenland: 20 Jahre deutschsprachige Popmusik*, Frankfurt: Ullstein Verlag, 1987.

Koenen, Gerd, *Das rote Jahrzehnt: Unsere kleine deutsche Kulturrevolution 1967–1977*, Cologne: Kiepenheuer & Witsch, 2001.

   Vesper, Ensslin, Baader: Urszenen des deutschen Terrorismus, Cologne: Kiepenheuer & Witsch, 2003.

Kommune 2, *Versuch der Revolutionierung des bürgerlichen Individuums. Kollektives Leben mit politischer Arbeit verbinden* (Berlin: Oberbaumpresse, 1969).

Korte, Hermann, *Eine Gesellschaft im Aufbruch: Die Bundesrepublik Deutschland in den sechziger Jahren*, Frankfurt: Suhrkamp, 1987.

Kotsopoulos, Nikolaos, *Krautrock: Cosmic Rock and Its Legacy*, London: Black Dog, 2009.

Kraushaar, Wolfgang, *1968 als Mythos, Chiffre und Zäsur*, Hamburg: Hamburg Edition, 2000.

   1968: Das Jahr das alles verändert hat, Munich: Piper, 1998.

   Die Bombe im Jüdischen Gemeindehaus, Hamburg: Hamburger Edition, 2005.

   Fischer in Frankfurt, Hamburg: Hamburger Edition, 2001.

   ed., *Autonomie oder Getto? Kontroversen über die Alternativbewegung*, Frankfurt: Verlag Neue Kritik, 1978.

   ed., *Frankfurter Schule und Studentenbewegung: Von der Flaschenpost zum Molotowcoctail, 1945–1995*, Frankfurt: Hamburger Edition, HIS Verlag, 1998.

Krebs, Mario, *Ulrike Meinhof: Ein Leben im Widerspruch*, Reinbek: Rowohlt, 1988.

Krohn, Maren, *Die gesellschaftliche Auseinandersetzung um die Notstandsgesetze*, Cologne: Pahl-Rugenstein, 1981.

Kruip, Gudrun, *Das "Welt"-"Bild" des Axel Springer Verlags: Journalismus zwischen westlichen Werten und deutschen Denktraditionen*, Munich: Oldenbourg, 1998.

Kuhn, Andreas, *Stalins Enkel, Maos Söhne: die Lebenswelt der K-Gruppen in der Bundesrepublik der 70er Jahre*, Frankfurt: Campus, 2005.

Kuhn, Anette, *Zero: Eine Avantgarde der Sechziger Jahre*, Frankfurt: Propyläen Verlag, 1991.

Kühne, Karl, *Neue Linke und Gemeinwirtschaft*, Cologne: Bund-Verlag, 1980.

Kundnani, Hans, *Utopia or Auschwitz: Germany's 1968 Generation and the Holocaust*, London: Hurst, 2010.

Küntzel, Matthias, *Bonn und die Bombe: Deutsche Atomwaffenpolitik von Adenauer bis Brandt*, Frankfurt: Campus, 1992.

Küsel, Gudrun, ed., *APO und Gewerkschaften: Von der Kooperation zum Bruch*, Berlin: Olle Wolter, 1978.

Ladd, Brian, *Ghosts of Berlin: Confronting German History in the Urban Landscape*, University of Chicago Press, 1997.

Landgrebe, Jörg Plath, ed., *'68 und die Folgen: Ein unvollständiges Lexikon*, Berlin: Argon, 1998.

Langer, Günter, "Der Berliner 'Blues': Tupamaros und umherschweifende Haschrebellen zwischen Wahnsinn und Verstand," in Eckhard Siepmann, ed., *Heiss und Kalt: die Jahre 1945–69*, Berlin: Elefanten Press Verlag, 1986, pp. 649–657.

Langguth, Gerd, *Protestbewegung: Entwicklung, Niedergang, Renaissance – Die Neue Linke seit 1968*, 2nd edn, Cologne: Verlag Wissenschaft und Politik, 1984.

"Protest von Links: Die Studentenbewegung in der Bundesrepublik Deutschland 1967–1976," *Aus Politik und Zeitgeschichte*, B12 (77) (1977): 3–24.

Langhans, Rainer and Fritz Teufel, *Klau mich*, Frankfurt and Berlin: Edition Voltaire, 1968.

Larkey, Edward, ed., *A Sound Legacy: Music and Politics in East Germany*, Washington, DC: American Intitute for Contemporary German Studies, 2000.

Lee, Mia, "Art and Revolution in West Germany: The Cultural Roots of 1968," Ph.D. dissertation, University of Michigan, 2007.

Lee, Pamela M., *Chronophobia: On Time in the Art of the 1960s*, Cambridge, Mass.: MIT Press, 2004.

Lefebvre, Henri, *The Production of Space*, trans. Donald Nicholson-Smith, Oxford and Cambridge, Mass.: Blackwell, 1991.

Lefèvre, Wolfgang, "Zum Spontaneismus in der Studentenbewegung," *Blätter für deutsche und internationale Politik*, 23 (1978): 568–579.

Leggewie, Claus, "1968: Ein Laboratorium der nachindustriellen Gesellschaft? Zur Tradition der antiautoritären Revolte seit den sechziger Jahren," *Aus Politik und Zeitgeschichte*, B20 (88) (1988): 3–15.

Kofferträger: Das Algerien-Projekt der Linken im Adenauer-Deutschland, Berlin: Rotbuch-Verlag, 1984.

Legrand, Hans-Josef, "Friedensbewegung in der Geschichte der Bundesrepublik Deutschland: Ein Überblick zur Entwicklung bis Ende der siebziger Jahre," in Josef Janning, Hans-Josef Legrand, and Helmut Zander, eds., *Friedensbewegung: Entwicklung und Folgen in der Bundesrepublik Deutschland, Europa und den USA*, Cologne: Verlag Wissenschaft und Politik, 1987, pp. 19–35.

Lehnhardt, Karl-Heinz and Ludger Vollmer, *Politik zwischen Kopf und Bauch: Zur Relevanz der Persönlichkeitsbildung in den politischen der Studentenbewegung in der BRD*, Bochum: Druckladen-Verlag, 1979.

Leineweber, Bernd and Karl-Ludwig Schibel, *Pflugschrift: über Politik und Alltag in Landkommunen und anderen Alternativen*, Frankfurt: Verlag Neue Kritik, 1981.

Die Revolution ist vorbei, Wir haben gesiegt: Die Community-Bewegung zur Organisationsfrage d. Neuen Linken in die USA und die BRD, Berlin: Merve Verlag, 1975.

Lerm-Haynes, Christina-Maria, *Nachkriegsdeutschland und "objektiver Zufall": W. G. Sebald, Joseph Beuys und Tacita Dean*, Göttingen: Steidl, 2008.

Lönnendonker, Siegward, Bernd Rabehl, and Jochen Staadt, *Die antiautoritäre Revolte: Der Sozialistische Deutsche Studentenbund nach der Trennung von der SPD*, vol. I: *1960–1967*, Opladen: Westdeutscher Verlag, 2002.

Lüdke, Werner Martin, *Literatur und Studentenbewegung: Eine Zwischenbilanz*, Opladen: Westdeutscher Verlag, 1977.

ed., *Nach dem Protest: Literatur im Umbruch*, Frankfurt: Suhrkamp, 1979.

Ludwig, Andrea, *Neue oder deutsche Linke: Nation und Nationalismus im Denken von Linken und Grünen*, Opladen: Westdeutscher Verlag, 1995.

Lumley, Robert, *States of Emergency: Cultures of Revolt in Italy from 1968 to 1978*, New York: Verso, 1990.

Marcus, Greil, *Lipstick Traces: A Secret History of the Twentieth Century*, Cambridge, Mass.: Harvard University Press, 2003.

Markovits, Andrej S. and Philip S. Gorski, *The German Left: Red, Green, and Beyond*, Cambridge: Polity Press, 1993.

Marks, Stephan, *Studentenseele: Erfahrungen im Zerfall der Studentenbewegung*, Hamburg: Verlag Association, 1977.

Martini, Winfried, "Die Schwabinger Krawalle," in Gerhard Fürmetz and Thomas Kleinknecht, eds., *Schwabinger Krawalle: Protest, Polizei und Öffentlichkeit zu Beginn der 60er Jahre*, Essen: Klartext, 2006.

Marwick, Arthur, *The Sixties: Cultural Revolution in Britain, France, Italy, and the United States, c.1958–c.1974*, Oxford University Press, 1998.

Matin-Asgari, Afshin, *Iranian Student Opposition to the Shah*, Costa Mesa, Calif.: Mazda, 2001.

Matthias, Erich and Rudolf Morsey, eds., *Das Ende der Parteien 1933: Darstellungen und Dokumente*, Düsseldorf: Droste, 1960.

Mausbach, Wilfried, "'Burn, Warehouse, Burn!' Modernity, Counterculture, and the Vietnam War in West Germany," in Axel Schildt and Detlef Siegfried, eds., *Between Marx and Coca-Cola: Youth Cultures in Changing European Societies, 1960–1980*, New York and Oxford: Berghahn Books, 2006, pp. 175–202.

May, Michael, *Provokation Punk: Versuch einer Neufassung des Stilbegriffes in der Jugendforschung*, Frankfurt: Brandes & Apsel, 1986.

Medick, Hans, "Quo vadis Historische Anthropologie? Geschichtsforschung zwischen Historischer Kulturwissenschaft und Mikro-Historie," *Historische Anthropologie*, 9 (2001): 78–92.

Meinhof, Ulrike, *Die Würde des Menschen ist antastbar: Aufsätze und Polemiken*, Berlin: Wagenbach, 1994.

Mergel, Thomas, "Überlegungen zu einer Kulturgeschichte der Politik," *Geschichte und Gesellschaft*, 28 (4) (2002): 574–606.

Mesch, Claudia and Viola Michely, *Joseph Beuys: The Reader*, Cambridge, Mass.: MIT Press, 2007.

Meyer, Thomas, *Die Inszenierung des Scheins: Voraussetzungen und Folgen symbolischer Politik*, Frankfurt: Suhrkamp, 1992.

"Die Theatralität der Politik," in Peter Siller and Gerhard Pitz, eds., *Politik als Inszenierung: Zur Ästhetik des Politischen im Medienzeitalter*, Baden-Baden: Nomis, 2000, pp. 117–121.

Meyer, Thomas and Martina Kampmann, *Politik als Theater: Die neue Macht der Darstellungskunst*, Berlin: Aufbau-Verlag, 1998.

Michelers, Detlef, *Draufhauen, draufhauen, nachsetzen! Die Bremer Schüler-bewegung, die Strassenbahndemonstrationen und ihre Folgen 1967/70*, Bremen: Edition Temmen, 2002.

Miermeister, Jürgen, *Rudi Dutschke: Mit Selbstzeugnissen und Bilddokumenten*, Reinbek: Rowohlt, 1986.

Miermeister, Jürgen and Jochen Staadt, eds., *Provokationen: Die Studenten- und Jugendrevolte in ihren Flugblättern, 1965–1971*, Darmstadt, Neuwied: Luchterhand, 1980.

Mirzoeff, Nicholas, *An Introduction to Visual Culture*, London and New York: Routledge, 1999.

The Visual Culture Reader, London and New York: Routledge, 1998.

Mohr, Reinhard, *Zaungaste: Die Generation, die Nach der Revolte Kam*, Frankfurt: S. Fischer, 1992.

Moses, Dirk A., *German Intellectuals and the Nazi Past*, Cambridge University Press, 2007.

Mosler, Peter, *Was wir wollten, was wir wurden: Studentenrevolte – zehn Jahre danach. Mit einer Chronologie von Wolfgang Kraushaar*, Reinbek: Rowohlt, 1977.

Muller, Jurgen, *Movies of the 60s*, Los Angeles, Calif.: Taschen, 2004.

Mündemann, Tobias, *Die 68er: und was aus ihnen geworden ist*, Munich: Heyne, 1988.

Münkel, Daniela, "Die Medienpolitik von Konrad Adenauer und Willy Brandt," *Archiv für Sozialgeschichte*, 41 (2001): 297–316.

Negt, Oskar, *Achtundsechzig: Politische Intellektuelle und die Macht*, Göttingen: Steidl, 1995.

Nehring, Holger, "'Westernization': A New Paradigm for Interpreting West European History in a Cold War Context," *Cold War History*, 4 (2) (2004): 175–191.

Neimann, Susan, "Germany Remembers the Sixties," *Dissent* (summer 2001): 18–21.

Neuss, Wolfgang, *Tunix ist besser als arbeitslos: Sprüche eines Überlebenden*, Reinbek: Rowohlt, 1986.

Nicholls, A. J., *The Bonn Republic: West German Democracy, 1945–1990*, London and New York: Longman, 1997.

Nirumand, Bahman, *Persien: Modell eines Entwicklungslandes oder die Diktatur der freien Welt*, Reinbek: Rowohlt, 1967.

"Die harmlose Intelligenz: Über Gammler, Ostermarschierer, Adorniten und andere Oppositionelle," *konkret*, no. 7, July 1967.

Oetjen, Hinrich, "APO, Gewerkschaften und Intellektuelle," in Hans-Erich Bremes and Maria Schumacher, eds., *Mit der Vergangenheit in die Zukunft: Felder gewerkschaftlicher Politik seit 1945*, Münster: Verlag Westfälisches Dampfboot, 1989, pp. 51–68.

Olenhusen, Albrecht Götz von and Christa Gnirss, *Handbuch der Raubdrucke: Verlag Dokumentation Pullach bei*, Freiburg im Breisgau: Raubdruck-Archiv, 2002.

Olenhusen, Albrecht Götz von, "Entwicklung und Stand der Raubdruckbewegung," in Heinz Ludwig Arnold, ed., *Literaturbetrieb in der Bundesrepublik Deutschland: ein kritisches Handbuch*, Munich: Edition Text u. Kritik, 1981, pp. 164–172.

Oman, Hiltrud, *Die Kunst auf dem Weg zum Leben: Joseph Beuys*, Weinheim: Quadriga, 1988.

Ottman, Antje, *Der Weltstoff Ietztendlich ist- neu zu Bilden: Joseph Beuys fur und wider Moderne*, Ostfildern: Tertium, 1994.

Otto, Karl A., *Vom Ostermarsch zur APO: Geschichte der außerparlamentarischen Opposition in der Bundesrepublik 1960–1970*, Frankfurt: Campus, 1977.

Paetal, Karl O., *Beat: Eine Anthologie*, Hamburg: Rowohlt, 1962.

Patel, Kiran Klaus, "Überlegungen zu einer transnationalen Geschichte," *Zeitschrift für Geschichtswissenschaft*, 52 (7) (2004): 626–645.

Peters, Butz, *Tödlicher Irrtum: Die Geschichte der RAF*, Berlin: Argon, 2004.

Pevny, Wilhelm, *Die vergessenen Ziele: Wollen sich die 68er davonstehlen?* Vienna: Europa-Verlag, 1988.

Pijnappel, Johan, *Fluxus: Today and Yesterday*, London: Academy Group, 1993.

Poiger, Uta, *Jazz, Rock, and Rebels: Cold War Politics and American Culture in a Divided Germany*, Berkeley, Calif.: University of California Press, 2000.

Praml, Willy, *Lehrlingstheater und proletarische Öffentlichkeit: Berichte, Texte, Materialien zur proletarischen Kulturarbeit*, Frankfurt: Verlag Jugend und Politik, 1974.

Proll, Thorwald and Dubbe, Daniel, *Wir kamen vom anderen Stern Über 1968, Andreas Baader und ein Kaufhaus*, Hamburg: Edition Nautilus, 2003.

Prützel-Thomas, Monika, "Macht kaputt, was euch kaputt macht: Die 68er Generation und ihre Ableger," *Jahrbuch Extremismus & Demokratie*, 7 (1995): 292–294.

Puchner, Martin, *Poetry of the Revolution: Marx, Manifestos, and the Avant-Gardes*, Princeton University Press, 2006.

Rabehl, Bernd, *Am Ende der Utopie: Die politische Geschichte der Freien Universität Berlin*, Berlin: Argon, 1988.

"'Geschichte wird gemacht, es geht voran': Über die existentialistischen Grundlagen des Marxismus der Außerparlamentarischen Opposition der sechziger Jahre im westlichen Deutschland," in Bernhard Kuschey, ed., *Linke Spuren: Marxismus seit den 60er Jahren*, Vienna: Verlag für Gesellschaftskritik, 1987, pp. 21–58.

"Die Provokationselite: Aufbruch und Scheitern der subversiven Rebellion in den sechziger Jahren," in Siegward Lönnendonker, Bernd Rabehl, and Jochen Staadt, eds., *Die antiautoritäre Revolte: der Sozialistische Deutsche Studentenbund nach der Trennung von der SPD*, vol. 1: *1960–1967*, Opladen: Westdeutscher Verlag, 2002, pp. 400–512.

Rappman, Rainer, *Denker, Kunstler, Revolutionare: Beuys, Dutschke, Schilinski, Schmundt: vier Leben fur Freiheit, Demokratie, und Sozialismus*, Wangen: FIU- Verlag, 1996.

Rauhut Michael and Thomas Kochan, eds., *Bye Bye, Lübben City: Bluesfreaks, Tramps und Hippies in der DDR*, Berlin: Schwarzkopf & Schwarzkopf, 2004.

Reichardt, Sven, "Is 'Warmth' a Mode of Social Behaviour? Considerations on a Cultural History of the Left-Alternative Milieu from the Late 1960s to the Mid 1980s," *Behemoth*, 3 (2) (2010): 84–99.

Reichardt, Sven and Detlef Siegfried, eds., *Das Alternative Milieu: Antibürgerliche Lebensstil und linke Politik in der Bundesrepublik Deutschland und Europa, 1968–1983*, Göttingen: Wallstein Verlag, 2010.

Reiche, Reimut, "Erinnerung an einen Mythos," in Lothar Baier, Wilfried Gottschalch, and Reimut Reiche, *Die Früchte der Revolte: Über die Veränderung der politischen Kultur durch die Studentenbewegung* (Berlin: Wagenbach, 1988), pp. 45–71.

Reinders, Ralf and Ronald Fritsch, *Die Bewegung 2 Juni: Gespräche über Haschrebellen, Lorenzentführung, Knast*, Amsterdam and Berlin: Edition ID-Archiv, 1995.

Reinisch, Leonhard, ed., *Permanente Revolution von Marx bis Marcuse*, Munich: Verlag Georg D. W. Callwey, 1969.

Renner, Jens, *1968*, Hamburg: Europäische Verlagsanstalt/Rotbuch Verlag, 2001.

Rinner, Susanne, *The German Student Movement and the Literary Imagination: Transnational Memories of Protest and Dissent*, New York and Oxford: Berghahn, 2013.

Robertson, Roland, "Comments on the 'Global Triad' and 'Glocalization'," in Nobutaka Inoue, ed., *Globalization and Indigenous Culture*, Tokyo: Institute for Japanese Culture and Classics, Kokugakuin University, 1997, pp. 217–225.

Globalization: Social Theory and Global Culture, London: Sage, 1992.

"Glocalization: Time-Space and Homogeneity-Heterogeneity," in Roland Robertson, Mike Featherstone, and Scott Lash, eds., *Global Modernities*, London: Sage, 1995, pp. 25–44.

Rolke, Lothar, *Protestbewegungen in der Bundesrepublik: Eine analytische Sozialgeschichte des politischen Widerspruchs*, Opladen: Westdeutscher Verlag, 1987.

Ross, Kristen, *The Emergence of Social Space: Rimbaud and the Paris Commune*, Minneapolis, Minn.: University of Minnesota Press, 1988.

Rostock, Jürgen, "Ost-Berlin als Hauptstadt der DDR," in Werner Süß and Ralf Rytlewski, eds., *Berlin: Die Hauptstadt – Vergangenheit und Zukunft einer europäischen Metropole*, Berlin: Nicolai, 1999, pp. 259–294.

Roth, Roland, *Rebellische Subjektivität: Herbert Marcuse und die neuen Protestbewegungen*, Frankfurt: Campus, 1985.

Rucht, Dieter, ed., *Research on Social Movements: The State of the Art in Western Europe and the USA*, Boulder, Col.: Westview, 1991.

Rupp, Hans Karl, *Außerparlamentarische Opposition in der Ära Adenauer: Der Kampf gegen die Atombewaffnung in den fünfziger Jahren. Eine Studie zur innenpolitischen Entwicklung der BRD*, 3rd edn, Cologne: Pahl-Rugenstein, 1984.

Ryback, Timothy, *Rock around the Bloc: A History of Rock Music in Eastern Europe and the Soviet Union*, Oxford University Press, 1990.

Sander, Hartmut and Ulrich Christians, eds., *Subkultur Berlin: Selbstdarstellung, Text-, Ton-Bilddokumente, Esoterik der Kommunen, Rocker, subversiven Gruppen*, Darmstadt: März Verlag, 1969.

Sarr, Amadou Lamine, "Mai 68 im Senegal: Fortsetzung des Unabhängigkeit-sprozesses in Afrika?," in Jena Kastner and David Mayer, eds., *Weltwende 1968? Ein Jahr aus globalgeschichtlicher Perspektive*, Vienna: Mandelbaum, 2008, pp. 130–142.

Sassoon, Donald, *One Hundred Years of Socialism: The West European Left in the Twentieth Century*, London: I. B. Tauris, 1997.

Sauer, Christel, *Joseph Beuys und das Kapital: vier Vorträge zum Verständnis von Joseph Beuys und seiner Rauminstallation "Das Kapital Raum 1970–77" in den Hallen für Neue Kunst, Schaffhausen, ergänzt durch Erläuterungen von Joseph Beuys und seinen "Aufruf zur Alternative,"* Schaffhausen: Die Hallen, 1988.

Sauer, Thomas, *Westorientierung im deutschen Protestantismus? Vorstellungen und Tätigkeit des Kronberger Kreises*, Munich: R. Oldenbourg, 1998.

Scharloth, Joachim, *1968: Eine Kommunikationsgeschichte*, Munich: Wilhelm Fink, 2010.

Scheerer, Sebastian, "Die ausgebürgerte Linke," in Henner Hess, Martin Moerings, and Dieter Paas, eds., *Angriff auf das Herz des Staates: Soziale Entwicklung und Terrorismus*, Frankfurt: Suhrkamp, 1988, pp. 193–429.

Schenk, Herrad, *Die feministische Herausforderung: 150 Jahre Frauenbewegung in Deutschland*, 2nd edn., Munich: Beck, 1981.

Schewe, Egon, *Selbstverwaltete Jugendzentren Entwicklung, Konzept und Bedeutung der Jugendzentrumsbewegung*, Bielefeld: Pfeffer, 1980.

Schildt, Axel and Detlef Siegfried, eds., *Between Marx and Coca-Cola: Youth Cultures in Changing European Societies, 1960–1980*, New York and Oxford: Berghahn Books, 2006.

European Cities, Youth and the Public Sphere in the Twentieth Century, Aldershot and Burlington, Vt.: Ashgate, 2005.

Schildt, Axel, Detlef Siegfried, and Karl Christian Lammers, eds., *Dynamische Zeiten: Die 60er Jahre in den beiden deutschen Gesellschaften*, Hamburg: Christians, 2000.

Schläger, Hilde, ed., *Mein Kopf gehört mir: Zwanzig Jahre Frauenbewegung*, Munich: Frauenoffensive, 1988.

Schmidtke, Michael, *Der Aufbruch der jungen Intelligenz: Die 68er Jahre in der Bundesrepublik und den USA*, Frankfurt and New York: Campus Verlag, 2003.

"Reform, Revolte oder Revolution? Der Sozialistische Deutsche Studentenbund (SDS) und die Students for a Democratic Society (SDS), 1960–1970," in Ingrid Gilcher-Holtey, ed., *1968: Vom Ereignis zum Gegenstand der Geschichtswissenschaft*, Göttingen: Vandenhoeck & Ruprecht, 1998, pp. 188–206.

Schmierer, Joscha, "Der Zauber des großen Augenblicks: Der internation-ale Traum von '68," in Lothar Baier, ed., *Die Früchte der Revolte: Über die Veränderung der politischen Kultur durch die Studentenbewegung*, Berlin: K. Wagenbach, 1988, pp. 107–126.

Schmökel, Reinhard and Bruno Kaiser, *Die vergessene Regierung: Die große Koalition 1966 bis 1969 und ihre langfristigen Wirkungen*, Bonn: Bouvier, 1991.

Schneider, Franz, ed., *Dienstjubiläum einer Revolte: 1968 und 25 Jahre*, Munich: von Hase & Koehler, 1992.

Schneider, Michael, *Demokratie in Gefahr? Der Konflikt um die Notstandsgesetze. Sozialdemokratie, Gewerkschaften und intellektueller Protest, 1958–1968*, Bonn: Verlag Neue Gesellschaft, 1986.

Schorske, Carl, *Thinking with History*, Princeton University Press, 1998.

Schroder, Jürgen, *Ideologischer Kampf vs. regionale Hegemonie: ein Beitrag zur Untersuchung der "K-Gruppen,"* Berlin: Free University Berlin, 1990.

Schulenburg, Lutz, ed., *Das Leben ändern, die Welt verändern! 1968: Dokumente und Berichte*, Hamburg: Edition Nautilus, 1998.

Schult, Peter, *Besuche in Sackgassen: Aufzeichn. e. homosexuellen Anarchisten*, Munich: Tirkont, 1978.

Schuster, Jacques, *Heinrich Albertz: Der Mann der mehrere Leben lebte – Eine Biographie*, Berlin: Alexander Fest Verlag, 1997.

Schwartz, Frederic J., *Blind Spots: Critical Theory and the History of Art in Twentieth Century Germany*, New Haven, Conn.: Yale University Press, 2005.

Schwendter, Rolf, *Theorie der Subkultur: Neuasugabe mit einem Nachwort, sieben Jahre später*, Frankfurt: Syndikat, 1981.

Sedlmaier, Alexander and Stephan Malinowski, "'1968' als Katalysator der Konsumgesellschaft: Performativ Regelverstöße, kommerzielle Adaptionen und ihre gegenseitige Durchdringung," *Geschichte und Gesellschaft*, 32 (2) (2006): 238–267.

Seibert, Niels, *Vergessene Proteste: Internationalismus und Antirassismus, 1964–1983*, Münster: Unrast Verlag, 2008.

Seibold, Carsten, ed., *Die 68er: Das Fest der Rebellion*, Munich: Droemer Knaur, 1988.

Seidel, Wolfgang, ed., *Scherben: Musik, Politik und Wirkung der Ton Steine Scherben*, Mainz: Ventil, 2006.

Sell, Mike, *Avant-garde Performance and the Limits of Criticism: Approaching the Living Theater, Happenings, Fluxus, and the Black Arts Movement*, Ann Arbor, Mich.: University of Michigan Press, 2005.

Shell, Kurt L., "Extra-Parliamentary Opposition in Postwar Germany," *Comparative Politics*, 2 (4), Special Issue on the West German Election of 1969 (July 1970): 653–680.

Sichtermann, Kai, Jens Johler, and Christian Stahl, *Keine Macht für Niemand: Die Geschichte der "Ton Steine Scherben,"* Berlin: Schwarzkopf & Schwarzkopf, 2000.

Siegfried, Detlef, "Protest am Markt. Gegenkultur in der Konsumgesellschaft um 1968," in Christina von Hodenberg and Detlef Siegfried, eds., *Wo 1968 liegt: Reform und Revolte in der Geschichte der Bundesrepublik*, Göttingen: Vendenhoeck & Ruprecht, 2006, pp. 48–78.

Sound der Revolte: Studien zur Kulturrevolution um 1968, Weinheim: Juventa, 2008.

Time Is on My Side: Konsum und Politik in der westdeutschen Jugendkultur der 60er Jahre, Göttingen: Wallstein, 2006.

Slobodian, Quinn, "Corpse Polemics: The Third World and the Politics of Gore in 1960s West Germany," in Timothy S. Brown and Lorena Anton, eds., *Between the Avant-Garde and the Everyday: Subversive Politics in Europe from 1957 to the Present* (New York and Oxford: Berghahn, 2011), pp. 58–73.

Foreign Front: Third World Politics in Sixties West Germany, Durham, N.C.: Duke University Press, 2012.

Smith, Owen F., *Fluxus: The History of an Attitude*, San Diego, Calif.: San Diego State University Press, 1998.

Specter, Matthew G., *Habermas: An Intellectual History*, Cambridge University Press, 2010.

Stachelhaus, Heiner, *Joseph Beuys*, New York: Abbeville Press, 1991.

Zero: Heinz Mack, Otto Peine, Gunther Uecker, Düsseldorf: ECON Verlag, 1993.

Strassner, Erich, "1968 und die sprachlichen Folgen," in Dieter Emig, Christoph Hüttig, and Lutz Raphael, eds., *Sprache und politische Kultur in der Demokratie: Hans Gerd Schumann zum Gedenken*, Frankfurt: Peter Lang, 1992, pp. 241–260.

Sturken, Marita and Lisa Cartwright, *Practices of Looking: An Introduction to Visual Culture*, Oxford University Press, 2001.

Suri, Jeremi, *Power and Protest: Global Revolution and the Rise of Détente*, Cambridge, Mass.: Harvard University Press, 2003.

Tanner, Jakob, "'The Times They Are a-Changin': Zur subkulturellen Dynamik der 68er Bewegungen," in Gilcher-Holtey, ed., *1968*, pp. 207–223.

Thomas, Nick, *Protest Movements in 1960s West Germany: A Social History of Dissent and Democracy*, Oxford and New York: Berg, 2003.

Thomas, Richard Hinton and Keith Bullivant, *Literature in Upheaval: West German Writers and the Challenge of the 1960s*, Manchester University Press, 1974.

Thompson, Chris, *Felt: Fluxus, Joseph Beuys, and the Dalai Lama*, Minneapolis, Minn.: University of Minnesota Press, 2011.

Thränhardt, Dietrich, *Geschichte der Bundesrepublik Deutschland*, 2nd edn., Frankfurt: Suhrkamp, 1996.

Til, Barbara, "Anarchie und Kleiderwirbel: Mode 68," in Wolfgang Schepers, ed., *68- Design und Alltagskultur zwischen Konsum und Konflikt*, Cologne: DuMont, 1998, pp. 105–115.

Tisdall, Caroline, *Joseph Beuys: We Go This Way*, London: Violette Editions, 1998.

Tolomelli, Marica, *Repressiv getrennt oder organisch verbündet: Studenten und Arbeiter 1968 in der Bundesrepublik Deutschland und in Italien, Forschung Politikwissenschaft, vol. CXIII*, Opladen: Leske + Budrich, 2001.

Urban, Peter, *Das Buch vom Verlag der Autoren 1969–1989: Beschreibung eines Modells und seiner Entwicklung – Zusammengestellt von Peter Urban*, Frankfurt: Verlag der Autoren, 1989.

Van Dülmen, Richard, *Historische Anthropologie: Entwicklung, Probleme, Aufgaben*, Cologne: Bohlau, 2000.

Varon, Jeremy, *Bringing the War Home: The Weather Underground, the Red Army Faction, and Revolutionary Violence in the Sixties and Seventies*, Berkeley, Calif.: University of California Press, 2004.

Vogth, Hannah, *Parlamentarische und außerparlamentarische Opposition*, Opladen: Westdeutscher Verlag, 1972.

Voigt, Lothar, *Aktivismus und moralischer Rigorismus: Die politische Romantik der 68er Studentenbewegung*, Wiesbaden: Deutscher Universitäts-Verlag, 1991.

Voßberg, Henning, *Studentenrevolte und Marxismus: Zur Marxrezeption in der Studentenbewegung auf Grundlage ihrer politischen Sozialisationsgeschichte*, Munich: Minerva, 1979.

Vostell, Wolf, *Aktionen: Happenings und Demonstrationen seit 1965*, Reinbek: Rowohlt, 1970.

Waine, Anthony, "Fatal Attractions: Rolf Dieter Brinkmann and British Life and Culture," *The Modern Language Review*, 87 (2) (1992): 376–392.

Walker, John A. and Sarah Chaplin, *Visual Culture: An Introduction*, Manchester University Press, 1997.

Wallerstein, Immanuel, "1968: eine Revolution im Weltsystem," in Etienne François, ed., *1968: Ein europäisches Jahr?* Leipzig: Leipziger Universitätsverlag, 1997, pp. 19–33.

Warneken, Bernd Jürgen, ed., *Massenmedium Straße: Zur Kulturgeschichte der Demonstration*, Frankfurt: Campus, 1991.

Warnke, Martin, *Politische Kunst: Gebarden und Gebaren*, Berlin: Akademia Verlag, 2004.

Wartenberg, J. C., *Kreuzberg K 36: Leben in (der) Bewegung, Kreuzberg inside bis zum Fall der Mauer*, Berlin: J. C. Wartenberg, 2005.

Watkins, Renee Neu (trans.), *Storefront Daycare Centers: The Radical Berlin Experiment*, Boston, Mass.: Beacon Press, 1973.

Weidhaas, Peter, *Zur Geschichte der Frankfurter Buchmesse*, Frankfurt: Suhrkamp, 2003.

Weiss, Andreas von, *Schlagwörter der Neuen Linken*, Munich: Olzog, 1974.

Weiss, Hildegard, *Die Ideologieentwicklung in der deutschen Studentenbewegung*, Munich: Oldenbourg, 1985.

Werder, Lutz Von, *Was kommt nach den Kinderläden? Erlebnis-Protokolle*, Berlin: K. Wagenbach, 1977.

Westad, Odd Arne, *The Global Cold War: Third World Interventions and the Making of Our Times*, Cambridge University Press, 2005.

Wienecke, Jan and Fritz Krause, *Unser Marsch ist eine gute Sache: Ostermärsche damals – heute*, Frankfurt: Verlag Marxistische Blätter, 1982.

Wierling, Dorothee, "Oral History," in Michael Maurer, ed., *Neue Themen und Methoden der Geschichtswissenschaft*, Stuttgart: Reclam, 2003, pp. 81–151.

Williams, Emmett, *Mr. Fluxus: A Collective Portrait of George Maciunas, 1931–1978*, New York: Thames & Hudson, 1998.

My Life in Flux, and Vice-Versa, New York: Thames & Hudson, 1992.

Winkler, Heinrich, *Der langeWeg nachWesten*, 4th edn, 2 vols., Munich: Beck, 2002.

Wintjes, J. and J. Gehret, eds., *Ulcus Molle Infodienst: Jahrgaenge, 1969–1974*, Amsterdam: Azid Presse, 1979.

Wolfschlag, Claus, *Bye-bye '68: Renegaten der Linken, APO-Abweichler und aller-lei Querdenker berichten*, Graz: Leopold Stocker Verlag, 1998.

Index

CPSIA information can be obtained
at www.ICGtesting.com
Printed in the USA
LVOW13s1233200917
549286LV00031B/332/P